INSPIRING
WMEN
LEADERS

Leigh Bowman-Perks

Fisher King Publishing

Inspiring Women Leaders
ISBN 978-1-910406-16-8
Copyright © Leigh Bowman-Perks 2015

Published by
Fisher King Publishing
The Studio
Arthington Lane
Pool-in-Wharfedale
LS21 1JZ England

Cover design by

Sam Richardson

Author Image: Photography - Helen Jones

Stylists - REISS

Make-up - Faye Quinton

Hair - Mint Hairdressing & Day Spa

Contents

*This book is dedicated to my family who
are my greatest inspiration of all
- Daniel, Alanadh, Mum and Tania.*

*Also, the two inspiring mentors and
powerful advocates in my life
- Jonathan Bowman-Perks MBE and
Dr. Reuven Bar-On.*

*Finally, to male and female leaders alike,
around the world, who are making a positive
difference and inspiring others each day.*

Acknowledgements

This has been an exciting journey filled with inspiring and extraordinary people, without whom this book would certainly not have been possible.

My deepest gratitude to my family who have supported me every step of the way and, most importantly, put everything back into perspective!

My mother, Marguerite, who without her own strength, guidance and love I would not have had the determination to succeed.

My two children, Daniel and Alanadh who never cease to surprise me with their talents and insights that frankly quite often leaves me speechless, as I wonder how anyone so young can hold such wisdom beyond their years.

My sister, Tania, who has been the real backbone of our family and a powerful influence in my life; even though I forget to tell her that!

To Jonathan Bowman-Perks – my most trusted partner, mentor, motivator and husband! You were the real catalyst to me finding courage, self-belief and pursuing the dream. You espouse everything that you inspire others to do and be – a rare and irreplaceable gift.

Dr. Reuven Bar-On, a wonderfully talented, generous and intelligent thinker. You have taught me so much and stretched my learning to a whole new realm.

I would also like to thank the contributing authors for their shared expertise and insights; Dr Donald Bosch and the Headington Institute on Resilience, Dr. Henry Ford on Mindfulness and Robin Kermode on Communication.

To the countless women, men and businesses that have made the research and book possible. The stories, insights and positive support have given the energy I needed to get beyond the wall and reach the finish line.

In particular, Kezi Silverstone for the immense inspiration, encouragement and support. Andi Keeling and Chris Sullivan at RBS for their sponsorship and advocacy.

A special thank you to Isobel De Carles, one of the most talented rising stars I know, and the inspiring Ian Pearce who are helping turn the dreams for our charity, the Inspiring Leadership Trust, into reality.

Also, Isabelle Santoire for stretching me beyond my own imagination with the launch of the new expeditions for women leaders.

i

To Shola Awolesi of Save the Children for seizing the concept of Inspiring Women Leaders, and generously opening up her global network to extend our influence.

To my assistant, Bridget Steiner, who kept me sane (for the most part) and supported me tirelessly for the last three years.

Appreciation also goes to the companies and colleagues that I have worked with along the way, in particular: Unilever, Scandinavian Airlines, Centrica, Barclays, HSBC, RBS, Chemistry Consulting, BP and the Ministry of Health in Botswana. Some of my greatest moments, and of course some of the most challenging, have been through the experiences and sponsorship I received.

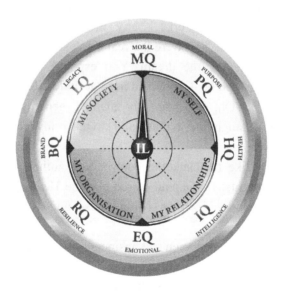

Foreword

"Nothing is so strong as gentleness.
Nothing is so gentle as real strength."
Saint Francis de Sales (1567-1622), Roman Catholic Saint

Leigh has explored the lives of over 100 truly inspirational leaders, with her passion for listening and a deep interest in the issues that lie at the heart of leadership today. Her fascinating conversations with such a diverse group of people reaffirms the fact that leadership styles may vary, but the essence of success lies in authenticity. It is in listening to one's inner voice, and in being able to dream.

The magic of life is making a difference and it is powerfully uplifting to read the many stories all filled with humility, integrity, courage and hope. This book is filled with practical tips, techniques and sound words of wisdom. Leigh and her team have backed up her research with the latest thinking in 21st century leadership, which they have underpinned with
sound psychometric data.

Leigh has not only brightened our lives with this collection of wisdom but has also added a philanthropic angle and in doing so will light up the lives of many, many more.

Pinky Lilani OBE
Founder & Chairman
WOMEN OF THE FUTURE

Prologue

"Perfect and bulletproof are seductive, but they don't exist in the human experience. We must walk into the arena, whatever it may be – a new relationship, an important meeting, a creative process, or a difficult conversation – with courage and the willingness to engage. Rather than sitting on the side-lines... we must dare to show up and let ourselves be seen. This is daring greatly."

Brené Brown, *Daring Greatly*

This Prologue is my own personal story, which after the privilege of hearing many leaders' interviews, felt only right to share.

To my children, Daniel and Alanadh, as maybe some form of encouragement to:

1. *Be courageous in doing what is right and authentic for you, even in the face of adversity.*

2. *Live a life of substance by giving in abundance to those that will benefit from your talents, gifts and compassion.*

3. *Follow your passion and always 'Dare Greatly'. Success and happiness are the descendants of purpose and perseverance.*

Remember, you are completely loved...unconditionally.

My Story…

I consider myself to be very fortunate today.

I'm updating this chapter as I look at the views from my new home in the country with a deep sense of pride and appreciation; my marriage to my soul-mate Jonathan, my beautiful children, who bring me such joy and my work as a coach, consultant and philanthropist, which gives me a true sense of purpose.

Life, however, wasn't always like this: I am also a survivor.

When he met my mother, my father Bev was a night Nursing Officer at Royal Air Force Akrotiri in Cyprus. Mum was actually still married to an RAF Sergeant, called David based out there with whom she had a child, Tania. She was in a desperately unhappy marriage at the time and so a passionate affair with Bev ensued. After my mother found the courage to leave David and return to England, she dedicated her life to motherhood and teaching. Bev swiftly followed her and it wasn't long after that before I arrived on the scene! As I was writing this book I asked myself, "Which women leaders actually inspire me?" I feel that my one consistent *source of inspiration* and *role model* has been my Mum. I have learned so many qualities from her that I aspire to live up to today, including passion, courage, fairness, independence, compassion and resilience.

Having been pressured the leave the Armed Forces due to their affair, my father found a senior leadership position at the local hospital. Whilst committed to his work, where his patients adored him, he never quite recovered from leaving what was a very promising career in the RAF. Bev's early discontentment turned initially to resentment and then finally a deep anger, often fuelled by alcohol. Again, Mum found the courage to leave my father and created a new home for us, so we could re-build our lives in a safer environment. However, my estranged father still had access to me, and therefore a strong and controlling hold over Mum. In our early lives, whilst we were joyfully happy with Mum, we witnessed occasional outbursts of mental and physical abuse from my father, whenever he turned up unexpectedly at the house. The final straw came one day after we returned home from shopping; my father broke into our house and whilst holding a knife he grabbed me, then threatened to kill us all, if Mum ever attempted to leave him.

Knowing we were in severe danger, Mum secretly booked flights for my sister Tania and I to go to her hometown in Bundoran, on the west coast of Ireland, where our grandparents were waiting for us. My father unfortunately found out and caught up with us at the airport. He insisted I was removed from the aircraft. After much begging and pleading, my father agreed we could leave if Mum went back home *alone* with him. Later in life, she described to me that bitter-sweet moment; knowing that I would be safe but also believed, as she returned home with my father, that she might never live to see me again.

Although she had an unpleasant battle to go through, Mum fortunately remained safe. She escaped from him a few months later, leaving everything behind, except the clothes in her suitcase. We were together again and so happy. I was five when I learned my father died of a massive heart attack. At my young age, I knew the right emotion to feel at the loss of a father should have been one of sadness, even trying to make myself cry, but it was different from me. More mature now, I understand my emotion was actually one of relief. We were finally safe.

As I reflect back, I now realise the level of **courage** Mum must have had, and yet she clearly hid so much from us. Mum like any inspiring leader, *protected us* from her worries, fears and what kept her awake at night. As a result, Tania and I can only ever recall the *'craic'* (or *'crazy fun'* to the non-Celtic readers) that we had and the depth of love we always felt from our mother.

We had wonderful times being at home with our very large Irish family. To begin with, we lived on the poverty line and Mum struggled financially, as a single parent. She has always been (and remains) a proud woman, so would never ask for financial maintenance payments from our either of our fathers, or any help from others. In fact, her life has been spent giving completely to us and to others in any way she possibly could; even to complete strangers! Mum's pride was her strength, but also her weakness. I see now that she would work extremely hard holding down three demanding jobs, to ensure that we had wanted for nothing.

Whilst I think Mum made life a little more difficult for herself than necessary as a result, I absolutely applaud her for her strength of character to pursue *financial independence* and *sense of empowerment.* This is in stark contrast to the extreme *'sense of entitlement'* that appears to be an emerging modern-day trend, without taking any personal accountability for what this means! Whether it's motivated by fears, the need for safety, limiting self-beliefs or just plain materialism, it is the kind of stuff that holds back the equality agenda. I believe this increasing issue must become a mantra used by feminists and any decisions by our legal systems, if we are to be true to the 'F' word – and I'm not talking feminism but *Fairness*…for all. This of course would challenge our thinking as we enter a new, and arguably more progressive, era for feminism that goes beyond the realm of a single identity to consider the macro issue of actual inclusion.

Mum was told it would be *"highly unlikely"* for her to teach in Ireland, as she had to pass the *"virtually impossible"* teaching exam, which was in the Irish language. As a divorcee she was also warned that was also *"unacceptable"* for her to teach in a Catholic school. She never once complained that it wasn't fair and she didn't get caught up in the downward spiral of believing their words, by adopting a victim mentality. Mum knew teaching was not just what she did, but it was who she was; it was *her calling*. So, she spent 13-weeks completely dedicated to studying for the exams and re-learning the Irish language. With the support of an inspiring *mentor and teacher*, Mrs. Connors, she proved the naysayers wrong and passed her exam with flying colours. Despite much protest from the local priest, she became a teacher at the local *Roman Catholic* primary school. In fact, she earned a reputation for being one of the most talented teachers. This taught me that we simply cannot be talented at everything, but by *knowing our talents* and *pursuing what we absolutely love*, we can achieve anything. Through the advocacy and support of Mrs. Connors, she had all of the resources she needed to succeed. And what about the naysayers? Well, their fears don't become ours. In fact, whilst sometimes their comments can be informative, they become irrelevant in the end.

It took time to re-build our lives from scratch; our family remained on the poverty line for some time. From snuggling under the covers, because we had no heating, to hiding behind the sofa, because the bailiffs were pounding at the front door! Tania and I didn't really appreciate the severity of the financial burden for Mum. We always felt surrounded by pure love and happiness, even during times of inevitable tension. Mum was such a vibrant character with a warmth and positivity that attracted people to her. With her twinkly eyes, she would grasp life with both hands, stating that she planned to (pardon the crudeness in advance), "…slide unceremoniously into her grave with a glass of vodka in her hand, a man underneath her shouting *'yeeeehaaaa, what a hell of a ride!'*".

It was only when we heard her sometimes cry in bed at night, when she thought no-one could hear, that we understood that all was not right. I recall one year, as Christmas approached, she knew she could not afford to buy much food, never mind buying Christmas presents. Instead we prepared a simple Christmas for just the three of us, excited over the fact that we were the 'Three Musketeers' and we always had fun adventures of our own making.

Yet, as Tania and I woke up on Christmas morning, we found lots of wonderful presents under the tree. Our wider family and community of friends had made sure that we did not go without. Whilst this was so unexpected, it is a day that I will treasure for the rest of my life. Not just because of the gifts themselves, which I still hold dear. It was more because of the sentiment behind them and the sense of closeness with a community that had helped us on a whole different level. Now remember…my Mum is proud!! This help wasn't asked for; they had a strong sense of community, caring deeply and compassionately about others. This was a wonderful *random act of kindness*!

Mum's fortunes picked up. Life became easier. She started to focus on herself a little bit more and got involved as an actress in drama. She realised she had another amazing talent and soon she was winning Best Actress awards all around Ireland.

Whilst Ireland has its great beauty and warm people, it also has a darker side. In a town steeped in religion, many saw that Mum, being the first divorcee at the time, had clearly committed a 'mortal sin' in the eyes of the Catholic Church. I know it was always not made easy for her and some people treated her like the 'town pariah'. Despite this, she has always been a beautifully vibrant and compassionate woman, blended with a quiet inner strength. So she would **elegantly and gracefully rise above all their judgments**. She had a voice and an opinion and used both extremely well. I recall her being 'removed' one day from the town's general meeting for calling out the issues relating to the dangers of local Irish Republican terrorism. She was advised to stay quiet on such matters, because "*you never know who would be listening*". She declared, "It was for this very reason that it was crucial to speak up, if progress was ever to be made". She has never believed in being the silent observer of wrong-doings. She feels accountable for calling out issues, so as not to appear accepting of, or even colluding with them by "turning a blind eye".

I had always been shy and introverted. That was until I started to experience the Catholic education system myself, where cruel corporal punishment was prevalent. The importance and power of the Catholic Church was very apparent in our small town, where the community was utterly accepting, rather than questioning. When I was younger and, fearful of the Nuns, I protested loudly and dragged my feet to school. Then I changed my attitude and took pleasure in rebelling against them and their controlling ways.

It was here that I realised that I had my Mum's feistiness and deep desire to challenge "the system" and people's basic human rights. Unfortunately, my voice and opinions then lack the maturity of today; they were more emotion than well-considered logic. Fighting the system for me became more about skipping school, avoiding home-work and not turning up for my exams, until finally I left the education system completely. My Mum, having experienced her own challenges with Catholic education, was a little too tolerant of my way-ward behaviours! As I reflect back now, I realise that I was cutting off my nose to spite my face. Much of my attitude was actually driven by my own fears; fear of not being accepted, fear of failing, fear of not being good enough. Knowing what I do now, about personal growth and ambition, I understand I would have better served myself, and others, if I had applied myself fully and focused my energy on bigger issues.

At fifteen years old, I told my Mum I wanted to go to England, where my sister Tania was already successfully studying fashion design. Of course,

Tania and I were the world to my Mum and so she packed up everything in Ireland and travelled to England with me.

Early on, the height of my ambition was to become a Nun (before hormones set in), or a primary school teacher (before Mum highlighted just how tough it was to teach well in the current education system). With my own limited knowledge of careers, I did not realise just how restricted and parochial my thinking was! Now I witness the progress we are making today in highlighting the breadth of career opportunities and subsequent role models, particularly with STEM subjects, I am very encouraged to see the continually increasing participation of women. I started my first job with British Gas on a youth training scheme within their Call Centre Operations. This first role and the *robust training and leadership support* launched me, opening the door to a wealth of opportunities over the subsequent years.

Careers were very different in the 1990's. As I consider today's highly competitive market, where there appears to be a more rigid view of what great talent looks like, I wonder if I would ever have the same opportunity today, without a degree, several languages and well-connected parents! I am concerned about the growing *social mobility gap* and differences between class systems, particularly the subtleties of biases and tribal mentality. Through my interviews with the education sector, it's clear that at a very early age we have treated, and continue to treat children differently and 'manage their aspirations'. With today's gap between the rich and poor at an all-time high, I believe we must take more ownership for changing how we create opportunities for the breadth of talent from a variety of social backgrounds and education. We should not just focus our resources on the select few, in the interest of fairer societal and economic growth.

It was also in England where I met James, who became the father of my two children. By the time I was 18 years old, I had my first child, Daniel, and had bought a two-bedroomed home. I took a great deal of pride in this, as I have never relied on the support and benefits from the state. I felt sufficiently financially independent and hardworking to support my own family. Within two years, I had my beautiful daughter, Alanadh, two months premature; she couldn't wait to arrive into the world and not much has changed since!

I felt I had the best of all worlds; an amazing job with British Gas and my own family. I was lucky to get a significant amount of investment in my job training and personal development. The balance between work and life became the main sacrifice, and would do so for some years to come. There wasn't the level of support structure then, as there is now, where organisations are more aware and far better at responding to changing demographics and employee profiles. Every penny counted in our household, but all of this just fuelled my ambition for success and recognition.

After a few years, James and I separated, but we remain friends to this day. We have always valued the relationship with our kids and creating a healthy upbringing for them both. Also, it was an important choice to make for ourselves, where we could mentally heal and move on; not just physically. I find it desperately sad to see how many couples are struggling to achieve the same.

It was at this point that an opportunity arose for me to work in London - on one of the largest multi-million pound investment projects in Europe at the time. It offered a significant career step, however, it was over 130 miles away from home. I did not have the financial stability, or trusted support network to bring my children with me. However, I truly believed that this was a chance for the three of us as a family to thrive and get greater stability in the long run. The project meant leaving my children with my Mum from Monday to Friday, then returning home for the weekend. I accepted the job with conflicting feelings.

I set off for my first day and the longest drive of my life! I waved goodbye, as my Mum cradled 18-month old Alanadh and held 4-year old Daniel's hand. Although this was only going to be a project for a few months, it was not an easy choice to make. Guilt and overwhelm set in, but I put on a brave face and blew kisses to my children. I slipped the car into gear to drive away. I watched as my Mum's face turned from sadness to shock! Like a cringe-worthy sketch from a bad comedy, played out in slow motion, I realised too late that I had slipped the car into the wrong gear and reversed at speed straight into my Mum's car! This wasn't the first time I'd dented my rear-end and I had no doubt there were plenty more to come! With no real damage done, I could try again. This time, slipping the car into the right gear, I set of on my new adventure. I went to work on one the most exciting business projects, with some of the most talented colleagues of my career. Finally, after eight months, I was able to move the children to join me in London.

This was a stretching and *life-changing career choice*; it created the catalyst needed to step into a whole new realm of opportunity, which helped me gain more confidence and inspiration. Importantly, it was clear demonstration of my own freedom and a drive towards greater independence. That was a driving force in me no doubt fuelled by my upbringing. It appeared that when I needed fresh opportunities in life, they would amazingly appear. Could this be the law of attraction? I'm sure it is. Timing is everything and I can say with certainty that I would not have been so open to embracing this opportunity before. I would have given myself *reasons why not to, rather than why*. I recall a speaker I heard once saying, *"we only ever really innovate in our lives when there is a driving force. Otherwise, we tend to settle for the status quo, often trapped in our own ignored discontentment"*. I see this often in client coaching, where the driving force is often an external force; redundancy, divorce, illness, a call from a head-hunter.

It was on this project I met Colin. He was fifteen years my senior and very different to me; adding to my need for a sense of security and stability. I secured a new role with Scandinavian Airlines as the Regional Head of Learning, at the age of twenty-four. Not bad for a high-school drop-out, I felt! In the years that followed, I moved swiftly through an *upward career trajectory* in a variety of roles for a variety of different organisations. Each move ALWAYS offered more responsibility, more stretch and more money.

I had a confidence, and no doubt naivety, that gave me enough courage to *ask for what I wanted*, even if I thought the request was a bit cheeky! But as I reflect, I realise I have never been turned down and I have never really been bored, or stagnated in a role. All of this was a 'quiet' pursuit of opportunities. However, what I often struggled to do was talk about any of my own achievements, or raise my profile beyond a interview. I felt this was self-promoting, which totally went against my value-set. Yet, as we know from research today and from my own expereince, successfully *managing your brand* is a key contributor to success. This meant I only really looked at progression within organisational structures as upward career moves, relying on quite narrow networks of support and influence. It was only later on in my career that I realised that by looking around me at potential opportunities, the world opens up more and the breadth of opportunity is vast. Maybe this is part of the journey, to consolidate learning and find out who you really are...

I recall once how a Chairman guessed I was a Cambridge or Oxford graduate, and I laughed inwardly at how so far off the truth this was! I'd often been to events like these and felt a fraud, completely outside my comfort zone. This was one particular moment where I realised that my own inner insecurities and fears were not what other people were seeing. This was a step forward in terms of embracing my *own authenticity* and accepting that *I was good enough*. Whilst I don't necessarily believe this has held me back at all, I do believe that a sound education can open more doors and can make a successful career journey easier.

During my years working in "the world of corporate", my experience spanned from the highs of developing competitive markets and customer-centric cultures, to the absolute lows of terrorist attacks in the travel industry and the financial crash in banking. What struck me through all of these experiences were the variable responses that particularly highlighted the role of *culture and leadership during significant times of catastrophe and chaos*. For example, following the horrors of the 9/11 terrorist attacks and our own air-crash, the ripple effect meant that our communities and the whole of the travel and tourism industry were caught up the shock-waves.

However, I have never witnessed so much strength of character as our industry became more united, employees became more supportive and leaders became inspirational; *everyone took responsibility for leadership*. During the economic meltdown, the good, the bad and the downright ugly emerged. Politicians turned on the banking industry, banking leaders turned on employees, whilst the people turned on everyone! Leaders responsible took no accountability and broken organisations developed a 'them' and 'us' attitude. Already tough environments became toxic environments; everyone looked for scapegoats and cultures became even more command-control, compliance-driven and transactional. It was also clear that these *crucible moments* are where real change and innovation can be nourished, or stifled. I have seen the expanse and expense of external consultants, crawling all over the resulting change programmes. Some consultant firms offer transformational solutions and value, whilst others make money building complex and unsustainable systems, structures and processes.

In one organisation, I recall how tough the environment was; a highly politically charged environment where self-preservation was encouraged, and we were challenged to re-present the facts to show a more 'positive' story. I found the "political game-playing" grated against my value system. Leaders would individually enter the boss's office to share the latest extensive presentation deck, which had taken teams of people weeks to prepare. We would watch anxiously, as our leaders came out of his office and walked down the corridor for signs of how each meeting went. We often called that humiliation: *'walking the green mile'*.

People were dropping off like flies; through stress-induced sickness, leaving, or being told to leave. I was barely getting time to see my children during the week. I knew it was unhealthy and it was now my time to leave. And let's be honest here, I knew had had to go before I was kicked out, as I have no doubt I would soon follow many of the others who didn't fit in! I handed in my resignation and decided to start my own business. Again, I notice through my current leadership work that this transition is becoming more popular and often for the very same reason. Today there is an interesting shift in attitudes, where corporates who want to attract and retain talent need to consider how they can create *a great place to work*.

In parallel, my marriage to Colin my husband of 15 years broke down. Well, in all honesty it had broken down a long time before, but I had lived in denial as my work and children became my focus! As the main earner, I was achieving career successes, whilst he struggled to get promotions. He would oscillate between caring and rage. As I look back now I realise I had been the victim of psychological abuse, where it escalated over time so in the beginning went un-noticed then later became accepted. I found I had lost my voice, fearing any kind of conflict. As successful as I was at work, I was deeply ashamed of who I had become at home. I had developed a persistent stress-induced cough and felt as if my whole chest was being compressed. After many visits to a variety of specialists, I was diagnosed with… full health!

Whilst I was able to make important decisions about my career, I was struggling to do the same at home. I persevered. After several earlier threats of violence, the crucible moment came when Colin twice threatened my life. After seeking professional legal advice, I realised I had very few rights. So I prepared. One morning, after he left for work, I quickly woke my two teenage children Daniel and Alanadh. We took only black bin bags filled with clothes and some belongings, leaving everything else that I had worked for behind us. We moved to our new rented accommodation. I knew that there would be challenging times ahead financially, and I was very scared. However, now at last I was also safe and free.

New business, new home, new beginning!

The shocking fact is that in just the UK alone, two women on average are killed each week, as a result of domestic violence. This does not even take into account statistics relating to incrementally increasing control, aggressive cultural practices and psychological abuse. These are known to exist, yet often not addressed, due to feelings of shame and guilt. Subsequently extracting women from highly toxic relationships and/ or communities are some of the biggest challenges that we face in terms of gender equality and empowerment.

Through my coaching and support of highly successful leaders, what has struck me is just how prevalent this abuse issue truly is. *You will note that I said leaders, and not distinguished this as a women's issue. Why? Because it is a growing issue for men too.* Whilst there is still much to achieve, in terms of addressing domestic abuse, I welcome the strong action being taken by our government, and in particular Theresa May, to criminalise these behaviours and highlight the issues. This initiative includes tackling psychological patterns of coercion and control, which will inevitably lead to the cultural shift and action that is needed to support victims; or as I prefer to call them, *survivors*. But let's remove the word 'domestic' and replace it with the word 'managerial' or 'organisational'; because, as many businesswomen and men know, abuse and bullying is not just reserved for the confines of the home. It is the dirty little secret, or *the inconvenient truth*, deep-rooted inside cultures, where denial is an easier option.

My new executive development business, Clareo Potential, created one of the greatest developmental stretches and opportunities so far in my career.

Fortunately, I had developed a strong network, which helped me to develop early business opportunities. I pitched for a significant piece of work with HSBC, collaborating with Harvard, to develop their top 60 C-Suite leadership talent globally over an 18-month period. In parallel, I also won a fascinating piece of work with Unilever to conduct a review of their participation in external awards and recognition globally and to build talent profiles for their top 100 leaders. Both opportunities helped me to kick-start my business, during a period of huge economic downturn. When asked, I used to put it down to luck. But on reflection, I realise that the actual secret was by keeping 'my finger on the pulse' I was able to spot opportunities, followed by hard graft, in order to win and deliver them. In the words of Thomas Jefferson, *"I'm a great believer in luck, and I find the harder I work, the more I have of it."* So true!

It was during this period of my life that I started to write *Inspiring Women Leaders*. It is only in this version, as I have begun the healing process, that I have been able to do a deeper exploration. No-body knew any of this on the outside, not even some of my closest friends, unless I dared share it in confidence with them. As I emerged through, I understand how my personal experiences were clouding my own appreciation of my strengths, as well as feeding my belief system. My conscious thoughts drove me on, but my unconscious thoughts (understood to be circa 95% of our brain-power) often reminded me that I wasn't good enough. I felt I was: not clever enough, not slim enough, not courageous enough, not talented and certainly not good enough as a Mum. Don't get me wrong! I was happy and successful, but a part of me, deep down, felt a fraud and I knew this was detracting from my performance and what I could truly achieve.

My dear friend and therapist to many celebrities, Marisa Peer, wrote the exceptional book 'Ultimate Confidence'. She shared with me that, as humans we continue to return to *what we know*, as it makes us feel safe, even when it is bad for us. Or at least, it gives the illusion of safety and so we fear **breaking out of the known into the unknown.** Having convictions and a belief system that hold us back, become our reality and so these need to be erased. Marisa also shared a technique with me to encourage self-praise and let this in; "Leigh, I want you to write on your mirror **'I am enough'** and I want to repeat to yourself every day, *I am enough*'". By accepting that we are enough, we are able to change the way we respond to praise and criticism. These powerful conversations with Marisa have been life-changing. So I now encourage others struggling with some form of discontent to use similar techniques.

Building a new business and life, whilst managing two teenagers, as a single Mum was no doubt tough, to begin with. If I hadn't made these *decisions and taken action*, I wouldn't be where I am today. I am convinced of that. As one door closes, many more open. Finding the courage to close the door on what is unhealthy – at work or home – can only lead to better things. But everything in my story that I have shared with you has prepared me for *who I am* and *how I experience life - today.*

Who am I?

I am a businesswoman passionate about inspiring leadership. Though my work as an author, motivational speaker, culture consultant and leadership coach, I am able to use my passion to help and inspire others. I have the privilege of working with fascinating people and businesses around the world. By linking my business with my new charity, *The Inspiring Leadership Trust*, I am helping change the platform, in order that women and men can thrive and the already successful leaders can *"pay it forward"*. These successful leaders can contribute their time, resources, energy and passions to supporting some of the most vulnerable in society.

Importantly, I am a loving Mum with two children to be proud of. I have married my soul-mate, Jonathan Bowman-Perks, who shares similar passions and so we often combine our work. We live a splendid life. I know that if I hadn't had the life experiences I had - witnessing great leadership, bad leadership and experiencing great relationships and bad relationships - I would not have found my calling.

I also have many fears; how do I grow the business, so I can pay the bills? How do I step on stage to deliver a speech, without being ill in the bathroom beforehand? How do I make sure I am a good mother, when I sometimes get my parenting so screwed up? Am I good enough to achieve my ambitious aspirations?

But, I am also fuelled by passion and purpose. And now I know *passion and purpose trump fear* any day!

Who am I?
I AM ME!

-

Nairobi, Kenya for my charity, Inspiring Leadership Trust

Speaking at the House of lords

Inspiring Leadership with the Ministry of Health, Botswana

Introduction – An Alternative Paradigm

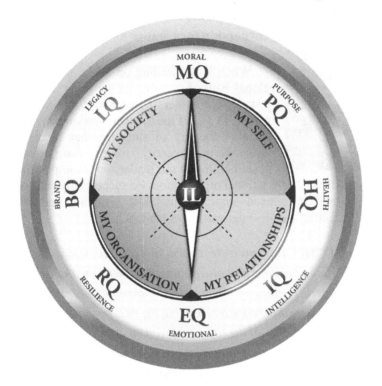

"Early on in careers, when people are promoted into positions of leadership, they talk about the structure and systems. However, the biggest challenge is leading and inspiring others. It is working with lots of different individuals across different departments. If you get this right, then everything else will fall into place. There are fewer people that can actually get the best out of others and it is harder to find. You can have different styles and the skills are less obvious, such as the quieter, more humble leader. We need to hunt deeper for great leadership that's respected."

Marie Nassor, Dep. Head Teacher

Ed Fox - Human Resources
The Inspiring Male Leader Who Takes
Ownership for Change

When I was leading on talent and diversity at a global bank, I met one of the most intelligent and progressive leaders that I had come across in my career. In one of the toughest working environments, Ed was the ray of sunshine that recognised the longer-term diversity issues that affected the sustainability of our leadership talent pipelines. In a highly data-driven, transactional organisation, Ed successfully challenged the status quo and introduced some of the most visionary and pragmatic solutions affecting our next generation of leaders.

Ed shared, *"My Gran was a strong feminist and an important role model in my life. I studied history and always found myself focusing on the gender angle. This interest continued when I came to management. It was great that I was able to make a difference by ensuring the next generation of leadership succession was inclusive of the talents of women.*

"When I started my career on an internal graduate scheme, I noticed that the future pipeline of talent all had similar backgrounds, approaches and thoughts on leadership. We were hiring very masculine, high-achieving outcome-focused individuals. There was an absence of the values orientated, collaborative and inclusive leadership mind-set that that I saw in many female leaders. There was a notable lack of NextGen leaders that brought this feminine approach to leadership. I was struck by the fact that over 80% of graduates recruited were male. Around 70% of retail employees are female and it is noticeable that as you go up the leadership levels this reverses. This happens even though we know our customer base and consumer choices are mostly influenced by women. It made no sense that we had an absence of women on our programmes. I set about removing the bias that occurred at the point of hiring and within the first year 55% of the graduate cohort were women. This had a tremendous impact in terms of diversity and the appetite for graduate hires shifted from an initial 15 to 55 and then finally 135. This was in a time of recession when many

organisations were reducing graduate hires. The next generation of the leadership pipeline was going to be more female; the thinking brought into the organisation immediately introduced new perspectives on our consumers.

"This isn't about gender actually. It's about a genuine attempt to reinvent ourselves as leaders for a modern age. The internet, social networking sites and modern technology have reset our values and expectations as employees. Modern leaders will only engage their employees if they have the humility to listen, reach out to seek better answers than your own, collaborate, inspire and transform. We are concerned by purpose, values and how to get things done with a strong sense of mission and duty. There are men with a more feminine mind-set and vice versa. Hiring by a single identity does not work. We were looking for the right style(s) to help deliver products that reflect the full diversity of consumers' values.

"Women are consistently identified as talent and yet they are not showing up on succession plans. Unless you really focus on it in order to drive the agenda forward it is so difficult to drive change. In order to get results, we need to set targets, otherwise it just doesn't happen. We live in a world where networks make a difference to who gets the job. When senior leaders know there is a target to hit, they make the effort to expand their network and understand the talent of those different to themselves. It is win-win. Obviously leaders seek out women that are good. No one appoints a woman just because of their gender. I've seen men get the right roles because they know the right people and targets refocus networks so that it isn't only the usual suspects who are discussed around the board table. Critical mass is needed. If you have just a few then you can get the 'queen bee' syndrome. It isn't helpful as it doesn't reflect well on women and stops progress. Targets force the manager to care about building an inclusive talented team.

"This isn't about positive discrimination either, it's about meritocracy, the best person for the job and the sponsorship needed to support a diverse range of talents. Women will come to lead more as they become more represented on succession plans. We often see women in Heads of HR or Marketing roles as they encourage a feminine influence on leadership styles. Yet with Finance and Risk, it's the more masculine. Other areas should embrace the feminine influence and they should have permission to do so.

"In the West we are in an aging workforce. The baby boomers have held power and influence longer than previous generations. We need these leaders to embrace an extended career through which they pass on their legacy through mentoring. This is really important. This generation loves work and we must find a way for them to hand their expertise over to a generation of leaders who value work/life balance and dual family careers. We must be careful that our unconscious biases do not lead to us assessing the potential of the next generation of succession by the values of the previous generation. There are clearly two very different mind-sets on the role of women in society. It will take its time to shift. We must not underestimate the difficulty for generations that find themselves in a different world. Things always make sense or don't make sense dependent on the generation and viewpoints. There are views on how things should be done."

Inspiring Women Leaders

For over twenty years I have been a quietly ambitious woman focused on carving a successful life both in my home and my career. I have always been curious how others achieved this. This fascination has grown even further, through my journey of developing talent and diversity strategies for global companies. It has finally led to me building my own international executive development business. Together we have worked with and coached hundreds of male and female leaders helping them to achieve their own leadership and career success.

Even with the highly anticipated, yet faltering, second wave feminist movement, there is no denying the evidence that gender parity does not exist across the leadership levels. It's become the hot topic of today, with many prominent female leaders taking a visible stance. We have not progressed sufficiently enough to unblock the pipeline of female talent. The heat has certainly been turned up for more to be done. The women's agenda is growing in its visibility and support. One could be forgiven for feeling consumed and distracted by the noise in the system about a lack of progress. It is of course an important matter, however, this is not the main rationale and purpose for the book.

I have been curious about a number of issues:
1. Responsiveness
2. Sustainability
3. Inclusion
4. Celebration
5. Inspiring Leadership

1. Responsiveness - *Our world is changing, therefore, so must our leadership*

The recent global economic crisis led to a well-documented loss of trust. In my view, there were at least three fundamental catalysts at the heart of this crisis: poor leadership decision-making; toxic organisational structures, and a severe breakdown in basic societal values.

Our expectations of leaders has changed significantly in recent years, and so too has our understanding of the art of leadership itself. This was caused by two seismic shifts operating in parallel.

The first group are environmental factors, which were: the complexity and pace of international businesses; political and regulatory environments; technological advances; socio-economic and global instability. The second group were: our understanding of people's neurology, psychology, biology and cultures which gives significant insight to our knowledge of humanity and, in turn, leadership. These significant changes mean we must evolve old models and views of how we recognise and develop leaders fit to face 21st century challenges.

We now live in a freer market with short-term change initiatives, where careers are in a constant state of flux. There is a far more tenuous psychological contract between the leader and the led. More than ever before people question, 'Are our leaders trust-worthy?' Organisations instantaneously determine an individual's social or economic usefulness, sometimes at the expense of their potential longer-term value. Such organisations also continue to advocate systems and structures that favour old working patterns and behaviours. How are they really thinking innovatively about enabling career participation for both female and male leaders with different needs over time? Working with technology enables this flexibility and there is an opportunity to harness these solutions - if organisations choose to!

I have observed archaic leadership models and systems, which are failing to address individual performance and potential. Our excuse for not letting go of these traditional approaches is that we are concerned that leaders don't have the capacity or ability to understand new concepts. We therefore fail to challenge the status quo. This results in infantilising leaders and tick-box exercises to managing our people. We should challenge HR to move from the role of 'policing' to one of 'pace setting' in order to anticipate and facilitate people's career aspirations.

If we were to scrutinise our reward systems, structures, infrastructures and leadership strategy, I wonder how relevant they are to today's climate. If our paradigm for understanding potential hasn't shifted, then how can we embrace new and diverse leadership? In Ed Fox's story, he demonstrates that significant change can occur with the right momentum and healthy attitude. With sufficient creativity and understanding, surely this is not as insurmountable as we are led to believe. If it can happen in Ed's example, then it can happen anywhere.

2. Sustainability - Short-sighted change brings short-lived progress

With the anticipated talent shortages, wider participation and unlocking leadership talent from a more diverse pool is crucial for business success. If women make up 50% of the full potential pool of talent, then enabling them to progress their careers in the workplace under more flexible terms, will help address this shortage. It is also a key factor in creating economic empowerment for women and a more diverse workforce.

However, as we look through the lens of statistics and debates around imposing quotas, I wonder how our obsession with numbers is helping us to address the real dilemmas for our genuinely talented and aspiring leaders, both female and male. In the race for gender balance, I question whether this is driving healthy and fair behaviours in businesses.

Through my own executive development business and corporate experiences, I have met, observed and coached many inspirational leaders. I have also witnessed what we call 'expiring leadership': those in leadership positions who suck the life out of others. I think you know the kind of poor leaders I mean!

I have seen how women have had to fight hard to make their way to the top of male-dominated, masculine cultures. You can achieve an equal 50:50 split of men and women on executive teams, yet still have a masculine culture, comprising Alpha Males and Alpha Females. This makes the data irrelevant. We need to see true leadership diversity which includes more of our local markets represented. This is not just a gender issue. If you don't bring diversity to the table then how are you going to be able to relate to and reflect the differences in your employee and customer bases?

Many of the women I have coached and interviewed have similar views. They have often shared with me, "*I look up and see accomplished women, but ask myself whether I am prepared to make the same brutal choices. Often I am not.*‖ The role models presented to us had often reached the highest echelons in business, yet other women felt they were so far removed from their own lives, that it has been difficult to connect with their journey or even their ambitions.

Let's also be clear on another concern that keeps arising: aspiring women mostly do not look at other women and make judgements based on their assertion and career success. More often, they are disappointed when that success is achieved at the expense of remaining true to their authentic selves, or too much has been compromised in order to get there.

Is this solely a women's issue? Or is it an issue of family and/or personal values, something that often transcends the lure of the corporate workplace to involve decisions that take place in our homes and private lives – a dilemma for both women and men.

By looking at the data on gender presented to us for today's leadership, aren't we also missing the more telling picture of a sustainable future pipeline and truly diverse leadership teams? We should beware of responding too hastily to today's gender data. It is a deeper issue within our organisations. The culture and our succession planning give a true indication of real movement in the agenda, rather than just 'today's figures'.

For example, let's consider the recruitment firms that actually pay women to go through the hiring process to the final stages, in order that they can 'demonstrate' to their clients they can deliver a diverse pool of interviewees.

In another example, within our education system in general it appears that girls thrive on practical assessment, whilst boys perform better in formal examinations. Poor educational performance results bring the highly anticipated political knee-jerk reaction with brutal decisions and newly enforced testing through more examinations as our governments strive to demonstrate 'progress'. What are our changes in favour of and who are the actual beneficiaries?

Alternatively, let's explore a little further the people metrics within business. My observation from all of the research and interviews is that you can report on achieving greater gender parity and yet still fail to create a diverse and inclusive leadership team.

I do accept numbers are important, however I believe we must know what we are looking for and reporting on. Data can provide the insight, but not the solution, and unfortunately they are often deliberately misrepresented. The "baby boomer" generation have vested interests in protecting their positions and the status quo, so it does not encourage the transformation and change that is required.

If our cultural environments are not shifting, then we will still fail to attract a diverse pool of talent. Playing the numbers game is a short-term strategy that is unsustainable. As we see talented women leave executive and board positions, where are the replacements coming from?

The time is ripe for progress. Rather than focusing on the numbers game and imposing blanket policies, governance or even quotas, by exploring many of these business initiatives we can get closer to the positive efforts being made by businesses to support and, more importantly, *sustain* gender parity. In the long term, it is in our economic and social interest to serve the upcoming generations. You can get blockers in the culture, which are hard to overcome. We must get to the heart of the issues that affect the talent pipeline and spotlight where the bottlenecks occur far deeper within our businesses.

3. Inclusion - Gender Parity is a Women's Issue: the paradigm shift

In her insightful and inspiring book *Lean In*, Sheryl Sandberg[1] eloquently challenges the philosophical arguments as to whether it is the institution or the women themselves that need to break down the barriers. She asks that we *'wage battles on both fronts'*. I recommend you read her book as I found myself nodding frequently in agreement to the stories shared and her sensitive and generous contribution to the topic.

In this book, *Inspiring Women Leaders*, I want to challenge the way that we think about this further. We talk about issues of gender and parity as if this is a women's issue, or something we need to fix by changing the system. And of course, being women, we are highly responsive to how we can address 'our' issues and assume the responsibility for making change happen. The result? We help women overcome these issues through 'self-help' gurus, we ask for women's viewpoints, we run women-only networks and we see the gender challenge through the monocular lens of 'women'.

With so many publications on how women can survive and thrive in a man's world, I have become increasingly concerned by terms like 'faking it, to make it', 'breaking through the glass ceiling', 'the sticky floor' and making it in 'the boys club'. As we try to differentiate women from men, we build stereotypes and divides: men are 'this' and women are 'that'.

When we talk about having diverse boards and leadership teams, I also didn't realise that our teachings must be about adjustment to 'fit in' for survival.

I wonder how our language, which reinforces biases and stereotypes, still serves us today? Surely, enhanced business results come from all of our differences, more so than from our similarities. I fully appreciate that we must all develop and grow.

Squeezing ourselves out of shape, in order to fit with traditional views of leadership, however, is not the way forward. I believe our language needs to shift to become more positive and progressive and, in particular, more collaborate and inclusive.

Are we not increasing social stigmas in how we craft our methods for addressing the issues? Of course, these are all great initiatives: creating visibility and mobilising people into taking action. However, I believe we need to be a lot clearer about what's going on here.

In an exceptional and thought provoking presentation Jackson Katz (TED Talks), shares how acts of violence against women 'are seen as women's issues that some good men help out with'. Jackson has a problem with this frame in that the dominant group that holds the power and privilege does not get paid attention to. On a personal level, this was a real 'aha' moment for me and became a significant paradigm shift for how I considered the issue of inequality.

This alternative lens resonated with my own and other women's experiences and growing frustrations. With messages from all around us about how we, as women, need to change in order to address the gender issue, we are reinforcing old patterns of responsibility for the issue. Women then incorrectly assume a position of guilt and shame when things aren't changing. I would like to take Jackson Kratz's concept back into the world of business and leadership. I would therefore argue that this is an issue of achieving diversity through addressing the issues of equality and inclusion.

Let's take this to the top of the tree. You can be a CEO, or even a political leader, with ability to influence the agenda. You may even have a diversity strategy and talk frequently about women in leadership. However, if you surround yourself with right-hand men in the most prominent and powerful positions and don't create your own personal change, then I question whether your actions speak louder than your words.

By removing or reducing men's involvement in encouraging women leaders, then those leaders that have some of the greatest decision-making influence are not part of the solution. The pervasive formation of the in-group and out-group conspires to reinforce this divide.

Times are changing and I certainly think that debates about what men bring to the table versus women will naturally become somewhat obsolete with generational shifts and role changes. This is illustrated by the wealth of male and female talent bringing feminine and masculine traits to the table and devising solutions in both work and home that encompass dual responsibilities.

So, whilst insightful, categorising differences by gender can become a bit of a red herring for us. If we are to move forward progressively and conquer gender bias, we must focus on the underlying social and cultural issues. Then we can form a paradigm shift where we *all* have a role to play in collaboration, equality and, importantly, valuing authenticity and true differences.

4. Celebration – Recognising that Successes Emerge in Different Ways

Messages of the growing frustration that the women's agenda has stalled are ubiquitous. Of course, the evidence is there and this cannot be denied. However, as I conducted my research, it became apparent that change is happening in some of the most crucial areas.

It is clear that women who are pursuing careers are co-creating solutions with their partners. Together they manage family and work, building boundaries to protect the most important things in life - the things that they truly love in both areas.

Numerous women's networks, speaking events, awards and recognition are in full flow. Inspirational women are becoming the catalysts for change in repressed and oppressed countries in the world. They lead on initiatives that hold purpose and meaning, such as Chime for Change, founded by Gucci; the Kezi Silverstone Trust whose story is in this book, and also Lucy Ndungu's Hope for Teenage Mothers, to name just a few. There are many more trail-blazing women working hard around the world who are making a positive and significant difference, mostly under our radar as the unsung heroes.

We haven't stalled at all. In fact, I would argue that we have more momentum than ever and just need to fully embrace what that means. Only then we can innovate in response to the future needs of our employees and not hold on to past structures and solutions that are, in effect, obsolete in today's economy.

The toughness of any transition period is that it is just that.

This is not the phase of the bra-burning feminism fighting for equal rights, certainly in the developed world. Nor is it the phase where generational beliefs have fundamentally shifted to the point of consistent behavioural change. We all know that changing structures and processes are easier tasks than changing the hearts and the minds of those with conflicting views. I believe that the space in between can be some of the most challenging. Unfortunately it has also become some of the most unappreciated. We must recognise and celebrate these changes that are happening on every level.

Clearly, there is more to be done. None of us are powerless to make a difference, even at the most basic level. We all have huge and, at times, unrealised potential for doing even more.

5. Ultimately, this is an issue of 21st century leadership

In essence, it seems the real enigma is all about what exactly is leadership. With leadership comes a celebration and appreciation of the progress that is really being made, not just at the most visible levels but also at ground level. With leadership also comes responsibility for taking the baton.

How can we develop cultures that respect and understand the value of equality and diversity through enabling inclusion? We have many amazing female trailblazers and even a few great men. Yet, the existing dominating leaders cannot sit by on the sidelines, quietly encouraging progress, viewing it as someone else's role.

We could just wait it out, as something that will naturally evolve with future generations. But isn't this a cop out?

Are we not more ambitious about our own personal development and power to influence as leaders? As Ghandi famously said, *"You must be the change you wish to see in the world."* We can all take courage and be the game-changer, if we choose not to get trapped by our societal norms and dogma, indifference, or (as described by Margaret Heffernan in her TED Talk) act in 'wilful blindness'.

Until we start to make leadership choices about our behaviours and infrastructures, only then we will find it hard to make a difference. Overcoming our fears to find courage and take that gauntlet is empowering for us all. That is the case, whether you are operating in some of the most developed economies such as the US or Europe, through to some of the toughest environments for women such as areas across parts of the Middle-East or Asia.

Let's be very clear, this is not an issue for women. This is an issue for everyone. This is an issue of ***Inspiring Leadership.***

About this book

We are already inundated with data and media comments about gender diversity. Whilst it is important to understand the information that's available to us, this book does not revisit these well-trodden paths and statistical arguments. In particular it avoids metaphors such as, 'glass ceilings', 'sticky floors' and 'the men's club', which hold little appeal. This book aims to create a new and more inclusive language.

We know that it is often a few courageous trailblazers within minority groups who enable the change. It is also essential to the success of the agenda to ensure that dominant groups embrace and live the change. This book is an encouragement for greater participation by *all* to achieve equality through inclusion.

I have been searching for an alternative path and language for leadership in its most integrated way. It needs to be one that values the combination of authenticity and equality. I have always personally found inspiration from the stories where people share their experiences, including their vulnerabilities as much as their strengths. *Inspiring Women Leaders* aims to combine real life and work, both of which go hand-in-hand, for greater resonance and wisdom.

Having interviewed over 100 women and men, I have been deeply humbled. I have identified leaders whose stories resonate with our own. I have purposefully selected inspiring women from around the world, those who offer very different insights and experiences. All are working hard day by day to make a greater difference through their leadership. Many are the unsung heroes that attempt to close the gaps in equality and societal challenges, so that others may thrive. Often these women had no such privileges as we experience now.

By getting these leaders to share their own highly personal stories, we can understand more about what drove them and how they achieved success. We can learn what they have in common and also what makes them so different, so they stand out from the others to be inspiring leaders. I interviewed high potential leaders and aspiring leaders from different sectors. They had different ambitions and were at varying career stages, thus providing a deeper review from a variety of perspectives. I delved into the cultural differences and how women have successfully navigated their way through these.

Through my research, it became clear that inspiration came in many guises. The level of diversity really struck me. What emerged was no single magic formula to success. Some were rebels and high school drop-outs, only to flourish later on in business, like myself! Some were highly academic, studious and attended some of the best universities in the world. Some may have been bound by their cultures, or challenging circumstances by anyone's standards. Yet they achieved the most admirable successes.

My research also uncovered some common, recurring themes. Through their profound experiences, often encountering what would seem insurmountable hurdles, they subsequently learnt a huge amount. They generously share this wisdom for us all to benefit.

In essence, the main thrust for this book is about inspirational leadership and cultures because I believe that *we all* have a role to play.

It is underpinned by current insights into the women's agenda from the stories generously shared by a variety of leaders. I combine insightful data with soul to tell stories that form an empowering journey that is deeply personal and sets the tone for change at both personal and social levels. This is because I truly believe that the catalyst for change is diverse leadership in its *sincerest* form.

So, if you seek a debate about the differences between men and women, the struggles of managing careers in a male dominated world, or if women can do a better job in leadership, then this is probably not the right business book for you. However, if you are keen to make a difference in your life, work and the community, in a short amount of time, then this book is aimed at providing you with inspiration and accumulated wisdom to support you.

What I cannot possibly do is give all of the answers. In a complex and diverse world this is impossible. Nor can the leaders in this book. We can only share experiences and perspectives so others may benefit.

For every insight there's an alternative viewpoint and for every argument there is a counter-argument. Life is a paradox; perceptions and perspectives are always going to be diverse and conflicting. The book acts as a catalyst for your deepest reflections and thinking, so you can make personal shifts and change by levering your individual talents and passions and having the courage to pursue them.

Inspiring Women Leaders is about what resonates and, equally, what has no fit at all, as both offer insights. Leadership success is situational and contextual, so very personal for you as the reader.

Who is this book aimed at?

You may already be a successful leader and aspire to become more inspiring and inspired by your work and life. You may be a follower looking for how to be led well and manage your leaders. As a leader, or advocate of the diversity agenda, you may want to know more about the work that other organisations are doing to support women in their careers. You may even be an undergraduate, keen to understand more about the world of work and how you can carve a successful career in the future.

From CEOs through to students, both men and women, in any part of the world, this book has been written for you. Therefore, I have made *Inspiring Women Leaders* relevant to anyone ambitious enough to create their own inspiring legacy. I encourage you to leave your positive legacy, in your lifetime, rather than after your death, no matter how great or how small.

Everyone has the potential and can choose to be a leader. Opportunities for leadership emerge in many ways. The leadership of others impacts us *all*.

My call to action is for our choices to be inspiring to others and ourselves.

About Inspiring Leadership

Inspiring Women Leaders looks at the results of my interviews with male and female leaders and is structured around the model for Inspiring Leadership. It contains the latest research into emotional intelligence and the Inspiring Leadership Inventory™ (IL-i™). This takes a deeper look at characteristics and behaviours to understand and celebrate differences, inspiration and real passions. I also explore useful insights, drawn from the disciplines of psychology and neuroscience, to understand how our thinking becomes either an enabler, or a blocker to achieving our life purpose.

In collaboration with Jonathan Bowman-Perks MBE and Dr. Reuven Bar-On (Bar- On EQ-i), we have looked to address 21st century leadership issues such as:

purpose, ethics, morality, health, emotional intelligence, neurobiology and sustainability.

We have brought this together in a simple framework and are surveying leaders and businesses from around the world. By combining empirical research and interviews with leaders, I have identified the common themes. From these themes I have created a set of tools, techniques and strategies to help model Inspiring Leadership.

Inspiring Women Leaders is the second book in the Inspiring Leadership series, the first being *Inspiring Leadership* by Jonathan Bowman-Perks MBE. The books are underpinned by the Inspiring Leadership model and the Inspiring Leadership Inventory^{TM} (IL-i^{TM}) and has been researched and tested with leaders from around the world.

The next book in the series is called *Inspiring CEOs & Their Boards* and we have already commenced our research. For further information about the series, research, supporting events and even participating in our future research, please see **www.leighbowmanperks.com**.

How to get the most out of this book

You could read this book straight through as a practical guide to leadership and to understand the underpinning philosophy to *Inspiring Leadership* and the research. Equally, you can dip into the various parts of chapters that are relevant to you at a given time.

For ease, I have divided the book into three key parts:

Part 1 – Provides background, context and research, including interesting results of the Inspiring Leadership Inventory^{TM} and psychometric analysis.

Part 2 - the 8 Inspiring Leadership components. Each chapter contains stories from inspiring leaders and some topical questions at the end to provoke our thinking and help us to generate some personal actions.

Part 3 - contains a variety of resources, tools, references and recommended reading and links to support your development. Further support and information is available via our website.

Although there are common themes, the content does not necessarily replicate the viewpoints of every individual, who have diverse experiences and perspectives. They are there to provoke thought and discussion.

It's all about action and not intent

How often do we hear reassuring words of intent from leaders? These words quickly become the rhetoric, rather than the reality. We have all seen the most inspired training programmes, coaching and workshops culminate in disappointingly little personal behavioural change.

We are comfortable changing processes and tasks. We may make some behavioural change. However, how much of our great intent drifts away over time? We then become self-critical, or feel shame and guilt when we look back and think about our broken promises. Behavioural change is like a muscle that needs focus and exercise to grow in order to become habit.

My hope is that *Inspiring Women Leaders* helps you in understanding the essence of leadership. That you might learn from other leaders, who have achieved success in work and in life, often in the face of adversity. It assumes that you are interested in hearing stories from inspiring leaders and are keen to develop your own self-awareness, in order to create some form of change.

Some areas may challenge you to revisit aspects of your own work-life to find greater congruence and alignment, through living your life "on purpose" and achieving your ambitions. With so much noise in the system, it is also my hope that you identify with, and find confidence in, your own authentic self.

Through taking a fresh view through an alternative lens, the book offers you the opportunity to make both subtle and transformative changes at a number of levels. In particular, it encourages you to make small acts of leadership that positively affect yourself and those around you daily. If you are leading or part of a broken system, it is a call for taking action to positively affect change rather than accept the status quo.

Through being open to experimentation and learning, you will find a fresh source of energy to take action in a constructive way. With intractable and complex systems, do not be overly self-critical if you are not successful in all of your goals. The important fact is that you participate and take steps forward, learning from errors and poor judgments whilst acknowledging and celebrating progress.

This book is not about faking it, playing the game, or squeezing yourself out of shape. I don't seek to make you fit in with others' preconceived ideas of who, or what you should be or do. It's certainly not about judgement of yourselves or others. You are unique and your choices are very personal to you. I encourage you to sit with any vulnerability from your experiences and take courage to stretch yourselves to be an even more inspiring leader. This is not about doing even more; we all know the challenge of balancing so many conflicting priorities.

In a busy and demanding world, this is not about working harder: it's about working smarter and on the things that are most important to you.

Rita Ross
Diversity & Inclusion (Finance) and
Executive Director of 'Cure Rett'

"My parents were both Italian immigrants. My Mum immigrated to England at the age of 21. She didn't know anyone here apart from an uncle who owned a fish and chip shop in Scotland; this was the only reason why her father allowed her to come to the UK. After working here for five years, she was due to go back to Italy, however, she met my Dad. He had come over with his family and had been here since the age of 16. They married and settled in London.

"Growing up I always felt like a foreigner. I would speak English in school and when I went home Italian was our spoken language and socially we mixed with other Italian families. At school I always wanted to fit in and be like everyone else as, although we lived in North London, in those days it was not as culturally diverse as it is today. My Mum wanted me to go to a Catholic school, however, I wanted to go to a mixed comprehensive secondary school like my friends, which, looking back, wasn't the best

choice. However, I did well as I mixed with the right groups there having the discipline from my Mum at home to make sure I studied and always did my best.

"My parents split up when I was 12. It was then that I realised my Mum had kept up the pretence of the stable Italian family for a long time up to the separation, always wanting to do the best for her family and being a very proud woman. She worked in a factory over the road from where we lived as the shift patterns worked well with managing the family. She was a hard worker and often worked very long hours and double shifts to earn as much as she could for the home. So, from a young age I was taught to work hard, be independent and earn my own money. I also needed to help my Mum around the house whilst she was working, so learned to cook and do the housework.

"My Mum was an extremely strong role model for me in terms of working hard, and she instilled in me that I always needed to be able to stand on my own two feet. Most of my friends left school at 16 but I stayed on for a further year, as my Mum was keen for me to get the best education I could. However I saw my Mum struggling financially and having to pay off the debts left by my Dad so I wanted to leave school to help her out too. My Mum said I could only do this if I got a good secure job. A friend of mine had got a job in one of the big banks, so I thought I would apply too and was quickly offered a place. I found that anything that my Mum thought was a good thing really influenced me at the time and she was delighted that I had secured a job in a bank.

"My original idea was to be an airhostess or something equally glamorous, so I thought I would only spend a couple of years working at the bank to build up my CV. I started as a back office junior then moved into roles serving customers, which I loved! I was given lots of new opportunities and I aspired then to be a Personal Banker or Office Manager, not appreciating how much was beyond this. As banking changed, the roles became more and more customer-focused, and, since I had good people skills, I continued to be promoted and moved into senior management roles.

"In the back of my mind I always thought I should also do something else career wise as my original plan was not to stay in banking. I applied for a

job with a new mobile phone business, which was just starting out, and they offered me a good role with them. When I approached my manager to say I was going to resign he took me out to lunch and convinced me that by staying with the Bank then I could continue to progress my career and would have as many opportunities open to me as I wanted. There were no real female role models at the time, so I decided to take a career break rather than leave and consider other options. I took the opportunity to work in Italy and use my Italian. I found a job as a PA/translator in a multinational company. Working in Italy really opened my eyes to how great my role and company in the UK was. I found Italy was still very chauvinistic and much more male dominated environment then I had been used to in the UK.

"That really made up my mind to return to the bank and continue my career. As openings came up I would apply and worked in many different roles from regional office to a variety of management roles. Every time I felt my career was slowing down, I would look around and push myself to take on a new challenge.

"One of the roles I took on was a Business Development Manager for a stockbrokers which was very different to anything I had ever done before. However, it helped me realise what I did and didn't like in terms of working alone and being on the road much of the time. Although I knew this wasn't the role for me, doing it gave me great profile to senior leaders and prepared me for my first senior management position. Being a woman made me stand out more. Nearly all my colleagues were male and very numbers driven where as I was far more people focused. So I achieved success through, what some would say at the time, less traditional ways. I was promoted to a Director position whilst I was pregnant; at the time there weren't a lot of women in these roles, so this was very unusual.

"My intention was always, once I had the baby, to just take a few months off and then get back to work, which I did. I settled Cameron in to nursery and then I returned to work and went back to being the kind of manager I used to be. I always believe that if you work hard you will get the results. I was never a 9 to 5 girl; I never stopped. For me, it was all about being with people, and motivating and inspiring others to be the best that they can be.

"I did feel the guilt of leaving my son at nursery. It was very hard.

Fortunately my husband was really great and I had very supportive line managers. Even though I sometimes felt like I wasn't doing as much as I used to, my husband would tell me otherwise as he thinks I'm a workaholic! This is really about 'who I am' rather than anything to do with the demands of the job.

"Two years later I was pregnant again with my daughter, Frankie. Again I took five months off but the week before I was due to go back to work, she had some seizures and we ended up in hospital. At the time they thought that Frankie had some kind of brain-damage. At this point they put her on steroids to stop the seizures. This was one of the worst periods of my life as it was full of so much uncertainty for us all.

"Shortly afterwards we did get some good news, in the sense that a neurologist found the hospital had made a mistake. They had compared Frankie's brain with an adult brain. Her brain was found to be normal with **no** *damage, however the worst news was yet to come. It was probably at this point in my career where I stopped thinking there's more for me to do and stopped thinking about my own career. I realised I'd got a good job and two children; I'd done my bit. Finally when Frankie was 3 years old, after going through numerous blood tests, brain scans and MRIs etc., Frankie was diagnosed with the devastating condition called Rett Syndrome. This meant she would require 24-hour care for the rest of her life. We were devastated once again but decided then that I would continue to work until we reached the point that she would need me more.*

"Just after Frankie was diagnosed, I found out about a Rett Syndrome Conference in Paris. I wanted to go to find out more about the condition and what research was being undertaken. It was there that I met with other like-minded women who also wanted to do something positive so we went on to found a new Rett Charity to progress the research in to a cure. I threw myself in that work and getting the charity up and running.

"My career had halted at that point. It wasn't until I had a female line manager that she asked me what was next for me career wise. I hadn't given any thought to that, as I really believed I couldn't do anything more given my personal circumstances. She said to me, 'I don't think that's true, I think you're limiting yourself', and really started challenging my thoughts.

"It was this conversation that started me being more open to doing something different within the bank, and led to the role I now do at headquarters for Diversity and Inclusion. It did take a number of conversations after the offer to convince me that I could make the change, which I think is very typical of women in general.

"In terms of key development points, I would say that a female leadership course I attended in my late 20s really helped. It made me realise other women are going through similar challenges. We had the opportunity to share ideas and think about how you can run your life and career. The networking that came from it was also very useful. My Mum had cooked, cleaned, worked, mowed the lawn, and done all the jobs around the house. In my head I had said, 'this was how a woman was meant to be'. To avoid burnout you can adjust your life. Change your mentality, and adjust everything in your life, otherwise you run the risk of failing in many areas.

"On my self-image and beliefs, even though I read and intellectually understand what I can do, it still doesn't stop my fears. I always tend to hear the negatives and not the positives in feedback. Even though I have been headhunted on several occasions, my fear of failure is definitely something that has held me back.

"I found that when I was younger I was a lot bolder about my career and happy to take risks. If I'd have continued to do this and if I'd taken more risks, would I have followed a different career trajectory? I found I stopped doing the stuff that would help me get on, some of this potentially to do with my family and personal circumstances but some with not being courageous enough. My advice would be to take every risk that you can. Go and do the roles that you think will stretch you, are right for your future and set your sights high.

"Deanna Oppenheimer [who has also recounted her story in this book] *was a huge inspiration for me. It was the first time I experienced an extremely successful yet 'real' woman; she had the ability to have conversations and build relationships with people at all levels of the organisation. She was surrounded by men, and yet stood out as a great female leader for all the right reasons. She gave the belief that you could do anything you wanted, totally inspirational. I am inspired by bold, bright*

leaders who show they care.

"My real passion is people and I love to be busy all of the time. I enjoy cooking and having people around for dinner. My balance is the home bit, being busy socialising with my family and friends is what I love most. My husband has always been very hands-on, helping a lot with the family, the house and the children, which allowed me to continue to focus on my career. I couldn't have done the roles at work and set up the charity without him. I really worried, and still do sometimes about the impact of Frankie's condition on my son and how it would affect his friendships or school. However, he is doing extremely well. He is popular with his friends and has a fabulous caring nature; I am so very proud of him. I have now learnt that you can't predict the future and that the best you can do is give yourself as many opportunities in work and life and make a positive impact on those around you. "

Chapter Reflection:
A Call to Action and Not Intent

As Rita Ross describes, being courageous in our decisions about work and life will help us to successfully navigate both. We don't know what the future holds, but we always have choice. *Inspiring Women Leaders* is therefore a call to action to understand inspiration and encourage you to draw the required lessons to help you become an even more inspiring leader.

For individuals

During my coaching or consulting conversations I often ask leaders the question, "What would your colleagues say about you when you are not in the room?" It's interesting noticing the different reactions - mostly ones of discomfort! Often when we describe our leadership it's with our own perspective on what we value about ourselves. We talk about our leadership as if for an interview. We are often blind to, or have a limited view of, what others think of our leadership.

Ask yourself, 'what am I going to do to ensure I give the necessary time to reflect, learn and take action as a result of reading this book?'

For Leadership Teams

As Madeleine Albright, former US Secretary of State, famously said, "There's a special place in hell for women that don't help each other". I'd like to extend this even further to include men. Of those leaders that hold positions of power and influence, how many of you take a real stance in breaking down biases and barriers? We can often talk about commitment and yet be wilfully blind to the reality of the challenges that face us day to day. Are we truly committed and taking accountability or just making rhetorical statements of support, whilst occasionally observing from the side-lines? This is not a 'tick-box exercise' to outsource to your diversity departments. This is fundamentally a behavioural change.

*Ask yourselves as an executive, or leadership team, 'What are **we** doing to* *role model the changes, behaviours and decisions that people need to see?'*

For organisations

With volatile careers and advancing technologies, the traditional fixed ways to structuring work cannot be the way forward. Whilst I generally respect Marissa Mayer, her imposition of sanctions to prevent working from home was not responsive to the altered psychological contract; it was a disappointing and retrograde step. Our micro-management, micro-conversations and decisions serve only to limit the potential for change and are disempowering. So we have to address our biases, desires to control and our supporting infrastructures. Instead of policing and controlling, I would encourage those in power instead to *empower* and *inspire* others by becoming the real catalyst and enablers for change. I particularly call out to the profession of HR to re-examine its role and think outside of the box. Now is the opportunity to take the courageous step to become key strategic and pragmatic influencers and shapers of the people agenda.

'How progressive and transformational are we in delivering HR infrastructures, policies and processes that enable diverse leadership to be rewarded and developed?'

Chapter 1
Inspiring Leadership – Defining Inspiration

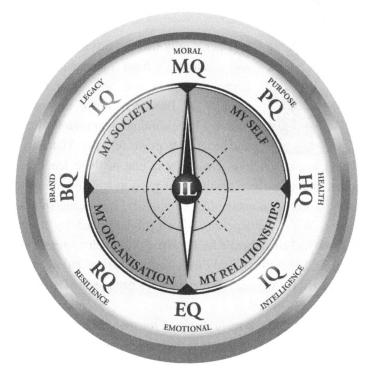

"My advice is, don't conform to the company norms. Be aware of them. Try to be your own person and if it's not in contradiction, always stay true to your own values. I'm so rigidly driven by values. I rely on them. I know what matters to me. It's the stick of rock that runs through me and keeps me authentic. It enables you to be resilient when you are buffed around and gives you inner confidence to believe in yourself. I think if you have an idea of who you are then that's easier, whatever happens."

Eva Eisenschimmel
Managing Director – Finance

**Deanna Oppenheimer
CEO of CameoWorks and
Non-Executive Director**

I personally had the privilege of experiencing and learning from Deanna's inspirational leadership when she was the CEO of Retail Banking at Barclays. There are many female leaders I have admired over time for their courage and progress to powerful roles. There are very few whom I feel inspired by, yet Deanna was one of these leaders. Deanna's success was undoubtedly a result of her passion and commitment to those she served – her customers, her employees, her leadership team and stakeholders. With a compelling vision, underpinned by a set of core principles, she had an authentic leadership style, which inspired those around her. The result? We all willingly followed her vision and even gave more discretionary effort. Anyone I've met who has been led by Deanna names her as an inspiring role model.

Deanna shared, "*I grew up in the small town of Parma, Idaho. Of course, the great thing about a small town is that you never know what you can't do because, due to lack of resources or numbers, they always need you to do something! As a result, I developed incredible breadth by participating in a wide variety of sports and activities. Also, I am the youngest of five and my next closest sibling is 7 years older. This was very helpful to me because I felt like an only child but had the network and support of a large family to help me along the way.*

"*My mother was a homemaker and my father had his own second-generation produce business, which is probably where I get my entrepreneurial instincts. Even though I loved growing up in Parma and appreciate all that it gave me, I also knew I wanted to move beyond a small town. I went to a liberal arts university near Seattle where we were encouraged to study a wide variety of disciplines such as sociology, psychology, political science, literature, and religion. By taking the lessons from one and applying them to another, I learned a lot about communication, problem solving, analytics, and making connections between concepts. Ultimately, I graduated with an honours degree in political science and urban affairs.*

"After graduation, I held a few different jobs, but ended up joining the bank Washington Mutual at age 25. There I had the opportunity to work for a great mentor, Lou Pepper. He was CEO of the company, and a terrific person with solid values. I recall many memorable coaching moments from him but one of my favourites was when I became his Chief of Staff and had to manage the government relations function. A planner for large industry event had contacted me and requested that Lou chair the event. When I told him they were set on him doing it, he said 'Deanna, remember one thing; they don't want Lou Pepper to chair that event, they want the CEO of Washington Mutual. Never confuse who you are, your title and the company that you represent'. That was a valuable lesson, and I think that happens frequently in business. People don't realise that they get to rent the title for a period of time, but that is not the core of whom they are. It is simply the role that they have at the moment.

"Washington Mutual was a fantastic growth experience for me. I went from having one direct report to over 60,000. The company grew from 67 branches to 2,000 branches and completed over 30 acquisitions along the way. It was an incredible growth story and was a great opportunity. However, I fundamentally believe that you always want to leave an organization at a high point if you can. That can be difficult because there is always more to work to be done and more to be accomplished. However, the art of knowing when to leave is something that I have happily developed over my career and, in early 2005, I felt it was time for me to leave but did not have a good sense for what would be next.

"I had joined a few boards and was setting up my consulting company, CameoWorks, when I got a call from a head-hunter who was looking at sourcing talent for Barclays. When I was a student at university, I spent a semester in London and had fond memories of two brands: McVities biscuits (I ate too many of those) and Barclays, where I opened my first account. I never thought that I would live outside the US but the opportunity in London definitely piqued my interest, and I was excited to be offered the CEO job for

the UK retail bank division after a short stint as COO. Unlike my time at Washington Mutual, which was focused on growth, the job at Barclays was focused on turning around a venerable, 350 year old institution, which was a daunting but very rewarding assignment. I grew as an executive there and expanded my role to ultimately wear three hats: Vice Chair for Global Retail Banking and CEO of the Western Europe retail franchise in addition to my job CEO of retail in the UK. Once again, there is an art to leaving at the right time, and by 2012, I felt like I had accomplished everything I had set out to do and there was a talented team in place to come in behind me.

"Leaving an executive role in banking and becoming an advisor through my boutique firm, CameoWorks, could have been a difficult transition. However, I am finding it to be very rewarding. I like being able to work with a wide variety of companies and industries and seeing them excel. With this experience, I've gotten much better at active listening and asking questions.

"Here are valuable leadership lessons I've learned along the way:

The first is on the people front. As I mentioned, at Washington Mutual we had acquired a lot of banks, and had to let a lot of people go. I developed a philosophy along the way was that can be summarized by the following: 'Anyone can hire to the brand, but can you fire to the brand?' This means that you must treat people with the utmost dignity, give them the time to transition with clarity and transparency on their options, and be incredibly organised to accomplish this quickly and effectively. By being clear about our intentions, people had control of their destiny and received a lot of support. Ultimately, this engendered a lot of loyalty, and, in different jobs in my career, I've rehired someone that I have let go in the past.

"Number two on my list is being authentic as a leader by willing to make yourself vulnerable. During my first year at Barclays as CEO, we had an incident where a journalist infiltrated a call centre and the results were broadcast on the BBC in a very unfavourable light. I initially had a horrendous feeling of violation and fought the urge to brush it off as an isolated incident. However, it pointed to some very bad business practices that needed correction. I knew that it was not a reflection on how the rest of the company operated, and I needed to give our employees inspiration and belief in themselves. My initial step was to embark on a series of employee meetings believing they would appreciate the candour and rise to the challenge. This honesty and candour had a positive, galvanizing effect on the culture of the company. To do that, however, meant that I had to be willing to make myself vulnerable. In those meetings I knew I was going to get asked hard questions but found that it made me more authentic to employees and resulted in their confidence in following me. People realize you aren't perfect and will follow the authentic leader above others.

"The third element that I learned is the importance of home and health. Throughout my career, I always thought that I could simply go, go, go. Finally, during my time in London, I learned that I need some 'down time'. Many leaders pay lip service to the concept but don't practice it. You must take time to focus on health. It's like what they tell you on the airplanes: put the mask on yourself first before you put it on anybody else around you. As simple as that may sound, it was a big lesson learned for me. Some of that personal time must be spent on reflection. It could be through prayer, it could be through music, it could be through yoga, but it should be time where you reflect on the greater good, the bigger whole, and something beyond what you are doing.

"Looking at these leadership lessons and my career so far, there are a few things that stand out to me that may be particularly applicable to women.

"I developed self-confidence because I was allowed to try anything and fail. I was not raised in a culture, social area, or a family that focused on what girls can't do, or what can't happen. I learned to play the piano when I was four, I was giving speeches by the time I was five. As a parent, I think the best thing you can focus on is raising kids that are self-confident without arrogance. When mentoring and managing women, I've observed that sometimes that self-confidence is missing. That is can be a real challenge, because if a person doesn't believe they can do something, how will they convince others that they can?

"Secondly, focus on what you really are good at. If you don't know, ask people, 'what am I good at' and then capitalise on those strengths. Frequently, we are told to work on our weaknesses but I believe it is a lot easier to capitalise on your strengths. Age 50 is where it gets very interesting. When I was younger, I knew that I wanted to do well, and there

31

were a lot of things that I should do. I should do well in school, I should get married, I really wanted to have children and I really wanted to have a great career. These viewpoints turned into a version of an action list, because if you want to do well at something the next steps are pretty clear. If you want to do well in school, then there are actions you have to take in a certain frame time. If you want to advance in your career, there are other actions. I was a very 'Type A personality' going through everything.

"Once I reached a culminating point in my career, however, I realised I didn't need to prove to myself (or anybody else) that I could be a CEO of a Retail Bank. I then had to consider a really fascinating question, 'What do I want to do?' That is where I had to reflect more on my greater purpose. I think my purpose is to help others achieve, be better, learn and be inspired. People frequently mention to me that I have the ability to inspire others, and I have been able to do that throughout my career. I have much more balance in my life now, am clearer on my purpose, and am enjoying the ebb and flow of life."

Definition of *'Inspiring Leadership'*

Drawing directly from Jonathan Bowman-Perks' book on Inspiring Leadership[1] and the copious discussions we have had over the years with Dr Reuven-Bar-On, the following is our definition of Inspiring Leadership:

To Inspire: drawing in of breath, infuse thought, or feeling into (The Oxford Illustrated Dictionary)

Inspiring Leadership is addressing a new era of leader that breathes life into the organisation and the people they lead. It is not one-dimensional, but holistic and integrated leadership, responsive to the vast challenges and resulting opportunities that face 21st century leaders.

As individuals, they are multi-faceted and respond sensitively to the paradoxical nature of leadership. They see their role as serving those that they lead and serving their own needs as an important component to healthy leading. They combine decisiveness and reflection with an ability to bring together the great teams and draw on the full intellectual capability, both from within and outside the business. They are sufficiently self-assured to surround themselves with a team that constructively challenges them, harnessing diverse perspectives. They don't spout the values; they live the values. They are intellectually curious, eager for themselves and others to learn and grow in order to never stagnate, always making themselves current.

Inspiring leaders avoid the hubris – the over-weaning self-pride, arrogance and complacency trap that comes with today's success. Instead they create a clear vision and focus and courageously pursue greater goals, confident with what they know and bring. Decisions are never made which compromise or are at the expense of the brand, of individuals or of society as a whole. They are adaptive and flexible in terms of skills, attributes and styles in order to meet diverse and evolving needs, whilst remaining authentic to themselves. They change things for the better, not just for the sake of change, and leave a positive impact and a sustainable legacy. There is no single type. Their leadership styles range on a spectrum from being larger than life and energisers to being more introverted and quieter leaders. They all bring humility. The most centred have established well-balanced lives.

Inspiring Leaders are also mortals like the rest of us. They have imperfections; they don't always get it right, or have the right answers. They certainly feel the pain of mistakes, like the rest of us. But here's a distinct difference. Their bounce back is swift and their openness to vulnerability is a useful source of learning, in order to become much stronger. Most important of all, they are not compromised. Their integrity is well-guarded, sustaining their authenticity no matter what comes their way. Their morality is never for sale, not at any price. Stylistically, I have found they are all very different

and have sufficient confidence to be themselves. The common theme is that they continuously invest in developing their leadership skills, staying relevant so as not to stagnate.

Lynne Graham describes the positive evolution of leadership.

"In the late 80s and 90s expectations of

33

leadership were very macho; there was a basic leadership deficiency. I breathe a sigh of relief now as, in the last decade, it has become okay to be yourself, it's no longer one size fits all. We now recognise different leadership strengths. The sheep-dip courses of the 80s and 90s created a language about leadership, but now we are far more respectful of differences and this continues to evolve. My son is into cars and using his language helps me to liken leadership development to the miniscule adjustments that complex sports car machinery requires to achieve maximum performance. This is the joy of leadership now - it is to find each individual's personal potential."

To be an inspiring organisation, we need to draw from our pipeline of talent, embrace diversity and create inclusive environments where individual leaders can be truly authentic. Instead of concerning ourselves with 'cultural fit' as the rationale for selection and development, it feels right that we should look for more of the 'misfits' rather than clones. These leaders who are authentically themselves are inspiring, yet at the same time also provide creative challenge. As described by Margaret Heffernen, *"We must resist our neurological drive to seek out people like ourselves, instead actively seeking out different people with different backgrounds, different ways of thinking and different experience, and find ways to engage with them."*

I believe that we are in a period of transition. We just don't have enough of those kinds of 'inspiring leaders' in the workforce yet. We don't have enough different types of leaders permeating through our structures, because not enough transition has occurred. Instead we continue to view leadership through the lens of old models and sustaining languorous cultures.

The changing nature of work demands a change in leadership behaviour. Through developing talented individuals who model inspirational leadership, we can get more of these holistic abilities into organisations. These qualities are rare in leaders, yet we have had our wake-up call with today's crisis demanding change. Call it the 'crucible moment' of the most significant order, striking us at the very macro socio-economic level across the world. Every ripple of which has a common underlying factor. This disaster is man-made.

A time for some change in leadership? Most definitely!

'Anonymous' - An Inspiring Woman Leader's Personal Story of Expiring Leadership

"Although I had bosses in the past who were idiosyncratic, this was the first time I had to deal with dysfunctional leadership.

"Prior to this particular situation, I was working with an inspiring male leader at a hugely important time in my career. He was challenging and fair. He knew when to push and when to support. He just kept things going and made complex things simple. He created this 'drumbeat' of expectation. We went through some really tough stuff, but he built a great team. There were other leaders in the executive team that, although they had big egos, could express their points of view appropriately and we had great mutual respect.

"When my boss left for a new role in another part of the Group, I started working for a different leader. His approach was to unpick everything that had been done by the previous leader. The first action he took was to sack a number of my colleagues and, given my role, I had to support this. It was a hugely difficult thing to do. I did what I could to do things in the right way and to protect those affected from being treated unfairly. But the brutality of the way the new boss behaved towards my former colleagues really compromised my own value set. I witnessed dysfunctional and bullying behaviour.

"Looking back I can't believe how this 'expiring leader' so quickly destroyed the confidence and resilience I had built up throughout my career. I asked myself how was it that one person could be so negatively impactful? Within a matter of weeks I was having panic attacks, not sleeping and really not coping well. I felt ill. He was always undermining me in front of others. Always wanting the immediate decision, he never allowed time for reflection or consideration on what was the right thing to do. He loved to pull people up publicly on mistakes. So many people would schmooze up to him, but being independently minded I refused to simply agree to anything he said just for an easy life.

"When I confided in a colleague and asked for advice in how to cope I was told to, 'just say yes - he needs 100% loyalty. If you become one of his, then he looks after you. Alternatively if you don't, then you have to leave the business. It's a binary decision.'

"I thought I would tackle the issue head on and arranged for us to discuss our relationship over dinner. Surely we could find some mutual ground and

35

resolve things? I remember as we headed to the restaurant, he strode ahead and chided me for not keeping up. He needed to impose his power on everyone around him. I left the restaurant that evening realising that he was never going to change.

"I then asked for an executive coach to help me up my game, rather than feeling so helpless. But through discussing what was happening with someone independent it became clear that I was being bullied. So I decided I had to tackle the root cause, which was his unreasonable behaviour.

"It felt great to regain control by confronting the issue and not avoiding it or trying to change to accommodate it. I arranged to meet with him away from the office and told him the affect his behaviour was having on me. I made it clear that I would not tolerate this and that we had to find a resolution. He refused to accept the impact of his behaviour and tried to blame me, but I stuck to what I had prepared and would not concede my position. Eventually we agreed that I would leave with a substantial financial settlement. It wasn't right and it wasn't fair but it was the only solution for me at that time.

"I took a year off, which was a very necessary recuperative period for me. It took me that time to rediscover my self-confidence and put my anger and resentment behind me.

"Even so, when I started my current role, I kept expecting something bad to happen. It was hard for me to trust others again, particularly my new boss, and I found myself over-reacting to criticism. This was the residual impact of working for a bully.

"Time has passed and everything is back in balance and perspective but I regret that organisations continue to put business performance and results ahead of leadership impact. The end doesn't always justify the means."

What is 'Expiring Leadership'?

Although we would prefer to avoid the topic, particularly when it comes to supporting women in business, we cannot talk about Inspiring Leadership, without also looking at its nemesis! The opposite of *Inspire* is clearly to *Expire,* which is 'drawing life or breath from another'. Inspiring and Expiring leadership sit at polarised ends of the continuum.

The 'personal story' shared earlier is an example of the affect that this can have for an individual or team. Unfortunately, this is not so unusual. I remember once being approached by a head-hunter for an opportunity. In the past, I would have jumped at the chance, naively focusing on the role itself which was an absolute dream, even the global brand was a strong and reputable one in the market. However, in my more mature years I have learned to be more discerning and turned down the opportunity, without any hesitation at all, based on two reasons. Firstly, the culture was known to be toxic and secondly, the hiring female leader had one of the worst reputations in the market. Interestingly, the head-hunter agreed and they had consistently heard similar feedback from many other candidates.

Sadly, this response is often as a result of wisdom gained through unfortunate and tough personal experiences.

As we celebrate the women who have climbed to the heady heights of power and authority, we measure success based on power, rather than on the ability to inspire and engage others. We, at times, incorrectly give credibility to their outer journey (impressive roles achieved) rather than their inner, more authentic, development journey to become an inspiring leader.

After playing the political game, navigating the corporate jungle and annihilating the competition along the way, some senior women quickly pull the drawbridge up behind themselves to maintain their status and exclusivity. Why not - they've worked damned hard to get there, haven't they? There is still an unhealthy issue with some 'alpha' women who, having muscled their way by climbing up to the top of the corporate tree, are determined to prevent other women following.

One specific type of leader – the Business Psychopath – can cause the most damage. Outwardly they present an image of charisma and care, whilst actually harbouring internal battles whether it's ego-centric, low emotional intelligence, or an inability to lead a diverse workforce. Their leadership style is a more manipulative one – creating elite in-groups and out-groups. Their deployment of tactics make life as uncomfortable as possible for those they hold little regard for and banish them to the out-group.

This is by no means an excuse for anyone to say 'we are the victim in this scenario'. Instead, I want to draw attention to the fact that we cannot hide away from the unpleasant existence of expiring leaders whether male, or female.

As strong, ambitious and talented as followers can be, the impact of these kinds of leaders above them is a significant issue for any diversity agenda. We must address these issues face on, so that we can enable the new era of emerging leader to survive and thrive.

Powerful and well-paid roles attract people who enjoy and are drawn by such power and money. So, let's be clear. Expiring leadership is not a style of leadership that is reserved for men. The global issues that we experience in today's climate cannot be attributed to testosterone-fuelled and ego-driven male leaders alone. There are as many inspiring male as there are female leadership examples and the same goes for really bad leadership. It frustrates me when we create this irrelevant gender divide. Indeed, the women in my research talk of inspiring men being their role models and not necessarily women. It is misguided to champion a narrow kind of feminism; one that holds the belief that equal rights for women is based on their differences and that their attributes and virtues offers better leadership.

The Expiring Leadership trap holds no gender bias. With the changing roles in society, the resulting power and liberation of women is increasing, enabling them to pursue their dreams more successfully. Therefore, the question for both the ambitious women and men carving out their careers in business is, 'how do I constantly reflect on my leadership to avoid these traps and the lure of power and status when ineffective?'

There are a number of Expiring Leadership personality types. Here are a few of the more extreme examples, which I'm sure many of you will have experienced them in some form at a variety of points in your career and lives.

The Narcissistic Leader

With a socially networked world and businesses playing a bigger role than ever before, today's leaders have higher profiles than they used to. We observe the mud-slinging tactics of many politicians, and the questionable behaviours and decisions of ego-centric business leaders. Some people over-stretch their finances to buy what they can't afford, in order to have the perception of the 'dream-life', often at the expense of basic fundamentals.

There is no question that we have our fair share of narcissists among us in very powerful positions and as in Jean M. Twenge and W. Keith Campbell's book *The Narcissism Epidemic: Living in the Age of Entitlement*, it is a growing issue that is corroding society and business.

Almost everyone has some narcissistic traits. This is actually healthy in the right context. Consider it like a continuum: too little, or too much is not good for leadership. Michael Maccoby (*HBR's Leadership Insights*) believes there is a need for 'productive narcissists'; they are risk takers with compelling visions coupled with the ability to attract followers. They *'break up big questions into manageable problems...extrapolate to understand the future, they attempt to create the future'*. They are the 'skilful orators' whose charisma and charm can convert the masses.

However, they are often power-hungry and aggressive pursuers of their own agenda. One inspiring leader described how her Managing Director declared, *"If I have a dog, why should I bark myself?"* whilst another described how they were encouraged to "*create compelling stories to promote their leader in the best possible light*". These leaders, convinced they are right, genuinely believe their own hype and fail to listen to the advice of those around them. They require adoration and are seduced easily by flattery. They are highly sensitive to criticism, which makes them extremely insecure and demanding.

With a sense of entitlement, narcissists can become the 'divas' among us, creating favourites whilst being emotionally cold to others. Paradoxically they can play the victim, whilst also being the puppet-master. The narcissist 'lack choices in their behavioural repertoire, like paying attention to the needs and wants of others' and have 'difficulty learning alternative behaviours... but can learn to moderate their behaviours and the negative effect they have on others', say Babiak and Hare in their book, *Snakes in Suits*. It is unfortunate that so many narcissists have become today's role models for our future generation of leaders; an issue which is crying out for rebalance.

The White Collar Psychopath

More antisocial and destructive than the Narcissist, are the growing numbers of white-collar psychopaths. Again, the differences between male and female are often misunderstood, as our interpretation directly links with expected behaviours, such as dominance and aggression. As described by

Babiak and Hare in their book *Snakes in Suits*, 'the same underlying personality structure may find different behavioural and social expression'. There is little variance between the acts of female and male counterparts and yet we look for possible excuses, or alternative labels for women.

The Business Psychopath proves to be a highly manipulative one, using powerful and irresponsible tactics to get what they want. Emotionally deficient, they show little or no remorse for those around them, as they play mind games to belittle and provide a source of personal stimulation. Many causes lie behind these unhealthy behaviours, including an 'under-responsive threat response centre' in their brains (the amygdala). They have narcissistic tendencies as well and use others mercilessly to their own ambitious ends.

The lure of advancement into leadership and the resulting power and money for these individuals can be at the compromise of their moral values. They often skirt just within the ethical and legal boundaries, without getting caught. For organisations, these expiring leaders can wreak havoc, with severe impact on the individuals they lead and the organisation's performance. Surviving these business psychopaths is extremely challenging for those around them, affecting their follower's confidence and even their health.

In one of my interviews an individual, who shall remain anonymous, said of her experiences with a white-collar psychopath, *"I didn't even realise the depth of impact that her behaviour was having on me. I began to think it was me.*

"I was so stressed and crying at home each night. Not until I was seated in the hairdressers, when they told me my hair was coming out in clumps, followed by a confidential conversation with my mentor at the time, did I start to understand that I was being manipulated and bullied."

If employees are constantly fighting to survive undermining tactics such as criticism, judgement, reprimands, power-assertion, discrimination and unfairness, then we must address the issues.

We should be acutely aware as leaders who are subtly and discreetly using these tactics under the radar. Once found, then we must help to facilitate different and healthier environments.

The Impact

An inspiring leader shared her experience of an expiring female leader, *"I don't work well with leaders who need a lot of attention. I moved into a role led by a very senior woman in the organization. She should have been more confident. She was easily threatened, even if there was no competition. She needed a lot of care and attention, constant feeding of her ego. I was liked by the team, so she tried everything to alienate me. She would give opportunities to others. The feedback she gave me was that 'I smiled too much'.*

"The generational gap was a real issue for her and so, as she came up through the ranks, it was achieved through adopting certain behaviours. She never thanked me for the work I did; she only looked for fault. Even when my work was published, she never associated me with the work and took the glory! I found myself handing work over to her and reporting to her. She favoured those who would take orders and were non-threatening. When the team was restructured, as her universe was not the same as my universe, I have found myself redundant."

These expiring leaders often evade penalty for their sinister ways, yet most eventually derail themselves. Unfortunately, it is often after significant damage has already been done to others. As we have seen in sector-wide scandals and poor business practices, organisations are certainly being more closely scrutinised by regulatory bodies and the public. Whilst heartening to hear the hard action that is being taken by new leaders focused on swift resolution, I wonder how much we are addressing the real leadership challenges. Often such executives are 'strategically moved' around the organisation, paid off with large sums in compromise agreements, fired, or, at times, even imprisoned, and we see new leaders move into their position. By their nature compromise agreements hide what has really happened. Consequently, the psychopaths can rewrite their CVs and continue feeding off new unsuspecting teams and organisations for their own benefit.

We must continuously review the unhealthy cultures we are allowing to develop in our organisations as a result of not tackling poor leadership. Thought leader, Peter Drucker, was insightful when he said, *"Culture eats strategy for breakfast."* With these new organisational structures and fresh business strategies posing a wonderful opportunity for change, what strikes me is the preservation of homogeneity and status quo, rather than differences and progress. I see all-male boards being replaced by... well, basically all men! What's not working in our succession planning that fails to see new and more diverse leadership emerge? What's really changing beyond their superficial statements of intent?

Diverse leadership teams make sense at more than the macro-economic level. They are a vital requirement at the very core of organisational structures for greater team cohesion and engagement, wise and ethical decision-making and overall performance.

This is contingent on the quality and strength of internal structures that encourage diversity, reward the right leadership behaviours and swiftly deal with poor managers and toxic leadership behaviour.

It's misleading to classify leaders into just two strict gender roles of male = masculine and macho *versus* female = feminine and nurturing. While we do need more feminine style leadership, gender balance in a male dominated culture on its own doesn't work for many men or women. You can also bring a more feminine leadership style as a man, without being accused of being effeminate.

Equally some women leaders have a very masculine leadership approach. Many people like to think of things in black or white and categorise for simplicity but it's really a continuum, with both men and women falling into different places on this spectrum of masculine-feminine brains and leadership behaviours.

In our research and psychometric results, inspiring leaders are consistently strong in each of the 8 components of the Inspiring Leadership model, with no difference between male and female leaders.

If we can get to a really diverse cultural blend of those traits the outcomes are much better for our communities, for our safety and for the effectiveness of our decisions. It encourages people to be more authentic. We must allow the feminine qualities within our organisations to reach the surface. It is not about tolerance of differences, it's about embracing them.

Inspiring Leadership and the Women's Agenda
With significant investment already made into achieving greater gender

parity and tackling the issues, we have yet to see the value realised in the results. It is important that we approach the agenda strategically, enabling a cultural transformation to take place with sponsorship from the top, which is the biggest catalyst for change. A tick-box exercise - merely to comply with new rules, regulations and even quotas - managed and facilitated by Human Resources or Corporate Social Responsibility teams is not enough as it abrogates the responsibility of the leader.

It takes a concerted effort that gets to the heart of our organisational cultures, creating environments that respect and value diversity through inclusive efforts.

This means challenging ourselves, as leaders and decision-makers by setting aspirational goals and being more challenging to achieve diverse talent slates, finding more creativity in the way we organise and structure work and, in particular, address the subconscious biases that reinforce in-groups to the point of exclusion.

Nadia Younes shared, *"People say they want to get past things like race and gender and that we should strive to be gender and colour blind. Whilst the intent behind this may often be well-intentioned, the statement in itself is naïve and the impact typically negative for all parties. Clearly seeing and understanding how these and other differences interact with the whole as well as how they could work together and strengthen the problem-solving and decision-making in organisations and communities offers far more potential for positive outcomes and mutual benefits than striving for 'blindness'.*

"Gathering a greater variety of perspectives and ideas across far more diverse groups of people can offer stronger, more innovative and more sustainable solutions. Intentionally seeking these sharpens rather than blurs our vision."

The ability to remain authentic as a leader has emerged as a key and consistent theme throughout the research. As leaders continue to change themselves to adapt to the cultural norm, there is a crucial issue for how we invite and respect full potential, valuing what diverse leadership offers us. Building a culture that is inclusive remains the important issue to address. We can achieve this by challenging our own and others' affinity and social biases that encourage the formation of in-groups. Only then can we start to make real and sustainable change occur which will be reflected in our numbers.

Because of a constant focus on what's not working and the lack of progress, we fail to recognise the extreme efforts and positive momentum behind achieving greater equality. It has been a very positive experience for me researching Inspiring Leadership and observing the level of genuine commitment there is for change. The passion of inspiring leaders is contagious, actions pragmatic and they 'walk the talk'. Cultural change takes time and is transmitted slowly through the generations. The efforts today reflect a difficult scenario that moves us from a 'game of numbers' to a far more powerful future.

There is certainly no shortage of talented and aspiring women. So the question is, how do we access and develop them? I have also found inspiration in the numerous male leaders advocating and sponsoring the agenda. There is an abundance of diverse talent, if we are prepared to search for and invest in it.

Society is crying out for inspirational leadership at every possible level. Such leadership poses important questions around: morality and ethics, purpose, brand reputation and the rippling impact of the decisions we make and the legacy we leave.

This opens up the opportunity for unfulfilled potential to be realised beyond oneself or even the organisation.

If we aim, not necessarily for gender, but for *inspirational leadership* through building inclusive environments that allow authenticity, then we will address much of the deeply embedded cultural norms of past generations.

The rippling implications of leadership approaches undoubtedly determine whether we *inspire,* or *expire* energy for or from ourselves and those around us.

The greatest challenge that faces our businesses today is not one of diversity – this is just the outcome. Rather it is providing inspirational leadership. As individuals, we ascend into positions of leadership as a matter of process. However, being an *inspiring leader* that role models excellence is a matter of choice.

Andi Keeling (UK)
The Consistently Inspiring Leader
Director of Women's Markets, Finance

Andi Keeling was recommended to me as a truly 'inspirational leader'. When I arrived at reception and asked for her, the receptionist responded, "Andi is really amazing, she always talks to us and has a great reputation here. She runs some really inspiring events for women". When other people are singing the leader's praises, you know you're in the right place!

What really struck me about Andi is she exudes intellect, drive and passion – a really powerful force, delivered in a genuinely authentic way. It was apparent just how energised her team were by her, and this is contagious. Generous in both her story and support of me personally, Andi and her team at RBS worked with me to help launch *Inspiring Women Leaders*. She is often recognised for her contributions, most recently she was awarded 'Inspirational Role Model' by the Gay magazine g3 and I can absolutely see the reason why.

Andi shared with me, *"I left school at 16 years old and joined the Bank. I wasn't thinking about a career, it was just a job to go into and it was the best job that I could find at the time. I like people and I built relationships with colleagues and customers alike, some of which still live on today, thirty years later. From my first day, I wanted to do the best job that I could, it's always been important to me not to let myself down and in this way I will not let others down either. Interestingly enough, as I did well more opportunities arose and doors opened for me. What I noticed was, when I had elements of doubt, I was never afraid to reach out and ask for help when needed. I have no issue with, when you see something you really like in others, 'stealing' these approaches for myself. At one point, I recall my mother sharing with me that my uncle had said that I would never be anything but a cashier. This helped to spur me on even further.*

"Another important factor was my ability to be mobile and this helped me to climb the ranks. To help me with these decisions I would compile a list of 'Why should I?' and 'Why shouldn't I?'. Writing it down on a blank sheet of paper was invaluable in helping me to spot the obvious and then the decision becomes very easy to make. I challenged myself to never say 'no' to something just because I was scared – there had to be a better reason if I was to decline an opportunity.

"There were a few key external influences that affected my life and career, including an early, short lived marriage. Two key things are extremely important to me: to really enjoy what I'm doing and to do the best job I can. I know it sounds a little cliché but it's so important to look to 'pay forward' and not look to receive the 'pay back'. I believe in helping others whenever possible.

"My mother has always been a strong influence on me, instilling core values. I had a very happy and stable background, which really helped me to believe that I could achieve. My core values today are based on treating people well, even if that means being tough sometimes. I would never ask someone to do something that I was not prepared to do myself whether it be writing a paper, pitching or presenting. For example, when I was Branch Manager and went to open up the branch one morning, I found that someone had been ill all over the pavement at the front door. It would have been very easy for me to have delegated the task of cleaning it up. I didn't, I did it myself.

"I realise and value the importance of sponsors. I was approached by the then CEO to apply for a Regional Director role and I wasn't sure I was ready. He persuaded me to interview and appointed me. He made it very clear that he valued the difference I could bring to his team. He encouraged me to have a voice around the board table, even though my thoughts and ideas often differed from those of my peers. He believed in me and told others too. His successor however, was very different and loathed anyone to disagree with him. I eventually started to try to please him and changed my ways. It didn't take long to realise that I wasn't happy and needed to get out.

"I saw a role advertised for Head of Learning & Development in HR. I had no HR experience other than leading big teams and I almost didn't apply as I couldn't 'tick' two of the requirements of the role. Again, I was appointed by someone who valued difference of thinking and approach. I later learned that she had spoken to the previous CEO who had valued my input and approach. What I lacked in HR technical experience was replaced with a valuable commercial approach and strong leadership skills. Again, my experience is: do a great job and doors of opportunity will open.

"As Regional Director, I was the only woman on the executive team. My peers and direct reports were all men. There was an assumption that I would be the one to take the notes at meetings or get the drinks. At one of our executive team meetings a colleague said to me, 'I will have a coffee Andi' to which I responded, 'So will I, thank you very much'. At client meetings when I accompanied one of my team, the client often assumed that I was the assistant. Fortunately, times are changing and I believe that people are getting more used to seeing women in senior positions. The media has an important role to play in profiling successful women in business as role models for the next generation.

"Another influence on my life and career was realising that I am gay. This wasn't until my mid-30's and it took a long time for me to come out at work. I didn't think it was essential to, as it was my personal life that was impacted not my work life. However, I soon realised that I wasn't bringing my 'whole self' to work and therefore wasn't being true to myself or others. I wasn't telling the whole truth if someone asked me what I had done over the weekend and I certainly wasn't being fair when colleagues started trying to set me up on blind dates! I also realised that as a relatively senior woman, I had a responsibility to be a positive role model to others. If I can make it any easier for just one person to be themselves at work, then it's been worth it.

"I made a conscious decision, when I changed roles a few years ago, to be open about who I am and, guess what, there was no big reaction, I was accepted for just being me.

"From that moment on, I was completely out. Being able to bring my whole self to work allows me to better support other people around me. I didn't realise just how much of a difference my story made. This was such a

great experience and looking back now I see just how bringing my true self to work each day has had a hugely positive impact. I now sit on the LGBT network (Lesbian, Gay, Bi-sexual and Transgender) focused on employees, customers and suppliers. My experience coming out within RBS has been a really positive one.

"My current job as Director, Women's Markets at RBS has three key strategic pillars: to support more women moving into senior roles; to support women who run their own business or want to run their own business; and to work with key strategic partners, like the other corporates, government and media, to help achieve our goals both internally and externally.

"To make this work we need more empowerment, autonomy and boundaries to do the right thing. By completely focusing on what matters most and always being respectful in communication is crucial to success in both performance and relationships. When I talk about diversity, I mean truly valuing the difference that each individual can bring and the strength that creates in teams."

Chapter Reflection:
What is my vision for my Leadership?

To achieve quantum leaps and to become an inspiring leader to others, you must first of all feel connected with your own perspective on your leadership and then cultivate this.

Consider these crucial questions:

For my leadership
- *Who are my Inspiring Leader Role Models and what, specifically, is it that I admire about them?*
- *What are my Expiring Leader experiences?*
- *What is important to my personal leadership style now?*
- *What have I done that has inspired me and those around me today, last week, last year?*
- *Am I a trusted leader?*
- *How do I diminish my 'expiring leadership' derailers?*
- *How do I leverage my 'inspiring leadership' strengths?*

For my organisation
- *What is important to the leadership of my organisation and where is it now?*
- *What are the cultural and diversity issues that we need to address?*
- *If we were to pick up the gauntlet, what action would we really be taking to make change happen?*
- *What can I do to develop the pipeline of female talent and help other women to succeed?*
- *What courageous acts in my organisation do we need to take in order to shift dominant cultures and leadership to make a greater difference for diversity?*

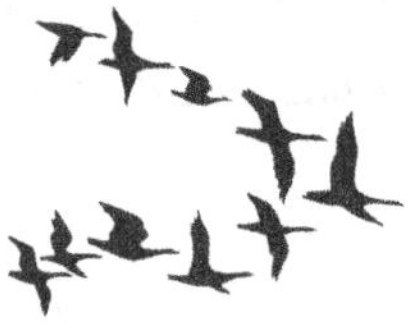

Chapter 2
Overview of the Inspiring Leadership Model

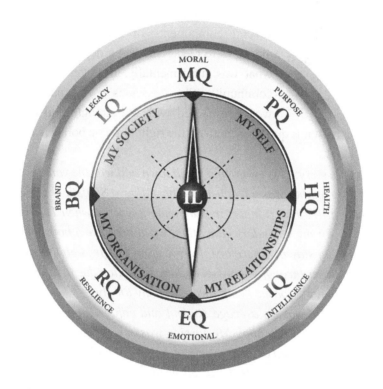

"I was going to work, with my colleagues, to bear witness to violations of human rights; to shine a light on the problems the world wanted to forget; and to demand accountability... My resolve was to give leadership: to use whatever tools I might have to bring home the need to prevent serious human rights abuses, to hold perpetrators to account, and in the culture and understanding of human rights worldwide."

Mary Robinson
Everybody Matters – A Memoir

Menaca Calyaneratne
Sri Lanka, Humanitarian – NGO

When I interviewed Menaca, her strengths across several components of the Inspiring Leadership model were clear. She had a deep self-awareness of what was fundamentally important to her and her community. She possesses a real passion for her work, combined with the strength and courage to challenge the status quo in order to do the right thing on both a personal and societal level.

Menaca's story: *"I grew up in a small town and was the youngest of three siblings. My mother was a teacher and my father a Statistical Officer in the Government. We had a house in our home town but when I moved to the capital city for my secondary education, we didn't have a house that was fit for all of us to stay in. Therefore, I grew up in lodgings similar to priming boarding houses throughout my secondary education due to its convenience. It was challenging for me being away from my family.*

"In school, I was an average student and enjoyed sports and drama. I played netball for the school. My passion was in writing, and I wrote novels that were often passed around in school, so lots of children read my stories. It was when I was about 16 I started writing poetry, which I wrote in the little English that I knew, as well as our local language. Then I started to get them published in the local newspapers. I created a penname for myself by coining two of my names, which had gender association and so no-one knew it was me writing under this name, which I liked. My primary schooling was the foundation for what I do today.

"As a child I used to write about the war. This was a time when Sri Lanka was really at the beginning of the war. I used to write about the war and soldiers at times from a very naïve perspective than I have now. There were people who were very upset about what I was writing about. Some sent me letters, some were given to me by the school and some were expelled. I had even received some threats. My interest in writing grew as a result. Because of this and my interest in writing and journalism, I chose to read English for

my first degree and also study journalism as an additional subject. I worked as a freelance journalist part-time. Then I got a really great opportunity to work for a television production house that were focused on creating programmes on human rights and development, but focusing on youth. This gave me the opportunity to really stretch my learning. One of the reasons I turned towards human rights was triggered by a single incident which was very close to my heart and still hurts me now.

"I was doing a series of videos on child rights, which I was interested in because nobody had thought of child rights before. I was doing a story about two children whose soldier father had died in the war. There was an organisation that was providing financial support, sponsoring them when their fathers had died. I poured my heart into telling the story. In the afternoon I was interviewing the 10 year-old boy, he agreed to do the interview with me on camera. At the point where I had asked him if there was anything he wanted me to say to his benefactor. I kept asking him the question and he never answered me, he kept avoiding the question. I stopped the camera to have a chat. At one point he said he would like to say, 'thank you'. I was pressing to say something that could be used in the story. At one point he said, 'If my father was alive I wouldn't need anybody's help'. That was the turning point in my life, to stop being the insensitive journalist I was and to become something different for children.

"I felt that there was more I can do than just telling stories. From the interview I went beyond the story to talking to the family. The family shared with me that the boy was upset and angry and he had a lot of pain that was not helping. I linked them with a child psychologist to help the child to come out of this state. This changed my whole life, career. All I do now is advocate for children. It was one child and one sentence that changed it all for me.

"I started as a very junior communications officer telling stories and helping children. This was one of my biggest inspirations and I listen far more now than I did years ago. In 2004, the tsunami in the Indian Ocean turned the world's attention towards the nations that had been virtually wiped out. I remember my humanitarian team leader saying we should go home. However, I really needed to do something. I needed to get over my grief. One of my colleagues had lost her 5 year-old son, whom I knew very

well.

"I knew many people with families and friends who had died, villages were totally destroyed. I was suddenly thrown into the situation where I became the spokesperson of my organisation. There was huge interest in the tsunami and the aftermath. Everyone wanted to know what was happening and the stories. I was not trained yet suddenly I spent the next six to twelve months on the other side, facing the media. It was affecting different parts of the world and so I had to work across the different time zones around the world, from the Vatican to London to Norway, I had to be up and about.

"We were working so hard but in such tough times, I really felt that we were doing something. From then on I became the spokeswoman for Save the Children in Sri Lanka. I had to be very careful about what I said and how I said it, as there was a lot of work that needed to be done and a lot of people impacted. People want answers. A lot is going on around you and constantly disturbing you. However, I have not experienced a fraction of the destruction these people have and yet they found their courage, which has been inspirational for me. Giving statements on broader national issues means you have to keep your emotions deep down and not showing that you are affected. You have to be the voice.

"During the war, it was a highly political situation. I was part of the majority and yet I found my voice in supporting the minority. The things that I saw and spoke about, I realised the risk to my life. When I came home and opened the gate, I would look around me sensing the threat. I had people telling me I was bringing them down. Friends and family would caution me not to say anything. However, I was speaking about the things that the children were telling me about. They would share their stories of suffering and cruelty, of how they were being treated. I felt it was my job to tell these stories, although never to have a negative impact on any of these children. I could do this, feeling that I have always had support around me. However, I needed to choose certain public statements and then convince others. This was frightening for me; it was a very emotional thing. I was aware how I could say the wrong thing or be in the wrong place, causing adverse reactions. You need to know when, where and how to make change. I remember a male politician asking me once, 'How have you survived all of

your statements?' But these were not just statements. They were facts and experiences. It's not always well received but that is what has to be said, it is the truth. I feel always held my head up high and believed in the things that I have said on behalf of children.

"In my professional career a key turning point for me was when someone spotted my potential and put me forward for a one-week programme on leadership. There were very senior managers being picked and I did not even fit this criteria. I was told that this was going to be the best week of my life and it was. I realised that the organisation had taken a risk on me and were investing a lot, therefore I had a real stake in it too. I knew I had to get the best from the programme so I grasped the opportunity with both hands.

"I started internalising the leadership qualities that I was learning about. I knew I had to make a real effort and then start to demonstrate the behaviours. I felt I had to give back because I was grateful for what I was given. I asked to be part of the team of facilitators on the development programme and I give 200% to everything I do. In the five days of this programme, you can really turn things around. It is great to see how leaders whom I facilitate go on to have greater leadership skills or take on bigger roles. There were lots of challenges, with the emergencies and also the culture with different people coming from different countries. With human rights you have to believe in the cause, as it gets very difficult. Learning about my own leadership style, I started to convince other people. I have (literally) small feet! I can fit into anyone's shoes. It is easy for me to think from the other side; emotional intelligence has always helped me. You really need to be able to empathise with the other person when it's on the topic of human rights. It's not just a business transaction, this really does affect the people. This strength has really helped me to overcome barriers as managing varying cultures is not easy, however, the underlying feelings as human beings are the same. Wherever I go I have friends and I feel good about this.

"I have always enjoyed and felt proud of the fact that I am female. As females I believe we can do and contribute a lot. As a female and a mother, I have always been able to use my skills to my advantage and in a positive way for others. It has helped me to reach out to more people. There weren't obstacles, I would just take my time, be slow and steady and always move

forward, never backward.

"I like myself. You have to like yourself in order to be able to reach out and like other people. This brings me back to being grateful for what I have. A couple of weeks ago, I was travelling back into the country when a woman pushed a trolley into me and knocked my foot. It hurt like hell and it broke my favourite shoe! We were both tired, but I stopped myself. I thought, 'there are so many people without feet, so why am I worried about a shoe?'

"We need to appreciate what we have. If you are constantly striving for something you will feel miserable. There are lots of distractions in this world preventing us from finding out who we are. We can waste a lot of time wanting, particularly if you aim to inspire other people. I have learned to appreciate the small things in life. You need to know your talents. If you are busy always looking at someone else and wanting to be like them, then it leads to dissatisfaction. First, find yourself because that's when you can really reach out.

*"There is a saying I always follow, 'Remember that the [job] titles you have are **only** to do a job of work. Use it only for that. Titles can be taken away at any time. But the people you win over are your real earnings.' It is my way of saying that the higher you go, the more you need to be humble. One must not forget that there are no leaders without followers. A leader without followers is only a manager.*

"Finally, you really need to have a good attitude and a good sense of humour to inspire others. You really don't realise how many people notice things, even the little things that you do. So you need to demonstrate the right behaviours. Everyone can be leaders of something. If you're a parent, a business leader, protecting human rights then you need to be a role model and you need to make choices that are inspirational for others. "

The Inspiring Leadership Model

That was aptly stated by Menaca; it is true that we all are leaders of something, whether it is at home, at work, or in our communities. The choices made around the type of leader are unique to each individual and cannot be defined by those around us. Certainly, we must learn from those that inspire us, but attempts to imitate someone else's life or style only serves to hold back our full potential and uniqueness. When you read through "Chapter 4: The Neuroscience Behind Inspiring Leadership" you'll see why this is such a drain on your energy.

In business today, the role of leaders has become far more physically and mentally complex and demanding than ever before. The Inspiring Leadership model provides a framework that has been developed to respond to the challenges facing today's leadership. It is there to value diversity and create insight. The model provides a holistic view and facilitates a depth and breadth of conversation and personal development that is currently absent from the language of leadership today.

You may easily identify which of the 8 IL-I components are your strengths and which hold possible gaps for you. However, the true power of inspirational leadership comes from the integration of these components. It challenges you to consider the choices to respect differences. It also allows for authenticity, helping you to become even more successful in life and business, but on your terms. It is not an idealistic view of leadership; it is an essential and very relevant view.

For example, there is little point to having a great vision and purpose, if it is not founded in strong morals and ethics. The ripple effects we witness today will leave a longer-term legacy affect on our economy, resources and society.

We just need to open the newspapers and read about the financial crisis, government policies and unstable countries to know this to be the case.

We have all witnessed highly intelligent colleagues promoted into leadership positions, but who lack the emotional intelligence to be successful as a leader. Subsequently they fail to successfully inspire those they lead. Or we can recall the damage caused to brand reputations, as a result of inadequate or unethical sourcing of labour and goods and the implications on the health and wellbeing of the disadvantaged people they have used to profit from.

How many of you have been, or seen others get, agitated by the individual in the team who goes on about a point of concern, challenging whether something is the right thing to do. This 'team conscience' has become the source of irritation and labelled as the 'blockers' to innovation and progress.

Are we really even surprised anymore by the whistle-blowers? We need to take a look at how we work together and fail to manage conflicts effectively! There is one thing that all of these issues have in common: leadership.

Many people say that they want to be advocates for a change in the way we lead, which is fantastic. However, this means that we have to stop and reflect on what's not working and why it isn't. We need to speak out and challenge each other, without getting defensive and taking it personally, in order to see and deliver the greater vision.

Whether we are accomplished, emerging or aspiring leaders, we must understand the dynamic and interplay, as it is in our responsibility to make change happen when it is not working. In order to make the changes, we must first start with changing ourselves. We need to bring this to life and champion inspiring leadership, both in the context of gender and other areas of diversity.

This is the true unleveraged opportunity to develop authentic, inspiring 21st century leaders. You may think this idealistic, yet it is not unrealistic. Fundamentally, both male and female Inspiring Leaders must find truth and confidence in their authentic selves. Organisations must respond positively by embracing this.

The Inspiring Leadership Inventory™ (IL-I™)

Inspiring Leadership creates a framework for discussion. The IL-i™ provides a set of tools to leaders and organisations keen to understand their strengths and development areas. The model directly correlates with performance and potential, and through benchmarking and profiling, provides a clear definition of what successful leadership looks like. It can be used for: assessment, benchmarking, leadership development, coaching, team and organisational performance. It includes psychometrics, 360 degree feedback, team and cultural diagnostic. We are also crafting and beta-testing a *'customer experience'* version, helping your organisation to understand the brand strength and customer impact.

The 8 *Inspiring Leadership Quotients* (components) describe the key predictors of leadership performance:

1. *MQ - Moral Integrity:*
    Living according to your ethics, values and beliefs.

2. *PQ – Purpose & Meaning:*
    Giving meaning and purpose to your own and other's lives.

3. *HQ – Health & Wellbeing:*
    Investing time in your own and other's health and wellbeing.

4. *IQ – Cognitive Intelligence:*
    Acquiring wisdom and judgement for sound decision-making.

5. *EQ – Emotional & Social Competence:*
    Understanding and managing yours and others" emotions.

6. *RQ – Resilience*
    An ability to sustain performance, learn and bounce back from adversity and thrive.

7. *BQ – Brand Presence:*
    Presenting an authentic and influential image of your own personal brand and reputation.

8. *LQ – Legacy:*
    Decisions you make today that creates a sustainable and positive impact.

Overview of The 8 Components of Inspiring Leadership

1. MQ: Moral integrity – you live life according to a clear set of principles, values and beliefs that guide your decisions, choices and actions. It is a focus on your irreproachability, character and discernment. It captures what you consider be right and what is wrong.

Each one of you as a leader has your own moral compass, and MQ provides a sense of 'true North' which points in the direction of your individual integrity to sustain values and beliefs, even in the face of adversity and challenge.

2. PQ: Purpose and Meaning – you strive to find meaning and purpose in your private life and at work, which leads to a more complete, satisfying and fulfilling life. Some refer to this as *spiritual development*. This process involves you being aware of what is perceived to be fundamentally important and meaningful, which goes beyond your self-actualisation and personal development to benefit others. You then strive to achieve these intra-personal, inter-personal and trans-personal goals.

3. HQ: Health and wellbeing – you strive to achieve and maintain good physical, mental and emotional health, which leads to a sense of your overall wellbeing. This manifests itself in you being physically fit, emotionally balanced, energetic and productive. *Healthy* leaders are infectious and inspire others, who are typically attracted to you and express a desire to work with and for you.

4. IQ: General intelligence and wisdom – you have the ability to learn new things, apply learned knowledge, solve problems and make good decisions, based on sound judgment and wisdom.

Your good decisions and choices incorporate a reasonable course of action, combined with past experience that has worked for you. Also you have openness to learning new things that could work in order to attain your desired results. You are able to make the complex simple, identifying the best course of action to drive the greatest value. Inspiring leaders are *wise* in addition to being *intelligent*.

5. EQ: Emotional and social competence – you are aware of and understand emotions, as well as effectively expressing feelings. You understand how others feel and relate well with them, manage and control emotions to cope with your daily demands. You have strategies for solving problems, managing through change and responding to your pressures and stresses. You are able to generate positive mood and be sufficiently self-motivated and fully engaged.

6. RQ: Resilience – you successfully cope with disappointment, crisis and catastrophe. You have the ability to quickly recover from these setbacks and learn from them. As a result of this process, you often become wiser and more *resilient* than before. It is your bouncing back from adversity and thriving, rather than merely surviving. Resilient people can handle difficult colleagues and toxic environments. You have the tenacity to pick yourself up after minor hassles or major crises. When you have high levels of RQ, then you have a strong internal locus of control and you are able to reframe adverse situations in an optimistic way.

7. BQ: Personal brand and reputation – you concern yourself with building a strong *brand* image and reputation. BQ is a combination of what people observe (your reputation), your ability to positively influence (your power), your personal track record (your value) and your image and presentation (your impact). Personal branding is a persuasive tool, its impact often overlooked and so underutilised. From initial impressions to a consistent image of who you are as a leader and what you represent, all have the potential to build confidence in those around you.

8. Legacy – This is what you leave behind after moving on from the organisation. Your *legacy* is the impact you have made and left on your organisation, colleagues, community and society in the end. You make a sustainable difference that adds value. The choices you make involve ethical decisions for the longer-term sustainability, avoiding negative implications through your areas of responsibility. Your systemic and strategic thinking includes the broader impact of your decisions.

The Four Environments of Inspiring Leadership - Achieving Focused Balance

The Four Environments are how and where you focus your time and energy: (1) Myself, (2) My Relationships, (3) My Organisation, and (4) My Society. They provide an important lens to determine who you are in service of, and highlight important areas that may be neglected.

You may have more or less influence dependent on your roles and responsibilities. As long as you are comfortable with the choices you make and the boundaries you set, then you do not need to be judgemental about yourself and others. Being judgemental is misspent energy.

You do however need to regularly revisit these choices to reflect and make sure that you are not compromising on your values.

Your energy and focus within these Four Environments and how consistently authentic you are:

1. My Self

The first area is the focus that you give to yourself. This deals with the confidence that you have in who you are, understanding of your deepest desires and passions, as well as the characteristics that give you strength to perform consistently in your personal work and life goals. The idea here is that if you are able to inspire others and to give in abundance, then you must first give abundantly to yourselves. To be a respected and trusted leader, you must have credibility. This comes with your own levels of energy, confidence and competence. Interestingly, across all of my interviews with women, 'myself' is the most neglected environment. Everything else comes first and 'myself' comes last. Inspiring Women leaders adjust this balance.

2. My Relationships

The second environment focuses on the relationships that are most important to you. This is about how you understand, interact and give priority to them.

Inspiring leaders recognise how essential these relationships are and establish a set of boundaries that help to protect the time spent on nurturing them. You value and utilise the support network that is available to you, enhancing the relationships in a positive way and reinvesting your energy with reciprocity. You maintain healthy relationships, discerning between energy drainers and energy radiators!

3. My Business

The third environment relates to your commitment to making an impact and driving value in your work as an inspiring leader. You establish organisational structures and ways of working with your teams to engender loyalty and commitment. You make organisational decisions that protect the reputation of the business and those you lead. In a fast-paced, changing and often competitive environment, inspiring leaders put the people they are there to serve at the heart of what they do, understanding this will pay dividends as a result.

4. My Society

The final element is the time and energy you give to playing a meaningful role in your communities and society. You understand your potential to bring your strengths to the fore and offer these to others who will benefit. You are passionate about making a difference and leaving a legacy beyond your own sphere of influence. You search for and align to initiatives that make a sustainable and positive difference.

Inspiring Women Leaders and the Four Environments of Influence

Alix Pryde
Director, Media & Entertainment

In my interview with Alix, she proved to be an engaging and intelligent leader who is inspiring and insightful about how she successfully manages both work and home. She has a real focus on what matters most to her, pursues her passions and has established the necessary boundaries around the areas that are most important.

Alix shared, *"The loss of my parents had a huge impact on me. My father died after a long illness when I was 15 years old and then my mother very suddenly 10 years later. So by the age of 25 I had no parents and no grandparents and had effectively become the head of the family. It taught me starkly and early that life is too short and too precious not to follow my passions and ambitions.*

"Both my parents were physicists and since primary school I had the ambition to become 'Dr. Pryde' like my Dad. My Mum would have been 'Dr. Pryde' too had the funding system been more supportive of married women at the time she was offered her PhD place. I drove towards that goal until I achieved it. Although my Dad never saw me get there, one of the last days I spent with my Mum before she died was my graduation ceremony in Cambridge.

"During the year my Dad was ill and then died, I discovered a new passion: radio. It might have come to nothing, but the wake-up call I'd had, or perhaps a desire for escapism, made me more adventurous in exploring it.

I volunteered to work at my local radio station and discovered a fascinating world. I found a kindred spirit in the now-famous presenter who invited me in, who had lost his father at a similar age and described it as "the shot that started the race". More importantly, it's also where I met my husband and father of my children, although that all came many years later.

"So I pursued radio as a hobby and physics as a career. As I approached the end of my PhD and was thinking about what I really wanted to do next, I shifted the balance towards broadcasting. I learned about management consulting and in particular about McKinsey & Co, which was well known for working with the BBC in those days. Working as a Business Analyst at McKinsey gave me a fantastic grounding in the world of business and the joy of applying my skills for the benefit of the BBC and learning from leading thinkers about public service broadcasting. It was as I was just putting the final touches on a major written summary of months of work for the BBC that I came home to find my boyfriend (and future husband) waiting for me with two police officers and a police car to drive me to the hospital where my Mum was dying. McKinsey was very supportive; I had a lot to deal with, first with the funeral and then sorting out the family home. Then a few months later, I was approaching the end of the analyst programme with McKinsey and it was time for me to decide what to do next. I was single-minded; it had to be radio. And fifteen fulfilling years working in broadcasting have followed.

"I've been called a role model a few times, but the first time I ever actually felt like a role model was when I found myself pregnant (after having all but given up trying) shortly after winning a great new role. I was the first woman to lead the BBC's distribution (transmission) team. Now with pregnancy and a promotion, I felt I was representing something that would have been a taboo not so long before, or at a less flexible company. I really admire women who take on new responsibilities around the time that they are expecting or returning to work after a child, and especially managers who put their faith in such women. My manager was absolutely brilliant about it. I knew I needed support and I worked with a terrific coach to help me approach my new responsibilities and plan for my maternity leave in a way that was fair to the team that I had just been trusted to look after.

"A big challenging moment for me came shortly after I returned from maternity leave to find that we needed to make cutbacks in the BBC, which would result in redundancies. It was six to nine months before everything began to feel on an even keel again. I felt a heavy responsibility having to reduce my team by 25%, holding people's livelihoods in my hands. It felt sickeningly horrible, but at least I had the opportunity to try to make sure it was done as thoughtfully and caringly as possible. I tried hard to be very open and transparent and as rigorous as I could be with this hard task. It was an uncertain time for me too and I was upset about some things that had happened. I eventually decided to share with the whole team my own feelings and vulnerabilities, which I think made me more authentic. That was only after I had got myself to a more accepting state of mind thanks to a female leader from a different organisation. She advised me to try to appreciate the differences in my situation and choose to find the positives. This really gave me a sense of integrity as I could start to tell my story in a different way that felt more true. Initially I felt frustrated, however, the more I stood up and demonstrated my vulnerability whilst holding my 'cabinet responsibilities' it worked for my team, who then felt able to share their anger and frustration with me in private. By approaching it with the mind-set that 'I am also on your journey but a bit ahead of you and I know we can get through this' helped me to lead others through.

"I have had the privilege of working with some fantastic women. I was Chief Adviser to a member of the BBC Executive Board and learnt an enormous amount from her. She showed me that you can be a very senior leader but also be humble and frank and show your human side. She is great at telling things straight, but also kindly. Time after time, people came away after raising a complaint to her feeling satisfied that they had actually been heard and treated with respect, even if the underlying issue couldn't be addressed. Also, she always believes the best in people and places her trust in people. And while the rare person might let you down, the rest of the time it cuts out so much wheel-spinning. I do believe that a lot of energy can be expended on being suspicious or playing corporate politics.

"Regarding work-life balance, I am by no means perfect. I try my best and don't always get it right. But I also try to tell myself, 'I am not at home to Mrs

Guilt'. It's is a really unhelpful emotion. I've chosen to be a full-time working mother and I'm better off expending my energies to do that as well as I can rather than feeling bad about it. I am very lucky to have a really supportive husband who easily does his fair share of the many things that go into making a home. We've made a priority of good quality childcare for our kids (son 6, daughter 3). I'm fortunate with the BBC as my employer and the role I have that I have a good deal of flexibility and autonomy. I can usually ring-fence and work around the big moments, like the class nativity. We try to make sure each weekend we do something special, however small, so we have memorable 'Mummy and Daddy days'. I'm conscious that as my kids get older, it will only get harder to get the balance right. For starters, they're now old enough to remember events for the rest of their lives and might replay my failings to me one day! The 'To Do' list becomes more complex too, with the arrival of things like spelling tests and fancy dress days at school. At the end of the day, I believe that bringing up my children is the most important job I will ever have on this planet. And at the same time, it can feel strange that I've 'outsourced' it in some way. But of course I haven't. And even though I might not be the person who spends the most time with them in any given week, I know am special to them as their mum; there's an irreplaceable bond. And it was really reassuring when working women who'd been there before me shared stories that illustrated that, especially at the point I returned to work after my first child. I'm very lucky that I can share my work with my kids because of the nature of what I do, and that the BBC and television and radio are part of their daily lives. When our city went through digital switchover, we made it into a big event at home, retuning the TVs together. And they share my excitement as we approach new channel launches and start to see the signs appearing on screen.

"The legacy I want to leave is two-fold. In my work, I get an enormous kick out of helping to make visible (or audible!) changes around broadcasting which benefit people that I might pass on the street. I help to bring people on in my team with great talents, which is very humbling. It is important for me as part of my legacy to show my son and daughter what a woman can do in the workplace.

"But above all, the thing I most want to be is a great mum."

Chapter Reflection:
How inspiring a leader am I?

It is very difficult for anyone to consistently meet all of the criteria across all aspects of the model at any given time. However, by developing aspects of the model that are most important and create the greatest value, then it will help you to become a more inspiring leader. In my workshops and one-to-one coaching, I often ask leaders to evaluate themselves using the Inspiring Leadership Model.

*1. Starting with the eight components and using a scale of 1 to 10 with 1 being low and 10 being high, where are you now? (Alternatively, visit my website **www.leighbowmanperks.com** and complete the Inspiring Leadership Inventory^{TM} on-line to receive your own detailed psychometric report.)*

2. Use this process to notice your strengths and your gaps.

3. Now allocate the percentage time and energy you give to each of the 4 environments: My Self; My Relationships; My Organisation; My Society.

4. Finally, compare each of the 8 components with your impact as an inspiring leader across all 4 environments, notice the consistencies or differences.

Questions:

- *How congruent are the results with who you are and what you want?*
- *How consistent and authentic are you being?*
- *How understanding, flexible and responsive are you to the needs of others?*
- *What thoughts do you have on the gaps and the resulting actions that may be required?*

Chapter 3
The Research Behind Inspiring Leadership, Confirming Its Importance

Contributing Author: Dr. Reuven Bar-On

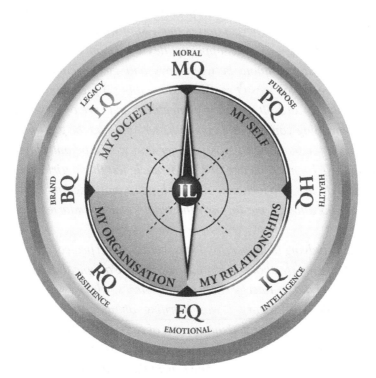

"I grew up believing there were no limitations. I received unconditional love and was brought up to believe you could succeed at anything you set out to do. My grandmother and mother's stories were parables of overcoming setbacks hardships and difficulties and taught me what women could achieve. I never noticed discrimination against me as a woman and I must have ignored it if I came upon it."

Elizabeth Corley
CEO Allianz

Jaz Rabadia
Chartered Energy Manager, Mechanical
Engineer and STEM Ambassador

"Coming from an Indian background, education was considered very important in our family. The perception is that Asian women are not offered the same opportunities as Asian men. However, my Mum did not discriminate between boys and girls, demonstrating huge independence, which wasn't really the done thing. I grew up with two older brothers and as a result was very competitive and sure of myself. I had the attitude 'anything you can do I can do better' and had the gift of the gab!

"I was a tomboy when I was younger and would be out playing tennis matches past 10pm at the age of 13. My uncle felt that a girl should not be allowed to do this. I'm fortunate that my biggest ambassadors have been my parents, who allowed me to push the traditional boundaries from a very young age.

"Whilst studying at university, I was working on a project at the time that I was not passionate about. I wanted to do choose a topic that would make a difference so I did an Energy study at Sainsbury's, where I was working part time. I applied the theory I was learning about at university into the workplace and this generated the interest of colleagues. The Head of Energy invited me into headquarters to present my findings and nominated me for a Sainsbury's award. At the ceremony I spent the entire evening sitting next to the Chief Financial Officer. He asked, 'Why aren't you working for Sainsbury's in the Head Office?' Six months later I started there, with no experience of corporate life. I had pestered a guy about getting this job and everything led from there; my persistence paid off. I could have been a quiet and polite person and hoped that I would have been noticed if I was good enough, but I'm not convinced that it would have been as quick. I've learned that getting people to notice and champion you may be the hardest thing to do, but it is extremely important.

"For the first six months it was pretty daunting. Property was generally full of middle-class older men. When I started I would get handed the post, or

people would think I was the PA (Personal Assistant). I found I always had to prove how senior I was. In the first year it was just about getting things done and I felt more of a barrier, whereas in my second year I felt a lot more comfortable. I had a different outlook and learned different approaches. I found that my difference didn't create a barrier; it actually got me noticed as I brought different ideas to the table. As a young and creative woman I was not typical in the field of Energy.

"At the same time as working at Sainsbury's, I started my Master's degree to become an Energy Specialist. As a female engineer I found that everyone was extremely supportive. City University gave me a hefty discount, as I wasn't in a position to take on the full price. When I got my MSc, I was very surprised by how Sainsbury's celebrated my achievements. That gave me the confidence boost that was needed. I had a lot of recognition and support from my manager, who would talk to me about development opportunities. My friends would call me a bit of a 'Kodak', because I was always seeking development and because of my photographic memory. I have always been academically minded and so this for me has been a measure of my success. I always think about what else can I strive for, my next challenge. I'd always seen the value of professional development, but it was after working in a corporate environment that I saw the bigger value of personal development.

"I needed to be able to empower others as much as myself. I wasn't from a particularly privileged background. You don't have to go to Oxford, Cambridge, or Imperial to be successful. I went to a poor performing state school and still made it. So I became a STEM ambassador and started to go into schools to attend career events, mentor students and give talks on environmental sustainability. The careers that students think about are typical roles such as accountants, lawyers, doctors etc. I like to raise awareness of the not-so-typical jobs.

"A big part of my life is the community base with about 1,000 people who are within my temple. I've built my confidence growing up in a supportive community and am a member of their Sports Committee. I started by just playing netball there, and now I've learned how to coach it and have a professional coaching qualification. I've also started a football academy and have become a key lead on activities that help more youngsters get into

sports. My Swaminarayan (Hindu) faith drives my morals; these were instilled in me from a very young age by my parents and grandparents.

"The temple places great importance on selfless giving, It was Churchill that said, "It is our blood right to make a living out of what we get, yet we make a life out of what we give". This has been the best advice for me.

"With my success in becoming the Asian Woman of the Year and winning the Energy Manager of the Year awards, I understand the importance of this recognition in helping to knock down barriers and create real life role models. The Asian Women of Achievement Awards have raised my profile, helped me to establish an amazing network and changed my life. I used to think 'A diamond doesn't need to remind everyone it shines; it just shines', but imagine how much more it would sparkle if you shone a spotlight on it. On the back of the awards I have learnt that women can do so much more to support each other and shine a spotlight on those coming through the pipeline. Something I hope to put into practice as I climb the corporate ladder.

"As I look at my Facebook status and then my LinkedIn profile, I sometimes feel like I'm leading a double life. The 'personal me' and 'professional' me are so different! However, my core does not change. It doesn't just switch on and off, it's just about putting on the 'right outfit'. So my advice would be don't be scared to be who you are and be comfortable in your own skin.

"I've taken a few knocks, whilst trying to climb the ladder too. I have put that down to my immaturity and inexperience at the time. I have sometimes unwittingly antagonised people; partly because I found myself working with people twice my age and partly because of my intense work output. It's taken them 20 years to get to where they are and so understandably they are demanding recognition and remuneration. I didn't understand that then and so I approached some issues in the wrong way. It was the support that I received from Helen Sachdev [an inspiring leader also interviewed for this book] *that helped me to get through this. How would I know any different, unless someone helped me with an alternative perspective?*

"Despite being Asian, young and a woman I have not felt at all held back, only supported by friends, family, managers and colleagues alike. This has

been the secret to my success. I've just started as Energy Manager at Debenhams, and I find there is a really positive attitude towards me. I think it's down to the fact that they value capability and fresh ideas I have the stamp of approval, because I know what I'm talking about. I have the qualifications, the experience and the championing to prove it!

"Achieving Chartered Energy Manager status was a very difficult mature application and I'd invested money and five years of my energy into it. I genuinely just want to experience as much as I can. I've got to where I've got to because of the questions I have asked, not the answers I have given; I'm genuinely inquisitive. I believe that you only know what you know. I want to be the middle-person in the seat on the plane so I can speak to the strangers either side of me. I'm hungry for knowledge and am very pragmatic. Having won awards, I feel ready to tell the world about it."

The Research Behind Inspiring Leadership, Confirming its Importance

This chapter is divided into three parts:

- Part One: Introduction and Context
- Part Two: Results from the Quantitative Research (IL-i^{TM})
- Part Three: Results of the Qualitative Research (Inspiring Leadership Interviews)

PART ONE: Introduction and Context

What was the primary aim of my research?

From the outset, my aim was to show that Inspiring Leadership (IL) is a viable concept that can make an important difference in the workplace. I believe it will contribute real value, especially for women in leadership positions. Consequently, it was imperative to demonstrate that this concept is intrinsically associated with performance and has the potential to predict high performers in leadership. I was also curious to learn whether women in leadership positions possess 'more IL', or 'less IL' than men. I intended to explain gender differences should they exist, as well as how to address them.

I aspired to obtain significant findings demonstrating the predictive ability and value of IL. This would give our IL concept credibility, so that it could be applied in selecting and developing more inspiring and high performing leaders. These must be leaders capable of contributing to their organisation's overall effectiveness, productivity and profitability. It was also thought that if gender differences do exist, then my findings could provide a 'roadmap'. Such a roadmap would indicate which IL qualities needed to be enhanced, in order to help level the playing field in the corporate world.

How do we prove that *Inspiring Leadership* is a valuable and applicable concept?

I began to address this intriguing challenge by first developing an operational concept of Inspiriting Leadership together with Jonathan Bowmen-Perks, based on his original work in this area. We began to comprehensively define the nature of this IL concept. This described a set of characteristics we thought inspiring leaders possess. Our many years of work in leadership coaching and development, as well as a systematic review of the professional literature, contributed to this phase of our research. The end-product of these efforts culminated in our initial conceptualisation of Inspiring Leadership, described in detail throughout this book.

The next step involved piloting this nascent idea by conducting a survey, designed to ask both lay and professional people what they thought about our concept in general. We also asked them what they would edit, change, or add to improve it. This piloting process was conducted over a period of nine months and succeeded in reaching nearly a hundred individuals in person, by phone, or online. The input received from the survey was used in carefully revising and moulding the burgeoning concept, making it more concise, comprehensive and comprehensible.

The next major phase of the research involved interviewing over 100 inspiring women leaders from around the world. I focused on interviewing women in leadership positions working in a wide range of industries. The women interviewed were 'highly recommended' by colleagues and professional contacts. This was primarily because they were "recognised as being very successful in what they have accomplished", but also because they possessed a number of very positive qualities. These particular qualities represent, in essence, the basic criteria I applied in selecting prospective interviewees.

They were selected because they appeared unique, authentic and stood out from others, as individuals who choose to lead and do so with focus, determination and passion. They are people who others look to, listen to and admire, in spite of a typical unimposing, modest and quiet presence. Furthermore, they usually make informed, well-thought-out and wise decisions that add value for both the short and long term. These individuals are typically humble and open to learn from their mistakes, past experience and the wisdom of others. They are also flexible, adaptive and able to recover relatively quickly from adversity, as well as to learn from setbacks when they occur. Additionally, they appear to generate energy, motivate themselves and feel fully engaged in what they do. They also tend to exhibit moral courage and live by high ethical standards at work as well as in their private lives. Last, these individuals appear to seek meaning in what they do and are focused on leaving a positive and sustainable legacy.

At the same time that I was involved in the interviewing phase of this project, Jonathan Bowman-Perks and I began to develop a psychometric instrument designed to assess this concept. This was done in consultation with Reuven Bar-On, an acknowledged expert in test construction, to assure that this instrument was being developed in an acceptable manner and according to the highest standards (Anastasi & Urbina, 1997). It is important to point out, moreover, that we were advised to base the development of our measure of Inspiring Leadership on the meticulous process applied in developing the *Bar-On EQ-i*™ (Bar-On, 1997, 2004 & 2006). The result of this effort was the creation of the 'Inspiring Leadership Inventory™' ('IL-i™'), which is briefly described here and elsewhere in this book.

In short, the IL-i™ is an 82-item psychometric instrument that assesses the 8 primary characteristics possessed by inspiring leaders as we have defined them in our conceptualisation of Inspiring Leadership:

1. Moral integrity
2. Purpose

3. Health and wellbeing
4. General intelligence and wisdom
5. Emotional and social competence
6. Resilience
7. Personal brand and reputation
8. Legacy

An IL-i™ user guide is currently being prepared for publication as well as additional manuscripts that will be submitted to professional journals in the near future. By visiting my website **www.leighbowmanperks.com**, you can complete this inventory online in order to get a better understanding of what it looks like.

While the interviews I conducted can be considered a semi-structured assessment tool, the IL-i™ is an actual psychometric instrument; one that meets acceptable standards of psychological test-construction (Anastasi & Urbina, 1997). I applied both interviewing and testing techniques, in order to increase my ability to obtain maximum information about the Inspiring Leadership concept, inspiring leaders in general and inspiring women leaders in particular. In addition to interviewing over 100 inspiring women leaders, it was reasoned that the IL-i™ could be administered to hundreds of individuals to gain additional information about this concept of leadership. This process of data collection would enable us to apply sophisticated and robust 'multivariate statistics' (Tabachnick & Fidell, 2001) to the results in an effort to learn more about inspiring leaders and examine the ability of the IL-i™ to predict leadership performance.

Forty-four women who were interviewed together with an additional forty-three men, who met the previously described criteria for being interviewed, completed the IL-i™ online. In their 1997 classic text on test construction, Anne Anastasi and Susana Urbina refer to this approach to validating tests as 'criterion group validation' and maintain that is a powerful way of demonstrating 'construct validity' (what they measure exactly) as well as 'predictive validity' (how well they predict what they were designed to measure – Inspiring Leadership in the case of the IL-i™). In addition to this criterion group of 87 inspiring leaders, more than 1,200 individuals have completed the IL-i™ to date.

The following was the approach I pursued in applying the quantitative part of my research. This allowed me to examine the potential importance, value and applicability of the Inspiring Leadership construct. This was then combined with the qualitative results I obtained from interviewing a sizable number of inspiring leaders:

1. Examine if there is a statistically significant correlation between the Inspiring Leadership construct, as measured by the IL-i™, and performance by first using bivariate statistical methods (Hill & Lewicki, 2006).

2. Apply multivariate statistics (Tabachnick & Fidell, 2001) to confirm, or disconfirm, the possible correlation between Inspiring Leadership and performance, as well as to see if IL-i™ scores actually predict performance and how well.

3. Confirm the IL-i™'s predictive validity, by examining its ability to accurately distinguish between average leaders and inspiring leaders, in the criterion group, by applying additional statistical methods (Tabachnick & Fidell, 2001).

4. Depending upon the nature of results obtained from the above approach, I would most likely need to do the following:

   a. First see whether there are differences between male and female leaders with respect to their IL-i™ scale scores

   b. Then examine if there are significant differences between inspiring men and women in leadership positions

   c. Finally obtain a more accurate picture of what inspiring women leaders look like. This would also depend, primarily, on applying sophisticated and powerful multivariate statistics (Tabachnick & Fidell, 2001).

The specific statistical procedures that were applied as well as the major findings obtained are presented and discussed below.

PART TWO: Results from the Quantitative Research (IL-i^{TM})

What were the results from administering the Inspiring Leadership Inventory™?

Together with my colleagues, we conducted a number of different statistical analyses of the data generated by more than a 1,200 individuals who completed the IL-i™. To reiterate, this approach was imperative for learning more about:

a. The nature, importance and applicability of the Inspiring
   Leadership concept
b. Inspiring leaders in general
c. Inspiring women leaders in particular

The procedures applied and the results obtained are discussed below.

What we know about the relationship between Inspiring Leadership and performance.

The initial analysis of the data was designed to address a question of fundamental importance for the continued conceptualisation of our model of leadership:

Is there an actual relationship between the Inspiring Leadership concept and performance?

This was done by comparing the degree of 'bivariate correlation' (Hill & Lewicki, 2006) between the 8 characteristics of inspiring leaders, as measured by the IL-i™ and performance. In addition to completing the inventory, respondents were asked to rate their daily performance on a 10-point scale, and this provided an estimate of their leadership performance, which was then correlated with each of the IL-i™ scales. The results are presented in Table 1.

Table 1: Examining the degree of bivariate correlation between each of the IL-i™ scales and a self-rated estimate of performance generated the following correlation coefficients (n=1100).

IL-i™	Performance
Total IL	.43
Moral Integrity	.28
Purpose	.20
Health & Wellbeing	.17
General Intelligence & Wisdom	.37
Emotional & Social Competence	.41
Resilience	.37
Personal Brand & Reputation	.47
Legacy	.39

The results in Table 1 suggest that Inspiring Leadership (IL) is indeed correlated with performance, albeit 'self-rated' performance which is thought to be biased to a certain degree (Anastasi & Urbina, 1997). Those *IL* characteristics that appear to be more highly correlated with performance are the leader's degree of:

1. General intelligence and wisdom
2. Emotional and social competence
3. Resilience
4. Personal brand and reputation
5. Focusing on the importance of leaving a legacy

Regarding the leader's personal brand and reputation, it is unclear whether this characteristic enhances performance and/or if performing well contributes to this apparently important characteristic of inspiring leaders. Additional research is needed to address the direction, or directions, of causality in this regard.

In addition to the above bivariate examination of the correlation between the *IL-i*™ scales and self-rated performance, a more robust 'multivariate' analysis (Tabachnick & Fidell, 2001) was then conducted and rendered an overall Canonical R of .52 [Chi-Square = 335.47, p level <.001]. This moderately high correlation provides additional confirmation that *IL* is significantly correlated with performance.

Findings that shed light on the ability of Inspiring Leadership to predict performance.

When a concept is correlated with a specific type of performance, psychometricians often examine its ability to predict that performance, as the next logical step in test development. We needed to take a closer look at the significant correlation between the Inspiring Leadership (IL) concept and leadership performance. In addition to examining the degree to which this concept can predict this type of performance, we ran a more sophisticated statistical application. The results generated by applying 'Multiple Regression Analysis' (Tabachnick & Fidell, 2001) appear in Table 2 and are discussed below.

Table 2: The results obtained from applying Multiple Regression Analysis to determine the ability of the *IL-i*™ and the concept it measures, Inspiring Leadership, to predict performance (n=1100).

IL-i™	*Beta* scores	*t* values	*p* values
Personal Brand & Reputation	1.13	7.98	<.001
Emotional & Social Competence	0.50	4.20	<.001
General Intelligence & Wisdom	0.39	3.02	.003
Legacy	0.35	3.28	.001

The multiple regression analysis of the data, that generated the results appearing in Table 2, rendered a Multiple R of .52 (*F* value = 65.45, p level <.001). This moderately high correlation strongly indicates that the concept of Inspiring Leadership (IL) is indeed capable of predicting performance. The most robust IL predictor of leadership performance appears to be the leader's personal brand and reputation, followed by emotional and social competence, general intelligence and wisdom, and the drive to leave some valuable and sustainable legacy for others. Apparently, these are the key *IL* predictors of performance based on the results obtained in the present study. When a regression correlation of .52 is converted to a 'squared correlation' (R^2), it suggests that more than 27% of successful leadership performance is based on the IL concept. It means that this concept accounts for a sizable amount of the variance that drives performance.

The ability to distinguish between average and inspiring leaders based on our findings.

After obtaining the above results suggesting that the Inspiring Leadership concept is not only significantly correlated with performance and is capable of predicting it, the next step was to see whether there are significant differences (i.e., equal to or less than a "p level" – probability level – of .05) between average leaders and inspiring leaders based on the scores they obtain on the *IL-i*™. A *p* level of .05 means that the probability that the results obtained are inaccurate is only about 5% or, phrased differently, the results are 95% accurate. The results from applying a '1-way ANOVA' – Analysis of Variance – (Tabachnick & Fidell, 2001) to examine the degree of difference between average and inspiring leaders appear in Table 3

Table 3: Differences in IL-i™ scale scores between average leaders (n=1013) and inspiring leaders (n=87) based on applying a 1-way ANOVA.

IL-i™ scales	Average Leaders	Inspiring Leaders	*F* values	*p* levels
Total IL	3.9	4.1	35.64	<.001
Moral Integrity	4.3	4.4	11.09	.001
Purpose	3.7	4.0	16.68	<.001
Health & Wellbeing	3.6	3.9	14.07	<.001
General Intelligence	4.0	4.1	08.37	.004

& Wisdom				
Emotional & Social Competence	3.9	4.1	21.05	<.001
Resilience	3.9	4.1	17.69	<.001
Personal Brand & Reputation	3.9	4.2	33.00	<.001
Legacy	3.6	4.0	34.36	<.001

The results in Table 3 clearly indicate that inspiring leaders are fundamentally different from average leaders, in that they are significantly more adept in all of the 8 IL characteristics measured by the IL-i™. It is important to note, moreover, that the highest p level is .004, which means that the accuracy of the results presented here, as well as the accuracy of the IL-i™ in obtaining those results, is more than 99.6% accurate. In re-examining this instrument's overall level of accuracy, an F value of 6.10 was generated with a p level of <001. This finding suggests that its overall level of accuracy is most likely higher than 99.9%!

Additional results that do not appear in Table 3 suggest that inspiring leaders invest significantly more energy at work and in the community than average leaders. They also outperform average leaders, even though they experience the same amount of stress at work.

At the time this book was being published, additional, larger and more diverse samples of average and inspiring leaders are being studied using a number of different methods in order to shed more light on the findings presented here. The next edition of this book will present and discuss this growing body of knowledge.

Differences between male and female leaders based on our research findings.

In spite of the fact that there are differences between male and female leaders, as the results in Table 4 reveal, there are no significant differences between inspiring women leaders (n=44) and inspiring men leaders (n=43) as can be seen in Table 5. These findings are presented and discussed below.

Table 4: Gender differences in IL-i™ scale scores between women (n=775) and men (n=325), who do not meet the criteria of inspiring leaders applied in the present research.

IL-i™	Women	Men	F values	p levels
Total IL	3.9	4.0	15.40	<.001
Moral Integrity	4.3	4.3	0.10	.724
Purpose	3.7	3.6	3.67	.056
Health & Wellbeing	3.6	3.8	13.44	<.001
General Intelligence & Wisdom	4.0	4.1	35.36	<.001
Emotional & Social Competence	3.9	4.0	8.03	.005
Resilience	3.9	4.1	29.32	<.001
Personal Brand & Reputation	3.9	4.0	14.31	<.001
Legacy	3.6	3.8	18.33	<.001

The findings presented in Table 4 suggest that men are more adept in 6 of the 8 characteristics of *inspiring leaders*; and the overall gender differences captured by the *IL-i™* and presented here is highly significant (F value = 14.63, p level < .001), which means they indeed exist.

The only 2 *IL-i™* scales that did not reveal significant gender differences beyond the accepted 5% level are Moral Integrity and Purpose, although the results suggest a tendency among women to find more purpose and meaning in the work they do when compared with men. Regarding daily performance in the workplace, it is also worth noting that men appear to outperform women in the sample that was studied. Additional results, not appearing in this table, indicate that women tend to exaggerate their positive attributes, which could possibly represent a 'survival mechanism' aimed at being competitive in a male-dominated corporate world.

The results presented in Table 4 suggest the need to develop 'remedial programmes' designed to strengthen Inspiring Leadership (IL) characteristics, through group training and individual coaching, in order to level the playing field and help women become more competitive in the workplace.

Based on these findings, such programmes could help women:
1. Make better decision-makers.
2. Become more resilient.
3. Develop their personal brand and reputation and.
4. Become more focused on the legacy they would like to leave for their colleagues, organisation and community.

Three of these IL characteristics, that appear significantly weaker in women, are 3 of the 4 characteristics that are the strongest predictors of performance based on our current research as was indicated by the findings presented in Table 2. It is reasonable to assume that if more women could enhance these particular IL characteristics, they would become more competitive and productive in the workplace.

After demonstrating that Inspiring Leadership is correlated with and predicts performance (Tables 1 and 2) and that there are indeed significant differences between average leaders and inspiring leaders (Table 3), I was curious to see if there are differences between inspiring women and inspiring men in leadership positions which is the centrepiece of this book (Inspiring Women Leaders). This was done by comparing the IL-i™ scores of inspiring women leaders with those of their male counterparts. The results appear in Table 5.

Table 5: Gender differences in IL-i™ scale scores between inspiring women leaders (n=44) and inspiring men in leadership positions (n=43).

IL-i™	Inspiring Women Leaders	Inspiring Men Leaders	F values	p levels
Total IL	4.1	4.1	0.60	.442
Moral Integrity	4.4	4.4	0.08	.778

Purpose	3.9	4.0	0.13	.724
Health & Wellbeing	3.9	4.0	0.06	.807
General Intelligence & Wisdom	4.1	4.2	0.90	.346
Emotional & Social Competence	4.1	4.1	0.08	.774
Resilience	4.1	4.2	0.97	.329
Personal Brand & Reputation	4.1	4.2	2.08	.153
Legacy	4.0	4.0	0.10	.759

The findings displayed in Table 5 show that there are no significant differences between inspiring women leaders and their male counterparts, based on the individual IL-i™ scale scores generated by this sample. These important findings indicate that the Inspiring Leadership concept is not gender-specific and possibly not influenced by gender. More succinctly, this concept is about leadership and not about gender.

Additional results not appearing in this table, also demonstrate that there are no significant gender differences associated with inspiring leaders regarding the energy and effort they invest in personal, interpersonal, organisational and community activities, which is significantly more than average leaders.

The only significant gender difference is a tendency in inspiring women leaders to moderately exaggerate their positive attributes more than men, which has possibly evolved because of a deep-rooted need to be more competitive than men for 'survival and adaptation' in the male-dominated corporate world as was previously suggested.

Current research findings that shed light on what inspiring women leaders look like.

Our research findings show that we are able to predict performance as well as distinguish between average leaders and inspiring leaders. Next, I began to take a closer look at what inspiring women leaders actually look like based on our research findings. To do this, we compared the IL-i™

results from our criterion sample of inspiring women leaders (n=44) with those of other women in leadership positions who were not included in this sample (n=775).

Significant differences were indeed revealed and tell us a great deal about this unique breed of inspiring women leaders, who are an invaluable asset to any organisation. The key findings appear in Table 6 and are discussed below.

Table 6: Differences in IL-i™ scale scores between average female leaders (n=727) and inspiring women leaders (n=44).

IL-i™	Average Female Leaders	Inspiring Women Leaders	F values	p levels
Total IL	3.8	4.1	17.63	<.001
Moral Integrity	4.3	4.4	4.77	.029
Purpose	3.7	3.9	6.39	.012
Health & Wellbeing	3.6	3.9	8.51	.004
General Intelligence & Wisdom	4.0	4.1	4.57	.033
Emotional & Social Competence	3.9	4.1	11.13	.001
Resilience	3.9	4.1	8.74	.003
Personal Brand & Reputation	3.9	4.1	12.43	.001
Legacy	3.6	4.0	19.79	<.001

The results presented in Table 6 show that there are several fundamental differences between average and inspiring women leaders. In fact, inspiring women leaders are noticeably more adept in all of the 8 characteristics of Inspiring Leadership described in detail throughout this book, and the overall difference between them is quite significant.

In addition to doing the correct as well as the right thing in leading others, making wise decisions and finding purpose in what they do, they are emotionally and socially intelligent, resilient and have built up a presence, personal brand and reputation based on what they have contributed at work and in their community. These qualities represent the key differences that distinguish these inspiring women leaders from other women in leadership. These are the individuals who possess the presence of a true leader and who know how to inspire and lead others; these are the leaders who others want to work for, with and follow.

What we now know about inspiring women leaders, based on the above research findings, confirms much of what I have learned from interviewing the women who met the criteria mentioned previously and were included in the criterion group used in validating our measure of the Inspiring Leadership concept.

The research results presented in this chapter have confirmed and clarified a number of important points regarding inspiring leaders in general (Perks, 2010) and inspiring women leaders in particular.

The key findings suggest that inspiring leaders are emotionally, socially and morally competent and strive to do the right thing in their interactions with others at work, in the community and in their private lives. They are also significantly intelligent, wise and resilient when compared with other leaders. Additionally, they are successful in building a positive image and reputation based on what they have contributed over time, in finding purpose and meaning in what they do, and are driven to leave a sustainable legacy for their colleagues, organisation and community.

Inspiring Leaders also possess good physical health, fitness and overall wellbeing, which have a positive impact on their performance as well. They were also shown to invest more energy, effort and passion at work and in the community than other leaders. All of these factors combine to create a distinctively unique type of leadership that we have referred to as Inspiring Leadership; a specific type of leadership that is highly correlated with performance. This means that leaders who possess Inspiring Leadership characteristics perform at a higher level than other leaders. Their strongest predictors of performance are apparently general (cognitive) intelligence, emotional and social competence, personal image and reputation, and the drive to leave a valuable and sustainable legacy for others.

Based on the above results, the four most robust and important characteristics of inspiring leaders are:

1. Emotional and social competence
2. Resilience and bounce-back
3. Personal brand and reputation
4. The desire to leave a sustainable and positive legacy

Additional results not presented here suggest that they focus less on themselves, more on their relationships with others and much more on their work and doing something constructive for the community.

The findings presented in this chapter also indicate that there are no significant differences between inspiring women leaders and inspiring men in leadership positions, clearly demonstrating that inspiring leadership does not depend on gender or follow a gender-related motif. This suggests that Inspiring Leadership is solely about leadership, in and of itself, and that the gender of outstanding leaders is irrelevant to their ability to lead and inspire others.

Last, the findings presented here suggest that the IL-i™, which was developed for the purpose of assessing inspiring leadership, is a valid and reliable instrument capable of predicting leadership performance in the workplace. Moreover, its applicability in selection and development appears to be justified although its validation needs to be continued on larger and more diverse population samples.

PART THREE: Results of the Qualitative Research (Inspiring Leadership Interviews)

What were the results from interviewing 100 inspiring female and male leaders?

Inspiration often comes from storytelling, particularly when there is resonance between the speaker's experiences and our own. With such an emotive and often personal topic of women in leadership, I was keen to gather stories from female leaders around the world. I wanted women who had achieved success, at times in the face of adversity. Through capturing stories, I could understand the essence of what made these women so successful. It was important in my research that the women selected were actually representative of every-day women. They needed to be women we could relate to more easily, rather than those who are far too removed from our own lives. The women selected were from a range of sectors, at different career and life stages, and represented a variety of cultures.

I also fundamentally believe there is a difference between *powerful* leaders and *inspiring* leaders; both attributes don't necessarily exist together in the same person. We have many powerful leaders around the world, however we know with recent global events in almost every sector that there is most certainly a dearth of inspiration! My intention therefore was to explore what makes a leader truly inspirational.

The leaders identified are successful in their own right, and have also been consistently described by others as 'inspirational leaders'. They positively affect the lives of others. I included male leaders in the interview process to gather alternative views. This is an essential perspective that is far too often ignored.

The interviews were *loosely structured* around the Inspiring Leadership model, so as not to detract from the quality of the personal story or influence the content. They included the following questions:

1. What was their personal leadership journey in both good and tough times?
2. What were their strengths and key lessons?

3. Who and what inspired them as leaders?
4. What are their views on the 'women in leadership' agenda?
5. What words of wisdom would they give to others?

These interviews represent all the qualitative results of our research to support the quantitative results from administering the IL-i™. I describe some of the key emerging themes below, however, you will find many more insights and stories throughout the book.

1. Social Background and Cultural Context

All of the women came from a variety of social backgrounds and cultures. Social status, education, financial resources and family structures varied. Therefore, these demographic parameters were not the key drivers and criteria for general success.

The consistently important theme was that the positively reinforced values from their early upbringing helped to shape their attitudes and beliefs. This included working hard and gaining financial independence. There were noticeable different cultural influences, such as the US, Australia, Canada and Nordic countries, which seemed to produce more self-assured and driven female leaders. For example, women in the US are twice as likely to be entrepreneurially active than in the UK. Asian families for example, place a stronger emphasis on education and pursuing professional excellence.

 **Susan Hooper,** a very successful CEO in the tourism industry described how, in her early career, she was a Product Manager in Carolina, when a position came up in Frankfurt. She shared, *"Although they wanted somebody fluent in German, and I wasn't, I knew I would manage. I got the role and, determined to learn, I studied using television and a dictionary to help me in the first couple of months! I believe that my American past has made me more confident."*

In particular, early messages reinforced their self-belief that there is nothing that they could not achieve if they set their mind to it. Family and social values play a vital role in attitudes to future work and also one's own view of self.

Penny Biggs shared, *"Sometimes it can feel hard to get through, but we can do more to help ourselves. In particular, we must connect ourselves more with the positives. My mother called this the power of positive thinking. My father, who was in the army, also said to me to work as hard as I could and to always deliver, never committing to anything that you can't follow through on. My parents taught me some really great behaviours that inform my leadership today. "*

Interestingly, in a growing narcissistic culture in many societies, the role models we endorse can gain instant notoriety for their looks, behaviours, outbursts and their arrogance. This is negatively affecting our future generations and whom they see as their role models. Furthermore, we find cause to critique and judge others in efforts to sensationalise or undermine. This distortion undermines our core value systems and skews what is deemed important.

I believe as a society we must take more responsibility for re-evaluating and intervening the messages that we communicate via various media. Finding inspiring female leadership role models in business is also a challenge, particularly when identifying women whose stories and styles resonate with our own personal aspirations.

Lynne Graham shares, *"I do believe that we have very few female role models in leadership positions. They're more the back room, support and analysts. All of my role models were male. I found my own way through. Having attended leadership development programmes, I've become aware of what I need to: 'Stop, Start and Continue'. I have found a way that suits my personality, which blends femininity with the toughness of the role that I do. "*

Gender parity and women's economic empowerment is recognised as a critical issue for the future of business and the economy. However, in a global context we still see some cultural challenges affecting women's status. Where traditions made it more difficult for women to find independent success, many carefully and respectfully challenged the status quo. They have become role models for what could be possible.

Whilst social status and education may not have been such an inhibitor in the past, with economic downturn we see short-term decisions to managing and growing talent. Youth unemployment also poses a significant issue; young people are three and a half times more likely than adults to be unemployed, as they are ill-equipped to exploit opportunities.

2. *Work-Life Balance*

In an on-going Project 28-40 by Opportunity Now, the latest results indicate that 81% of women aged between the age of 21 and 40 believe that having children will harm their career. The resulting impact is affecting the decisions both women and men are making between career and home life, or even whether they have a family or career at all.

Through my own research, I have found a variety of approaches to tackling work and life choices. Some people have opted for both, successfully negotiating a healthy balance between home and work where neither is compromised. Some leaders, particularly those who are ex-pats or working in highly mobile roles, have made the choice not to have a family at all. Then there are leaders who hold themselves back, tapping the 'brake pedal of their careers' to allow for having a family.

At times, past choices have been made based on a series of unchallenged assumptions. The resulting question is generally, "*What if...?*"

For example:

"What if I asked my manager for what I really need?"

"What if I asked for more support from my social network?"

"What if I had focused less on my career and more on my family?"

This is *not* about feelings of guilt and regret; our choices are based on the facts available to us at any given time. It does however highlight what we can learn from our choices and experiences and break down limiting assumptions (lived as true) in order to achieve what is possible.

Cilla Snowball is Group Chairman and Group CEO of AMVBBDO. I was inspired by Cilla's laser-like focus and dedication to balancing everything that is most important to her in work, in her relationships and in the community. She exudes a highly contagious passion and energy, centred around a real clarity of purpose.

Cilla was awarded the CBE in the 2009 New Year Honours list for services to the advertising industry. She is one of the BBC *Woman's Hour* '100 most powerful women in the UK' and an *Advertising Age* 'Woman to Watch'. Most importantly, she is Fred, Albert and Rosie's mum.

Cilla shared, *"I'm proud of my three - they are beautiful, funny and nice kids. Fred is a trainee solicitor, Albert is doing his PhD in Neuroscience and Rosie is at Oxford University reading French and Spanish. I am the youngest of three and my father was a clergyman. When I was at university I read French and studied at Birmingham. My first job was as a trainee in an advertising agency and I moved after two years, as I was looking for more responsibility and variety. I worked in the next agency for nine years, during which time I was married and had the two boys. I was commuting and juggling being a mother and a full time job. Then in 1992 I joined AMVBBDO as their first new business director. Rosie came along a year later.*

"I feel strongly that women have got to help each other. We talk ourselves into our own under-confident behaviours. We need to start by believing in ourselves and championing and mentoring other women.

"It is a huge privilege to be AMV's Group Chairman and Group CEO. I enjoy building big, productive relationships with clients to develop the ideas that will help grow their businesses.

"Luckily I have a lot of energy and pack a lot into home life, as well as at work .

"Bounce-back is important; when you take a knock it is important to put it into context, learn, plan and quickly move on.

"Work with people and organisations that you get energy from and make you feel good. You will get results with people who inspire and understand you.

"I have a full, busy and demanding work life. I work with amazing clients and a wide variety of talented people. We have strong people values and a team ethic based around delivering effective creative ideas for our clients that work in the marketplace. In an advertising industry where just 21% of advertising agencies are run by women, our culture embraces talented women at all levels of the agency: ability is what matters, not gender. Gender is no barrier.

"My philosophy is that you should be happy and learning in your job, whatever you do. That's definitely why, 22 years into working at AMVBBDO, I still love what I do and the challenges and variety it presents.

"I have always liked Madeleine Albright's assertion that 'There's a special place in hell for women who don't help other women'. I have set up an alumni mentoring programme at Birmingham University to help final year students with job selection and employment. I do two to three school visits and a year and speech days. I believe passionately in helping to inspire the next generation. Advertising is a wonderful career.

"We need to work together to provide moral support and provide equal opportunities. I don't believe we should be reluctant role models. We need as many women as possible telling their stories, inspiring others, showing it is possible to combine work and family, progress up the ranks and have fun, rewarding careers. You are never too young to be a role model, nor too old to need one! Lots of great women have inspired and helped me, so it's important to give back and recognise our ability to help others and make a difference.

"My advice to other women leaders is to build your knowledge and confidence, surround yourself with the best people and then support them to develop and do their best work.   There is great value in having a female perspective. We need to be confident about what we bring as women."

In my research, I also found that both men and women do feel the challenge of successfully managing the balance between home and work. For women, this is particularly evident at mid-career levels where financial means are often more limited and can restrict the type of support that can be put in place. To protect their career and income stream, a number of women have made the choice to return to work within weeks of having children, taking the minimum amount of time required. In Cilla's story, it is clear that our own and others' successes is underpinned by the strength our support networks, the talent in our teams and our philosophy of paying it forward.

With all of the investment for creating greater gender parity to date, we are not seeing the anticipated benefits. Shola Awolesi believes, *"There is so much that we can do around women and the agenda. There are pockets that are very male dominated. There is an opportunity to be more creative. There are amazing female leaders and we need to build, buy and leverage talent more than we do now. We also need to get more creative about flexibility and ways of working. This is not about handing it out on a plate. Women can speak up more and say, 'This is what we require'. It's a two-way deal."*

The digital age is still not fully leveraged, despite the fact that it has significant commercial and business benefits. These include reduced overheads, reduced absenteeism, increased wellbeing and morale, improved retention, as well as strengthening the overall Employee Value Proposition (EVP). This is a leadership issue, and not a technology issue. Highly controlling managers and an unaccommodating culture of presenteeism prevails. Being highly visible and working long hours continues as the unwritten rule.

Rebecca James shared, *"It's really challenging for jobs that do not allow sufficient flexibility, such as part-time working, alternative working patterns. Careers don't account for progression and flexible arrangements. It is generally an either/or."*

Women who have managed to negotiate flexible arrangements are often at more senior career levels. There, they have the benefit of flexible arrangements, which have formed part of contractual negotiations and informal arrangements. Alternatively, it is also prevalent where they are working in more open-minded cultures rather than traditional organisations.

When one inspiring leader was working on the women's network for a consultancy, she found a recurring issue was work-life balance, especially in regards to women. She shared, *"As a consultant you work very long hours, with lots of travel. As a result, when women (and some men) got to the point where they thought that starting a family was something they would like to do in the near future, then they felt the need to review other career options.*

"Another issue that emerged was women's response to the amount of feedback within a consultancy firm. On each project we get five or six aspects of feedback, but there's something about that approach that can be a bit alienating. Where you have worked hard on a job and things have gone well, getting a detailed list of failings with limited focus on what was done well can be disheartening. It's important to think about how feedback is structured in a motivating way for different individuals.

"This brought up ideas about what could be done to make it easier for women with children. However, dilemmas arose – for example, sending all the men on the projects in more remote locations when they also may have a family at home, which would not be fair. So, overall, there was a good acknowledgement on some of the challenges. There were changes made to the interview process and there was acknowledgement of the need to adapt parts of the feedback process. Unfortunately, I think the whole issue of part-time work and working when you have a young family has proved much harder to resolve. Even now in the big consultancy companies, there aren't many women Partners and one reason for this is the issue of the imbalance between work life and family life."

I have found inspiring male and female leaders have found the clarity of focus on what is most important, both at home and in the careers. They create boundaries to protect both. They work together with their partners and their children to share the responsibilities. They don't feel that they *have* it all, nor do they feel that they *need* it all. They have clarity about what brings them meaning and how they live their life on purpose. They are fiercely protective of the boundaries they create.

Let's be clear, for many leaders who've established clarity of focus and boundaries, this has often been achieved through trial and error. There has been a realisation, through pure exhaustion, that something needs to change. Often, in the literature and media that gives the illusion of the 'perfect world', the reality of the majority of people's experiences is less visible. As the saying goes, 'behind every successful man, there is a great woman'. In my interviews, the same is said for successful women. Furthermore, where both are successful in their careers, there is a great 'nanny' helping in the wings!

Some leaders have described darker moments where they have felt resentment, fears, doubt and even considerable unhappiness. Some even describe how being at work has been easier at times than being at home. Yet, those are often taboo conversations that are off-limits, with a sense of deep shame that these feelings even exist. I remember my friend and I having cocktails one evening. Both of my children are fully grown as I'd had them young. She had just started a family and confided how tough she was finding it all; she was exhausted. When I shared some of my own darker or calamity moments, she visibly relaxed; she was not alone in these feelings and felt relieved. 'Super heroines' do not exist, a crucial issue that we must acknowledge more for both men and women.

One inspiring leader shared in confidence, *"I needed to be physically in the London office and my partner was based in Liverpool as her business was there. The trade-off was being away from home. However, we wanted to have a child. This forced the issue of me 'coming out' and being gay. I had three weeks off when our son arrived. The reaction and support in the business was very positive. I found it very tough and I'd started to get a bit down. I'd put on some weight and started to feel a bit resentful. The first thing for me was to revive my exercise routine and change my eating habits. I got myself back into shape. It also helped me to start thinking a lot more clearly. For the first time I put myself first and stopped asking for permission. At last I started to have authentic conversations and taking back control. I found that resetting the boundaries was crucial. I also believe that you must create the time to think."*

Inspiring leaders experienced tough times and negative emotions; by acknowledging them they have then been able to take positive action and create coping mechanisms.

Carol Nicholls, a head teacher at an all-girls school, described her observations, *"When a woman goes off on maternity leave only to go back to work a couple of months later, that is tough. There is no black and white rule and individuals must decide what is right for them."*

The decisions we make are deeply personal and yet, some leaders continue to feel judged about these choices.

It is also disappointing when we continue to hear only a woman's perspective. There are a huge number of men that are supporting women with their careers and home. However, in our efforts to promote the cause of women, the men's contribution is being under-valued and unrecognised. This reinforces an unhealthy divisiveness of 'them' versus 'us'. These issues of balance, certainly in the developed economies, are not only for women to solve. They have become part of a family discussion, where diaries are negotiated and responsibilities are shared. Of course, many women express feelings of additional responsibility towards caring for the family, and equally men feel additional responsibility for providing financial stability and security. We know that these perceptions are evolving and maturing, as our roles are changing in society.

Lynne Graham shared, *"I feel uncomfortable about the gender thing, I don't quite get it. My father encouraged me to strive to achieve and my husband and I have always shared responsibilities for bringing up our children and for the household so I have not experienced gender stereotyping either personally or in the workplace."*

I suppose the provocative challenge is to be very considered when selecting a future spouse! However, with each generation, this is becoming more of the norm, than the unusual. There is not a single male leader that I've interviewed that has not described the importance of carving time with their families as being of utmost importance.

Mark Edwards shared, *"I have a wife and two children, so work-life balance is really important to me. I want to get home and see my family. Management by presenteeism is not reflective of expectations today."* Often, when I am coaching leaders, creating a healthy work-life balance and being successful in both career and with family is a core objective, particularly in today's manic and demanding society.

A number of the women do feel a strong commitment to their home lives. For example one female leader shared with me, *"Family and relationships are so important to me. They have stopped me from pushing too much in my career. I am always thinking about how I balance the choices that I make. I find that men in particular want more time with their families too."* The challenge for organisations is to make the work environment attractive enough for women to want to return to work, or to compete for the senior level positions.

Another leader in the professional services sector described how both she and her husband had highflying jobs. When she returned to work after maternity leave, they arranged for a nanny to look after the child, whilst they were at work. She found that in order to compete with her colleagues, she needed to work longer hours. She described how they had even considered employing a second nanny, so that they could have 24-hour childcare. They made a joint decision against this solution. So instead she took on a less demanding role, within the support functions. She was envious as she watched her peers successfully navigate through the organisation and gain promotion to more senior positions. Her colleagues are now making choices about early retirement. However, she feels this is not an option for her. She wonders whether she made the right choices early on in her career.

Leaders realise that they can no longer do it all. As a result, they outsource the things that are less important, which enables them to give their full energy to that which is most important; their relationships and their career. In other words, they get help in a variety of areas including: cleaning, childcare and grocery shopping. As they are time-poor and cash-rich, they focus on what matters. Many have helped their organisations to devise solutions on flexibility that meet their own personal needs, to great success.

Anna Mallett believes that having the right support has been fundamental to her success, *"For others like me with a young family, it's really important to make sure you have a good support network. This then means that you don't under-deliver in your job. I make sure I have 'bullet proof' childcare, a very supportive husband, who's happy for me to do whatever I want career wise and to help, and parents who will step in if there's an emergency. In terms of managing your career, when you have a young family, things will undoubtedly go wrong. However, if you set things up to work as well as they possibly can, then it means that you can put a lot of energy into your career*

when you're at work, rather than being distracted by things that are going on at home."

The times when this proves more challenging is when there is not a strong social support structure in place; managing the financial implications of childcare, or where they work in organisations that are less supportive and don't have more flexible arrangements.

Carol Nicholls shared, *"When I have 51% of my parents who are single, 50% of which are women then what does this say for the agenda? Their concerns are, 'I'm leaving my kids, I can't do this or that'. We need to structure ways of working in a more creative way. We can't have it all and do it successfully. I believe we first of all need to discuss what we have to do for the children, then discuss how we get there as a creative process."*

3. Career Navigation

There continues to be a limited focus on educating young people around the vast array of career opportunities. This is a concerning issue with an anticipated global skill shortages for 18 out of the 30 leading economies (Hays Global Skills Index). There is more that can be done by businesses, governments and education to unleash this potential, which can secure the future pipeline and prosperity.

With the inspiring women leaders, it was mostly the case that they did not feel held back in their careers and did not experience bias, or discrimination. They certainly didn't let it get in their way. What was clear is their clarity and focus on what they wanted to achieve, how they could get there in the most authentic way and being courageous in asking for what they want and need.

One leader described how, *"We have made it a topic of conversation, including flexible working, maternity leave and equal opportunity, but I still don't see a lot of women. So I question, what is it that we're not doing? I do believe that the women's network does not mean that you don't connect with men. I find that we don't talk enough about our families and challenges. We need to give ourselves permission to do so. This will help us to challenge some things. So the fact that I got speeding points, whilst rushing from the organisation to the nursery and had a meltdown at home - we shouldn't hide these things. Lots of women decide to have a better quality of life by making different choices, hours, life etc. That's okay. There are lots of different ways to have a career."*

Approaches to career navigation differed between the leaders. These ranged from structured plans and focus through to a more fluid and opportunist approach to career progression. There's no one single way, but rather a multitude of approaches. What is clear is that women benefited greatly from making their career aspirations known. They were also astute at spotting potential opportunities and proactively pursuing them. Their career steps were mostly based on stretching roles and significant steps that contribute to greater opportunities in the longer term. It is not about playing small or safe. They actively took risks. This fundamentally shifts when children arrive on the scene and security and safety start to play a major factor. This is when careers start to plateau. This isn't exhibited so strongly when the support system is strong for example, they have greater financial security, or a spouse who is the main carer of the home and children.

We are seeing increased participation of women in work and significant evolution in independent wealth in developed economies. There were more than 126 million women starting or running new businesses in 67 economies in 2012 (Global Report on Women and Entrepreneurship, GEM 2012). The growth of female entrepreneurs and self-employed has been staggering, which plays a major part in the contribution to Gross Added Value for any given economy.

However, according to a report by RBS Group 2013, 'Women in Enterprise: A Different Perspective', the majority of start-ups are by men, who are more likely to be entrepreneurial active. With a high rate of business deaths, we find a high churn rate (start-ups and closures) for women. Women are less likely to attribute closure to 'business failure' and more likely to cite 'personal reasons'. RBS Group has been taking proactive action to tackle this issue and encourage more women entrepreneurs, including addressing preferred supplier lists (see RBS Case Study at the end of this chapter).

As a woman running my own business, it is fascinating to observe supplier and corporate behaviours. For example, in a recent tendering process that saw two suppliers in the final stage of selection, the final decision came down to who could deliver the service at the lowest possible cost. I know the CEOs of both suppliers and their value systems. One supplier has a poor reputation in the market and 'wins business' no matter what the cost. The other supplier has a strong reputation in the market for fairness and quality, underpinned by strong values. Whilst able to compete in a fair way based on market-rates, the second CEO would not compromise the service and quality delivered.

With such a narrow process for selecting and encouraging new suppliers, I wonder how corporates are taking responsibility for ethical and fair decisions. This is not a unique situation. How can we honestly say that we are encouraging entrepreneurialism and new business growth, when it always comes back to the bottom line? In a cutthroat world, is the answer to 'surrender our souls', or do we diligently stick to our core values for running healthy businesses and relationships?

In today's global context for leadership, there are certain skills and experiences that become important the more senior you are in organisations. This includes international exposure. An inspiring leader shared in confidence, *"I became pregnant when I was working in China. There was no policy there for what to do with ex-Pats and their spouses. I could have stayed, as it was quite lucrative to be there. However, I decided I wanted to go back home to have the experience. I returned at 36 weeks pregnant and worked up to the latest possible point. I struggled going back to work. Interestingly, my fastest career progression was at the times when I was having children. I got promotions on both occasions that I was on maternity leave. I always felt 'I've got my default option to stay at home with the kids and you (the organisation) have got to compete with that'. The work and my role had to be satisfying, as I was very conscious of the sacrifice I was making. This made for much better negotiations on both sides."*

There are a number of women who have applied for and been successful in securing new opportunities, when pregnant or on maternity leave. So it is clear that many organisations are recognising the importance of talent retention. One challenge that has emerged in my interviews is around ex-pats and those serving abroad in the armed forces, which often start to create limitations in terms of opportunities for their dependents in remote locations.

This is a particular organisational paradox, as key global leadership roles look for international experiences, often in emerging and growth markets.

One of the most influential factors in career navigation is having a form of down-time. This helps the oscillation between (1) performance and drive and (2) recovery and reflection.

Pavita Cooper describes this as her third place to go to. *"When times have been really tough, I need to emotionally and physically recover. Not enough executives create this. Personally, this is my religion. It helps me to reflect and learn; not just a post-mortem on what's going badly, but an appreciation of everything that is going well. I work really hard to stay connected with my network and reach out to give, or ask for support and guidance."*

Sandi Rhys Jones was appointed OBE in 1998 for her work promoting women in construction, became a Fellow of the Chartered Institute of Building in 2002 and was awarded an honorary doctorate by Sheffield Hallam University in 2005. In 2012 she was appointed a Companion of the Chartered Management Institute and listed in 'Who's Who'. During our interview Sandi shared the following insights about women in the property and construction business:

Sandi shared, *"The representation of women varies widely across the various disciplines. For example there are many women in town planning and the number of women engineers is increasing, albeit slowly. There is a large number of women studying architecture (30%), but this plummets once people move into practice. It is male dominated world in construction and personally I believe that blaming the low representation on the industry being different to all others is a big cop-out! We only need to see what has happened in medicine, law and accountancy to know that change is possible. What's more, women are badly needed – there simply aren't enough of the right people in the sector, particularly in engineering.*

"I believe there are both cultural and practical issues affecting the low numbers of women. For example, the size and structures of contracting companies or surveying firms are often larger and broader than architectural practices, giving more opportunities to take on women. There are also recent findings indicating unconscious bias in assessment centres for new engineering graduates, resulting in fewer women getting first jobs than men, despite achieving better grades.

"On the positive side there are some fantastic fearless women who are building great careers in construction, engineering and property. During the past ten years several have become the first female Presidents of their professional institutions. What is fascinating that nearly every one of these women run their own business – which tells us something about the corporate environment!

"Indeed many women in construction and property leave in midcareer and often we only find out when it is too late to do anything about it. This presents a big challenge, because there is little point recruiting more young women when we don't know the causes of the leaky pipeline.

"We need to increase the visibility of women who are building careers in construction and work with employers to recognise and develop this talent. We need to create more opportunities for shadowing and work placements, encourage multi-disciplinary mentoring and training and be creative in dealing with the 24/7 work culture. It is important to involve people from different industries to discuss issues, particularly clients - not only to share knowledge and experience, but also to build better relationships, understanding and performance. Many issues are the same, even though the context is different."

We consistently hear that females are following typical career routes and, in particular, failing to pursue STEM (Science, Technology, Engineering, Mathematics) pathways. Numerous studies have tried to explain why we have a dearth of female talent in these fields, some suggesting that women lack ambition or ability. The latest research in neuroscience first of all refutes these theories and certainly when we look at similar academic achievements in Asia, where education is understood to be the root to success and social mobility. There are clearly opportunities to make a difference by defusing misinformation, stereotyping and societal views on the roles of men and women. We can start to alter perceptions through addressing our education in STEM subjects and confidence building to consistently increase achievement and participation levels. We can also create greater visibility of the breadth of career opportunities and visible role models and organisations taking actions to invite and welcome women into STEM careers.

Regarding the Women's agenda, inspiring women leaders believe there are several things that we must have. One is to have men and women in the workforce together, rather than just a single gender. One particular gender, or even group, means we can get blindsided and fail to capitalise on the value of diversity. For example, we know that women are responsible for circa 80% of purchasing choices, controlling more than $20 trillion of world-wide spend whether it is on vacations, homes, healthcare, or consumer brands. The majority of new products fail, as they don't connect with the market's needs. So, this is really not even about feminism any more; this is about harnessing the power that already exists in women. With global changes virtually affecting every industry, balanced workforces are not just nice to have, they are a necessity.

What is great to see is the level of momentum that already exists, with issues of diversity very visible with a huge level of commitment at every level.

4. Culture of Fairness with Managing Talent

Issues of gender parity are a global problem. Organisations and leaders alike are investing huge energy in achieving gender parity. Corporate executives have sunk significant resources and money into tackling the issues and presented us with creative solutions as a result. However, it is clear to see that the value has yet to be realised. The process of coming to see oneself and to be seen by others as a leader is a fragile and complex one.

David Cameron, the British prime minister, stated that, *"The case is overwhelming that companies and countries run better if you have men and women working together at the top."* Global statistics show, however, that there are still not enough women on executive boards and in key leadership decision-making positions. There is a vast amount of research available, which demonstrates that there are valid reasons for achieving greater gender parity, including significant bottom-line benefits. Diverse teams are also essential to providing a breadth of thinking, by breaking down the exclusive in-groups for greater corporate governance and management of risks. Ironically this remains an issue in the male-dominated senior levels of British government.

Mark Edwards is General Counsel for Global Retail and Business Banking. As a talented, inspiring leader, he is a powerful advocate for driving greater diversity and cultural change. He shared in his interview with me: *"This is achieving diversity through creating an inclusive culture. It has to be part of the DNA and philosophy of the organisation. It must not be through symbolism, tokenism or paying lip service to an agenda. Leadership comes in many forms and is not a narrow or singular view. I believe it is about authenticity and capability, which means not losing who we are and changing ourselves to the extreme. Therefore, cultural change can only truly start when the tone that is set from the top.*

"Our messages must be crisp, clear and driven. This starts with our very foundations and permeates through; there is absolutely no short-cut. We have been good at talking about these things in the past, but we have lacked full execution. As leaders we are trusted to do the right thing and so we must be in it for the long haul as we are dealing with deep-rooted issues. It means we need to think and behave differently. People feel very let down when they don't see this."

This is a powerful acknowledgement of the commitment that is required of organisational leaders to make positive change. Leaders recognise there is no quick fix. We must tackle the issues that sit within the very heart of our businesses if we are to address this issue in a *sustainable* way.

A number of women spoke of the cultural challenge, and one inspiring leader described how, *"Leaders still struggle with defaulting to promoting people in their own likeness. Bias of all kinds is still rife, holding us back from creating diversity through promoting more inclusive cultures. Then women try to play the rules using the men's playbook and so they become bad leaders. Not because of the mirroring, but because of the inauthenticity. If we understand that this is not the way that we are wired to be, and we actually bring our own strengths and something magical to the mix, then we can make the fundamental shifts to being confident in and authentic for ourselves."*

In the chapters on Neuroscience and EQ, we explore in more detail why unconscious bias occurs. The formation of in-groups and exclusion is a key blocker, which holds us back from the creation of truly inclusive environments. The language in much of the literature on this agenda, describes the tactics women can use to help their careers. For example, we say that 'feminine' attributes are essential to business, but then we ask women to adopt 'masculine' attributes to be successful. Whilst there is clearly some relevance to the literature, it provides us with a narrow view of the real challenges, which are cultural and not just individual or gender specific.

Pavita Cooper's experience of managing talent is not so unusual, *"Running talent management at times was in the presence of toxic leadership. It shocks me how ugly things can get at the top."*

There is also significant issue with the number of really challenging jobs that are decided off-screen, even though it's claimed to be 'open and transparent based on merit'. In practice, it is widely believed that the real jobs are already spoken for and in some cases not even advertised. Leaders describe how it can get highly political at the top. For some of the big jobs, you really need to have very strong relationships. This also means having sponsors who are willing to advocate for diverse leadership and individuals.

Leadership gets 'lonely' at the top and so we tend to surround ourselves with our most trusted confidantes and advisers. In other words, we like to appoint people from our in-group. We can have a diversity strategy and the best will in the world to create diverse lists of candidates for promotion across the organisation, however, we must role model this within our teams too.

Unconscious bias include 'affinity bias' which is where we ignore the faults of people we like and hypocritically notice the errors of people from groups we unconsciously don't like, or don't have an affinity with. It also includes 'social comparison bias' which often manifests itself through talent assessment and recruitment processes; a game where we like to appoint from within our 'in-group'. Finally there is 'confirmatory bias' which is where we search for information and data to support our existing perceptions and decisions.

In Asia, the US and across Europe, companies mainly promote women through support roles such as HR and Communications. Research also shows that functional roles attract female leadership talent, and yet it is these roles that often become the target in tough times.

One inspiring leaders stated in her interview, *"Metrics are the focus and the current economic climate affects things like attrition and performance. This is a big issue as people stay for reasons of security and not because of passion. It is clouded by the current climate.*

"However, are women excelling to their true potential? Often the gender balance achieved in our succession plans are made up of women in functional roles, rather than operational roles. In a volatile economic climate, where we go through restructuring and downsizing, then these are often the roles that are eliminated. So we must get more women into the operating roles, in order to combat this. Otherwise it's a vicious circle and we will continue to see the lack of movement. We need more female engineers, technical people, P&L (profit and loss) leaders. We need to continue to build plans to bring women into our operating roles."

Whilst we change the language in job advertising and create some great role models, we continue to use traditional models of leadership to assess and make judgements about the pipeline of talent. In increasingly horizontal organizational structures, it becomes more difficult to advance vertically. The question is, are women being fairly assessed and their talents utilised? Many inspiring leaders are proactively challenging recruiters and HR to produce more diverse 'talents slates' of potential candidates, and push back when this falls short.

Some HR teams have been struggling with this, due to the extra pressure it causes. However, there is a surplus of qualified and experienced female talent available and it is no longer acceptable to not have this reflected in attraction, development and retention strategies.

Some women cited that when they look up to the highest echelons of their organisation they do not find what they see to be appealing. This is a trend for certain sectors to still fail to address the traditional working cultures and behaviours. These tend to prohibit women from succeeding, or women make a conscious choice to opt out, because they are not prepared to make the unhealthy sacrifices that are involved. They resent giving up on their own values to feed 'the beast of the machine'. There is, however, a small body of determined women that push on to succeed. We know there are capable and talented women out there, and so certainly this would suggest the issue is less about ability and more about motivation. This must not be confused with limited self-belief, which has become much of today's mantra for why women aren't successful.

When women are making choices between home and work, organisations must be able to find ways to develop a more attractive proposition. The critical point where women become eligible for key promotions is at the same time that they are also evaluating life's purpose and meaning. With the bitter after-taste of capitalism gone wrong, the lure of 'more' and working our way to the top may pose a challenge if we don't start to address some of the fundamental issues in our leadership and structures.

Women were vehement in their views on quotas. Most of them were against the very prospect. Carol Nicholls states, *"I do believe we must base leadership on merit, rather than gender. The law has become over complicated. Sometimes both men and women have been promoted to a point of incompetence. Everyone is quickly judged and if we force it, then we will get the 'I told you so' and make it even more difficult to achieve success."*

It is believed that positive discrimination, on the main, is unfair and actually undermines the agenda. Responding to quotas does not guarantee progress and women are keen to be brought to the table for the right reasons. It's not believed that there is a talent gap, although we often see the same names re-appearing. It is felt that targets do give organisations something to aim for, and metrics provide us with insights to help us address issues.

Lady Susan Rice shared her views, *"You can have regulations in place, or quotas, which I don't necessarily think is a good thing. However, it still doesn't solve the problem unless women desire to go through that open door. There is a disconnect between the perceptions and reality; people perceive they've got to be a certain kind of person to get to certain organisational levels.*

"However, in my experience it's all there for the taking, each in their own way. We do need to respect the choices that individuals make. Being female is one of the things that I can bring to any role that I do. I understand that even more now than ever before.

"I also believe in meritocracy. I would not want to be on the board where people were tacitly thinking – as they would not say this overtly - that they had made their quotas! If that was how I was perceived first and foremost, that's not what I desire.

"My role is to bring my experience and knowledge and contribute to a particular organisation. It takes a little while to find your voice. It would be much harder to find my voice if I was there as a woman first; how do I legitimise my expertise?

"My expertise isn't being a woman; it's a characteristic that can add to everything else.

"Most of the executive women I have spoken with would say the same thing. Not all, I've heard a couple say it's just a transitory thing. I think that quotas give you a false construct.

"Having a difference in views is extremely important. I have found that I offer different views at the board table, often being the only woman, and this empowers me to find my voice but if I was there because of being in woman then it would not be the same."

Of course, there were a number of women disappointed by the lack of progress and so are more open-minded about the possibility of quotas to force an issue that does not seem to be resolving itself.

What we know about inspiring leadership, inspiring leaders and inspiring women leaders

My qualitative research fully supports the quantitative findings. Both research methodologies indicate that Inspiring Male and Female Leaders demonstrate the following characteristics:

- *High performers and very successful*
- *Unique, authentic and stand out from others*
- *Choose to lead and do so with focus, determination and passion*
- *Others look to them, listen to them and admire them*
- *An unimposing, modest and quiet presence*
- *Make informed, well-thought-out and wise decisions that add value*
- *Humble and open to learn from their mistakes, past experience and the wisdom of others*
- *Flexible, adaptive and able to recover from adversity as well as to learn from setbacks*
- *Generate energy, motivate themselves and feel fully engaged in what they do*
- *Exhibit moral courage and live by high ethical standards at work and in their private lives*
- *Seek meaning in their work and are focused on leaving a positive and sustainable legacy*

Inspiring Leadership Research - What's next?

The next step in my study of Inspiring Leadership will be to continue validating the IL-i™ on larger and more diverse populations, which is essential in test construction (Anastasi & Urbina, 1997). A multi-rater version of this instrument has already been developed, the IL-i360™, which will also need to be normed and validated across cultures.

My team is also considering the development of a semi-structured interview based on our concept of Inspiring Leadership. We will also need to build a 'library' of occupational profiles to be used in selection and development.

Last, these instruments will need to be translated from English to a number of different languages and standardised for use in other countries to facilitate and expand their applicability.

In addition to administering our psychometric instruments to an ever-increasing number of individuals worldwide, I intend to continue interviewing inspiring leaders, both men and women, to gain a greater understanding of our approach to leadership in a wide variety of industries, occupations and professions.

My team will develop programmes for group training and individual coaching designed to enhance leadership performance. We are also considering the development of IBT (Internet-based training) programmes for online and remote e-learning to expand our reach to more remote global sites. After building these programmes, their efficacy will need to be examined, and this input will be vital for improving the programmes themselves.

Last, we will need to publish and present our findings in professional forums to reach larger audiences around the world.

Case Study
RBS Women's Markets (Gender Inclusion) Approach

Andi Keeling shared some of the inspiring work that RBS is driving forward to make a genuine difference with the gender agenda and increasing women's economic empowerment.

RBS and their NatWest network are passionate about creating greater economic empowerment, in order to support women in business. Due to the growing success of their various initiatives, they were all pulled together under one umbrella called 'Women's Markets'. A clear strategy was developed and a senior steering group was put in place to make decisions and drive progress.

Women in Business (WiB)

Anne McPherson, MD for Diversity in Business, leads the approach to supporting Women in Business in RBS and NatWest. Women own only 19% of Small and Medium Enterprises (SME). However, women represent 52%

of the population, so there are sound commercial reasons in encouraging more female entrepreneurs. Since 2007, the UK Corporate team, led by CEO Chris Sullivan, have been developing a unique proposition, through creating innovative initiatives to support women-owned SMEs. They have over 200 Women in Business (WiB) specialists across the country, all accredited through Chartered Banker to support this growing market.

The role of the WiB specialists is to be the centre of excellence for women's enterprise, both internally within their team and externally with their professional networks. RBS Group equips them with skills and expertise, supporting them in setting up and growing their businesses including providing access to finance and giving them a wide range of personal development opportunities. Their Inspiring Women in Enterprise programme pledges that by the end of 2015 RBS will inspire and enable an additional 20,000 women to explore and unlock their enterprise potential.

Nicola Short is a very active accredited Women in Business Specialist. Nicola says, "*For a lot of the female business owners I've looked after, their highlights include taking their first proper wage, moving from a home business into commercial premises, or being recognised for their achievements in their sector. It's those things that I love to hear about the most because it means we are helping them to achieve their individual ambitions.*"

Her customer, Annie Armitage, is a photographer who endorses this approach, "*To have Women in Business Specialist support from my relationship manager has taken away the stress of having to deal with the bank, which can be daunting. I have benefited from great customer service and also the business knowledge that Nicola has given to help my business grow.*"

Anne also shared, "*We are not ignoring our own business either and are keen to support more of our female employees to rise up their career ladder. To help achieve this, we have built a programme of support called Achieving Ambitions - this is aimed at our junior manager population. The programme includes mentoring, personal development discussions, CV writing and interview practice, presentation skills training, confidence building, peer-to-peer learning and regular access to senior role models in business. Through this programme, we have seen many more women progress and people are starting to consider opportunities that they would have previously ruled out as too much of a leap. In the first six months of the programme we saw 30% of participants achieve a promotion, so we are already making a difference."*

Led by Heather Melville and sponsored by Chris, a small group of RBS volunteers set up the first RBS internal women's employee network. Its purpose was to support the attraction, retention and development of women across RBS **Focused Women's Network (FWN)**. The success has led to other employee networks being created across the business. Members enjoy networking, development opportunities and support offered through FWN. The network is inclusive; men are currently the fastest growing population. It has grown to over 10,000 members across over 30 countries and FWN is a powerful and influential voice of change within the culture of RBS. Over the last two years alone, FWN have organised and delivered over 100 personal development events. They believe in giving back to the community and have raised over £250,000 for a variety of charities.

The initiatives have led to more women asking for stretch opportunities, more female promotions and better statistics for women at all levels.

RBS have also adapted their recruitment process, including changes to language used in role profiles and a healthier interview style to ensure we attract more women to apply. Our graduate intake is now almost 50/50 and our talent proposition for senior management has gone from a ratio of 92% / 8%, men / women to 62% / 38% within just three years.

Supplier Diversity

RBS has worked on understanding the diverse make up of their supply chain. They have set about making it easier for SMEs to do business with them as suppliers. This culminated in the RBS Supplier Diversity Code of Conduct being launched and endorsed by WEConnect International in the Houses of Parliament in May 2013. It is now being presented by the European Commission as the model for large corporate companies to work with.

RBS has carefully selected partners to leverage relationships and to maximise effectiveness through collaboration. They work closely with media and government to ensure awareness of actions and progress, including participating in the Government's 'Think, Act, Report' scheme.

As a result of their great progress on this agenda, RBS and its leaders have received significant recognition and awards, and has been featured in *The Times* Top 50 Best Employers where women want to work' every year since its inception seven years ago.

Elin Hurvenes,
Founder of the Professional Boards Forum

Following Norway's controversial proposal in 2002 forcing companies to increase the number of women on corporate boards from 6% to 40%, Norwegian chairmen and investors were despondent claiming, *'We don't know where to find qualified women'*.

The response by Norwegian entrepreneur, Elin Hurvenes, was to set up the Professional Boards Forum. In a series of pioneering events she brought leading chairmen and investors together with talented women ready and capable of taking on non-executive directorships. Elin has expanded and set up the Professional Boards Forum in the UK, the Netherlands and Switzerland with local partners.

"When the quota system was introduced I thought it was incredibly sad, but I didn't know it was going to become such an issue. There were a lot of negative comments that the quota was a ridiculous suggestion, that women were neither interested nor qualified. Chairmen and investors were saying, 'We don't know where to find qualified women'. Traditionally board members had been recruited from Chairmen's network of business associates and friends and clearly in these networks there were not enough women. I already knew several women who would be an asset to almost any board – they just needed to raise their profile and visibility with the people who influence board appointments. There was no natural arena where these two groups could connect and that's what I wanted to do with the Professional Boards Forum – bring these two groups together.

"Board roles are about experience and ability but also about trust and personal chemistry – this is something you build in a face to face meeting. The Forum events are highly structured and centres round what I have called a "Simulated Board Meeting". It is a bit like a Harvard Business School case study that we create especially for each event. It is designed to give the women a chance to shine and excel and affords the chairmen an instant insight into the skills, experience and potential these women would bring to a board.

"When I held the first event in 2004, I was very nervous. Would the Chairman and Investors turn up on the day? Would the concept work? Would the women impress? I needn't have worried. The atmosphere was fantastic and we made the national TV evening news where chairmen and women non-executive candidates were interviewed and profiled.

"I found it sad that a quota was needed to recognise Norwegian women's ability to serve on boards but I am glad it was done as the Norwegian quota legislation helped put the issue of women on boards on the global agenda.

"There is no shortage of qualified women – I can say that for sure because I meet incredible, successful and talented women on a weekly basis. Many of them are fantastic role models and help and encourage other women. I believe that is so important. Role models are only of real value when they make themselves accessible and share their experience and knowledge. We need successful women to share their experience with other women and help narrow what I call the 'confidence gap' - when women align their confidence levels with the quality of their CVs - the effect will be astronomic!"

Chapter 4
The Neuroscience Behind Inspiring Leadership

Contributing Author: Jonathan Bowman-Perks MBE

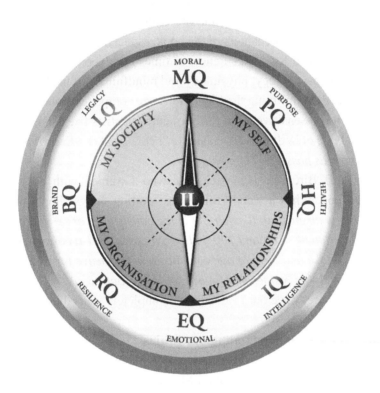

"Emerging findings in neuroscience research suggest why inspiring and supportive relationships are important - they help activate openness to new ideas and a more social orientation to others. Insights such as these may move the primacy of a leader's actions away from the 'results-orientation' toward a relationship orientation. Neuroscience tells us what we need to know to be good, even great leaders."

Dr. Richard Boyatzis
Professor of Organisational Behaviour

Why we should study neuroscience to become more inspiring leaders

The aim of this chapter is to take the highly complex subject of neuroscience and make it simple and clear enough for us to apply practically and pragmatically in the way we lead others every day.

We will firstly provide a quick guide to the brain and then reflect on what happens when it all goes wrong and our brains become ineffective.

As we'll see in later chapters of the book, especially those on HQ - Health and Wellbeing and RQ – Resilience, in times of adversity we find that the neuroscience, psychology, physiology and mindfulness of meditation are all closely linked. Simplifying the highly intricate components and functioning of our brain is a sensitive topic for our neuroscientists friends, however we take the advice of William of Ockham (c. 1287 – 1347): *"Everything should be as simple as possible, but no simpler."*

Dr. Geoff Bird, the Neuroscientist who I trained with as a Meyler Campbell coach, has a wonderful way of putting things simply and said, *"The brain is disgusting. It smells; it is the consistency of set yoghurt; very soft; 100 billion neurons and 100 trillion synapses, and it consumes 60% of our sugar intake and 30% of our calories. It is expensive for us to keep. So why is this 1.4kg vulnerable mass so important to us?"* Let's aim to understand more, since our leadership is completely shaped by it.

A quick guide to understanding our brains

A simplistic model to help us understand the functioning of different brain components is provided by Dr. Paul MacLean's triune brain model:

Example diagram to illustrate above model

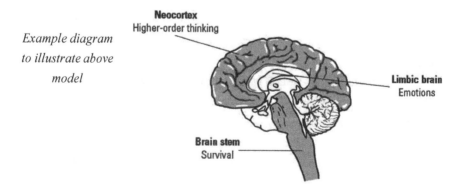

Neocortex
Higher-order thinking

Limbic brain
Emotions

Brain stem
Survival

1. **The Reptilian Brain.** This is seen as the earliest part of our brain to be developed in humans and is similar to the brain functions in a snake, or reptile. The focus is on the basic, instinctive, "autonomic" functions of: breathing, heart-regulation, food, sex and survival, rather than focusing on emotions, or relationships. Much of the functions within this part of our brain occur below the level of our conscious awareness.

2. **The Mammalian Brain.** The second developmental stage of human's brain is called the mammalian, limbic, or 'chimp' brain. It is here where we learned to form relationships and socialise in groups and teams and from where many of our emotions are generated. Other mammals, such as dogs and monkeys, have such a brain system, hence they can tell when we as humans are upset, angry, or feeling loving. This is the most authentic part of our brain; it is an expression of our raw, unfiltered emotions.

   As leaders motivating others to follow us, we need to be aware of the amygdala, our 'threat response centre' within the limbic system and how to manage it. In many ways we find it hard to *control* this part of our brain; rather we need to learn to *manage* it and find strategies to calm it and bring the best out of the poor responses we sometimes take within milliseconds.

3. **The Cognitive Brain**. The neo-cortex is the third part of our brain; this allows humans to think about thinking. It is within the cognitive brain that we have developed amazing skills such as language to make sense of and communicate about the emotional experiences we are having in the mammalian, or chimp brain. From a very early age we are told that it is not appropriate or acceptable to do things that our limbic brain would like us to do. Consequently in some ways the cognitive brain is the part that learns how to lie and deceive. Hence this part is aptly known as the human brain. Of especial interest is the prefrontal cortex part of our Neo-Cortex. This part is crucial to generating our finest thinking and problem solving in our working lives.

Of great importance are the neurons within our brains and the synaptic connections that are made between them. Synapses are the links between the neurons in our head. They make the key connections for us that keep us thinking, laughing, crying, shouting, and responding to our environment. The synapse is created by dumping electron chemicals into the gap between them to make a new link and create a thought. The strength of the connection requires repetition to increase the power of the connection. This is why we encourage the practice of new leadership behaviours to make it habitual. Harder personal and leadership problems take time because they require lots of neuron-to-neuron connections to get to a solution.

Our brains are highly plastic. They show how our life experiences have shaped us and this is focused into the wisdom we have accumulated. If you imagine the analogy of our brain being like the Cloud storage system, where we can save information to it (our experiences) and we retrieve data from it when prompted by external stimulus. The more experiences we have, the more robust and adaptable the data and concepts are within our own Cloud profile.

What happens when it all goes wrong?

In the 100 interviews conducted with inspiring women leaders, they all spoke of moments that were especially challenging. These were times when they were working with others who were intimidating and in very tough situations, which they called their 'crucible moments'. I would like you to recall a situation you have been in, in which there was great pressure of time and money. There may also have been concerns about failing and a power struggle between individuals seeking to protect their personal egos, reputation and pride. I give you the benefit of the doubt that normally you may be someone who remains calm under pressure. I expect that you also have a reasonable amount of empathy to connect with others, can build rapport and have a sharp mind to cut through the noise and make a clear decision.

However, on this occasion that we asked you recall, perhaps things did not go so smoothly and so you didn't think well, nor did not behave at your optimum performance. You probably found that your colleagues then became rivals and the debate turned fractious and personal. You may have discussed about whom and what was right, wrong, or you found yourself arguing over a point of principal. Within your brain, many untrue limiting assumptions (lived as true) would have been made by both you and others involved in that heated debate. Perceptions were becoming reality for both you and your opponents. A casual observer would have noticed that, as you got involved in a more heated discussion, you and they were then more interested in speaking, rather than listening.

We call this 'the dialogue of the deaf'. Your body language would have been most interesting to watch. The additional blood rushing to your brain would have flushed your face, your muscles would have tightened and your breathing would have become shorter and sharper. Under the table the agitated movement of your legs and feet would have been most telling. Even your hands may have been clenching and unclenching. Micro muscles in your face would have sent subliminal messages to others in the room, indicating your heightened level of arousal and stress. You may even have begun to sweat slightly more. Many signals would be emanating from you, you are always communicating whether you intend to or not: 'You cannot not communicate!'

There would have been some interesting physiological signs, if at the time you and the others, who may at this stage have become your opponents, were wired up electronically, or had your brains scanned by a neuroscientist on an fMRI scanner. Your hearts would have been beating faster, your breath shorter and faster and higher up in your rib cage. Muscles in your jaws, shoulders, back and hands would have been tightening.

So what was going on in your brain and physiology?

In simple terms what would have been happening in your brains may have been as follows. The amygdala is a vital component of your brain and acts as the guardhouse and your threat response centre. In his book first book on emotional intelligence, Daniel Goleman speaks of an 'amygdala hijack'. This is where as a result of such a stressful situation, as in the example we created, your limbic brain gets flooded with an excess of adrenaline and cortisol. In response to this threat, your initial reaction is: freeze, followed by flight, followed by fight, in that order. In this respect very little has changed from our ancestors, padding barefoot across the Kalahari Desert with spears and responding to a physical threat.

If you are in a very highly stressful meeting with someone, then you may freeze both physically and mentally for a fraction of a moment. However, following 21st century business etiquette, you feel that you are unable to either run away from the meeting room, or that it would be inappropriate to physically fight with your opponent. Sometimes, both have been known to happen; recent television coverage of Italian members of Parliament, as they threw punches at each other, still sticks in my mind. Your shoulders will hunch up in preparation for flight, or fight, with the impact that by the end of such a day you will have very tight shoulders, a stiff neck, headache and your stomach will have tightened. Your stomach is a key indicator, since your basic human instinct is sometimes, when suffering from extreme shock, for you to feel queasy, or be sick in order to empty the stomach in preparation for a quick getaway.

Your amygdala may have identified a perceived threat within 80 milliseconds (ms), but you only become consciously aware of that threat and your subsequent response is within about 250 ms. Such a response is below your conscious awareness. Within the limbic system the amygdala triggers the pituitary gland to convert glucose into energy and produce cortisol (the stress hormone) and adrenaline if you find yourself in a stressful situation. On the other hand, it will produce the 'vitality hormone' DHEA, if you are in a safe, emotionally positive and high performing situation.

In the stressful situation, where you may become overwhelmed with fear, or anger, then your amygdala and orbital frontal cortex will draw metabolic energy away from your prefrontal cortex (PFC) region. That PFC region is vital to help you think well and solve the very problems you are now facing. However, sadly your brain works against you in this situation. Without the cognitive brain working well (especially your crucial PFC), then you are left with the emotional, limbic brain in charge. That is the point where your impulsive, animal instincts take over.

The results are rarely ones you are proud about, when you honestly reflect later.

Indeed when you recall how badly you may have acted and the

accompanying humiliation and perceived slight, it actually causes you pain. If you are someone who pauses to reflect in life, rather than rushing ahead, without ever learning, then you can relive stressful moments and agonising failures again and again. Each time they cause you pain and anxiety. This is because physical pain and emotional pain are located in the same region of your brain. The difference is that physical pain generates endorphins, which act as pain suppressants. Emotional pain does not generate endorphins, so you unfortunately relive that pain all over again, at the same level of intensity as when you first had the stressful, or anxious emotional moment.

This is just one, isolated, stressful situation for you. However, imagine what would happen to you if you were living in a tense, intimidating, fear producing, highly competitive environment, continuously. It is important at this stage to point out that the triggers for stressful situations and threats to the amygdala vary between cultures and nations. So, for example, someone from Beijing in China will get far less stressed about another person pushing in front of them in a queue, than someone from Britain who will take serious offence. Your brain and associated endocrine system (made up of many parts including: adrenal gland, pituitary gland, thyroid gland) were initially designed when your ancestors lived in far more primitive situations, such as the Kalahari. Now you are spending hours in meeting rooms and on conference calls. This was not something the body was designed for. There is consequently a very unhealthy impact on you, your brain and your body, when you find yourself living and working in such toxic situations.

You will read more about this later in HQ health quotient and the RQ resilience quotient. In summary, your body reacts very badly to the accumulation of too much adrenaline and cortisol. Those two hormones are designed to help energise you to respond to the body's fight, or flight command. So the excess cortisol is often stored around your stomach, like an extra tyre, or less visibly around your vital organs. Your immune system is worn down by too much cortisol in situations of constant toxic environments at work. Then you, or others who are working alongside you in such situations, frequently become ill, at regular intervals, often at the start of your holidays, when you finally relax.

This viewpoint is a simplification. Remember everybody responds differently to specific stressful and intimidating environments. Different people have different levels of physiological resilience. Not everyone will be so badly affected. Indeed a few unusual people, who gravitate towards the very top of many organisations, have an under-functioning amygdala. Consequently they do not feel threat, or danger, as most other people normally do. Instead they thrive in toxic and highly dangerous environments and are often perceived as bullies. Yet on the brighter side, some might consider that they would make excellent Special Forces soldiers, since they can remain cool under fire and are supremely self-confident.

Those with under-functioning amygdala display similar characteristics to a group of people referred to as 'business psychopaths' in Bob Hare's excellent book *Snakes in Suits: When Psychopaths Come to Work.* I also touched on this earlier in 'expiring leadership'. These people form about 5% of the population and get into highly influential positions of leadership such as CEOs, politicians and key roles in the Emergency Services. While they can achieve results and hold positions of power, they are extremely dangerous colleagues, or opponents. They would definitely not be described as 'inspiring leaders' when benchmarked against the qualities we are describing in this book.

How to manage our own brains and emotions to inspire ourselves first

If you aspire to inspire, then you must first look after your own health and well-being. You should be able to handle stress, keep yourself fit, have a healthy diet, manage your breathing and develop moments of mindfulness. To be a high performing leader the key is sustaining your level of energy and how you're able to excite the circuits of your brain, rather than inhibit them, as we described earlier. Everything is a learned behaviour and your brain is shaped and indeed described as 'plastic' by the way you learn from the experiences that you have had. Daniel Goleman, in his latest book *Focus,* has written about the importance of having an inner sense of calm and mindfulness combined with an outer sense of focussed attention.

Choose with whom you spend most of your time. An old Chinese saying is very apt, 'you are the company you keep'. Live and work with people who give energy, happiness, fun, love and life to you. Then you will be a far more successful and happy person than many other people. Alternatively, if you surround yourself with negative, miserable, cynical, ungrateful, energy draining people, then it will have affect your health and well-being. It will ultimately undermine your leadership performance and enjoyment of both your work and life.

When you're in a challenging job, then, of course, you will be working hard. However, when the pressure increases, the answer is not to work ever harder and harder. That will certainly lead to eventual burnout and breakdown. Instead you need to work smarter, take a 'coach approach' to leadership and fairly delegate, empower and bring on those around you. Then together you can achieve extra-ordinary performance from what other people might mistake as just an ordinary team.

Our brain is an energy system. We need to manage it to focus on doing anything and everything that adds energy to our life. It is estimated that our body uses 95 Watts of energy and the brain uses 20 to 25 Watts of energy. So consider eating a healthy diet that feeds your brain and your body and do take regular exercise. This is something that, when combined with keeping good company, will generate crucial hormones like serotonin, oxytocin, endorphins and dopamine to give you that feel-good factor. The brain also needs time to recharge and refresh. Sufficient sleep, breaks from work and holidays of 1 - 3 weeks are not 'a nice to have'. They are essential if you are to perform at your optimum and remain 'in the zone' of high-performance.

Neuroscientists estimate that you have 89 billion neurons in your brain, 40,000 neurons in your heart region and 100 million neurons in your gastrointestinal tract (gut). Consequently as well as realising the power of your brain, you should not overlook the 'mini brain', which is your heart, and the communication messages you get from your gut. That is why you need to treat your body, mind, emotions and mental state as closely interrelated systems, which should all be maintained, nurtured and sustained.

As we shall touch on when enhancing your HQ and RQ, there is a wealth of research and experience to back the importance of mindfulness practice, such as diaphragmatic breathing, or 'belly breathing'. What works especially well to calm you in stressful situations, and help you to think well, is focussed breathing involving five seconds inhaling followed by five seconds exhaling. When you combine that with the practice of remembering and generating positive emotions, then you will have a more powerful control over your heart and mind. That will both enhance your health and well-being and more importantly help you perform and think well in difficult situations. The result is greater focus and an increase in your hormone dopamine, which improves your fulfilment and satisfaction. You may also enjoy travelling to sunny holiday venues and that is of benefit to you since the associated bright sunlight helps increase your serotonin levels, without drugs.

Inspiring leaders stand out for their energy and drive. Testosterone is one of the hormones linked to drive and in many situations is ten times higher in men than women. However exercise, especially training with light weights, can increase your levels of testosterone. Drive on its own is insufficient, unless we can create 'followership' by building rapport with others. The left and right hemispheres of our brains are connected by the corpus callosum. This is a lattice of neural connections that is far more densely connected in women than men. It is estimated this is five times more effective in women, who in general can understand feelings and emotions more easily than men and access the language function from their left hemisphere to describe emotions that they are feeling in their right hemisphere. This is something that some men find more difficult to do, but with practice in emotional intelligence techniques, they can improve.

It is our various neural connections that lead us to behave the way we do as leaders. Repeated, familiar old behaviours are habitual and therefore easier to perform than new behaviours we are seeking to adopt and embed. If you want to change behaviours, then we need to literally 'change our minds'. The brain is remarkably plastic. We have now learnt that the brain is completely shaped by our experiences - throughout our lives. You actually *can* 'teach an old dog new tricks'. So, in a similar way to getting fitter and more toned by going to the gym and working out, if you want to have more healthy leadership behaviours then you need to consistently practice new ones. It was found that when your new behaviours were practised consistently for over forty days, then, within the brain, the connections between neurons are 'Myelinated' by Glial cells. These Glial cells wrap Myelin (a fatty substance) around the connections between neurons, which makes these pathways 100 times faster than the other older connections.

How to get the best out of those we lead and inspire them

As inspiring leaders, the first and most important thing you must do is to create an environment where your team can think well for themselves. At work, for people to be effective members of a high performing team, they need a feeling of camaraderie, safety, clear vision and sense of meaning and purpose from an emotionally intelligent leader who cares about them. With such a powerful combination then they give discretionary life energy that adds 20 - 30% to their effective levels of productivity.

In neurobiological terms this means you need to provide a high-performance environment, where the amygdala of your followers is calm and they are not feeling threatened. Psychologically this is known as a 'secure base'. This in turn allows their adrenal glands to produce DHEA, rather than cortisol, so triggering the prefrontal cortex (PFC) and the neo-cortex to work at optimum levels of thinking. Do all you can to create a safe, fun, creative and innovative environment, rather than a fearful one. Fear and intimidation in a team is highly infectious. It triggers the fight, flight and freeze response in their amygdala, so the pituitary (master) gland turns glucose from their food into energy. This energy and other finite resources, such as blood, are drawn to the limbic system and away from the areas you need them to use for their thinking such as the hypothalamus and prefrontal cortex.

To illustrate this point with a real-life example, one client, who was working in the tough environment of a global bank, then went to work for the world-famous technology company, Apple. Whereas previously they had found themselves in a highly competitive, intimidating, fear-based culture full of jealousy, criticism and stress, in Apple things were very different. They laughed more, found their ideas were readily accepted and built upon by their peers and not stolen, as they had previously experienced. They now loved coming to work and with far lower levels of stress and the brain producing DHEA, rather than cortisol, they no longer suffered from frequent bouts of illness, which they had previously suffered consistently every three to six months for the last five years.

The high levels of trust and openness amongst their new colleagues in

Apple generated large amounts of the high performing hormones: endorphins, dopamine, serotonin and oxytocin.

What also would have been happening was 'limbic resonance' where the brain of one person picks up the mood and emotions of the others. This can work in both positive and negative ways depending on who you choose to keep your company with and which organisation you work for. In the case of the client at Apple, they were so excited about their new work environment that they willingly gave huge amounts of discretionary life energy.

As an inspiring leader attempting to get change in your team and your organisation, there are varying ways of approaching this change, with different levels of success. Traditional carrot and stick methods have short-term results in attempting to influence and change the neural pathways in somebody else's brain.

The next more effective approach is to build rapport and use high levels of emotional intelligence to manage your own emotions, then read and manage other people's emotions. In that way you can achieve the fundamental aim of leadership: to get people inspired to do something they didn't really want to do and now feel good about doing so for you. However, be careful: there is a significant difference between manipulation and inspiration. Inspiring leaders, who understand the workings of our brain, realise that the 'coach approach to leadership' is more effective than a directive/tell style of leadership.

There are obvious moments where a directive/tell style of leadership is the only approach. For example, when there is a fire you must quickly direct people towards the exit and there is no time for discussion. However, on the whole, your brain works best in the presence of a question and when you are given the chance to decide on how to solve a problem yourself. As an inspiring leader you need to provide the 'why' and give meaning and purpose to the work they should do and the outcomes you want from them. That is about you setting the goal and clearly outlining the results and standards required.

When your followers can be encouraged and coached (and not manipulated), then their amygdala is calm, they generate high levels of DHEA and, so, levels of cortisol are low in inverse proportion. Consequently they are far more innovative and come up with the best possible solutions. They are then highly motivated to see their task through to a successful completion. An additional, welcome by-product is that their brains generate the pleasure hormones (endorphins, dopamine, serotonin and oxytocin) from working well with peers who are open, trusting, appreciative and believe in their capability to deliver.

Richard Boyatzis has gathered some interesting work on the research behind neuroscience and leadership. He suggests that: *"Inspiring and supportive relationships are important as they help activate openness to new ideas and more social orientation to others; to move the leader's actions away from results orientation towards a relationship orientation."* He used fMRI brain scans to compare resonant, high quality relationship leaders against dissonant, low quality relationship leaders. Resonant (inspiring) leaders activated the parts of the brain involved in arousing attention, social networks and approach relationships. Meanwhile dissonant (expiring) leaders deactivated systems involved in social networks and connections and instead activated regions associated with less compassion and more negative emotions. They could see from the brain scans that dissonant leaders seem to turn people off, alienate them and sap their motivation. Such followers were less open to new ideas and social orientation towards others.

Boyatzis' research also looked into emotional contagion and empathy. From the fMRI scans he drew the implications that, as leaders, we bear the prime responsibility for knowing what we are feeling. We should be aware that our negative emotions are more powerfully transmitted than our positive emotions. If we think we can disguise how we are feeling, then we are misguided, because we 'emotionally leak' and others pick up that contagion from us. So if you are to become an inspiring leader, then you need to manage your internal state to generate more authentic, positive emotions, which then in turn motivates others to learn, adapt and perform at their best.

Also we should be aware of the biological impact of rank, power, or status differentials on those we lead. When a senior leader is meeting with someone more junior in the organisation, then the hierarchical inequality has a hormonal and electrochemical impact. The leader's brain and body generate more of the hormone testosterone (ambition and drive) and reduce their levels of cortisol (the stress hormone). For the more junior person they have the disadvantage of the exact opposite response. Consequently inspiring leaders must respect this reaction and practically seek to reduce the physiological impact, by creating more equality through their humanity and humility, self-deprecating humour and by increasing our appreciation of the other person.

Even simple tips make a real difference. Examples include: an inspiring leader squatting down, or sitting down beside a more junior colleagues' desk, which helps. This is more preferable, rather than towering over their more junior colleague. We should really understand our impact as leaders on others – this gives physiological underpinning to the saying, *'be aware of your shadow that you cast as a leader'*.

Dr Geoff Bird shared some common myths and truths about our brains:

False: In make-up male and female brains are different. (This isn't true in make-up but is true in size.)

False: Left and right sides of the brain do different things. (This has been proved to be false.)

True: Exercise positively affects our brain. (This has been shown in cyclists, except those who cycled on busy roads and breathed fumes.)

True: Mood affects our brain. (Mood is both a product of our brain and created in our brain and has a big effect on our learning.)

False: 'You can't teach an old dog new tricks'. (This is an Urban Myth - there is no loss of plasticity in older brains; we are just slower to learn as we age.)

True: Stress affects your brain. (The pre-frontal cortex, hypothalamus are the learning areas and stress kills the neural connections here. If you are young they come back, if you are old 'keep calm and carry on'.)

True: Self-esteem affects your brain. (The view of self affects all areas of the brain.) A famous experiment in the US involved Maths PhD women. They scored one point lower on an exam when on the front of the test they were asked if they were male or female. When they were asked at the end of the paper if they were male or female, the scores went up.

True: Location and Place matters. (If you are learning at home and try to apply in a very different environment, you lose 30% of the ability to apply the learning. If you learn on a mountain top and try to apply it at sea level then the same thing: there is a 30% differential in success. Most of the time the learner has greater success of applying the learning if they are in the same environment.)

True: Culture affects brain development. (Our brain learns how to adapt to the culture. Brains in the West (USA and Europe, for example) are developed for the self and the brains in the east (China and Tiger Economise, for example) are developed for the collective.

Chapter Reflection:
How can you apply your knowledge of your brain more successfully?

1. **Focus our attention to be more successful**. We can enhance our ability to focus our mind through practicing mindfulness meditation. We now know the brain changes as a function of where we put our attention.

2. **Manage our breathing and our emotions**. By learning techniques to generate positive emotions and calm and steady our breathing in moments of stress, then we will think better and people will 'buy' us and our ideas, rather than us having to oversell ourselves.

3. **Practice new behaviours to make perfect**. By purposeful practice over 40 days, or more, we will create and embed new, faster neural connections and behave differently.

4. **Manage your brain; don't try to control it**. When we have an 'amygdala hijack' and our brain is overwhelmed with excess adrenaline and cortisol, then it is hard to control. Instead learn techniques to break the emotional stranglehold, such as taking a short "time out", walk, deeper regular breathing and generating positive emotions to overwrite the negative ones.

5. **Take a coach approach to inspire leadership**. Rather than directing and telling people exactly what they should do, instead ask insightful questions. That allows them to let their brains work the solution out for themselves. In that way they take greater ownership and are more likely to see through the change.

6. **Focus on what we want, rather than what we don't want**. Our brains open up and work best when we begin interactions with questions such as 'what is working well?' (WWW) and appreciation of good work already done. At that point we can then go into greater detail by asking questions like 'what would make it even better?' (EBI). To go straight into destructive criticism of them is a great mistake, as it closes down the crucial creative centres of their brain.

7. **Healthy body and healthy brain**. Work in the area of Psycho Neuro-immunology is a fascinating development area. Early research shows a

strong link between stress, helplessness and various life-threatening diseases such as cancers and brain tumours. If we want to strengthen our immune system, general health and well-being then we need to change our lifestyle and our thinking.

8. **Use our brain and our positive mental attitude to live longer**. Early research has shown that people described as 'attributional pessimists' see events happening to us and being beyond our control and are likely to both generate more cortisol throughout their life and die younger. Those who have 'self-efficacy' feel they have a greater ability to make things happen and be in control of their lives and so naturally generate more DHEA and live longer.

Chapter 5
MQ: Moral Integrity

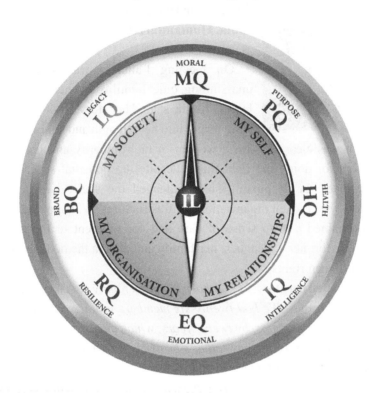

"At what point in time did we sign up to give our souls away? We need to know that we have to bring something to the table; it's what we've been recruited for. As leaders we become 'loyal' and start conforming, running with the pack, as it's such high exposure. We stop sticking our head out and use people as sacrificial lambs. We can't be afraid of mistakes and do what feels right, at times risking getting it wrong. This means that we also need to celebrate when we get it wrong."

Jackie Uhi
Managing Director, Finance Sector

Latha Caleb
The Inspiring Leader with Courage and
Passion for Doing the Right Thing –
India, Humanitarian

On meeting Latha, I was struck by her unassuming, quiet humility and her grounding as a leader. As she shared her story, I felt privileged to gain insight into her strength and courage. Absent of ego, it was clear she was a woman of high integrity and had a strong conviction for doing the right thing, despite the potential severity of the consequences. In its pursuit, she challenged the societal rules and the bureaucracy of broken organisational infrastructures. Whilst doing that, she also maintained a deep sense of care and commitment to those she felt responsible for: her colleagues, her family and also in the dedication of her work for human rights.

Latha shared her story: *"I was born to a joint family including my parents, siblings and uncles. We had twenty-six members in total. I have two elder sisters; I am the youngest, by twelve years, which meant a whole generation gap between us. In reality my father's brothers' children were younger and so I had to take care of them.*

"My leadership journey started then, managing a group of young kids. If something went wrong, then I was asked, 'Why were you not looking after them properly?' I had to keep a watch on everything. I grew up in this environment of joint family, where I had to negotiate space. In high school, I also took on leadership positions by doing army training and being in the National Cadet Corps, where I was leader of the battalion. I was seriously thinking about a career in the army at the time. My father was a businessman and my mother a housewife. They were of different religions. I was the first graduate in the family. At every stage I had to challenge the status quo in the family. The society was patriarchal; I was often out of joint with the family.

"I graduated in sociology. I met my husband, who is a Christian, but different caste. As it was considered unacceptable to go around with him, I had to keep it a secret at that time. It was only when I was at college that I

felt I had the freedom to be myself. My father expected me to take over the business. However, I was very interested in social science and psychology and so I forged my father's signature on the application forms, so I could complete my Masters in social work. Although we'd heard lots of stories about others who married from different castes, such as emotional blackmail and threats, my husband and I were determined to marry. To force our marriage, so the family had no choice in the matter, we went ahead and registered the wedding and then told them. It was not an easy thing to do, but I believed that I was doing the right thing. As expected, all hell broke loose at home! In the end I was asked to leave and was excluded from my family. His family, on the other hand, welcomed me as a daughter.

"My view now has made me so aware of how our caste system has been entrenched in our society. Reading psychology helped me to see this [caste system operate] in real life. What I believed in was the equality of people; when you make an important choice to be with someone, it is for the rest of your life. I was now making decisions and taking accountability for myself and I think my Dad found this the hardest thing to contemplate.

"I never saw my father again after I left home. Seven years later, he died in a foreign country. None of my family had a passport, so couldn't bring his body back; so this was something that I had to do.

"As my father had no son to deal with the last rites, then one of my uncle's sons performed the last rites for my father. At that time I felt, why can't I do this? If I could go to another country and bring back my father's body, then why can't I do the final rites? They told me that I couldn't. I was happy to let this go.

"Because I was very clear in my thinking and making decisions about what needs to be done, or can't be done, people started to look up to me - even my older sisters. They would start to consult me for advice. I didn't realise, until much later, the trauma that came with losing a parent. Mum was very insistent I would take responsibility. In India the parents usually live with the sons, but my mother decided she wanted to live independently. She said that she was born a Christian and wanted to die a Christian. It was unusual that the youngest in the family deals with both parents' last rights, but in my case this was the case.

"I started working in 1986 to help to establish an organisation for children with multiple disabilities. We started in a garage and then created more space as it grew. My grounding in leadership happened here. I had to understand the challenge of the bigger picture and the impact of decisions on the wider organisation. I would get involved in many things, including fundraising.

"I remember meeting with a businessman, who listened to our story. He then opened his desk drawer and handed me a wad of money, which he told me was unaccounted for and so I could use it. I recall the dilemma, as to whether I could, or should take the money? It was for charity and we knew the children needed our support. Everything must be receipted. I asked my colleagues what was the right thing to do and we agreed it was ethical and good practice to receipt the money, if we were to accept the donation. This is what we did.

"We are often faced with ethical questions, both personally and in business and sometimes you don't know the right way out. You must respect the need for disclosure. This is crucial in terms of staying clear about, and true, to your values. The importance of this grows as you work in bigger organisations, as it gets challenged more, as boundaries become blurred. It is important to debate, create clear guidelines on what to do and what is not the right thing to do.

"I have found this where systems and processes are not well defined, and then you need to keep refining this with growth. It can lead to situations, where you're dealing on a case by case basis, and so there are no equitable dealings. Not everyone gets treated the same way with different prioritisations.

"I was married, but had no children. As a social worker, I was working with parents. Yet I didn't know what it was like to have a child and didn't know how to handle disabilities. Dealing with disability is a 24-hour job, but I felt I didn't have the experience that would help me to create programmes to equip parents and build into the routine of the family. I knew I needed to create the experience. We raised money for new wheelchairs, which I had to get across India. I had requested that they would be road-worthy. I had some doubts and so wanted to try them out for myself. I put myself in a wheelchair

and pushed myself along the streets, where I could see how behaviours and traffic would change, if at all. It helped me to go back to parents; to help them understand and manage this. I continually fought for changes and creating greater awareness.

"When I got pregnant, mothers would all the time say to me that I should leave my work, because seeing children with disabilities may cause me to give birth to a child with disabilities. I understood the scientific side and knew this not to be the case. I felt it was my role to show this to others, so I worked right up to my last day.

"In 1989 my daughter was born; fully healthy. When she was five years old I came to study my Masters in the UK. This was the moment when I realised how much support I had in my husband and family. My sister-in-law took full care of my daughter, while I went to pursue my higher studies in the UK. It also highlighted my responsibilities. I had thought that when I left the organisation for a long time, that things would fall apart. This temporary separation from the organisation made me realise that people would come and go. Things go on at work, even if you're not there. Of course, not in the way that you would have wanted, or planned! You have your own standards, but you cannot enforce these on others. Organisations can go on, no-one's indispensable.

"On my Masters, I met leaders from around the world, including from the Gaza strip, Africa and Europe. It made me realise how Indian I was deep down. It was at the very core of me.

"When my husband went on an official trip to Tokyo, I wanted to go with him. I left my daughter with my sister-in-law. Whilst he was there, I had some distant cousins to stay with. The landlady in Tokyo didn't speak English and I didn't speak Japanese. It made me realise that you really don't need to speak the same language in order to communicate. I brought back to India new expertise on how to develop support aids for people with disabilities.

"By working for four years on a primary health care project with the local government, I became absolutely fascinated by how the government works. The scale is enormous. I met some fantastic people who were passionate about what they do. It made me rethink. In the past I would deep-dive into who I was and was so anti-government. I had people working there

who challenged me saying, —The government has its own challenges too, you know.‖ I had always put government people in a box, when I was on the outside. I now I understood so much more. I was working to set up 400 health centres, which gave me a wealth of experiences, including construction. When deciding priorities, there was so much hierarchy in meetings; I was such a non-hierarchical person. Over the years I have come to be comfortable with who I am. It doesn't bother me. Who cares what religion, caste or position a person is. I believe in respect, no matter what. It is the person that matters most – a personal value that I carry which transcends everything that I do. People are comfortable coming to me about anything, even when they have made a mistake. They trust me.

"On the government project we had an Indian staff association. I was elected to be president, which I did not expect. Firstly, because I'm a woman and secondly, because of the clear north and south India divide. There was a lot of politics, but I tend not to get involved in factions and divides. I try to counter and challenge them.

"I took a six-month break. My daughter was in a major accident – a hit and run. She was nine years old. My husband was with her. It was a traumatic experience. She had a fractured skull and blood clots. She was having seizures. I drove through the night to get to her. The doctor, who I knew from my work, said that the prognosis was not good, but he couldn't give any indication of how bad things would be though. This put me in a situation that the other parents with disabled children go through. Their crisis had become my own reality.

"I was volunteering at that time in my daughter's school. The entire school went on a fasting prayer for her. I didn't know what we had done to deserve such appreciation. It was very special. She was on medication for two years. We didn't know what the prognosis would be. They had removed part of her skull. I was working for the government health programme at the time. My husband and I talked a lot about what we should do. He saw the potential for my growth and he wanted me to continue work.

"We agreed he would take early retirement, which was absolutely unheard of in India. We really challenged the social construction of traditional gender roles. People were paying a lot of attention and both

families thought we would have problems with this. However, we worked through this and we believed that we had the right kind of support in place for our child. My husband has no problem cleaning, although he didn't have a clue about cooking! In order to organise the home well, we hired people to help out with both and created a framework for providing the right nutrition. The system worked and it gave my husband some freedom too. Now my daughter has fully recovered. She's completed her degree in Space Science and Engineering at the University College in London and is now doing her PhD in Australia - researching Astronomy and Astrophysics. All three of us are like friends and we have special moments.

"When the tsunami happened, I felt disturbed that I could not help. I joined Save the Children and worked in one of the Response Units. I didn't know anything about emergencies. We were responding to seven different sectors – such as in health (HIV / Aids), shelter, and construction with a budget of £25m. The volume was so high. This was a serious situation, where I had to hire, induct and train 75 emergency response staff. I worked flat out. During this period, I realised many things. I learned a deep appreciation for my family. I was returning home and just crashing into bed.

"The home was running by itself. I also learned how important it is to find the right people for the job. They don't necessarily need experience, you just need the right people, with the right attitude, to learn and do the job well. Over the years, I learned leadership skills across the wide spectrum of people: on one end dealing with the UK Board and then at the other end dealing with charities and children. It's a vast stakeholder group and so important to be on a good team. I experienced that no amount of planning ever prepares you for a crisis. When you are leading and dealing with volume, delegation is important. With so much money involved, there tends to be far more controls.

"But when you're dealing with an emergency, you also want things to happen quickly to provide the right support in the hour of need.

"When I was Country Director in the Philippines, there was a major typhoon where 80% of Manila was under water. We needed external help as we weren't able to cope. But like I experienced in India, the local team were rebelling against having ex-pats. As an Asian woman, who had previously

been accepted, I suddenly felt the shift on this occasion. Instead I was seen as another ex-pat bringing in more people. People were saving face, as they had huge pride and it was all so visible – this is something that I have experienced in many parts of Asia. It was hard for them to accept help.

"I set high standards for myself and expected others to follow the same high standards. Over a period of time, I have learnt that I have to allow for people to set their own standards and not impose mine on them. What's important is their commitment; the quality of standards can be worked on. Some of the biggest battles in my life have been internal. We are often the external voice advocating for change outside. However, we sometimes forget to also hear the internal voices: those that help us to advocate for change.

"The work that I do inspires me and I admire the commitment that people come with. People give so much of themselves; their engagement and commitment is heartening to see. As a leader you need to trust people to do their best and they will do it. You need to give them responsibility. You may need to make judgements on who you need to monitor and support more closely. I struggle with organisations that do not inspire me, where personal connection is lacking and they are not genuine. Sometimes we incorrectly focus on our own importance, or the importance of process, rather than on the people. We can be very clinical in some of our engagements and it doesn't make people feel good."

What is Moral Integrity (MQ)?

In writing this chapter, I have personally explored my own rationale for making choices.

For example, I make my choice on political alignment, not because I value the *number* of women in leadership of any political party, but because I value the *quality* of leadership and the *wisdom* of their policies. I make my choices about my careers based on my own values about how and where I want to spend my time. Not forgetting with whom I want to spend my time! As my eyes have been opened to organisations and their behaviours, I make my decisions based on my understanding of their reputation for *truly* doing the right thing, from my banking arrangements right through to my purchasing choices.

With so much free choice these days, when people feel uneasy about who you are, or what you stand for, it helps them to make a decision about whether to be loyal, or not. Thanks to the newly connected World Wide Web and social media, the worst-case scenario is no longer people just 'talking with their feet'. This is not about whether mistakes are made and we all make them and know 's**t happens'. However, it is the responses to those mistakes that are the real key.

I believe one of the greatest challenges in our society today boils down to a widespread and prevailing issue, that of MQ: our morality, values, integrity and ethics. Both our developed and undeveloped worlds present different challenges. Both impede progress in some form, whether it's the decisions that are made by our business leaders, issues of disempowerment, or basic human rights.

It is, therefore, of great significance that we begin the Inspiring Leadership compass with Moral Integrity. Our moral principles highlight the importance of our integrity, values and beliefs. A sense of morality governs all our behaviour; it is vital to our sustained success in our relationships, organisation and society. It therefore must be founded upon our understanding of universal principles and how these should be applied to our own actions.

MQ on the Inspiring Leadership compass is not the incrementally changing 'magnetic north', a vacillation, or dithering for what is moral and ethical. MQ points to a 'true north', that which is steadfast and fervent, providing us with the reassurance of our discernment between what is right and wrong. It is our integrity and irreproachability. This quotient in Inspiring Leadership measures our integrity to remain consistently true to our values and beliefs. It highlights our ability to understand and resolve differences with others and our confidence to take action, in order to do the right thing. It is often integrity and values that cause us to react in some form when challenged, as conflict calls upon us to compromise our beliefs. Having the confidence and courage to embrace our differences, rather than complying with norms, means that we bring diverse thinking and challenge to any leadership decision or act. Surely this is what we are hired for?

It is clear that morality transcends the boundaries of our societal rules, to something far greater, requiring us to consciously live by a set of principles that govern our behaviours. This is not just about the behaviours that adhere to imposed rules and regulations. In Roger Steare's book, *Ethicability*, he describes how the 'Ethic of Care' takes us beyond a set of rules and regulations that command obedience to a way of behaving, because it is the *right* thing to do. The world exists in several shades of grey, not just black and white. We cannot possibly have a rule for everything. As inspiring leaders, we each have our own moral compass. When challenged, finding our way back to this compass will guide us and give us courage. We must all live our lives according to a common set of humanistic principles; ones that provides a 'duty of care' and fairness to those around us, whose lives we impact.

Importantly, we are all unique and none of us are perfect, by any means! Every person has their own sense of integrity that guides them according to their set of principles, which aren't always visible to us. As you begin your leadership journey, you must be very clear on what you stand for. It is important to then seek to understand what others value: whether it's your customers, your family, or your colleagues. We must understand both the logic and the emotion that we attach to our attitudes, decisions and behaviours. We need to recognise the biases that we sustain, both conscious and unconscious that hold back progress. We must also acknowledge the similarities and the differences that may exist among leaders. Responsible leadership and stewardship is at the heart of this MQ component.

Consequences of a Lack of MQ

The majority of leaders are honest people passionate about their work and doing the right thing. They are keen to serve for the greater good, yet sadly they are often caught up in the decisions and impact of poor leadership. However, we only need to observe the breakdown at every possible level on a macro scale that occurred in the global financial crisis, as well as the stories of cover-ups, of abuse and tragedy that have only begun to emerge years later. It is also shocking to unearth the actual price that is placed on someone's head when it comes to budget cuts. Within the corporate world, we have also all witnessed highly intelligent individuals, in some of the most influential positions, with unquestionable wealth and lifestyles, who turn out to have been involved in utterly fraudulent and deceitful acts.

From a battered economy through to violation of basic human rights, I have been inspired by the emergence of great leadership in response to the aftermath of such events, which is undoubtedly shining through. It is, however, more often in retrospect that change occurs and rarely pre-empted.

With a growing separation from a purposeful and moral existence, there is a deep disconnect and isolation from basic humanistic values. This is resulting in highly questionable behaviours from the most rudimentary, to those of the highest order. Imposed societal beliefs and cultures continue to challenge the agenda for women. At best it is constraining the full potential and economic progress and, at times, at its worst it involves victimising and bullying those who challenge the boundaries and fight for equal rights.

The issue of moral integrity and principles is not just exclusive to the few people 'without conscience' and the scandals that we hear about. It may make us feel safer believing these issues exist beyond our own reality. However, they are not so far removed. We can personally be challenged on a day-to-day basis about the right thing to do in its simplest form.

I recall an experience in my career, when one of my HR Directors was facilitating the annual talent review session with an executive board. She invited me to observe for consistency, and consult me for my professional guidance. As the board worked their way through the '9-grid talent matrix' and discussed specific individuals, some concerning behaviours emerged.

Frustrated with one employee's performance, their discussion turned to how the team could work together in order to make this individual's life as uncomfortable as possible. Their hope was that this under-performing individual would choose to leave the business, rather than have to go through the arduous and costly process of performance managing them to be made redundant. The discussion escalated into them finding creative ways of operating within the confines of business. I observed the group with dismay, as the events unfolded. There was no intervention, or challenge from the group, although there were clearly many who shifted uncomfortably in their chairs. I became deeply concerned with the dysfunctional behaviours and direction of the discussion. I intervened in the session, challenging the group to reflect on their discussion and the highly unethical nature of it. Achieving a desired result, no matter what the cost, is completely unethical.

Corporate Rhetoric Versus Reality

Indeed, for one of the interviews for this book, I had a disappointing experience where their espoused corporate values conflicted with the actual leadership behaviours. Having made it through the security, I reached reception, which provided a most impressively sophisticated and professional setting. It had been some time since I'd been to the office and I noted just how much things had changed. The employees were super-efficient and looked elegant in their newly tailored uniforms. I gave the name of the woman I was there to meet for an interview and waited.

I looked across at the five plaques proudly erected in positions of prominence. The plaques reinforced the new corporate values and the recent public statements, trumpeting that significant change was afoot for this business. Things were very different in practice. Having signed in, I sank into one of the generous leather chairs and waited to be collected. I waited. Then I waited some more. Twenty minutes later, I checked to make sure everything was okay and I hadn't been forgotten! "No, the PA is on her way," I was told. A further fifteen minutes later the PA arrived. No apology, just a finger pointed in my direction, as she summoned me to follow her. I attempted to make conversation – a hard thing to do with the back of someone's head, I realise. I was escorted to the corner office and waited at the door, observing the exchange between the leader I was due to interview and one of her colleagues. It took all of my strength to stand firm and not walk out – at this point I was tempted to comment that 'maybe I had come to the wrong place'! However, again, I waited and told myself to be patient.

Finally the exchange was over. I was summoned into the room. As I took my seat, I still had not received even a hint of an apology, or acknowledgement of the long delay. Don't get me wrong, we have all over-run and been late for meetings, at various points. However, some humility and respect would have gone down well. Instead, the leader assumed a dominating frame in her chair and asserted herself. With strongly overt words of culture change and value statements and symbols 'in your face' throughout the office, I was not perturbed by the demeanour. Instead I was curious about the difference between the organisational rhetoric and the reality of daily leadership behaviours. Fortunately, I was pleased that I persisted and had my interview with her. Albeit a far shorter interview than planned, her story was fascinating and emotional, her advice wise and different given her unique perspective and experiences.

Dangerously Competitive Women

In a separate interview, I learnt of one female leader's experience. Hers is representative of the norm, rather than unusual. She told me, *"My concern is that many blocks to advancement are not caused by men, but rather by some women. Such women display toxic behaviours, but yet are put on the pedestal as role models. This teaches other women that you have to behave a certain way, in order to succeed. Consequently, we will get a repeated cycle, slowing down the whole women's agenda. Women can be our own worst enemy and we must break the patterns. Men still struggle with promoting people in their own likeness and bias of all kinds is still rife. This holds us back from creating diversity, through failing to promote more inclusive cultures. Women try to play by the rules, using the men's playbook and so they instead become bad leaders. Not because of the mirroring, but because of the in-authenticity. We must understand that this is not the way that we are wired to be. Instead, as women, we can actually bring our own strengths and something magical to the mix. Then we can make the fundamental shifts to being confident in ourselves and truly authentic."*

Support, Don't Judge

On another occasion, when Jackie shared her story, I was deeply moved. *"I'm married and adopted two kids at the age of 22. My brother's wife had passed away. Suddenly I was an instant mother; I had a family."*

Blown away by this insight into Jackie's life, I asked, "How on earth do you cope with something so traumatic and life-changing?" She replied, *"I did not really stop to think about it, I just got on with it – like most women do. My husband is a stay-at-home Dad and I decided to not take long for maternity leave when I then had my own kids. No-one really knows how personally challenging it can be, juggling everything and so they make judgments. I returned to work four weeks after my first child, six weeks after my second and was actually forced to take twelve weeks off after my third. My choices were seen in such a negative fashion and some people never really sought to understand. You see, the longer I stuck around the more difficult it was for my husband to get the routine he needed with three young children."*

What is concerning, is that we have forged a culture of judgement and criticism. We mistakenly make assumptions about others' lives, based on limited sets of information. We are all judging in some way: whether it be about the stay-at-home Mum, the stay-at-home Dad, or the 'mover and shaker' that challenges the status quo. The power of disclosure is deeply personal and yet shifts worlds. However, we should not need disclosure. If we are compassionate and respectful leaders then we will accept people for who they are and the choices they make, stepping in to support in the spirit of 'community' instead.

It is easy to get caught up in organisational culture and personally identify with the job title bestowed upon us, which boosts our ego. However, we must be aware of and take responsibility for our interactions and the signals that we send to those that we lead, or work with. The challenge with attempting any form of culture change is that it requires leadership from the top to advocate and for us to role model the necessary behaviour to embed it.

Toxic Environments and Bullying

Unfortunately, these simple examples are not so rare. I was told stories of toxic environments and leaders making life difficult for others. Such leaders cause disturbing results, affecting the health and livelihoods of those they lead. As we continue to witness decisions taken by many powerfully influential leaders, it is disturbing to hear of the level of manoeuvring that continues to take place, with blatant disregard for what is right. Such leaders persist in replicating failures of the past. This is despite a history littered with poor decisions, where rules and regulations are by-passed in the interest of more sinister purposes, such as short-term greed, status, position, or just plain ego. With the blurred and grey boundaries that exist between operating within, or outside, the realms of the law, we must be able to decide what is right and wrong in human terms.

Bullying has become the intellectual mind-game; a strategy to undermine with little regard for consequence. This has escalated even further, with the pervasiveness of social media, and subsequently cyber bullying. Cheating has become the advantage and the 'only' way some seek to win, with unfairly large rewards. Sophisticated charm and coercion has become the methodology for manipulative and deceitful managers. There has clearly been some moral decay. We have made it possible for these individuals to prevail. There has been an explosion of opportunity through the complexity of our systems. These manipulative managers have so little MQ and only, what one female leader described as, just a 'wishbone for a backbone'. Disturbingly, the high integrity, reforming leader creates enemies in all those who profit by sustaining the old order of things.

We observe some of those that hold the greatest power create sacrificial lambs and hang out to dry either single institutions, or individuals. We have governments blaming capitalists, capitalists blaming regulation and society and some people blaming everyone. In the absence of responsible leadership and widespread defensiveness, how on earth can we really embrace the learning that comes from mistakes? From a neurobiological perspective, we may overestimate how much people are similar to us. Then we are surprised when they think and act differently.

Listen to the Integrity of Your Advisors

We have functions like Risk, Legal and HR in place to help provide guidance. Often they act as the organisation's conscience by challenging the organisation's thinking. Yet, I have observed how much we 'shoot the messenger' when leaders don't like what they hear! Do we want 'echo-chambers' in our leadership, or diversity of thought and collaborative conflict? Such fresh thought helps us to slow down, reflect and think about the decisions that we are making. This, of course, requires a lot of patience and energy. But time is money and the next innovation, or task is seductively beckoning. The response therefore is to swiftly move on, or remove the naysayers from the situation. When we attempt to bring diverse groups together, we fail to effectively develop the integration. Jonathan and I facilitate a very simple 'thumbs up, or down' exercise in our team coaching to help unpick these challenges in a safe and trusted environment. This way all of the issues are on the table and the team get highly creative to form a solution that has been fully debated and everyone respects the decision.

Bystanders and Wilful Blindness

In Jackson Katz's powerful TED Talk, he defines the 'Bystanders' as a group that are separate to the perpetrators, or the victims. These are the rest of the people embedded in our social structure - you and me. When we take this concept into the business world, I witness how often we correctly hire for the knowledge, integrity and leadership that individuals can bring to the table. However, we throw this away once they are hired and find ways to drown out this integrity.

As we embark on making important decisions, or judgement calls, how often do we ask ourselves, 'Is this *really* the right thing to do?' When faced with the majority challenging us, do we stand up for our beliefs? Do we intervene for what is morally and ethically right in the moment? Jackson calls this the 'Interrupter' and acknowledges how tough this can be when challenging the dominant group, even when you're part of that group. How often do we buckle under the pressure of our peer groups and allow our confidence to waver? Do we justify our passiveness and silence with the excuse of supporting the majority, or most powerful? Maybe we close our eyes to what's happening around us, working in 'willful blindness' as outlined in Margaret Heffernan's excellent book. She gives examples of when people, just like us, are fearful of putting our heads above the parapet, remembering the emotional shame of having been 'shot down' before.

Sayyeda Salam shared with me, *"I believe that there are times when it is important for us to protect universal human rights and to not accept things, such as discrimination, and the way things are."*

Courageously Challenging the Unacceptable

My own grandfather, Bilshie (aka 'Pop' to his grandchildren), was a strong and influential figure in our hometown, Bundoran in Ireland. You name it, he did it: actor, singer, political influencer, sportsman, barber, comedian, poet, Lord Mayor...! He would also write articles for the newspapers. In one article he produced, he condemned the abominable acts of the IRA. One night, my grandmother, Mary-Kate (aka 'Mum', because she was Mum to just about everyone), heard a knock at the front door. When 'Mum' opened the door, IRA sympathisers burst through, knocking her to the ground. Placing a hood over Pop's head, they kidnapped him, and in an attempt to intimidate him and bring him into line with the IRA propaganda, they pressured him to withdraw his defamatory comments. He refused. He kept to his moral true north. Fortunately for Pop, he was dealing with sympathisers and not the real IRA, and so he was returned home safely into Mary-Kate's loving arms. Years later, when I asked him how he found such courage in the face of so much intimidation, he responded, *"Leigh, the day that we buckle to terrorists is the day we sell our soul. I will not sell my soul to the devil."*

It's an uncomfortable, and sometimes frightening, place to be to challenge others. However, if we live in collective silence then are we not condoning these acts? Wilful blindness has been at the core of some of the world's greatest tragedies and injustices. But let's be clear, this is not just about the issues of a significant nature. By only playing witness to the daily acts of discrimination, injustice and bullying and not taking a stance, we are contributing to the bigger issue.

During my interviews, it became clear that whilst we continue to value certain behaviours as part of a cultural norm, we would struggle to create inclusive environments that recognise the strength of truly diverse leadership teams. As we continue to formally report on the number of women in leadership roles (and rightly so), I would also challenge you to reflect on the subject of diverse cultures.

One inspiring leader shared, *"There aren't too many women here in our organisation. It's the unintended consequence of a set of moves, or some more unconsciousness. We don't hold leaders and suppliers, such as head-hunters, to account to come up with diverse lists. We could make a difference if we really tried."*

If an organisation's rhetorical statement of intent is to achieve 'gender parity', yet in practice it is devoid of any truth, then this will destroy the trust that women have in any diversity agenda. As they look to the executive teams and fail to see any change, they ask, what's really happening? Both men and women in positions of influence must start to take greater responsibility for advocating and demonstrating real and sustained change.

Intentions Versus Actions

It is often easier for us to judge others based on their *actions* and not their *intentions*. However, for ourselves we judge ourselves by our fine intentions and never our questionable actions. As we take such moral high-ground, is there some hypocrisy in such a perspective? As Stephen Covey quoted in his book, *The Speed of Trust*, 'If you think the problem is 'out there', that very thought *is* the problem'. Judgement, pressure and ridicule more often come from our own inadequacies, rather than those of others who we are attempting to put down.

One good thing that has come from our global financial crises is that it has created a new wave of ethical leadership behaviour with low tolerance for deviations.

I also want to acknowledge the inspiring leaders who are stepping forward and taking the helm, helping to craft the change that is needed for better judgements and behaviours.

When Trust is Broken

High MQ offers a clear signal of strength and capability that generates trust and respect, resulting in followership. With a clear focus on challenging objectives, in what is often politically charged environments, issues of trust and transparency are often at the very core of successful leadership. When I have been coaching teams and individuals, I have encouraged equality of dialogue that explores their values, vision, concerns and vulnerabilities. When trust is broken, although tough to achieve, it is redeemable. This requires honesty around the causes of the breakdown in trust, which requires a level of vulnerability, some principals and agreement for how things should be done around here, followed by sustained behavioural change. The solution does not involve the usual empty promises, subsequent U-turns, or seepage of old behaviours.

Consider the true story of Jeremy (name altered), a highly intelligent entrepreneur building a new technology business. He was a truly creative maverick with a real passion for making money, who had built a team of 20 people that had been won-over by his vision. He had hired Anthony, a talented IT Director, and together they worked on the strategy for growing the business. Anthony was a highly principled and methodical man, deeply committed to the engagement of the team and passionate about doing the right thing. In their meetings with investors and the board, Jeremy presented over-inflated and ambitious views of the business. His presentations stretched the truth on many levels.

Over the years Jeremy continued to fail to get the desired investments and was unable to demonstrate sufficient trustworthiness to persuade the board. He returned to the team filling them with more false promises, such as that their salaries would be paid on time, for once. He encouraged them to hold on, whilst exciting them with the latest new idea for products to develop. Needless to say, communication and trust had broken down on every level. We worked closely with each individual executive to explore mutual strengths and also the behaviours that were causing the breakdown that would 'de-rail' Jeremy. We brought the leadership team together, to explore the results in 'safety'. Through developing a greater awareness of self and others, we opened up a level of vulnerability and created the catalyst for more positive conversations. They adopted Nancy Kline's transformational approaches to create a better thinking environment by holding dialogues to solve their conflict and team challenges. As a result, the culture of the business suddenly shifted and the renewal of trust occurred. Of course, sustaining the behavioural change is the most important intervention of all.

How can 'MQ: Moral Integrity' help you?

The question I ask often of leaders, when I'm coaching or training them is, 'Who are you in service of and why?' I follow this by asking, 'What are you in service of and why?' When the answers are absent of MQ, we all know there is some work to be done!

MQ is intrinsically linked to your brand and personal reputation. Will your customers buy from you? Do your team trust you enough to be honest with you? Can your boss rely on your sound judgement? Can the people you care about rely on you and believe that you will not be judgemental about them? People are loyal to the leaders that they can trust to do the right thing.

Claire Hall shared one experience in her career, *"I remember when I was working in the retail sector. One of the managers was in a compromising situation with an employee. He had abused his position on numerous occasions for his own ends. They had lost respect and trust in him. They achieved good results and so I was told to give him a 'slap on the wrist' and send him back to work! He led 120 people and I felt by doing this I would be letting them all down and compromising their positions. [Instead I formalised his performance management process]. Unfortunately the press got hold of the story, which became front-page news. He was genuinely upset and realised the seriousness of what had happened. He had a family. Although I'd had full senior management support in what I did, I was the one pushing this and I felt responsible for destroying this guy's family. However, it was the right thing to do, although difficult at the time. The experience made me more reflective and determined to always think things through and appreciate the consequences. As a leader, you need to be seen to be doing the right thing and operating with integrity. This means that you may need to be bold and courageous at times when this is challenged."*

Even when you have the full capabilities of your team around you, leadership can often feel like a lonely place. In terms of the choices you make, the accountability, 'the buck', firmly lies with you! As a leader, you take responsibility for your decisions and the full consequences of your actions. Now this is hugely empowering and offers the power to leave a positive legacy behind you. However, we have also seen where badly made decisions, made in the absence of sound moral judgement and wise ethics, have completely unravelled careers, businesses and lives.

People love to work for leaders and organisations that hold strong values and beliefs. This must not be just statements of intent, but grounded in reality through their ethical and consistent decisions. The very act of speaking up for what is right is an act of inspiring leadership. I see with my clients today, in these tough times, the return to basic values. This is creating a renewed energy, as people recognise that somehow we all got a little 'lost' along the way.

Following Your Moral Compass

It is therefore essential for you as a leader that you have your own clear *'moral compass'* and so does your organisation. This must not waver, under the pressure of achieving results, or through the desire to win, if it is at the expense of doing the right thing. This can be deeply subjective and interpreted differently, as one Professor recently challenged me. Of course I acknowledge that this is the case and said, *"I cannot claim that there is one single set of morals and values that is universal today, as much as I would like a baseline. Unfortunately, I also cannot solve the issues that have permeated our society for centuries. However, by exploring high levels of MQ, we have the power to create new dialogue and understanding."*

In the ideal world, we would not be creating solutions to address the causes and symptoms of past poor decisions. However, in reality sometimes the results, or longer-term impact of such bad decision-making can be highly unpredictable. Quite often, the decisions of the past become the inheritance for today.

In times like this, the true inspiration comes from not the fact that a mistake has been made, but in the ensuing courageous act that acknowledges and takes responsibility for resolving them. By making the choice to accept that we make mistakes and learn from them, we engender trust and subsequent loyalty. If instead we make the choice to defend, make excuses for what went wrong, or avoid these mistakes, then we send a different signal that engenders a culture of cover-ups, fear and mistrust.

Rather than imposing our values systems on others, we are better to really understand them and be sensitive to their impact on others. From here we can ignite new ideas and generate solutions that will move us from a place of conflict and disengagement to a place of opportunity and collaboration. Through creating an open and trusting environment, where people can think effectively and contribute openly, we will be rewarded with honesty and even innovation. As a leader it is important for you to make strong public commitments and stay true to your promises.

I was once attending a course on the subject of 'Mindfulness'. Trudi Ryan, the Managing Director of Coachmatch, a top executive coach and an inspiring leader in her own right, was also there. She described how she went to dinner one evening with her father. She stopped mid-conversation and said to him, *"You know, Dad, I have just realised that through our whole lives together, I have never, ever felt judged by you"*. The whole room fell silent. This was a crucible moment for me as this one sentence made me think about the type of Mum I was and how my children would describe me. I know my children and I have always had a fantastic relationship and feel like an un-breakable force. However, I realised in that moment that I had recently been quite judgemental of my son, Daniel. It was out of pure love and concern, but the way I managed it was not helpful. He was applying for the police at the time, which is his absolute passion. However, their recruitment process was extensive and long-winded! I felt he was spending too much time on the X-Box. I wanted him to get a full-time job and work harder, whilst he was waiting to get into the Metropolitan Police. The more I critiqued (or nagged as Daniel would say), the more he withdrew. I value the relationship that I have with my family, more than anything else in the world. I knew I had to change. I was making him feel de-valued and unwittingly damaging his confidence.

I purposefully set out to change the language and conversations I had with Daniel. I started looking for what I valued and also what he valued. I would catch him doing the 'good stuff' and appreciate him in the moment. Neither of our sets of values was wrong; what fundamentally needed to shift was my strategy for enhancing our relationship. Our resulting behaviours and subsequent dialogue allowed us to move it to a more positive space. I'm really pleased to say he's thriving in the Police. Ironically, now I'm concerned that he's working too hard! As a Mum, I realise it is also my prerogative to concern myself with the kids welfare; no doubt I will do so for the rest of my life.

We don't always get it right, in business and in life. Sometimes we just need a wake-up call.

Bob Bond - US, Finance
When Leaders Do The Right Thing

Leaders need to really buy into the value of women in leadership. Bob Bond is one of those truly progressive, emotionally intelligent and outstanding leaders that have had a hugely positive impact on the people he has led.

With a dynamic personality and courageous spirit, he has no qualms in challenging the status quo and calling things out. He was recommended to me on several occasions as a leader that I must interview for the book. However, I remembered Bob from my days in banking and so knew only too well that he was an exemplary leader and humanising force. He has been a vocal advocate of gender and diversity issues, leading the way on challenging executives to 'walk the talk' and take some real action to address the lack of gender parity.

Bob said, "*I have always believed in creating a healthy mix of leaders on the team. I have seen the business benefits that this balance brings. I also believe that it's just the right thing to do. As I watch how gender parity is not progressing as quickly as anticipated, it's important to me that we all take responsibility to do something to make change happen. As our daughters, my own included, grow up and enter employment, it's vital that we remove the barriers that affect their opportunities to progress and achieve their full potential.*

"*I knew I needed a more diverse team around the table. I believe we need to be more purposeful in managing great talent. We have become so institutionalised and we hang on to the wrong things. This is not just about hiring good women. This is not about a better mix. This is about creating a more powerful leadership table around you. We need to get support for women and help them to get to a place that they weren't before.*

"At Washington Mutual we had an even 50:50 gender split, which was by accident, rather than design. I have never been involved in a better team. It was dynamic, successful, stronger and more rounded. When I went to Barclays I'd inherited a team of highly capable, corporate bankers. However, without any diversity amongst the team, it was a stark contrast. When we discussed things, I felt we were all in agreement, without any diverse perspectives to challenge our thinking. I felt we were just going to be doing the same things and not fully realising our ambitious vision. I had to take the mantle, and built a stronger, more diverse team. You need diversity of thought and opinion around you as a leader and to be open to listening to those wide ranging opinions.

"I had two mid-management level female Area Directors who were very successful. When I was interviewing for a Regional Director role and asked them, they said to me that they weren't ready yet. Retail Banking is about dealing with people, but they gave me every reason why it wasn't the right role for them at that time. If there are ten boxes to tick for a role and these talented women leaders ticked nine of them, then they feel uncomfortable. It's a big journey to break down the stigmas. We need to think more about the mix and give them more confidence to step forward.

"The pipeline that we see now shows growth throughout our management and leadership positions. We are now showing a higher proportion of female leaders, but we still have work to do to get women into director level positions. It's about getting the best mix in the team. I feel frustrated that this has not caught on elsewhere in executive teams. We have a bunch of men saying the right words, but they have not consciously done more. I believe they value men, or the alpha female. We must have individual leaders making the change happen. We can't change the business, but we can showcase what makes great results and then ask, 'how can you get involved?'

"We need to build better role models. It does concern me when I hear lots of fine words being said. At senior levels there's a lot of outward championship, but not really a lot happening at the leadership table itself. "I had a recent open position heading up the mortgage division. Recruiters were telling me 'there were no females out there'. My response was that I believed there were talented females out there. I said if they

couldn't find them, then I would need to find new recruiters who knew different kinds of talent. Doing the recruitment process fast would have been great, but mentally I could not justify leaving out the best female talent. I knew there were plenty out there; we just needed to work harder at tapping into this talent.

"As a leader, people know where I stand. I'm pretty much black and white and they feel confident that there's not too much variance. I make sure that I don't get emotionally too high, or too low. So in the bad times, I don't get too upset. In the good I celebrate, whilst maintaining balance. This inner calmness helps me to maintain my health and keep my blood pressure low. For the most part, I am easy to read. I take care of my team around me and they take care of me. We achieve great success and we do this through working our butts off! I choose to trust people first; this has led to great successes very quickly.

"We set up a dual mentor programme with our executive committee and worked hard to help remove 'unconscious bias'. We need to force the issue, no matter how unpopular it may be. We need to take chances on people to balance out the team more. I have never been in a team that's not been a good mix. As a large-scale leader, 'presenteeism' persists in organisational culture. I never doubt that they aren't working as hard as everyone else. One of our leaders works from home a lot, as he values balance and family. He's one of the most effective people and hard-working people I know, yet he's concerned that he's not seen enough at work. This is an issue for male and female leaders that needs to be addressed."

Principles and Behaviours

I believe that there are a number of key behaviours (the 5 Cs) that are essential to MQ:

- Conscience
- Consideration
- Compassion
- Courage
- Commitment

There is a growing ethos of maximising personal economic wealth and opportunity. These virtues encourage us to regulate our thinking for more rational and caring choices that contribute to the greater good. With values and beliefs often deeply buried in our psyche, understanding these at a conscious level is important to making the right choices, when conflict does arise. Appreciating differences, as much as the similarities, is key to our relationships. Equally critical is the ability to discern between misguided loyalty and sound moral judgement intended to seek the truth and do the right thing.

Conscience: *The choice for doing the right thing, not because it's governed by laws and regulation, but because we fundamentally believe and know it is the right thing to do.*

Consideration: *The choices we make taking in all of the facts from those around us. Listening to our own internal dialogue and intuition, to make considered judgements and decisions with the absence of bias and the presence of equity and fairness.*

Compassion: *We live by fundamental basic human rights and universal principals. We see others through compassionate and caring eyes, recognising our differences. We are not judgemental about others' choices.*

Courage: *We are not the silent witnesses, or should live in 'wilful blindness' ignoring what is morally wrong. We take action and become the catalyst for change. Leadership is often a lonely place, particularly when the dominant culture is being challenged. It is everyone's right and it is everyone's duty.*

Commitment: *We must empower others, and ourselves in order to become more accountable for the changes that need to take place. This means creating strategies that are sustainable beyond today. We must role model excellence ourselves or run the risk of breaking other's trust.*

Know that you are far from powerless; you are more powerful than you can possibly imagine. You have huge potential that must not be limited by fear. Each day we hear stories of courageous acts. Take the story of Malala Yousafzai, the Pakistani girl shot by Taliban gunmen on a school bus because of her campaign for girl's rights to education. The attack has only served to make her more resolute in her campaigning. Whilst extreme, we all have the potential and power to create acts of leadership, at varying levels, in our daily lives.

Case Study:
Unilever – When Businesses Do the Right Thing

Unilever and their powerful commitment to delivering a 10-year Sustainable Living Plan have impressed me. They make a difference right across the value chain. It represents each of the components of the Inspiring Leadership model and I believe at its foundation is a vision based on moral principles and ethical behaviours. They have taken direct responsibility for creating better lives, through their decisions and actions. They run Sustainable Living Labs to create a global dialogue between governments, consumers, NGOs and other businesses to generate solutions for key topics. They are making significant progress at every level, setting the tone for inspirational leadership. As a consequence Unilever leaves a positive legacy, including how they ethically source materials, setting the highest bar for nutritional standards right through to enabling better livelihoods.

Unilever aren't new to making sound judgements, based on what's right for customers. Dove's advertising campaigns celebrate the natural physical variation embodied by all women and inspire them to have the confidence to be comfortable with themselves.

Their latest campaign, 'Dove Real Beauty Sketches' available on YouTube, is a three-minute video showing a succession of women sitting behind a curtain. They describe themselves to a forensic sketch artist, who is unable to see them. The women use uncomplimentary language as they describe what they look like such as a chin that protrudes particularly when smiling, a large forehead and a fat rounder faces. The artist dutifully draws, including the imperfections they've described.

The exercise is repeated, but this time asking both men and women to describe the women in question, whom they had met earlier in the day. How others saw these women were far more gracious and admiring than the women had described of themselves. Both pictures were presented to the women at the end. They were visibly moved by the more flattering pictures based on the descriptions made by others.

I will be the first to acknowledge that I have at times been my own worst critic. I realise the implications this has had for my daughter, Alanadh. As one woman in the video describes, *"I should be more grateful of my natural beauty. It impacts the jobs we apply for, how we treat our children. It impacts everything. It couldn't be more critical to your happiness."* Whilst another observes, 'How we spend a lot of time analysing and trying to fix the things that aren't quite right. We should spend more time appreciating the things that we do like'.

This Dove campaign was a simple exercise that shifts so many women's views. I'm convinced I'm not the only one who breathed a sigh of relief at the very fact that an organisation had taken an ethical stance in advertising. It certainly influenced the purchasing choices that I made thereon in, feeling compelled to reward the courageous and compassionate choices Unilever's Dove brand had made.

P&G have also released their latest Pantene 'Be Strong and Shine' advert, which tackles labels against women. Clear and striking, both approaches are very poignant.

For me however, there is a subtle - yet crucial - difference between the two. One campaign is responding to the hype surrounding a topical agenda. It reinforces the 'trendy' language that raises emotion. Yet, it sustains a certain stereotypical image of beauty and women. Whereas, the other campaign gets to the heart of a deeper issue in our society, tackling the cause of perceptions and uses images, which is more reflective of the real consumer sentiment. **Both** are receiving widespread acclaim. Each engenders different attitudes, triggering different emotions. I think it's important that we become more *discerning* in these attitudes and our resulting solutions as leaders and consumers. We must aim for real and authentic change. Only then we will get to the heart of the issues.

Please take the time to look both adverts up on You Tube to experience the full impact of two different advertising campaigns:

1)   Dove 'Real Beauty Sketches Campaign - 'You are more beautiful than you think'

2)   Pantene Campaign – 'Be Strong and Shine'

Inspiring Women Leaders' Words of Wisdom

1. A strong work ethic offers independence and career success

"I've always had a strong work ethic and worked through my school and university years. I've been working since I was 9 years old, my first job was shovelling horse manure. It gave me independence and money to buy myself books and sweets."

2. Establishing boundaries based on what you value

"I always made a career decision never to have to commute. I decided this early on and so always made sure that I was within a good radius of home and work, always only ever 20 minutes away."

3. Remain authentic to yourself and your relationships

"My husband passed away a few months ago. We motivated, coached and supported each other in our marriage and as parents. For me, there is no difference between roles of: wife, professional and parent. Be caring, dignified and honest. You don't just do it outside work. You need to have balance and you need to know who you are."

4. Appreciating others' values and needs

"My husband was a typical Uruguayan-Italian man and I feel our relationship was affected by my success; he felt threatened. Instead of enabling him, I would tell him not to worry and that I was going to look after him. Eventually he became emasculated and so instead of helping, I had made things worse. If you don't respect their needs, then this is detrimental."

5. Courage to do the right thing by being the 'Interrupter'

"I find it disappointing when people say one thing and then do something else. I tend to call this out, which gets me into hot water at times! I like to think that I'm doing a tiny bit where I can to change behaviours."

6. Being the steward for sustainable decisions with positive impact

"We need to be guardians of the organisation for now and in the future, make a difference and leave the business in a better shape."

7. Be culturally aware and sensitive, choose the right battles

"It's important to keep your values but to understand how these fit culturally. Do things in a way that make the business feel comfortable. Choose your battles, learn at what point you need to call things out. The coaching I was provided enabled me to notice the signals."

8. Aligning values so what's most important is not compromised

"Who you work for matters. You need to line up your value system to match for whom you work. I now work for a family man, who absolutely believed in the importance of family, devoting his time to them. He has strong values, whilst also being successful in his career. He is a mentor to me to this day."

9. Always treat people with dignity and respect

"The MD left me to close things down; we were making most of our people redundant. It was the most formative and informative time. I learned how I could be empathetic, but also sensitive to the business needs. How do you achieve your own values, with a corporate that must make lots of money? How do you behave? You don't have to treat others badly in tough circumstances. You just need to think about how you would like to be treated; tempering expression of your own needs with those of others."

Chapter Reflection:
Are we doing the right thing?

Moral integrity is so fundamental to the trust that customers place in organisations. It is also key to the trust that society place in their governments, or families place on each other. When it becomes fractured, it has the potential to detrimentally affect all other components of the Inspiring Leadership model - such as health and welling, brand and reputation, social intelligence and empathy. Starting your journey with MQ is a key to success across the entire model. Ask yourself the following questions:

Myself: *How do I live my life, based on my values and with integrity, by making choices and speaking up about what is right?*

If my values and beliefs are being compromised, what are the courageous actions I need to take now to make a positive step forward?

My Relationships: *What would those people who matter say about how I live my own values and understand the importance of others' values?*

What are the boundaries that I need to create to protect what I value in my relationships and ensure they are not compromised?

My Organisation: *How does our culture embody our values and create transparency and trust by enabling people to have the confidence to know that they are doing the right thing?*

How effective is our strategy in ensuring we operate in a fair and ethical way; one that positively impacts our stakeholders and environment?

My Society: *What power do I give myself to be the 'interrupter', rather than the bystander?*

What is my unrealised potential and passion for doing more?

Chapter 6

PQ: Purpose and Meaning

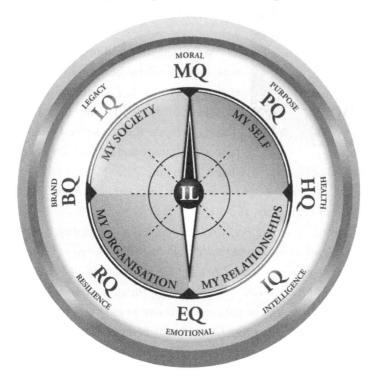

"We think we have to be superwomen, however, actually we need to shift this to being a role model. I have learned to pay attention to what matters most. I don't always get it right. What I do appreciate, as my kids have grown up, is how very important being present is – being in the here and now. Their decisions and life-changing events that occur for them now, require my attention more than ever before. I have become far better at managing the family now. It's OK me being in the mix and having a career. It's so important that the kids see that. This way I become a role model for them. We need to readjust our mentality to consider the things you love versus the things that you hate."

Ginny Ertl
Director of Executive Education in Consulting

Isabelle Santoire
The Inspiring Woman Who Lives her Life on Purpose, Mountain Guide, France

On first meeting and interviewing Isabelle, I was so inspired by her combined passion and energy to bring her own ambitions to life. Against all the odds she had fulfilled her dreams, despite the naysayers! She adopted a powerful strategy and attitude for achieving her goals and has chosen to live her life 'on purpose'.

"I'm a 45 years old, French speaking woman from Quebec, now established in Chamonix, France.

"My parents were teachers and I completed university and also became a teacher, as it all seemed to fit really well. In 1989 I moved to Geneva, started working as a primary school teacher and continued my studies doing a Master in Adult education. Then I met my (now) husband. He had a very unusual way of life. His ambition was to live in the present and explore his passion for mountaineering. He didn't own anything, not even a pair of shoes. Everything had to fit in a rucksack: a pair of rock climbing shoes, mountaineering boots and flip-flops. I thought, 'How can you not be in the "system" like everyone else?' It was his attitude towards life that moved me. I absolutely loved the outdoor sports, however I couldn't steer away from my upbringing, values and the need to have a 'proper' job.

"We decided to share a project together; to ski across the Alps starting from Austria to Mont-Blanc. I was strong physically, but had never done anything like this. It was really fabulous, although we did have our up and down moments. Whilst we were away, I had sub-let my place in Geneva. When I got back there, absolutely everything had been stolen, from my clothes, my computer, and right down to my photos. It was very distressing. I was left with my pair of skis and my Volkswagen. However, I felt I could either just cry, or move on with my life. I didn't know where I was going, but I had the confidence that I had to go! Sometimes you need a wake-up call in life. Instead of feeling miserable for myself, I perceived this event as a

chance. This was my chance to detach myself from any material bonds and explore the outdoors, as a way of life.

"My husband went to the Antarctic for 18 months, which gave me space to figure out what I needed. By the time he got back, our roles had reversed and I was taking him out climbing.

"I realised I wanted to find a job in the outdoor industry. Becoming an 'accompagnateur' (which is the qualification to take groups on hikes) would be a great way to continue my outdoor pursuits. I asked for the application forms. All my walks/hikes had been approaches to start climbing a mountain. I hadn't realised just how much experience in the mountains around the world I had gathered for being a Mountain Guide.

"People would say to me that, because I was a woman and very petite, in addition to not being French, it was really unlikely that I would break the barriers and become a mountain guide. That was enough for me to go for it!

"I had to complete an application, which was followed by a series of exams. One of the physical tests had changed, due to poor weather conditions and we had to run/jump through a boulder field within one and a half minutes. It wasn't really a fair test, with too many candidates; it was set up for many to fail. This first year I failed drastically. Three women had tried and all had failed. Everyone said I should complain, but no - I wanted to come back the following year. I didn't want people to think that I was given special privileges for being a woman.

"The failure made me really determined. I got very focused on my training, including interval running, and made myself even stronger. The next year I applied again. I prepared myself mentally for the possibility of failing and told myself that it was OK; I would just do something else. But I passed! The director of the school came to congratulate me. People said, 'Do you realise why he did that?' It was because I had got the best average of the 235 candidates that had applied.

"There are about 23 women and over 1500 men that are qualified Mountain Guides in France. Only about a handful of these women actually work full-time in mountaineering. People recognise me as we stand out; it feels very strange to be a local icon!

"Climbing, mountaineering and skiing had been my main focus for ten

years. I had only been fully qualified for two years, when I decided to have a child. I was 38 years old at the time. I knew it meant that I would also have to change my aspirations. I had a trip booked to South America, when I found out I was pregnant. I sought advice from my doctor, as it was planned for when I would be six months in. He said he wouldn't give the same advice to all women, but in my case, it wouldn't be a problem, as long as I listened to my body, and I would just need to get acclimatised because of the high altitude. To prepare, I climbed Mont Blanc a few times to make sure that I was ready to go. I went to Peru and hiked with a group of eight 'strong women', sleeping in tents at an altitude of 5300m. It was a wonderful experience and I gave birth to a healthy son with very healthy lungs!

"During the birth I dislocated my pelvic bone. Initially we didn't know what it was and the pain had completely blocked out my memory of how to walk. It was a very scary moment of my life; I could not remember the simple movement of walking! I was bed-bound for two months, using a Zimmer frame and wheeling my son around. By the third month I was back ice climbing again. I put this down to my positive attitude; physically and mentally I was very strong. I find it very hard to sit down and being in bed for two months was just the incentive to get moving again. I always like to push my limits and yet, at the same time, to listen to the advice I am given. I was absolutely rigorous about getting back into shape. I had my daughter a couple of years later.

"As a Mountain Guide, I go through life at an intense pace. However, I do believe that behind every good female leader, there is also a good man. My husband helps a lot with the house and the kids. In fact, he does probably more house chores than me. We have the same profession and we organise ourselves, so that one of us is always home with the children.

"However, I feel I am still responsible for a lot of the family logistics. It's very demanding both at work and at home. I am a worrier and I find it hard to let go. My husband is different to me in this way. He's more relaxed about it and he goes off to work, without thinking about it. Whereas I'm still thinking about what needs to be done and the logistics of it all, such as school, food, vaccinations, kids' activities, winter clothes, etc. As women I think we are perfectionists. We want things done our way and we worry more

about unnecessary details. I do notice that when I am away, it all does get done! The difference is my husband can be away for days back to back, whereas I now take on fewer contracts than I used to and I manage to create breaks. I organise my schedule to look after my health and wellbeing. My family is a big part of my life and it is also a big part of my wellbeing.

"What I do to personally let go is rock-climbing just for me. It's like my own form of yoga; it helps me to get focused and centred which is great for keeping a balance.

"My children are now 7 and 4 years old. I finished in 2005 as a qualified Mountain Guide and I've now built up my business to provide different and customised experiences for people, giving them the 'WOW' factor. I've noticed the combination of being a woman and my personality helps put people at ease, allowing them to relax and enjoy their leisure time in the mountains. It's not about reaching the summit for people; it really is the journey. They come with their work, or families and their life stories. It is incredible for me to be able to meet people with such diverse backgrounds and to be able to share with them. I often meet high-powered people, who just love to let go of their responsibilities. Mountaineering is accessible to most people. I help to challenge their perceived limitations and push their mental barriers; to move them beyond their comfort zone. At the same time, I respect their needs and levels, so they enjoy the whole experience. It's a great way for people to really learn about themselves, face their perceived limitations and the reality of what they can actually achieve. These are empowering moments.

"As a guide, I need to respect my body physically, taking time to rest. When you run your own business, then it is hard turning work away, as you are concerned about maintaining you contacts and the momentum of your business. My focus is to develop more quality work around what I want to do. When I take a break in between work contracts, it helps me staying fresh. It is important that I'm physically and mentally well. I also feel that the quality time, I am able to share 'en famille', gives me a lot of energy.

"I believe that you have to do something that you really enjoy. It has to be authentic for you. It's not about just doing things because others say you should be doing them. You need to work in accordance with who you are. At

first, I didn't think I wanted to be a Mountain Guide, as I didn't fit the stereotype. Now I believe that you just need to connect with what you feel inside, even if you cannot justify all the reasons that make you do it. You need to move on and go, even if you don't know the final destination.

"I do feel guilty for things that aren't necessarily within my control. If there's something happening, I take it as my responsibility, or my problem. I'm always saying sorry, even if it was nothing to do with me! I wonder if it's a personality trait, or a woman thing. It's the same with my work. I give it my best every time and I always want to bring the best out of people, but if it doesn't go quite as I'd planned, then I feel responsible. With experience and maturity, I've learnt to accept that you can't do everything and please everyone.

"I've also learnt that you have to take things step by step. If I were to look at me becoming a Mountain Guide as a whole project, then I would have felt over-whelmed by it. You just need to take one objective, do it and then move on to the next. When I take people up Mont-Blanc, by the time they reach 4,000m the altitude slows down our progress. At that moment, when they look at the summit, they feel intimidated. I advise them to take it step by step, setting achievable objectives and moving on from there. To me this just all makes sense.

"I am now launching a project called 'Inspiration 4,000m' to raise greater awareness about mountaineering. Over the last 20 years, I have shared and guided people who have extraordinary life-stories. I have decided to find a framework to capture these authentic 'voices' of passion for the mountains. In the next few years, I will be focusing my climbing and skiing on ascents of the classic 4,000m peaks of the Alps. This is not about performance, but a journey with people I have met and will meet along my guiding career. The project is about sharing other people's stories in the most amazing mountain setting of The Alps."

Want to get involved? Isabelle and I are working together with a team of executive coaches to launch new and exciting expeditions to support women in their leadership and wellbeing as part of the many fundraising initiatives for the Inspiring Leadership Trust, a charity established to help positively change the lives of some of the most vulnerable women and young people around the world. See www.inspiringleadershiptrust.com for further information and to get involved.

Definition of PQ: Purpose and Meaning

My son, Daniel, came home from the Metropolitan Police, after another 16-hour shift. Not surprisingly, he looked exhausted. At the end of an already long shift, he had spent the rest of the night in hospital with a victim. The team had rescued this man who'd been horrifically attacked with multiple knife wounds to his face and body. After eating his food, Daniel came to hug me goodnight and said, *"You know, Mum, I really look forward to going to sleep, because I'm excited that when I wake up I can get back to my Police work"*. Daniel is an MSC – Metropolitan Police Special Constable, which means he's a volunteer. He was recently promoted to Sergeant after a mere eight months. His lifelong ambition has been to join the police and he is passionate about what he does. At 21 years old, he is very clear that his purpose in life is to keep people safe. How powerful is it that? He has found a purpose that not only compels him to make the choice to go to work each day, but one that he actually loves and is excited by. The challenge is that, in our hyper-busy world, we may start out with such clarity but, along the way, we often lose sight of the 'why?'

Choosing to get up and go to work each day, when we have the 'draw' of staying at home with the family, or life outside of work, is directly correlated with the value of our work. It is a dilemma. We may ask, "Does my work make a difference? Do I believe I add value? Do other people feel that I add value?" I acknowledge that we all have a purpose and we all believe that we have been gifted with talents that help us to make a difference. At some point in our lives, most of us gain a really clear vision for how we can add value. Sadly, somehow this becomes diluted by life's louder demands.

PQ is not about 'what' we do. This is not the thing that compels us to do our job. It is all about 'why' we do what we do. It is about accessing our deepest sense of purpose and meaning in our lives. This is the reason for why we exist and it is our *'life calling'* (Jonathan Bowman-Perks, *Inspiring Leadership*[1]).

Through a forensic examination of the *'why?'*, *then* we can discover what truly drives and motivates us.

What is important is our view of the world and how we fit within it. By the mere act of building a clear personal vision and goals, that we confidently pursue, we are more likely to achieve them through the 'laws of attraction'. Go after it. Paradoxically, you also need to be flexible and spot opportunities. The women I interviewed have found their greatest successes came, not through traditional career structures, but from the unexpected leads to discovering their PQ. They have embraced these opportunities, rather than feared it. It is the subtle difference between career stagnation and career success.

I am observing a fundamental shift in societal rules around PQ. While somewhat unusual for many cultures, it is no longer the assumption that the woman alone manages these issues of balancing work and home. It has become a positive discussion for joint ownership about what it is that's most important when establishing boundaries between work, home and relationships.

When reflecting on the importance of having a clear sense of purpose in one of those three areas (work), I am inspired by Walt Disney. In Capodagli and Jackson's book, *The Disney Way*, they crystallise the secrets of Walt Disney's success and his strong PQ. When he was asked about his success, he explained, "I *dream*, I test my dreams against my *beliefs*, I *dare* to take risks, and I *execute* my vision to make those dreams come true." *Dream, Believe, Dare, Do*: these are deeply rooted values that permeate across the Walt Disney enterprise. There were plenty of naysayers, "no-one will sit through a 90-minute cartoon", but he tenaciously carried on, pursuing his 'life calling'.

This requires cultivating a deep awareness of ourselves and curiosity for understanding what inspires us, leveraging our strengths and passions to best effect. It means that we don't get caught up in someone else's plans. Let's not be blind to our own needs. This awareness and experience gives us confidence to take control and determine our own 'life plan'. Through pure ambition and drive, we are not held back by our inner voice, one that constrains and inhibits us from achieving what is possible. We are able to align ourselves and our business to a powerful cause that holds greater meaning.

When we are clear on our values and beliefs (MQ) and we are living our life 'on purpose', then we find the confidence and resolutely pursue a worthy goal, or cause. It helps us to make the courageous decisions on our direction, especially when we experience conflict. It drives us to take more risks – calculated risks, of course! By defining the 'why we do what we do', then a compelling vision and story emerge. This has the capacity to capture the hearts and minds of those we are in service of.

Maintaining Balance

A common theme that has emerged strongly in all of my research is the grasp that inspiring leaders have on creating the right balance across all of the Four Environments of Focus: My Self, My Relationships, My Organisation, My Society. They are supremely protective of what's most important to them in order to sustain their passions in a healthy way. They are very clear on what cannot be compromised. They achieve this by establishing clear boundaries and negotiating the rules of play with their spouses, their children and their work. They have a clear vision for their relationships and their work and it's based on their own terms. This conviction gives them the courage to ask for what they need. Their plans are not infallible and watertight, of course. When they make mistakes, as we all inevitably do, however, they understand this to be an opportunity to re-evaluate, learn and, if need be, alter their direction.

The challenge, in our fast paced world, is to not let our vision get blurred! It is clear that those who feel truly successful are those who take the time out to reflect and evaluate on PQ regularly. It allows us the time to become more introspective, exploring what we desire most, in order to think creatively about our futures. It creates the space for a healthy perspective about what is most important and enables a re-alignment when we are slightly off course. By thinking about our future, it helps to bring context and rationale for what we do today.

Of course, all of this firmly focuses us on the future. We must have something to strive for in order to learn, grow and realise our full potential.

Without this, there is the risk of complacency and stagnation. In this respect, there is a strong correlation between, on the one hand, the quality of our learning (IQ), enhancing the potential opportunity for discovering our purpose and, on the other hand, achieving the full possibility of our vision and goals. By expanding our horizons to establish breadth, we are able to make wise and informed decisions, whilst holding on to what's core to us. It gives us the leadership gravitas through being relevant, whilst also progressive.

Searching for Meaning

PQ is, importantly, about a sense of gratitude for 'what is' in the *here* and *now*. As eloquently described by Isabelle in her personal story: *"It's not about reaching the summit for people, it really is the journey."* Counter-intuitively, by slowing down our pace and being in the present, we notice more and are far more creative. This is not just a soft statement, but also a hard fact, based on the latest in neurobiological research. For example, when we are in a hyper-busy state, we impede our ability to think effectively, as our body releases too much of the stress hormone, cortisol. By combining presence and reflection, at a more controlled pace, we instead release chemicals such as the vitality hormone DHEA, which enables more creative thinking and enhanced relationships.

Viktor E. Frankl, a psychiatrist and holocaust survivor, wrote an outstanding classic, *Man's Search For Meaning*. He identified that hope and courage is derived from the profound realisation that, 'love is the ultimate and the highest goal to which man can aspire... I understood how a man who

has nothing left in this world still may know bliss'. This is a powerful message for an appreciation of what, in the end, has true meaning and so ultimately make us sincerely happy.

As **Sayyeda Salam** said, we need to take action to fulfil our passion and truly make a difference: *"I was fascinated with Middle-Eastern politics and passionate about understanding the world. Yet I was* *never quite sure how to challenge it. I went on lots of political rallies, but then came to the realisation that I had not changed the situation. I needed to change the situation from within and so pursued a career that helped me become more influential and make a greater impact. I wanted to work in a part of society that was for the betterment of society as a whole."* Doing what truly adds meaning and purpose gives us great fulfilment and happiness.

Happiness is our birth-right. When we define happiness, we take it back to its essence. In the pursuit of happiness, we find energy and thrive. The achievement of happiness is essential to healthy, abundant and successful living. When we build a vision for our lives, does it encompass having fun, or have we just become a bit too serious about it all lately?

Once we have a clear understanding of the 'why', it's essential that we get to work on the how!

Setting the Purpose from the Top

Working for Scandinavian Airlines, I was deeply privileged to have experienced the leadership of one of the most influential and inspiring leaders of my career - Jan Carlzon. He took over the helm as CEO when the business was in financial difficulties. It was losing $17m per year and internationally renowned for all the wrong things, like poor service. He revolutionised the airline industry through his unrelenting focus on customer service. He introduced a number of 'firsts': decentralised the organisation and building a cultural change programme that delegated responsibility for making decisions and, so, empowered employees within the organisation to resolve issues themselves.

With a complete overhaul of the corporate identity within the first year and increased morale, SAS became the most punctual airline. This was swiftly followed by improved bottom-line results turning into profit. The turnaround has been used widely as MBA case studies and Carlzon wrote a book, which translates into *Tear the Pyramids Down*, documenting the turnaround. This was later translated and called *Moments of Truth*.

When I was leading SAS's talent and learning agenda, I was working on a requirements diagnostic for the business to enable leadership performance.

Ground staff recounted the many times they had come into contact with Jan, describing him as authentic and walking his talk. One check-in agent described how, when there was a queue, she had offered for Jan to fast track through. He thanked her but declined, wanting to share the full customer experience, whether good, or bad. Carlzon famously said, "Mistakes can usually be corrected later; the time that is lost in not making a decision can never be retrieved".

He created a compelling vision, yet enabled the organisation to deliver to achieve success. This engendered trust and loyalty, which has the capacity to deliver positive and radical change very quickly. Our people notice our leadership; hence, walking the talk is essential for any inspiring leader.

Consequences of Lack of PQ

Continuing the story, in Jan Carlzon's latter years, he came under increased pressure from stakeholders, as the competition caught up. In Michael Maccoby's contribution to the book *Leadership Insights*, HBR, he describes Carlzon's deathly fall from the heady heights of leadership for SAS, cutting short what was a brilliant career. In it he describes how Carlzon ignored the issue of high costs, even when many observers pointed out that SAS could not compete, without improving productivity. He threw money at expensive and unnecessary acquisitions... propelled by a need to expand his organisation, rather than develop it... leading the company deeper and deeper into losses, he was fired. In the spotlight of success, leaders can get seduced by its opulence, very quickly destroying an impeccable track record. In this fast-paced changing world, we must be able to hire leaders who can shape the future. However, it comes with a risk. If they do not have the finger on the pulse of their business and do not listen to the sound advice of their teams, the potential for these leaders is to self-destruct. A leader's arrogance and appetite for the grandiose and high-risk strategies has been proven to ripple out from the leader to affect organisations and our society.

PQ and the Dark Side

There is a darker side to PQ. Sometimes leaders can use the 'why?' to justify everything they do, even when it is lacking MQ. On the extreme we have Adolf Hitler's aggressive and racially motivated leadership, who justified why he launched his 'final solution' and extermination of Jews and Gipsies by his need to create a pure, Aryan master race.

Some business leaders justify unethical behaviour by their need to make profit through an obsessive focus on results. In turn, this leads their supporters to go to any lengths to hit their imposed targets. It is inspiring leadership we are seeking, not manipulation.

On a lighter note, in Joachim de Posada's TED Talk, 'Don't Eat the Marshmallow', he presents a humorous account of the marshmallow experiment. It was carried out on 4 year olds in Columbia and was a repeat of an experiment conducted by Stanford University. The children were told they would be left in the room, alone with a marshmallow, for 15 minutes. If they didn't eat the marshmallow, they would receive a second as a reward. Two out of three children ate the marshmallow. Years later, 100% of the children that didn't eat the marshmallow were successful in their lives and careers. With impulse control and self-discipline being a key factor to success, it presents us with a stark reality check about the significant benefits of 'delayed gratification'.

It would appear that we have built a purpose with the sole aim of economic growth. As Roger Steare, the Corporate Philosopher warns, "*the concept of exponential growth, year on year, in a closed system that is the philosophy of the cancel cell!*" The culture of commercialism and 'get rich quick' was thought to be a good thing. With no sense of responsibility for its implications, it has led to perilous results. We have built structures that reward short-termism. Our focus has been on creating greater personal power and delivering ever increasing shareholder value. We have witnessed now how these decisions to deliver profits, above all else, offer dangerous pretence. By establishing a vision and strategy that fails to balance risk with certainty, or ethics with immediate gain, it has been underpinned by poor quality products and services. If the purpose is to be the biggest and the best, we see resulting toxic behaviours.

Leadership traits, such as greed, narcissism and even white-collar psychopaths, have compromised our establishments and society as a whole. Our television screens and media are filled with the inept and talentless opportunists talking drivel. They are looking for a quick road to success and incredibly swiftly become role models to some of our children. Our political leaders play power-games, or popularist politics, in order to win, at the expense of the countries they lead. Many of our financial institutions have been gambling and their out-of-control alchemy has pushed our economy to the brink of collapse. Our health and education systems are buckling under the pressure of bureaucracy, micro-management and disempowerment. Short-term reward systems lacking long-term, sustainable meaning and purpose (LQ and PQ) are apt to lead to disaster.

One leader recalled when she started her new role, "*I naively thought that I could get three months maternity leave and go part-time. I was told by my boss at the time "...you have to cut the cord and choose between your home, and your career responsibilities." I swiftly realised that I couldn't do part-time and although I continued to work hard, I had no extra passion and energy and didn't give any more discretionary effort. It's hard, when your heart is no longer in the job. Who you work for really, really matters. You need to line up your value system and it has to match with whom you work for. I worked for a family man, who was devoted to his family, with strong values, whilst also being successful in his career. He is a mentor to me to this day.*"

Many of us live in a fast-feedback based culture, where our structures and systems reward pre-defined success criteria. We often judge ourselves by others' definitions of success and it becomes very personal. We lose sight of our own view of what contributes to our real purpose and what provides meaning in both our work and life. Even when we know our purpose and how to get there, fear can be one of biggest blockers, causing us to procrastinate and avoid taking any action.

Chasing the Dream

I am a recovering busyness-aholic! In my early career, I believed I had a real sense of purpose. I had bought my first house when I was 18 years old, I had my two beautiful children and had an amazing career. I had a great balance between it all. As my career grew, so did its importance in my life. I started chasing the dream: more money to buy the fancy car, the bigger house and the perfect life. All were material symbols of success. The more I chased the dream, the more that the present life I had, whizzed by. With the juggling act, I became only partially present with others. When I was at home, I was thinking about work and when I was at work, I was thinking about family logistics! I never really shut my mind off from work.

My days were booked up with meetings. So my real work had to be done in the evenings after midnight, after I'd cooked and cleaned. I remember asking my husband if we could have a cleaner, because I couldn't do it all. When he refused, I felt guilty about two things. One, that I couldn't seem to put it all together and two, that I didn't have the courage to stand up for what I needed and outsource the things that didn't matter to me. I remember my kids would use the opportunity, when I was working on my laptop, to get me to agree to things, which I'd normally say no to! Working on four hours sleep a night, I was drinking Redbull during the day in order to keep me going! As I reflect and look back, I know that I had a deep subconscious fear driving me. I never wanted again to be in a situation where I felt insecure. I wanted to know we would always have a home, no matter what. I believed that if I had plenty of money, then I would avoid the terrifying situation of the bailiffs knocking at my door, as happened to me when I grew up.

At work, we were being asked to do the dreaded 'deep-dives'. These intense inquisitions into every minute detail were popularised by 'neutron' Jack Welsh in GE. They were then mistakenly copied by other unimaginative, over-controlling managers. We would spend weeks and weeks analysing and re-cutting data for the executive team, creating HR presentation decks that must have been about three inches thick. Everything in terms of delivering for the business came to a standstill. It was such a waste of everyone's time; it was madness! The onerous task was more about proving our worth and protecting the team. In such a culture of fear, our presentations were grounded in appeasing the leader. It was so tense and intense; you could cut the air with a knife. No one was truly *thinking*; we were just reacting and protecting ourselves. As the latest casualty emerged from the deep-dive, you didn't really want to be next person to be presenting your results. We couldn't wait for the process to be over, so we could get back to real work and our day jobs. 'What was it all for?' was the question in everyone's minds. Developing talent in the organisation had started to become a data exercise, rather than a leadership exercise.

The crucible moment for me came during a two-week holiday in Johannesburg. It created much-needed time and space to reflect and re-evaluate. I realised my life was seriously out of control. I needed to regain some 'focused balance' - on my work, my relationships and myself. I also believed that I had the capacity to add greater value and I needed more meaning and purpose from the work I was doing. I knew I wanted to experience the world and not be so insular. I knew I wanted to make a difference in society. With my friend, I had created a 'bucket list' - listing all the things we wanted to do before we died.

I returned to London and resigned from work. I started my own company, Clareo Potential, with a vision for developing leadership excellence that was fit for the 21st century. As I was keen to have a clear purpose to my business, I built a 'tithings' model, where we reinvest a percentage of profits and time back into community projects. I invested in my personal development, which has enabled me to deliver leadership programmes around the world: from the Ministry of Health in Botswana to the Arctic Circle with high net-worth individuals, to FTSE companies across Europe and the US. I restructured my work in a way that now works for both my family and myself.

Looking After Ourselves

In writing this book, I have come to realise the importance of giving to 'self', as much as to those around you. It is a crucial component of leadership. Admittedly this is often the area that is the last area to get focused on and the first to go! Stepping out to do my own thing was not an easy step, particularly as a single Mum again. I have felt the weight of responsibility and of dependency and so almost lost my nerve. My coach, who's been extremely wise, observed how this was the time to reflect on what is most important, as I'd lost my sense of self. With a big vision, but shallow pockets, I have learned that holding onto my purpose, whilst building successes for today, is crucial to the bigger game. Knowing and experiencing this in 'real time' has helped me to hold my nerve and enjoy the ride.

Establishing Boundaries

There was a clear distinction between specific groups in my research. One group is those that are living life 'on purpose' and have defined clear boundaries around what is most important. They have either reached, or are working towards creating, a more *'balanced focus'* between work, their relationships, their society and themselves. They were noticeably centred and content. There was also another group that talked openly about their compassion and commitment to a particular 'cause'- this was mostly their work. They recognised at times this was at the cost of something else. Often it was at the expense of their relationships, either destroying them, or even possibly not having a relationship at all. Mostly though, it was that it was at the expense of 'self'. It often took a 'crucible moment', a life-altering event, which resulted in a re-calibration of their PQ.

Goal Obsession

Research shows that once our basic needs are met, in the endless pursuit of more - more success, more money, more status – then we are not actually increasing our level of happiness. On the contrary, it has the reverse affect. With the unrealised benefits of working harder and faster, in order to achieve the next goal, a restlessness and dissatisfaction emerges. In the obsession for achieving the goal, you can lose sight of your true purpose and meaning; what is most important to you. In striving for a 'better' future, then the 'present' has the potential to slip right by you, barely noticed, never mind savoured. Why does it often take a 'crucible moment', which involves a seismic shift or an unforeseen crisis, to make us re-evaluate meaning and purpose?

I recall the tragic story of the 1996 ascent of Everest, which illustrated the danger of 'goal obsession', misguided PQ and the unwise focus on achieving big, hairy, audacious goals (BHAG). Despite pushing on past the 2pm turn back time and receiving bad weather information that should have alerted them to terminal dangers, they continued to summit Everest. It was the worst year on record for disasters, when fifteen of those climbers achieved their goal of climbing to the top of the world's largest mountain. The problem was they never came back. They died in their obsession to reach the top and didn't factor in coming back! They also endangered the lives of many people who tried to save them from themselves. How often do we pursue our goals, despite all of the warning signs telling us to turn back and reassess?

Sense of Perspective

In my interviews with women in the humanitarian sector, I was struck by their passion and dedication as the 'unsung heroes'. The stories they shared were deep and emotional in a way that no leadership book could convey. These leaders had a sense of purpose, one that transcended any internal structures, or politics to a greater cause. By serving the most vulnerable and needy, they had a real sense of perspective. They, in particular, had made sacrifices on very personal levels. When you are dealing with the after-math of wars, natural disasters and issues of the Third World, I can empathise with their dilemma of turning the focus to oneself, when there is so much out there to be done to help people who really need you.

Societal norms and cultures have a significant impact on our vision of ourselves. As a result, we often live our lives based on others' expectations of us, rather than living life on purpose. Many women have found the courage to *respectfully* challenge the status quo and these norms. Fortunately, we are now seeing more women strive for what they truly believe in.

Liz Satow describes her own determination and independence, "*I grew up in a very conservative part of North India, where there was no local education in English. As a result, I attended an international boarding school, which was for more liberal than the environment at home. When we were older, my parents had us volunteer in a local hospital during the holidays. When people had baby girls, they would often cry – everyone wanted sons. All of this filtered in. I remember my parents combatting this by saying things like, 'you were our first child and we were so happy to have you'*`. But it was difficult to combat all the critical messages of the culture around me.*

"*When I became a teenager, the 'aunties' in the community noted that I shouldn't go out without my brother. My friends started staying indoors, learning how to cook. I was a tomboy; it was so difficult for me not to be outside running around with the boys. Unlike life at boarding school, there was a real limitation on what I could do when I went home. All of this has impacted my life decisions. So I am ferociously protective of my independence."*

The leaders I interviewed were all very determined and focused on succeeding. Success always looked different, so too were their styles and approaches. But their attitude and hard work ethos were consistent.

Nikki Flanders shared with me, "*I have a great desire to succeed, not just personally, but for the business. If I'm going to do something, then I must totally believe in it. Then I put my complete heart, force and effort into achieving what we set out to do. I recognise that with this comes a certain intensity. This can be quite disarming for others, as I expect the same type of passion and commitment from them. Sometimes it can be misinterpreted as more heart and less rational. I have had to learn to read different situations and adjust my 'dial' up, or down, as necessary. As a leader, you need to galvanise people to take action, which is more powerful than getting caught up in the doing. The key to success is taking a step back, to let people grow.*"

Creating Meaning

In our coaching, we have worked with leaders around the world to address their ability to make meaning and create a sense of purpose for themselves and their firms. We address such fundamental questions such as, "Why should anyone be led by you?" or "Why do you do the work that you do?" What quickly becomes clear is that something does not resonate, most noticeably in the somatic reaction to the question. They are comfortable explaining *what* they do, yet far less comfortable explaining the big reason *why* they do what they do. At times we're met with inertia, or apathy. Alternatively, a quiet desperation, or discontentment is apparent. For the highly creative, they seek to dull their anxiety by constantly chasing after new and shiny things!

It is in our nature to need a form of identity and purpose; it keeps us healthy and alive as human beings. However, our business is often confused with our ego's identity and we don't stop to re-evaluate. By spending too much time dwelling on the past, or striving hard for a better future, we forget about living for today. As described by Robert Holden in his book, *Success Intelligence*, "*People crave success, because they hope it will deliver salvation from the ego's self-attack. They hope that being able to say 'I've made it' saves them from their inner taunts... A busy life is not necessarily a life well lived. A busy work schedule is not evidence of any great accomplishment.*" If we learn to appreciate what is, then we will notice that the good already exists in the present.

Reassessing Meaning and Purpose

When writing *Inspiring Women Leaders*, I was 39 years old. What struck me from the research and interviews was just how much I recognised myself in others" stories. In my early career, how driven and focused I was on achievement, often came at the cost of something I cared about. It was about logistics and management for balancing family, work and finances! It was all about fitting in, at times adjusting myself to fit with other's views.

In my 30s, having achieved so much, I now have a desire to recalibrate to what is important to me. I asked myself, 'What's it all for?' This resulted in changing the work that I do and how I do it. This led to the end of a relationship that had grown apart. Then I shifted my emphasis onto the quality of relationships, rather than the quantity of my pay packet. Also I concentrated on a new belief; that I could make a greater difference, and I really want to. Letting go of an old identity, with its recurring unconscious patterns, is a tough move. They felt familiar and safe. However, as I got older and wiser - well just a little wiser – then I realised I needed to get back to my authentic self. I believed that, as I entered mid-life, it's now or never! I need to fulfil my dreams.

I started looking to my future and how I would work towards slowing down. However, listening to the interviews with women who represent my (potential) future, it caused me a huge paradigm shift about age. As much as I had recalibrated my expectations of mid-life, to determine what success looks like, they had done a similar exercise.

Given everything they'd accumulated, their wisdom and experience, they were energised and vibrant about their plans. It made me realise the level of potential, contribution and success that comes with each phase. It was also apparent how less stressed, less anxious they are. That was a deeply thought provoking revelation for me, as it felt like their 'outer journey' was far more in sync with their 'inner journey'.

In Jane Fonda's insightful presentation on TEDx Women, she describes how the, *"third act...is the developmental stage of life and it has its own significance...and we should all be asking how do we live this life successfully?... It's not having the experiences that make us wise. It's reflecting on the experiences that we've had, that makes us wise and helps us to become whole. It brings wisdom and authenticity and it helps us to become what we might have been."* I suppose, the big question is how we can live each act in our lives successfully, by our terms, and what can we derive and learn from ourselves and others to achieve happiness.

The Inner and Outer Journey

By the way, finding meaning is not the fluffy stuff. It is very real, hard and can't be avoided. One of the most frequent reasons for leadership dissatisfaction is the lack of PQ. I have seen leaders struggle and get very emotional during coaching and workshops, because they have lost their sense of purpose. Even more concerning, some leaders have never identified what their life purpose really is.

One example is Richard (name changed) a coaching client, who when viewing his 'outer journey' appeared to be a successful entrepreneur and a millionaire by the age of 40. However when discussing his 'inner journey' he felt depressed and that he lacked a sense of purpose about what to do for the rest of his life. There was a complete misalignment between what he was doing and what he wanted to be doing. It is often the case that we let old life patterns determine our present and our future.

There is acceptance of what is, because it has always been so. Neurobiological research gives a compelling reason for re-evaluation. These patterns are experiences that are neural pathways that become accepted and the norm.

Creating time to think of what our true life purpose is, then practicing behaviours that align with that vision can change these neural pathways.

Neuroscientists reveal that these neural connections are not 'hard wired' as has been the urban myth.

Within the brain the glial cells myelinate these new connections between their sister neurons and over time make these neural connections up to 100 times faster than our old connections and behaviours. Richard was creating brain plasticity and, literally, 'changing his mind' in order to produce an alternative, positive view of his future. The result? Richard became a leader who was calmer, more present with work and family, less anxious, no longer depressed, more inspiring and connected to those he led and starting to live his life "on purpose", not "off purpose".

How can PQ help you as a leader?

The sheer enthusiasm that is generated from a compelling vision, that is founded in purpose and meaning, is energising and motivational for any team. In Zohar and Marshall's book, *'Spiritual Capital',* they describe it as *transformative intelligence* that enables *meta-strategic thinking* and for us to create paradigm shifts. It allows us to, *'criticise what is from the point of view of what might be…imagine situations and possibilities that do not yet exist… and the ability to dissolve old patterns and ways of thinking.'*

Commercial astuteness is an essential expectation of leadership. So spending time leveraging the knowledge from both inside and outside of the business will help us to provide logic, whilst pushing the boundaries. There is no point us having a great vision that is completely out of touch with reality! This enables us to align the team to the most salient issues and opportunities to drive the business forward.

When we feel that we are adding value and have a sense of identity, we become loyal to and driven by our cause. What is so compelling and, yet, so under-utilised in organisations, is the powerful implications of this for us all. Being able to articulate the story for our business that is so compelling makes people want to work for us, buy our products, have us on their team. This has major positive effects at a neurobiological level. It releases chemicals such as the vitality hormone DHEA, dopamine to help us feel good and serotonin for healthy mental balance – all factors in creating excitement, energy and increased levels of thinking and creativity.

Eva Eisenschimmel shared with me, *"What I learned was that my fascination with language is really core to my leadership. What most people want, myself included, is a picture painted in a way that engages and inspires you to want to contribute. So they need a story or picture of where the business is going, what its values are and what it stands for. It must appeal to head and heart - both things.*

"Most businesses operate with the 'head' and yet I know I need to engage emotionally. I don't leap out of bed with excitement, because I believe that I'm going to do 2,000 sales this week. It's much more about doing something that matters. Working in the Energy market is deeply profound; it's fundamental to society. Like money, of course.

"I found a way of translating that into a more emotive and compelling story: we were helping people to warm their homes, live comfortably and help businesses keep the lights on, quite frankly. So it wasn't just about selling energy, instead we had a purpose. So helping to facilitate this as a purpose, helped people to feel that they were part of something much bigger and even more exciting and positive. A real recognition for me was that language skills, marketing, branding, the ability to communicate a vision in both a tangible and an inspiring way, is something that people respond to... So what difference is an advertising campaign from thinking about how to engage 5,000 people on where you're going and what you want to achieve? What I observe is that many companies don't naturally have this and yet this is what colleagues are looking for and it's a natural part of leadership. "

Defining the 'Why'

In Simon Sinek's stimulating TED Talk, he describes what makes leaders, who inspire people to take action, so different. He challenges us that most people don't know why they do what they do. As leaders, we communicate the 'what' and the 'how'. He describes the 'golden circle', at the centre is 'why'. Why do we do what we do? Great leaders communicate from the inside out; the 'why', appealing to the limbic part of the brain that holds emotions, feelings and drives behaviour and loyalty. The goal therefore is not just to work with a team who can do the job. The ultimate goal is to work with people who 'believe what you believe...in this way people will give blood, sweat and tears'. Of course, the latter is not quite what you're looking for but maybe somewhere in between if you want your people to be committed for the long haul!

Eva went on to tell me in her interview, *"I had my own business quite early in life, as I was brought up by a corporate Mum and an entrepreneurial Dad, so I had two clear role models. I always thought I was the more entrepreneurial side of that and I set out to have my own business. I recruited people to work for me and it was very successful commercially. However, I found it deeply unsatisfying personally. It was quite hard to rationalise because it had been everything that I was aiming for in my career. I had to go back to the drawing board and start all over again and think. I wasn't the person that I thought was; I found that very hard. It was what I called my long dark night.*

"But it wasn't clearly just a night, it was six months of my life. I like to think I'm reasonably self-aware in a moment-by-moment basis. However, I really had to do a forensic analysis of myself and my purpose. I've actually had a lot of coaching around 'self-awareness in the moment', which I think is quite a high art form in personal leadership. Up to that point, my goal was to build a business and then when I achieved that goal, I believed it would feel different. By external standards it was winning awards and everyone was saying, "Wow, this is amazing". Yet I was deeply unsatisfied and unfulfilled by it. How do you reconcile public success and recognition with private disquiet?

"Running a business was worrying about the people that you'd hired, the real personal responsibility never stopped and I could never stop thinking. I realised that I couldn't compartmentalise my life anymore; the company was my whole life. My job was chasing money, and although my clients were good purple-chip companies, they had unreasonable payment terms for my type of business. I thought it would be glorious and grand. I became just like a bill chaser. All sorts of things made me realise I had a very naive and ill-conceived view of what being an entrepreneur and running my own business really meant. I suppose because we grew so fast, it did complicate matters

too. So it forced me to be 'forensic' about what really does make me tick. I thought it was all about building something, doing great work, making money, having a really tight knit team and being successful and, yet, still I wasn't satisfied.

"Two organisations helped me through this. Working for a top global consultancy was like being self-employed whilst still in a big business, which allowed me to channel my way back, as I couldn't do this in one single step. The other was a coaching organisation that almost counselled me and helped me to structure my thoughts to make some sense out of what I was motivated by. I came to the simple realisation that I was motivated by the big corporate. I liked playing with the big train-set, I like scale and reach. I understood that I could still be challenging, creative and entrepreneurial in the right big business.

"I'm really obsessed with brands because it's about the promise. I find them intellectually stimulating and fascinating entities as they encapsulate everything that you want to convey. Then the challenge of creating the alignment between your promise and ability to deliver it, speaking through humans, as opposed to electronic devises, is great fun and it's harder to get consistency from humans.

"I've also become more of a student of a CEO's ability to be able to tell the story of the business. You may have someone who is brilliant at telling the story in numbers, but I want to be part of something beyond the numbers. I coined a phrase 'helping Britain prosper'. It was actually more for myself because I wanted to know what I was doing here. I wanted to know, beyond making so many billion in profit, what is our higher purpose. It's literal as well as emotional. It's real, it's not fanciful and it's not an unrealistic promise. It's also very motivating; it's a big thought. It's not just about prosperity, it's about wellbeing in its total sense. This has helped me."

Believing In What We Do

As an individual, finding our own life purpose and meaning helps us to become a more centred and trusted leader. We believe in the work that we do and, therefore, those led by us trust and respect us. Once we have this cracked, everything seems to fall into place. We attract the very things that we seek. Whilst being grounded in the present, we are able to appreciative the full experience that life has to bring without it whizzing by us. Taking a pit-stop every so often helps us to make sure that we're on the right track and our tyres are not about to blow-out!

When our crucible moment is potentially life threatening, this really challenges our perspective and thinking about meaning and purpose. Liz Satow's harrowing account of her own experience does just that.

Liz shared, *"I was on deployment in Gaza. I was out with my team when a man pulled out a gun and grenade. I thought, 'I'm going to die here.' In that moment I felt so alone. Fortunately, it was okay.*

"When I next spoke to my Dad he told me he had woken up at 3am and prayed for me. This was about the same time the confrontation happened. It was an incredibly powerful connection and very comforting. I knew I was never alone. I felt protected and loved and therefore it would have been okay, even if I had died."

It reminds me of a piece of research that a palliative carer carried out on the patients who had gone home to die. She asked them about any regrets they had, here are the most common 5;

1. I wish I'd had the courage to live a life true to myself, not the life others expected of me.
2. I wish I didn't work so hard.
3. I wish I'd had the courage to express my feelings.
4. I wish I had stayed in touch with my friends.
5. I wish that I had let myself be happier.

Fedelma Good shared the importance of her relationship with her husband, *"We met for a dinner-date on Friday 13 August 1993. There's not been a day since that we have not connected with each other in some way. He's the reason why I am a leader today. He's a trained chef but became the house-husband. I have to admit if I were the one at home, my children would probably be malnourished by now as I'm not as*

good a cook as he is! Tony is my rock; he makes the difference between being comfortable and having my inner confidence. He gave me self-confidence as he was confident in me."

When we have a vision and purpose for our lives, having the right social support network is essential. Not just to success, but also to our wellbeing. From my research, it's clear that career management works extremely effectively when there is clarity on how to create the right environment, and the family works together to put the right 'structure' in place. This is always different for different people, and it's about finding the right way that works for us.

Principles and Behaviours

The conversations that I have had with leaders from around the world combine to create some core principles and behaviours for PQ:

Dream: Dare to dream to understand our own purpose and path to success, as we define it for ourselves. Consider the things that are most important to us with a 'Focused Balance' on the inner circle of the compass: yourself, your relationships, your organisation and your society.

Dialogue: By gathering insights, feedback and listening to the wisdom of those around us, we are able to avoid the pitfalls of misdirection and misalignment. We can use this understanding to validate our vision, negotiate terms and establish boundaries. Become our own storyteller, creating the compelling vision for others to follow us.

Dare: Finding the courage to take action and move towards our vision. Beware the naysayers that will stall us, make us procrastinate, or generate unnecessary fear within us. Push the boundaries to realise our full potential in life and in work. Dare to be different, but more importantly, dare to be ourselves. It is better to be a first rate version of ourselves than a second rate version of someone else.

Deliver: Live our dream, role model the inspiring leader and drive through at pace. What's the worst that can happen to us? Help ourselves to be successful by focusing on what matters most and leveraging the capabilities and resources around us to create maximum value in everything we do, whether it's the quality of time with our family, or the quality of work that we deliver.

Deliberate: Paradoxical to delivering quickly, then we need to take our time, be methodical, thoughtful and unhurried to encourage the best thinking to take place from within and from those around us. Notice when we need to keep going, re-evaluate, or, like the Everest climb, turn away! This is not an act of failure, just the best learning that we could ever get. Through our review check, 'Do we add value and do we experience the value of what we are doing?'

Alison Traversoni
The Inspiring Leader Who Lives Life on Purpose

"At 14, I had no thought of what I wanted to do. I was very strong-minded and knew that I did not want private school education, so I refused. Instead, I went to private secretarial college, which I absolutely loved. I was always two steps ahead of everyone else and I really liked this feeling.

"At 16 years old, I left school. I was offered a commercial apprenticeship at Jaguar Cars, but, despite the dismay from my parents, I just didn't want to work in a factory, so I turned it down – in my view I wouldn't get noticed for adding value. Instead, I joined a youth training agency and had about five different jobs in six months – one only lasted two days – each job wasn't satisfying and I thought, 'I can do better than this'.

"So I then joined a builder's merchant and soon started dating the assistant manager; even at 16 I viewed this relationship as unprofessional, so I moved onto another company. I went into surveying which wasn't particularly glamorous but ended up running the office. I worked extremely hard and I got noticed. This resulted in me getting promoted to assisting the Regional Manager. I created the blueprint for how to do things and so was able to share best practice for the region. I always had this hunger for learning more and a desire for people management. If ever the situation was new and I felt I was struggling, I picked up a book and read about it. This

has contributed a lot in terms of how I learned to do things.

"1993 was the age of the early office computer. My employer needed an office to trial the computers. I learned all about computer systems, DOS and networks, which led me to getting involved in a nationwide office roll-out.

"I never subconsciously put myself forward for opportunities. However, I always put myself into the right position and strived above everyone else.

"I always felt Regional meetings were so high powered and intimidating. I felt there was no way I could contribute and everything would be above my head. When I was I promoted to Operations Manager and started attending the meetings, then I found that my peers were keen to hear what I had to say, respected my contribution and I knew I was adding value.

"Since joining the surveying company in 1987, I have never really had to apply for a job in my career. I always wanted to be the best that I could be, but was still grounded and in touch with all people throughout the business. Following many promotions, I was then approached to become part of a team of thirty-five management individuals, who invested in the business through a Management Buy Out in 2004. Later, in 2006, the company successfully floated on the FTSE. In 2008 I was asked to take a seat on the PLC Board, and I thought, _There was no way I could possibly do this!' although I felt very flattered and happy. Simon, the CEO, really knew how to work me though! He came to me and said, 'Right, we need to get a coffee, Ali'. After much persuasion, I had to ask, 'If this is the poison chalice tell me now; it's a tough market'. He said to me, 'it's exactly for this reason, that we want you. You know the business, our clients and systems'. If I hadn't had that nudge, then I have no doubt that I would still be a COO.

"I found the PLC Board with the non-executives such a daunting and confrontational place. As someone who had successfully ran businesses, I'd had little exposure to the coldness of the boardroom; throughout my career, even with clients, there were really no battles to be had. We had strong, trusted, stable relationships. So the board was a whole new battlefield! In the boardroom it was cold and sterile environment and, at heart, I was a people manager. Understandably, non-executives wanted to see the 'whites of eyes' of the executive team, but in the early days I found I felt so tiny and I really did struggle to overcome this.

"I acquired an executive coach, Jonathan Bowman-Perks, which was fantastic in helping me to manage these complex relationships effectively. Through the coaching I received, I found I just needed to understand that as accountants, their brain was geared to operate very differently. I learned to listen, understand and not 'to have a go'. In other words, to understand their world. To manage this, I picked off each of the executives, outside the boardroom, so I could lobby and canvas their support.

"I helped bringing the board's attention to the people in the business; we needed to focus more on people. When people initiatives weren't happening across the group, then I created best practice, which then infiltrated the Group, so as to build a consistent beneficial people culture. Soft skills are highly under-estimated. The seat on the PLC Board was the pinnacle of my career.

"For me, money wasn't my primary driver. I have never asked for more money, or a pay-rise. I get massive kicks out of nurturing and bringing people through, which in turn created an army of supporters.

"I took small amount of maternity leave, two months, when I had Matthew, who then went to nursery. I was an Operations Manager at the time. I was in a far wealthier position when we had Olivia, my daughter, so we were able to make choices. I was still in the lock-in arrangement with the business and the day after Olivia born, our company floated. Whilst on maternity leave, I kept in touch with the office and had calls every fortnight. I really wanted to get back. I always loved working and was not overly maternal.

"Mark, my husband that I met at the builder's merchant when I was 16, had been headhunted and although he enjoyed his role at the time, it was more of a 'means to an end'. I encouraged him to resign his role and take over looking after our family and our home. He agreed, but couldn't agree to being a kept man and wanted to do something. So he continued working, until they found a replacement for him, but in his spare time his interest turned to magic and magic tricks. We then bought a lovely house in the country, which Mark decorated and he took over looking after the children, so I was free to work. He started a children's parties company in 2006, which has been a phenomenal success. He has gone onto to create his own magic

tricks and continues to grow the business further, and we're now looking at franchising and brand development.

"In terms of the women's agenda, I thing we must advocate better flexible working. We need to give people opportunities to coax them back into work. At headquarters we take more women on, but why do we restrict this opportunity? We need to be more innovative.

"There are lots of fantastic women, who don't want a taxing job and, as they return to work, we must help them to dip their toe in the water. We took loads of women on to our typing pool under these circumstances and then we took them on a career journey, nurturing the talent that was there. The result was very loyal, knowledgeable and long serving staff.

"In October 2012, it was evident that my Mum's battle with cancer would come to an end within the next 12 months. I decided to step away from the business world, so I could spend valuable time with her and my family. I needed time to think. In the past I'd never allowed myself any 'self' time. I find I am no longer stressed. With my Mum's illness, I felt stronger to be able to cope with and deal with it.

"I used to have the feeling of guilt, when I couldn't even find time in a day to ring my Mum, but now that I'm not working we are taking every opportunity to do some wholesome stuff together and create lovely memories. I've finally started focusing on me and have begun to feel really whole again and so well and healthy. Family life is wonderful. It's much calmer and we're not shouting or rushing. We have a real quality of life. Women add a whole different dimension to the home and business."

[***Authors note:*** Just before this book was published, Alison's mother passed away peacefully, surrounded by her daughter and those she loved.]

Inspiring Women Leaders' Words of Wisdom

1. Know Your Passion

"I love my job and I do say that I'd prefer be at work, rather than being at home. I made sure that I had good help to support me. When my son was recently offered a fantastic job with similar pay, this would have really cut into him and who he is. I told him to make sure he was following his heart. I personally feel so passionate about making a difference, I really buy into it and it feels great to do it. This means that I love my life every day."

2. Define Success

"On defining success, you set out to do something and you achieve it. You need to understand the cost along the way, the cost to oneself, and the cost to one's energy. In order to have energy and create success for others, you must first of all care for yourself."

3. Now Find an Alternative Success Definition

"I am noticing that we use language like 'bigger' and 'bolder'. I struggle with this language, it disturbs me and I believe that it is actually the opposite of what we are trying to achieve. It's important to define what success is, as an outcome. More importantly, check 'where is the definition coming from and what is the experience that it's creating?' "

4. Create a Compelling Vision

"Only once you are clear on what drives you and your priorities, can you then create a vision that you can successfully achieve without compromise."

5. Choose a New Role Model because Superwoman isn't it!

"We think we have to be superwomen, but we need to shift this to being a role model. One of my big "Aha!" moments was in realising the importance of being very clear on your own personal definition of success. It cannot be someone else's. Failure is not about making the choice to leave, it's actually staying in the same place when you're unhappy."

6. Take Control of your Career and Life

"Now you have a vision for where you want to get to, it's really time to drive it forward. You will get the naysayers at times, just accept that. You don't need to ignore insights and wisdom, but you really do need to know your own un-wavering truth, potential and limitations."

7. Choose Your Timing

"Know when to ask for things. The timing is crucial. The time to ask for more is when people want you. Go in super-confident. I found out about a project, which was affecting Retail. I said to management that I could do it and wanted to run this project. They said only a Retailer could do the role but I pressed on, until I got the job and they put a Retailer beside me - to run the project jointly."

8. Maintain Focus Whilst Being Open to Opportunities

"I never had a career plan. I focused on making the most of the job and took opportunities as they presented themselves. I have strong values around working hard and trying your best."

9. Reflect and Reframe

"Withdraw once in a while to reflect on whether you are still on the right path. We do not need to compromise, we just need to reframe, rescript and get proactive. Nothing is ever insurmountable, no-one is ever truly trapped... it is only in the constraints of their minds."

10. Manage the Busyness for Simplicity

"Life is cluttered and busy, you get 'blizzarded' with communications and the deluge of stuff that's coming at you in big business. You can't keep up and you don't know what you need to know. So, it's important to get coherence. Anything that helps you make sense of stuff in a simple narrative is very important and helps with your engagement, motivation and productivity."

11. Prepare and Plan

"You have to plan stuff. That's one of the tricks of leadership – to make things look effortless and spontaneous, when in fact you have been very well, scrupulously prepared. I have a motto, which is 'to plan for the worst and hope for the best'. I am a real optimist but if you plan for scenarios, then at least you'll be better prepared. I also feel that it helps me to organise my thinking and have a point of view."

12. Just Do It

"One piece of advice I give to women is that there is no 'best time' to have a child. There is no point in waiting for the stars to align in terms of your career, as it just doesn't happen that way. It's about when you feel brave enough and ready to have a child."

13. Always ask, 'Do I Add Value?'

"Focus is important. A lot of people do it once a year, setting out goals for themselves and never look back at them, until review time. I don't set goals in such a formalised way, more informally. I always then sit down and assess the day and ask myself, 'Did I add value today?' That to me is the real criteria: are you adding value, do you feel you're adding value? Think what you are really doing. When I had a lot of consecutive days where I felt I was no longer adding value, then that was when I knew it was time to leave."

14. Remember the Balance

"Experiment, learn and play. Find a way to have fun whilst working. There's a guy I work with who has a calendar with the number of days to retirement on the bottom right, which he tears off each day. I never want to do a job that I hate that much."

15. You Can Say 'No'

"This was a significant role, at a mid-size business, managing a significant client and recruiting all of the under-grads for the office. I've observed that, as women, we don't push back when we get more work. Instead, we see being given more work as a vote of confidence in our capability. But we are our own worst enemy by doing this, as, by the law of time, we cannot do everything that we take on. We think we can do it all, but we must change our mentality. We believe that by giving something up, it is a sign of failure, rather than by giving stuff up, it helps us to become even more successful."

16. Take Time to Reflect, Celebrate and Adjust

"Human nature is to focus on what's wrong with our lives and how can we make things better. We need to turn this thinking completely around. For example, if we think all of these ten things are important, so they all have to be great all the time, then we will be disappointed. That's because that's just not life…for anyone. And even when we look at other people's worlds and think how perfect they look from the outside, most often they are not. Because that's not life, there's always uncertainty and nothing is ever going to be as perfect as we define it and want it to happen. We must start celebrating what is great."

17. Know That You Can Use Your 'Lottery Ticket'

"I've never had the type of psyche to have a plan, that I must aggressively stick to it. I'm more of the type of person to see an opportunity and just have a go. I truly believe that what I do does not define who I am. When things get tough, or I no longer believe in the cause, I can use my 'invisible lottery ticket' any time. I imagine that I've won a lottery ticket and I've cashed it in so can move on."

18. Making Your Own Luck

"As I speak to graduate trainees, my key advice to them is that you have to make your own luck and not just wait around for things to happen. My concern is that there is a real attitude of entitlement. As working parents, I do think we over-compensate. I find I have to explain to my son the 'economics of life', so he can appreciate what it takes to get to the same earning power. As a baby boomer, I have benefitted from the Thatcher years. I see how we've all experienced great times through the 60s-80s. However, this is short lived and we are now experiencing the results of short-termism."

19. Let Go Of Your Ego

"I don't want to be jockeying close to first position. My biggest learning has been to let go of the competitiveness. With everyone wanting to be the one closest to the leader, I realised it just wasn't where I wanted to be. You can't get caught up in the ridiculous ego thing. You just need to let go of 'not feeling important'."

20. Creating a Shared Goal

"By bringing leaders together, we created a unity that never existed before. They could see a common goal that they shared. They would get excited by it and get behind it. They were getting the best out of each other. So they weren't just depending on their own wits. When Deanna turned around to me and said, 'Now we had the right 100 in the room. These are leaders', I thought she was absolutely right. We've worked very hard to get here and it felt right. The top leadership team were also on message. So when I would say to them 'this is where we're at with the culture right now and you need to steer the ship a little this way or that', they completely got it."

21. When the Going Gets Tough, the Tough Gets Going

"I have had some incredibly inspiring bosses, which has played a massive part in my commitment to stay. I believe my own leadership is most effective when I am delivering with a team. When the work gets tough and the team is in a bad place, which happens because of the [humanitarian] work we do, then I help the team by trying to bring them right back down to our cause asking, 'Why we are here, why do we what we do?' I also invite someone really inspirational to talk with the team about the wider situation that we are helping and the difference we make."

Chapter Reflection:
Living Life on Purpose

In Isabelle's story about the mountain climbs, she reminded us that it's not about reaching the summit (destination) for people, it *really* is about enjoying the actual journey itself.

For 'Focused Balance' for My Self, My Relationships, My Organisation and My Society, how do you divide up your time and create boundaries around what's most important?

Take an imaginary pie. Now divide it up into slices to represent the amount of time and energy you currently give to:

1. The Past
2. The Present
3. The Future

Consider the implications of this. Are you too caught up by old patterns of the past that they are holding you back from realising your full potential? Or are you so focused on future and the 'need for more' that the experience of today goes whizzing by in a blur? Finally, are you spending enough time experiencing the journey in the present?

- What is your vision of success?
- What has meaning for you?
- When is enough, enough?
- What are your strengths?
- What are the resources that you need to build around you, to help with success?

Ask yourself, if this is your journey, how do you make sure it's one that is travelled well and with gratitude?

Chapter 7
HQ: Health and Wellbeing

Contributing Author on Mindfulness: Dr. Henry Ford

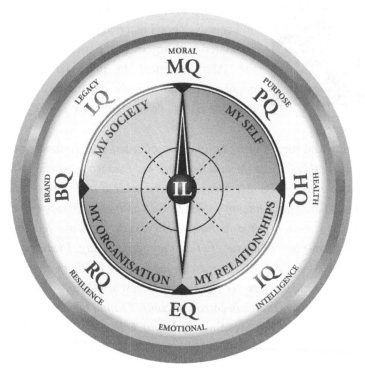

"In Holland it is common to take a three week vacation; they recognise the importance of recharging the batteries. Sometimes you can get lost in work and the company. Yes, of course we have to work hard, but how hard do we really have to work? Nobody's gravestone says, 'I didn't spend enough time in the office' and we lose sight of this early in our career."

Heather Melville,
Head of HR

Monica Singer
A Centred, Inspiring Leader - South Africa

When I first interviewed Monica, I was completely blown away by her vibrancy, passion and energy. Then I listened to her story and so much resonated with my own experiences, as she caused the 'Aha!' moment in me. Her life changing experiences had brought out the best in her, since her persistent drive had had some unintended consequences.

Monica told me, "*I grew up in a complicated and dysfunctional family. With two brothers, I was the middle child. My Dad was a workaholic and my Mum was an alcoholic. My Mum was very critical and always telling me I wasn't good enough, while my father had no ambition for supporting me as a woman. As a result, I had abandonment issues. I always felt the need to prove to myself and to my family that they were wrong. I worked very hard and achieved good results. As a strong person, my brothers always resented me and my achievements. As I grew up, I knew something was wrong, as I felt like I was living in a concentration camp. I found huge inspiration in the book,* Man's Search For Meaning, *by Viktor E Frankl. It showed me that, if he can survive the horrors of the holocaust, then I could certainly survive the pain caused by my family.*

"*At 19 I fell in love. Being Jewish, the love was not accepted, as my boyfriend was Christian. Out of spite, my brother would lock me in my room, so that I couldn't get out to him. When I was 21, my boyfriend said he was going to emigrate to South Africa and I said, 'I'm going with you'. I stood up to my family, even though they bribed me with money, clothes and cars. I gave it all up. Not just for love, but more importantly for my values and beliefs. But when you have been through hell and you give up absolutely everything that you know, then you are no longer fearful.*

"*A friend paid for my plane ticket and I left with absolutely nothing but the clothes on my back. This for me was the start of 'The Hero's Journey' [Joseph Campbell]; when confronted by darkness you just have to go out there on your own. This was in 1983, in the middle of the apartheid in South Africa, which was absolutely horrific. We stayed with my boyfriend's Mum. It got very tough with the government asking me to leave. I was trying to get work permits and my papers, but in the end the only way I could stay was if I married my boyfriend. He worked in a hotel and so we also lived in one of the rooms there. At the time, hotels were the only place that liquor could be sold and so I ironically ended up being surrounded by alcoholics, having escaped this in my past.*

"I worked during the day and then studied part-time at night, as this was the only way I could afford it. I would walk back to the hotel late at night, after my studies. Even with this and my broken English I managed to pass all of my exams. There has been a recurring theme for me through my life, which reminds me of the saying 'when life throws you lemons, then make lemonade'. That's my attitude.

"In my early life, I felt I was always the ugly duckling; having been told that I would never amount to anything. As I went to therapy, pursued a more spiritual journey and reflected back through my younger years, the things that kept me alive were often the fairy tales, fables, Disney movies and books from authors like Hans Christian Anderson. The fact that the heroine would go through absolute hell, then the fairy godmother would come along, or things changed, there would always be a happy ending.

"In South Africa in the early years, I found I was completely ostracised because of my own value system and I didn't follow the norms in many ways. For example, I didn't follow the culture norm; I didn't speak Afrikaans and didn't follow the practice that says you change your name to your husband's when you get married.

"When I was approached about the role to manage the re-engineering of the financial markets in South Africa, by introducing electronic settlement for the Stock Exchange, I said that I was a socialist and I wanted to make a difference, so didn't feel this was right for me. The leader told me I was wrong; that this is something I could do to positively develop South Africa and make a real difference. He trusted me to do this. The fact that I would make a difference is what drove me forward. South Africa was rated one of the worst markets in the world for settlement risk and today we are rated

amongst the top markets in the world – with only five countries ahead of us. "Nothing has ever stopped me; it was like a motto for my life. I would never take sick leave and even though I had many small operations, nothing ever slowed me down. Last year I started feeling very sick, which was unusual for me. I continued working hard and travelling. I started feeling very dizzy, until eventually I couldn't walk. I went to the doctors and had an MRI (Magnetic Resonance Imaging) scan. They found several very large tumours, which had been growing in my brain. They had clearly formed over some time. I had just been denying they were there and that something was wrong. I had always remembered to concentrate on my work, relationships, spirituality and emotions. But the last thing I would ever focus on was my health. I had them operated on and, all but one that's attached to a vein, were removed.

"The tumours in reality came with a clear message. You see, I was always a saviour; I would always be saving people around me, like my husband, or 'changing the world', no matter what happens! But I had never bothered saving myself. I sought advice from a neurological expert in Psychoneuroimmunology (PNI) which is research looking at the correlation between tumours and emotions. By looking at my tumours, he described my personality 100%; more than most people that I know. He told me I wasn't generating enough dopamine and asked what I did in my life to help create dopamine. My answer was my passion and love for my work. 'There's your answer' he told me, 'In order to produce more dopamine you need to stop thinking the lions are always chasing you in the jungle'. When I connected the dots, I realised that I have worked so hard to move on from my parent's legacy of pain and trying to prove myself, believing that I would overcome it through over-achieving. As a result, I do everything to the extreme. However, my passion and drive is what almost killed me. I realise I should have been more chilled. I needed to stop giving to the world and give more to myself.

"It reminds me of a saying – 'When I was clever, I wanted to save the world, when I was wise, then I wanted to save myself'. When I realised that I was potentially going to die and that I could hardly walk, I asked myself, 'how could I possibly save others?' Emotionally I'm very strong, but I had become tired of picking up the pieces. When we thought at first *that it might be cancer, I was adamant that I was not going to have chemotherapy. My family's response was 'Says who?' and they made me realise that by me making a decision like this, to throw in the towel, was a selfish one. This decision was not mine to make.*

"We totally sacrifice our lives to raise a family, do our own work and support everyone, but we have to ask ourselves 'where am I in this movie and am I the main actor?' My price was not my children; it was my body. You have to be able to learn to say 'no' and also to ask for help. When I'm travelling I'm not good at packing lightly! I normally have the full 32 kilos, as I carry my life with me and so I travel business class. I ended up hurting my back lifting my suitcase. I never asked for help, feeling that as I packed such a heavy suitcase, so I should suffer. I notice that many women are good at asking, but I haven't been. I should have just asked for help, but instead I ended up being hospitalised.

"Every operation I had was because I had neglected myself. So it's important to know that for every action you take, there is a reaction. Just be aware of the consequence. This does not mean to not do things. It's all about balance. I nearly died because I did not have this balance.

"When do you create any 'me' time? I know that the lack of 'me' time is what nearly killed me. I paid the consequence and every lesson now is coming through my body. My body is teaching me. We must be able to look after all areas: spirituality, mind, body and emotion - all at the same time. I'm really trying to slow down. So I now come in late at times and I attack my own diary to block time out. So, I spend my life only reading books that I can learn something from; I don't read novels and magazines. I have been in a spiritual journey for most of my life. I take time every day to meditate and I attend retreats. I have a place in Cape Town and I sometimes just go there and do nothing. This is permission I give myself to get balance and focus back for me. When you are in the eye of the storm, everything becomes absolutely alright when you become centred, find your balance and meditate. Not the kind where you're up in the mountains, but where you can bring yourself into the world and be centred.

"I still really have to learn balance; it takes time and I am always helping someone and wanting to make a difference, whether in the financial markets,

in charities or my family. I really do not have an option though. I have one tumour left in my brain; so I need to change my attitude.

"When you get to a crisis point like this, the option for me was to stop working and do nothing because I'm scared of dying. This is not for me. I would rather live one day intensely than fifty more years of doing nothing out of fear. What's life about?

"I have learned three key pieces of advice through my personal experiences:

    1. Be the best that you can be

    2. Be balanced

    3. Be centred and at peace with yourself and others"

What is Health and Wellbeing - HQ?

What strikes me about Monica's lifestyle, is that it sounds so familiar. Why? Clearly it resonates with me. Also there are so many parallels with most of the male and female leaders that I've worked with in the past, researched, or coached. In our manic, busy and connected world, it is easy for us to become overwhelmed by the sheer volume of demand, consuming our time and energy. Often we can't manage our external environment. However, what we can do more of is to manage ourselves internally - for our own health and wellbeing.

The challenge with leadership interventions is that they tend to deal with competence. Consequently they are very knowledge and experience based, primarily in the context of the job. Health and wellbeing are often the neglected components. Yet there is a significant difference between someone operating in the high performance 'zone' and someone operating in the spectrum between being both lacklustre and under-stimulated at one end, or being over-stressed and in over-drive at the other end. What we have to find is that sweet spot of being consistently in the 'zone' as leaders. This is what will make us Inspiring Leaders.

In Bean & Laing's book, *Turn Back Your Age Clock,* they state, *'maintaining our health is like going down an escalator – the longer we stand in the same place, the further we get carried down, until we eventually reach the bottom.'* An apt, if a somewhat brutally honest analogy, that hits you right between the eyes.

We know that we are living longer than ever before. However, many studies show that longstanding illnesses are set to rise. Many of them are linked to our lifestyles. According to the World Health Organisation, wellbeing is achieved when an individual, *'realises his, or her own potential, can cope with the normal stresses of life, can work productively and fruitfully, and is able to make a contribution to her or his community'.*

The health and wellbeing quotient, HQ, is when we have the optimum physical, mental, and emotional wellbeing, linked to living our life "on purpose". This means that we are able to capitalise on our entire potential, not just for work, but also for maintaining happy and healthy lives. By seeing ourselves as an energy system, we can understand how our mind and body are symbiotically connected for life's top performance. Neglecting any one of these components has a detrimental affect on all the others.

By bringing HQ to the fore, we start to look more deeply at what is happening for us physically, mentally and emotionally. We generate more energy, stamina and resilience, helping us to perform well regardless of what's thrown our way. So, a bit like the metaphor of a high performance car: if we use low quality or contaminated fuel, don't change the oil filter, or don't take it out for a run, then performance starts to dip. Then what happens when it comes to the chronic stress of our hyper-busyness? Well, that's like pushing your foot flat down on the accelerator, whilst simultaneously keeping the car in first gear. Worse still, we intermittently pump the brake pedal at the same time. The consequences? We catastrophically break down at 70 mph in the fast lane of the motorway. Time for a new model! Unfortunately, we don't quite have the same replacement choices, as we do with cars. We're unique, so need to take extra care of ourselves!

Emotional and Mental Wellbeing

Anna Hemmings MBE, one of the Inspiring Women in this book, has trained me in the HeartMath Institute approach and techniques. I have found these techniques incredibly powerful in making the difference to a leader's performance and the ability to build their resilience and manage stress. To bring out the best in our health and wellbeing, from the perspective of the mental and emotional side of our health, we need to look at two systems of the body: the Autonomic Nervous System (ANS) and the hormonal system. The ANS regulates 90% of what goes on in our body and most of the time we aren't even aware of what it does, such as our sweating; it goes on automatically. A network of nerves connects all of the vital organs such as breathing, digestion, heart, brain, immune and hormonal systems. What we are thinking, or feeling, triggers the ANS to either speed up, or slow down. When it speeds up, we call this the sympathetic nervous system, such as increased pulse, which is triggered by the hormone, adrenalin.

When it slows down, and our pulse slows, we call this the parasympathetic nervous system, which is triggered by the hormone, acetylcholine. When we've got the sympathetic part of the ANS firing up, this is when we get a high heart rate and energy and we can sometimes feel the adrenaline surge through our bodies. When we slow down, the parasympathetic part of the ANS is like a break that takes us to a lower energy state and slower heart rate. So, in the working environment, when we are under great pressure to perform, the sympathetic nervous system of the ANS will be fired up, adrenalin will be coursing through our body and our heart will be pumping fast. Whilst at night when we're tired, the parasympathetic nervous system will slow our heart rate down and lower our energy levels, ready for sleep. The challenge we have in the work environment is that the link between the threat response, which is managed in the brain by the 'amygdala', triggers the three survival responses of: freeze, fight, or finally flight (in that order). However, unlike our ancestors in primeval times, we generally can't immediately respond to these natural and understandable impulses. Instead societal norms force us to conform and, against our intuition, to stay and carry on working with the very people who we perceive are most threatening to us.

After the ANS, the second crucial part affecting our health is our *'hormonal system'*. Here we will focus on two key hormones; cortisol and DHEA. Both originate from the same chemical basis, which means you can have either cortisol or DHEA, but not both at the same time. Cortisol has the nickname of the "stress hormone" and is associated with negative emotions and low performance. DHEA, in contrast, is known as the 'vitality hormone', which is associated with positive emotions and high performance. For greater longevity, health and wellbeing, we need to generate situations, which naturally create more DHEA and so minimise the potential for cortisol production.

Research has shown that high levels of DHEA help with anti-aging and general wellbeing. According to the HeartMath Institute, the dangerous combination of chronically high cortisol with low DHEA is prevalent in a variety of clinical conditions. These include: heart disease, obesity, diabetes, chronic fatigue syndrome, migraines, fibromyalgia, osteoporosis, high cholesterol and many more. It can also cause premature aging. We've all seen photographs of US presidents before and after four years on the job. They have become haggard and excessively aged. Chronic stress = more cortisol = accelerated ageing.

If you can both generate positive emotions and also manage to calm and steady your breathing, then you can reduce the cortisol and increase your DHEA. This will improve your vitality and heighten your performance. There is further research to be done, however, there does seem to be a strong link between continuous stressful work-life situations and chronic illnesses, possibly even triggering cancers and tumours. We may consider that the toxic work environments, which many of us struggle to cope with, are a contributing factor. As inspiring leaders we have a duty to create a healthy work environment for those that we lead. This is one in which there is a sense of appreciation, a supportive work environment, positive emotions and a practice of catching people doing things right in order to generate lots of DHEA. In that way people will think innovatively and perform at their optimum. The added benefit is there will be less sickness absence, higher engagement and maybe we can even help our employees to live longer!

Physical Wellbeing

As an energy system, a number of key factors are at the centre of our physical wellbeing:

1. **Physical** exercise
2. **Dietary** habits

3. *Pace* of our lives
4. *Balance* between conflicting demands
5. *Environment* around us

1. Physical Exercise

Any of our healthcare professionals would tell us that exercise is the miracle cure we've always had, but for too long we've neglected to take our recommended dose! Our health is now suffering as a consequence. Unfortunately, we don't always notice until we move into a state of overwhelm, or burnout. We all know that exercise delivers oxygen through the body. It also creates endorphins, dopamine, serotonin, DHEA and oxytocin. These chemicals and hormones positively impact our overall wellbeing, including happiness, cognitive processes, health and confidence. The list goes on. Dr. Donald Bosch of the Headington Institute also shared with me that, *"Research indicates that exercise promotes neurogenesis in the hippocampus [short and long term memory]. Simply put, it helps grow your hippocampus, even if you are on the older side of life - like myself! We don't know why this is the case although evolutionary psychologists have speculated about it. But we do know it happens... hopefully you feel so enlightened and compelled that you will go out and exercise! Just don't expect that your hippocampus is going to be bigger when you get back from your jog. It takes six to eight weeks for neurogenesis to occur. Sorry, no quick fix here!"*

Let's think back to 2012; we were fortunate to host the Olympics in London. Around the world, we were all united in our pride for the strength and stamina of our athletes, who performed at peak performance. These athletes are at the top of their game, relatively consistent in their overall performance and, for many, even their success. However, all athlete's time preparing is a combination of *competing, training* and time out *recovering*. Extensive research in sports science and also research carried out by Jim Loehr and Tony Schwartz in their paper, *Making of the Corporate Athlete*, has confirmed that our ability and 'capacity to mobilise energy on demand' drives greater sustained performance. They have demonstrated that, *'...effective energy management has two key components. The first is the rhythmic movement between energy expenditure (stress) and energy renewal (recover).'* They have given the term "oscillation" to describe this process. They go on to say how, *'Athletes enjoy several months of off-season, while most executives are fortunate to get three or four weeks of vacation a year. The career of the average professional athlete spans seven years; the average executive can expect to work 40 to 50 years.'* When we consider our lifestyles, how much time do we really give to our energy renewal and recovery? Evidence would suggest, very little.

When I met with Deanna Oppenheimer, one thing that really struck me is how centred and focused she is as a person. I was keen to understand more about how she achieved this. Deanna attributes her sense of wellbeing to one thing in particular. She described, "I really got into yoga, kundalini yoga in particular. It is all about that idea of aligning to make sure that you are not just spending your life 'doing' but you are spending some of your life 'being'. This means lining up your physical and spiritual wellbeing - in a kind of metaphysical way."

Many leaders have incorporated some form of exercise into their life's routine. Equally, many will admit that this is the main area that gets neglected. When it comes to looking after 'me' and, in particular fitting in some form of exercise, this is the stuff that tends to get squeezed out of the diary! As there are a proliferation of exercises and approaches, this chapter does not focus on physical exercises, instead it urges us to reflect on how we create more activities that help us to oscillate between high energy and regenerative energy.

2. *Dietary Habits*

We know that many of the more common health problems can be prevented, or alleviated, by a healthy diet. It's rare these days that we don't see something in the media about our bodies. They highlight the issues of poor diet linked to diseases, some at record levels: obesity, anorexia, cardiovascular disease, or diabetes. Again, like physical exercise, there is a wealth of supporting material available on the Internet about food and nutrition. Consequently, while it is crucial, we won't be exploring diet plans and the detail of nutrition here.

Instead, we will just explore some of the habits that may be occurring, as we try to manage our hyper-busy lives! We often skip important meals, or replace them with quick foods like microwave-meals, which strip the goodness out. We grab sugary snacks for a 'quick hit of energy'. Of course, this is an energy spike and soon our pancreas kicks in, producing insulin, in order to return our blood sugar levels to normal. As the brain releases serotonin, our energy dips down again. So, then maybe we add a coffee, or several, to keep our energy levels up there! Much of our networking occurs 'in the city' after work, or over lunch, and so we fill ourselves with rich foods and wine late at night where it sits dangerously, turning to fat around our waists.

When we are under a lot of pressure, or in fear-based environments, we start to generate the stress hormone cortisol. When it's not used up by physical activity, unfortunately it also gets stored as extra fat around our midriff and vital organs. We turn to comfort eating to give us the energy for the pituitary gland and adrenal glands, when we are in fight or flight situations. However, it doesn't get used and so it can be a bit of a vicious circle. Simple choices to make simple lifestyle changes can have a huge difference on our health.

3. Pace of our Lives

At the same time, we are becoming more pressured by the demands of our work and a culture of immediacy. Modern technology and ways of living have automated much of our lives. Processed, microwave and fast foods have made our mealtimes far more efficient. We now even have working lunches, or we bring our lunch back to our desk! Most of us drive - everywhere! Well, this is understandable because we need to get to places faster, so we can get on with our next task. We don't even need to get up from the sofa to switch TV channels. Now we don't even need to go and visit our friends and family regularly, because we are so virtually connected by social media and technology. So, managing our relationships is far more efficient too! We also have one-minute bedtime stories for our children, or even toys that tell the story on our behalf! We know that most of us believe our relationships are the most important thing in our lives - over money and career. Yet these most important people must compete with our permanent state of busyness.

Of course, progress is important. In the *'era of convenience'* where everything is done faster, we are able to use the saved time to create lots of 'white space' in our diaries. Don't we? Sadly, not so. Instead we cram our lives with even *more* stuff! We miss the opportunity to utilise the 'white space' as moments for regeneration, reflection or maintaining our relationships.

Naturally, there are often times in all of our lives, which require the easiest and most efficient way of doing things. By creating awareness and some boundaries for ourselves, however, we can make sure it's more occasional than habitual. By looking after ourselves, we not only feel better, but have more positive energy to give to others too.

4. Balance between Conflicting Demands

There is a metaphor that the human mind is filled with *'Drunken Monkeys'* jumping around, screeching, chattering on endlessly. It describes how our thoughts jump from one branch to the other, jabbering, out of control and selfishly calling for attention. Fear, for example, is an especially loud Monkey, which can grab 100% of our focus. We have all experienced those frantic moments, when it seems a thousand thoughts are jumping in our minds. Each perhaps evokes anticipation, fear, anger, and joy as they flash up in our window of consciousness. Even outside of our minds, we have other people's Drunken Monkeys vying for our attention. They delegate Drunken Monkeys and pass us even *more* workload, that maybe on reflection we should have politely turned down. Our needy friend with their 'Drunken Drama Monkeys' zap our energy and the 'Demanding Drunken Monkeys' in our families pull on our attention.

Science has confirmed that the human mind can only successfully attend to one thought at a time. Think of it as a single window looking out onto your stream of consciousness, which flows past your window and the focus of your attention. The human mind can perceive up to 5-10 thoughts per second, again only one at a time. And all the time those Monkeys are jumping in, vying for attention in your window.

Our interpretation of events seems to be invisible, outside of our conscious cognitive processing. We believe in our interpretation and don't realise how this is determining our moods. Most people don't realise that stress is not the result of life's events. Rather, the damage is caused by our emotional responses to those events. Whilst we adopt strategies for coping with the stress, we don't do much to understand and manage our emotional reactions. Our tendency is to address the symptoms, rather than the cause - in other words better able to managing our emotional response. We actually have greater control over our emotions than we realise.

5. Environment Around Us

The environment around us affects our overall wellbeing. One leader shared with me, *"When I was working all of the hours under the sun and yet doing my own house-cleaning, I would fall behind. I never really asked for help, as I felt it was my failure. I started to tell my friends to give me advance warning, if they planned to come around, as I was so embarrassed. It was never dirty, just disorganised.*

"When it came to the weekends, I just had to get away from it all as everything felt like it was closing in on me. I just couldn't keep up with it all. I asked my husband if we could get a cleaner to help out, but he refused, as he didn't want strangers in the house. I was the bread-winner and in the most demanding job, yet I didn't empower myself to make this a non-negotiable. I struggled for years. Eventually, I took control and outsourced to a cleaner (and a new partner!) and it was the best thing I ever did. It's meant sacrifices in other areas but it's worth it. When I get home now I can concentrate on my relationship with my family and consequently my home environment is much more welcoming."

It is hard not to be affected by the chaos around us, whether it's our own or someone else's and whether at work or at home. Having the right kind of environment around us not only helps with our health and wellbeing, it can make us think more clearly and feel more positive. Many of my clients are 'imprisoned' in their stark, unfriendly offices. Often the meeting rooms are dark and airless places, yet, ironically, they are intended to be places where people are brought to think, innovate and make good decisions.

In summary, Health and Wellbeing is about seeing ourselves as an energy system. If we want to really perform effectively as leaders, then we need to maintain the system to ensure its on-going sustainability.

The Consequences of Lack of HQ

As leaders in organisations, we expect people to manage their own hectic workloads and mistakenly call this 'empowerment'. Yet, in a highly competitive world, operating at high pace, we squeeze our structures, our budgets and our people – in order to get every last drop from these 'resources'. Every organisation talks of saving costs, 'letting people go' (redundancy) and focus on performance targets. Our classrooms sizes have increased, our prison systems are over-crowded, our health service manages beds, rather than patients, and our organisations are concerned with getting more for less. The very first areas to be hit during these tough times are the very things that help leaders to thrive, such as capable people and their development.

As inspiring leaders of organisations, or countries, at what point do we start to challenge ourselves? Do we check whether we are making decisions that aren't detrimental to the longer-term sustainability and wellbeing of our people? In Robert Holden's book, *Success Intelligence*, he challenges the traditional view of success as being about '*more*': 'more money, more work, and more material belongings'. In a world where there is no such thing as infinite resource, time and money, he suggests an alternative perspective by offering the beauty of '*less*': 'less busyness, less waste and less greed'. Maybe it is time for us to alter our view of *more* by focusing on: more inspiration, more wisdom, more vision and more compassion.

One inspiring leader shared, *"Interestingly for me I had to change a lot. In 2011, I had a breakdown. I was just staring at my computer screen and didn't know what was going on. I used to think that panic attacks were for neurotic people. I had a panic attack, which I never expected would happen to me. I went through the whole meltdown, with all of the physical symptoms. It was then that I decided to change jobs."*

Stress induced illnesses often have early warning signs and, yet, we tend to ignore them because we are caught up in the intensity and hyper-busyness of our work. Many of the executives that we work with describe the early warning signs of acute stress caused by working in a toxic environment: shortness of breath, chest pains, sleepless nights, sweating, frequent illnesses, headaches, to name but a few. Sadly far too often all the symptoms are ignored.

Many high performance leaders thrive on playing the heroic role of 'fire-fighter' - constantly finding and extinguishing fires. These highly-strung, adrenaline junkies thrive on the fires. And if they don't find them, then they create them, whilst people around them get caught up and, before we know it, we *all* take on a part in the psychodrama. It gives some people an identity and sense of self-importance. As they persecute others, the spotlight is taken off themselves. We have all experienced high-pressure manic environments, and when sustained over periods of time, it becomes unacceptable for our people. Chronic stress, without recovery time is lethal. Without time to spend reflecting, regenerating and nurturing our relationships, it leads to burnout. The environments that we create are unsustainable in personal health terms, and we know it. We're just not sure how to stop it. Instead we are wilfully blind because, of course, we are all under pressure. 'That's just the way it is, around here,' they lamely say. But does it need to be? As leaders we have the power and capacity to intercept the mania; if we choose to. By being focused on priorities and deflecting the madness, this not only helps overall performance, but also creates a greater sense of wellbeing within our teams.

Throughout my research I have found far too many examples of 'expiring leadership'. Claire Hall shared with me, *"When I was working in a Pharmaceutical company I worked for a female leader. The experience felt like the 'tissue rejection by the business'. She had in mind who she wanted for the role and had connection with someone else. As two women, I think she felt she could be more critical because she was a woman. I find that men are more sensitive when dealing with women, more collegiate. I have never been so upset in a job, it was so undermining and damaging to my confidence and I would bring this home with me on numerous occasions."*

When we facilitate executive team leadership events, we often use the Inspiring Leadership Inventory (IL-i^{TM}), hold 360 interviews and observe teams in 'real time'. It is clear that the team health and their relationships are frequently at the core of deciding the team's performance. 'Expiring', dysfunctional teams suck the life and energy out of its members. Even if the majority of the team are collaborating well, the impact of one or two 'organisational terrorists' (those critics who undermine everyone behind the scenes) is significant and consuming. I see how lip service has been paid to decisions made in the boardroom, with dissent and rebellion outside of meetings. Lives are made uncomfortable for people, in the hope that they make the personal choice to move on, without expensive pay-offs. The 'yes' person is taken advantage of.

Interestingly, I often see divisive 'them' and 'us' when creating 'in' and 'out groups': functions versus the operation, the leader versus the team. The dominant characters consume the airspace and energy of others. As collective leadership teams, we need to take more responsibility for how we work together and role model healthy team behaviours for others to see. When we were working with a Health Department it became clear that the leadership team had clear divides, but were all venting their frustration on the leader himself. The onslaught began to sound like a 'free for all whine', were not solution based and had lost the context and power of their messages as a result. Venting frustrations in the moment may give us immediate satisfaction, however, it only leads to further frustration, as it does not get the desired result. Finding an adult-to-adult relationship, where conflict and issues are addressed and solutions are jointly found, is imperative to the team performance.

Now, imagine yourself in a workshop with your team. The facilitator gives you all an instruction: 'For anyone who has ever seen or experienced bullying in (this) company, please move into the right hand-side of the room?' In a real live event on diversity, all the 50 male and female delegates moved to the right-hand side of the room. A simple example, but toxic leadership and cultures happens in the most simplest and complex and forms. These environments create high stress, fear and disengagement. They compress the full intellectual capability that exists and are detrimental to the health and wellbeing of our employees. Acting as either the 'Persecutor', remaining 'wilfully blind', or being the 'bystander' affects the health, not just of our organisations and our colleagues. It affects us too. We may fear challenging the status quo. However, every leader I interviewed finds peace and assurance in their courage to break the silence and challenge unhealthy behaviour and practices. They also reflect on their sense of remorse, or guilt when they've kept their silence. As inspiring leaders, we are the 'systemic disturbers' in the organisation's, or team's conscience.

We are strongly affected by our moods as are the people around us. We interpret situations very differently and so our mood, the environment and our old patterns of thinking and experiences have a huge part to play in how we respond to situations. Our mood-swinging pendulum affects the relationship that we have with our teams. Whilst it keeps them on their toes, it is a bit of a drain on people. I have heard countless stories of times when people have to choose their moments very carefully, in order to have an honest conversation with their leader, if they dare to have it at all. Or, stories of the time people spend appeasing the leader and responding to their moods. Being a consistent and approachable leader, rather than a moody one, means that we earn the trust and respect of our colleagues.

There is a persistent, familiar theme that emerges from the research - guilt. Men feel guilty about their work, and actually enjoying being there, whilst their wives look after the home. Women feel conflicted between being a Mum who is 'present' with her family and also enjoying her career. Women and men have feelings of guilt; sometimes the context is different, however, the feelings are the exact same. These are unhelpful emotions. They can, however, indicate dissatisfaction with some aspect of our arrangements and focus, so is an issue worth exploring to identify the real issues that are causing our discomfort.

In our hyper-busyness, there are different things that we struggle with. The leaders I interviewed and researched that had a level of calm and control around their lives were the ones who'd established boundaries. They let go and outsourced the things that gave them least satisfaction, let go of the sense of guilt for the personal choices they made because they were personal. A relatively consistent theme is that 'self' is always the thing that gets squeezed. The time needed to personally re-energise, or re-generate is compromised. It is often the warning sign, a crucible moment and even a scare that jolts us into a different attitude.

As leaders we must do more to change the world of work. People are working harder than ever before. However, often when they ask for some flexibility in return, then it's not forthcoming. It is not a fairly balanced psychological contract between employer and the employed.

Claire Hall shared, "*I've seen bad examples such as, 'You can't go to the nativity play'. What's the right thing to do? You need flexibility in the system and when times are tough, then you need to look after each other. People give their lives to their work and, although we need guidelines, we also need to exercise judgement. There is real strength in my team, we feel like a family.*"

The flip side of the coin is that we must also personally ask for what we need as leaders. Many of the leaders interviewed were able to negotiate based on their terms but cite pragmatism and negotiation as key to making this happen. We also need positive support, with less judgment, when we do so. In the past, I missed most parent teacher meetings and school plays, because I was working in an environment where I was afraid to ask. Everyone around me was working from dawn until dark, every day. Feeling guilty, I never approached the subject of time out for the children, unless it was structured around holiday and illnesses. I recall one teacher saying to me, '*You are not a good parent – you're never here for your children*'. She made this judgemental remark when she was frustrated that I didn't attend all of the parent's meetings. This cut through me like a knife and, although I tackled her in the moment, that night I cried for a long time.

As I reflect back on my own experiences, I realise how I would have benefitted from the advice that these women have shared, as it would have made my own journey an easier one by staying true to such compelling words. I would have also challenged the environment in which I worked – one that had zero flexibility, if you wanted to be seen as successful. And if that didn't work, I may have even challenged whether it was the right environment for me, in the first place. Consistent feedback from the women I interviewed in the BBC highlighted their positive experience, which was supportive and helped to facilitate their home and work needs. This showed in their positive attitudes to their work and loyalty to the BBC. Many more organisations would benefit from adopting some of the same principles and work ethics; if they are truly to address the issue of achieving gender parity and supporting work-life balance. Many organisations have stated flexible working policies and processes. However, it is rare that the culture truly embraces this new way of working in practice. The reality is very different to the rhetoric and it's a big factor in losing talented people.

Sayyeda Salam shared with me that she always tries to *"Anchor myself before a meeting"*. It reminded me of just how manic we can be and how this seeps through into our activities. In the mad dash to get from one place to the next, one meeting to the next and one task to the next, we often forget to take both a metaphorical and physical breath in between.

I often found I would carry my emotion from one place to the next, with no downtime. It was also the same at home; I forgot to activate the switch-off button. My own daughter Alanadh, who's highly astute, would often have to remind me of this saying things like, *"Mum, you look stressed, shall I make you a cuppa?"* or *"Mum, we're your family not your client!"* It's important for us to find ways to switch off from work and be present with our family and friends. Also not bringing our 'baggage' from one business interaction into the next one is essential to the quality of our attention, interactions and relationships.

How Can HQ Help You As a Leader?

The scientific research demonstrating the beneficial effects of even moderate **exercise** on health, attitude, outlook and happiness is endemic. We have all felt the benefits of a new exercise programme, a regular training regime, or even a long Sunday walk. We know that exercise also releases healthy hormones such as oxytocin, dopamine and serotonin. These hormones help us to think well, create even more energy and help us to build better relationships. When we eat well, care for our body and exercise to create and maintain a healthy state, it shows in our posture, tone and flexibility. When we look and feel at our best, it has a significant positive impact on leaders attracting followership and our capacity to be even more successful.

There are simple exercises for a ***healthy mind***, which can be learned. They improve cognitive processing, emotional responses and are proven to enhance wellbeing. One powerful and learnable set of mental skills is classified as 'mindfulness', or meditation. It gives us the ability to cultivate and maintain a mental posture in which we become more self-aware, non-judgemental, open and able to choose the way we act and think. The central skill is the ability to direct the focus of our attention. It is that simple.

Ray Dalio, founder of $130 billion hedge fund firm Bridgewater Associates, stated, *"Meditation, more than anything in my life, was the biggest ingredient for whatever success I've had. Meditation gives me a centeredness, it gives me an ability to look at things without the emotional hijacking, without the ego, in a way that gives me a certain clarity."*

As life deals us the 'cards of our circumstances', our skill is what we do with the cards we are dealt. Practising mindfulness gives us the ability, rather than 'reacting' to our lot, to choose how we respond. Exercising control over what we attend to gives us the mental space to choose how we act and what we focus on. It helps create a reputation for being a centred, balanced and controlled leader. This is an essential skill that often appears as a key development need for many top leaders in our talent assessments. This is not to be confused with lack of passion and energy; quite the contrary. It is more about being less frantic, aggressive, or out of control.

Mindfulness has been shown to improve clarity of thought, personal presence, perspective and creativity. It has positive impacts on relationships, authenticity and emotional intelligence – all of which are beneficial to our leadership. Further, it has been shown to create specific peripheral benefits, including improved emotional wellbeing, reduced physiological stress and job satisfaction. Mindfulness helps us to experience long-lasting physical and psychological stress reduction; we are less likely to get stuck in depression and exhaustion, and are better able to control addictive behaviour.

In order to give quality attention to the important issues that we face (and, in fact, to be able to determine which are the important issues), we need the ability to attend to and focus upon the issue. Mindfulness is a technique that helps us to create that focused attention; it is the skill to sober up and train the 'drunken Monkeys' to take their turn at our window. This requires the skill to direct the focus of our attention and exercise control over what flows by the window constituting our stream of consciousness. Mindfulness exercises enable us to develop and hold a mental posture in which we can attend to on-going events and experiences in a receptive and non-judgmental way. It is a process of deliberate non-judgmental attention to present moment experiences.

Mindful practice has also shown to be at least as effective as pharmacological treatments in improving a variety of pathological syndromes. Anxiety can be seen as a dysfunctional 'brain loop' between the imagination, emotion and planning centres of our brain. Depressive rumination can arise from a dysfunctional loop between our memory, emotion and imagination centres. Mindfulness training strengthens our executive functions enough to interrupt these dysfunctional loops and redirect our attention elsewhere. Better said, mindfulness is good for sitting our Monkeys down! When we are acting mindfully, we must give ourselves the ability to choose how we respond to events. For example, when acting mindfully, despite that personal attack from our boss, we are aware of this urge to react, arising from the reptilian brain, and yet we remain able to decide how to respond, perhaps to fight, flight or freeze, or reply with a more measured response.

In essence mindfulness helps us to: increase the mass of the area of our brain linked to regulating emotion; improve our attention; reduce our blood pressure; reduce the risk of us developing hypertension, and reduce the risk and severity of heart disease. I'm sure you'll agree the research is extensive and provides us with a compelling case for acting mindfully!

We know from all of the research that ***work-life balance*** remains an issue.

Mariam Elsamny a Chief Marketing Officer in Dubai shared, "*At one stage of my career I didn't have much balance. I then realised that I needed to create balance; whether it was to go shopping, exercise, or just read a book. I have certain things I don't compromise on. It is very critical, for women in particular with multiple priorities, that you create those boundaries. Work will never stop; there's always more work to do. Decide what you want to cover that day and find something else that's of importance to you to, whether it's to be with women, do an art class,*

whatever it is. "

Leaders find it beneficial to establish the boundaries around the areas of their lives that are most important to them. This makes it far easier to calibrate and tackle the difficult decisions when conflict arises. Also, by incorporating other areas of interest in our lives, it's no longer a case that we live to work but, instead, we choose to work to live. Finding meaning beyond work makes us more rounded and grounded.

The 'bucket list' I mentioned earlier captures all of the things I want to do, places I want to see and new experiences that will break out of my comfort zone. It forces me to push the boundaries about possibilities. I constantly check this list off for progress and keep building on the list to keep it fresh. As a result, I have travelled more than I ever had, to far more exotic places than I'd ever experienced before and met fascinating people from all walks of life.

I have done some crazy things, some repeatable and some less so! I have belly-laughed, until tears streamed down my face. Some of these experiences included work, the kids, or even my partner, some didn't. I wonder, *'If we all had our bucket list, how much richer would our lives be as a result?'* When I coach leaders, we often explore this as a concept. On life's treadmill, we forget to live in the present and lose sight of the joy that life's experiences can bring; if only we would embrace them. Pushing the boundaries of our existence is essential to fulfilment. With this as the basis for our thinking, maybe when different opportunities arise, then we will look for the reason why we should do something and not for the reasons why we shouldn't do it.

With regards to the *women's agenda,* creating a balance between home and work can be challenging, to say the least!

An inspiring leader shared in her interview, "*When you first come back to work, there are so many options in terms of childcare and so it is an easier period than you realise. You clearly need money to finance the options. I did, however, find this the easiest period. You know the children are probably having more fun, than if they were with you all the time. You also know that they are safe. As they get older, the kids are more different. It's not as physically demanding, but it is more intellectually demanding. You need to be available at any time, be far more flexible and far more intuitive. At the mid-point in your career, it's not always obvious that you're doing what you should do. You often get guilt fired at you by others, that shouldn't do so. They don't always understand that you are recovering from kids. You always feel that you've done a full day's work, by the time you get to the office at 9am. It's physically exhausting."*

We have heard many times that it is impossible to 'have it all', particularly simultaneously! In the interviews, women acknowledged that it is challenging, with all areas demanding attention. Having clarity of purpose and meaning is the first step. This helps us to create boundaries and outsource the stuff that's not important to us. My interviewees were very clear that managing work and life was not a personal issue; it was a family issue. This not only helped with creating structure and boundaries, it also created a shared responsibility and understanding.

When we try to take too much control, we disempower those around us and lead to unnecessary tension, stresses and relationship breakdowns. Many of the men I spoke to felt a little more relaxed about things and so often felt criticised and disempowered by their actions to help the family at home. This often led to them opting out. Maybe, as women, we would benefit from just loosening the reigns a little and delegating more responsibility to others. Instead of critiquing, we could welcome the opportunity for the support that is there and fill our hearts with appreciation instead. It really is okay to ask for what we need from others. Asking for help, or letting go is not failure, and it's vital to our overall health and wellbeing. Go ahead and take the risk! What's the worst that could happen?

Finally, our wellbeing relies on the strength of our social support network. Building strong relationships, both inside and outside of work, has physiological, as well as emotional, benefits for us. When time is so precious, it is often our relationships that suffer. Many of the women found the strength and love of their partner as being the crucial component to their success. Some women had experienced very different relationships, some traditional ones, where they were not supported and some very toxic. My own personal relationship fell into this camp; it was having a detrimental impact on my health. I sustained the toxic environment for too long. Actually, I should have realised earlier that it was in my power to change things. As I enter a new phase of my life now, I realise how significant the impact was. Although I felt I was firing on all cylinders, it was often a façade. I recall once my sister, Tania, saying to me, "We just want to see our Leigh back." As I've taken greater command of my own life and relationships, I realise now what she meant. We often hear about body detoxing; maybe we need to also remove the toxins from our lives too!

Anna Hemmings MBE
6 x World Champion and Olympian
Founder & Director of 'Beyond the Barriers'

"I grew up in Middlesex in England. My Mum had a huge influence on my career, she is the sporty one; even now she is a keen golfer, and she goes to the gym and enjoys running. At 8 years old my mum took my brother and me to a weeklong canoeing course at my local club. I absolutely loved it. I was a super-sporty child and competitive person. I loved being outside and enjoyed the buzz from training and competing. I progressed quickly and by the time I was 14, I was on the Great Britain team.

"My first recollection of the Olympics was the 1984 Los Angeles Olympic Games and I remember watching Sebastian Coe, he was one of my heroes. From that point on I dreamt of becoming an Olympian. Having a dream or a vision is the essential driver of life. Without a vision you are in danger of drifting along aimlessly. A vision is what gives you the motivation; it is what ignites the passion. I had a pretty clear vision of my ambition from a young age. I wanted to become an Olympian and a marathon kayak racing world champion.

"I went to the Royal Holloway University in London to read Economics and Management (BSc) at the same time as competing. I believed it was important to me to have a strong qualification in a completely different topic than physical education. This turned out to be a good balance.

"When it came to kayaking, luck would have it that I had a bit of talent. But I realised that talent is not enough. When you sit on the start line of the world championships, or the final of the Olympic Games, every other athlete

on that start line is talented, otherwise they wouldn't be there. What makes the difference is in the mind, along with the little extra things that you do throughout the year that give you the competitive edge. I ask my clients, 'What gives you the competitive edge, is it the product or is it the package around the product, the quality, the customer service, your people, your values, your brand?

"It's a given that as an Olympic athlete you train hard, really hard. But in addition to that I constantly asked myself, am I doing everything that I can? What can I do differently this year that is going to make the difference, is this really the path to my desired  *outcome, am I getting the right diet, the optimum recovery, have I worked enough on mental preparation, have I really left no stone unturned? It's a holistic approach. In the corporate world, you might ask yourself, how do I become a better leader, am I doing everything that I can, are we doing more than our competitors, how do we become a better team, how can we offer better customer service, are there new and even better ways to do things? But it's not just that I ask these questions on occasions, its all the time. Keep fine-tuning your engine, constantly checking and rechecking, because talent is not enough.*

"I won my first European Championship in the K1 marathon in 1997. I was then the youngest woman to win the world champion title in the same event two years later. I went on to compete at the Sydney Olympic Games in 2000. In 2001, I won both the K1 (singles) and K2 (doubles) world marathon titles, becoming only the second person in the history of the sport to do that. In total I had accumulated seven European and world gold medals. Standing on the top of the podium, champion of the world, that feeling was like nothing else. Words cannot describe it. I realised that it was that feeling and that experience, the sense of fulfilment, the sense of achievement that I was chasing after again and again. That is what motivated me.

"Those feelings are basic human desires that we are all striving for – achievement, recognition, praise, challenge, power, competence, meaning.

Winning the world championships, all of the training along the way, the people that I worked with, all of that satisfied the basic human desires, desires that we all have. These are the things that motivate us.

"By the age of 24 I was a three -times World Champion and an Olympian, I was on cloud nine and thought it would last forever. However, just two years later the whole thing came crashing down around me. I was about to face the biggest challenge of my journey so far.

"Gradually my energy was being drained and eventually I reached the point where I couldn't roll off the bed, get my feet on the floor and sit up. My body felt like I was on strike. I was eventually diagnosed with chronic fatigue syndrome (CFS). CFS is a serious condition; it's not an illness that a couple of days in bed were going to cure. This kept me out of my sport for two years! I wasn't bad enough to lie in bed, but equally I didn't feel well enough to be out and about in normal everyday life. It was like being locked in a halfway world. Not fully in the 'sick' world, yet not fully in the 'well' world.

"There is a lot of mystery and mystique regarding the illness, what it is and its causes. I wasn't suffering from a broken arm, something that people could see and understand. Some days I actually wished I was covered in spots, or that my skin was see-through, so that people could see the pain and understand it. But they didn't. People doubted me; they thought it was 'all in my head', or that I was just being lazy.

"When it felt like things were spiralling out of my control I realised that there would always be one thing in my control. Even when you're feeling low and things are going wrong, then you can always choose and control your attitude. So, I chose my attitude and to endeavour. I chose to stay positive and to focus on finding a solution. It's the attitude that you bring to the table that determines where you go and how successful you are in the tough times, as well as the good.

"So I used my dreams and ambitions to inspire me and keep my spirits up. As long as I had a goal I had the motivation to keep persevering. Not once did I ever think about quitting. Of course I was afraid that I wouldn't be able to return to the sport at the highest level, but at the same time, I never gave up hope. In fact it's what used to inspire me and keep my spirits up on my worst days. You can cope with so much more than this.'

"So, although I was at rock bottom I realised that it was actually the perfect place to start again. My body was limited but my spirit wasn't, I had a dream and I had the will and determination to find a solution to the illness.

"I had become too consumed by my sport, I'd lost perspective, and my work-life balance had completely gone out of the window. I wanted to succeed at all costs, despite the fact that the way I was going about pursuing my dream was making me unhappy and, ultimately, ill. I isolated myself and didn't let people help me. I should point out that it was nothing to do with the actual training, the volume, or intensity of training. It was everything outside of training. I didn't realise that if I wasn't happy, if my heart and mind were not healthy, then I was never going to achieve my goals, no matter how diligently I trained.

"The symptoms are like alarm bells going off and I didn't listen to them. My body was crying out for me to get a bit of balance in my life, to chill out, to see my friends more, to go out and to let go of some of the conditions and pressures I was placing on myself. But I didn't listen, I was too consumed by what I was doing and, so, my body's way of speaking even louder was to give me the symptoms.

"Reverse therapy recognises that the mind and the body are connected and that emotional health is linked to physical health; this is evident in that a common trigger of symptoms for many people is non-expression of emotion. This was true for me; I wasn't good at speaking up and asking for help. Instead I tended to struggle along on my own. Only once in that first year of the illness did I break down and cry in front of someone else. I cried plenty of times on my own, but only once in someone else's company, despite the fact that I have good relationships with my mum, my sister and many close friends. That might seem strange but I think that it might be a scenario that many other people might find themselves in.

"For example, in business people regularly take on more and more work – either too great a volume of work, or tasks which they don't know how to achieve. Eventually they become overloaded, but they don't ask for help, instead they keep going on their own, without speaking up. In the end they are unable to deliver. They end up blaming other people and when it continues they become more and more stressed, until it becomes so big and

burdensome that it leads to their breakdown. You might wonder why we do this – perhaps it's a fear of showing weakness, looking vulnerable, not wanting to look incompetent in a work environment, or pride? I look back now and realise that I didn't want to let down my guard, to show a weakness or vulnerability. I felt compelled to maintain my athlete's poker face. This was even when deep inside I was desperate for people to see what was behind the mask.

"This experience taught me the power of letting down my guard and that it is OK to show weakness. In fact, I think it requires strength and demonstrates an inner confidence.

"With the changes in place and the training done, then I was finally on my way to Australia for the 2005 marathon racing world championships. This is what I came back for; to win world championships and gold medals. And I did, I won my fourth world title. It was a victory sweeter than all the others. I had climbed a larger more arduous mountain to achieve that particular gold medal. It wasn't an easy journey, but nothing worth achieving was ever easy. Just to make sure it wasn't a fluke I went back to the world championships in 2006 and won my fifth world gold medal and then to make sure that it really wasn't a fluke I went back again in 2007 and won my sixth world championship gold medal.

"I am now the owner of my own business, Beyond the Barriers. Our programmes are designed around three fundamental components – peak performance, resilience and health and wellbeing. I'm absolutely passionate about all three of these areas, because when I started out as a young professional canoeist, I was quite naïve. I thought that all I needed to do was train had; I just needed to focus on my performance, set my goals, do the physical training and work on my self- belief, my mental strength, and I worked with a sports psychologist. I thought that if just took care of all of these things I could reach the highest level. And I did reach the top of my sport but I wasn't able to sustain it for very long and not only that, at the peak of my career I was diagnosed with the debilitating illness I mentioned before.

"If employees want to be able to not only keep up but perform well under pressure and on a regular basis and still have energy left at the end of their

day for family/friends and work life balance, they need to be resilient. Because when you're low on resilience, you tend to dramatise problems, feel victimised and become overwhelmed and that's when performance suffers. And it's at that point that it's a lot easier to turn to unhealthy habits, behaviours and coping mechanisms. The bottom line is that the organisations with the most resilient employees will be the ones to emerge successful from these challenging economic times.

"The good news is that the skills of resilience are not reserved for the extraordinary and the exceptional. We can all build resilience and you can build your capacity to maintain flexibility and balance in your life as you deal with challenging situations and setbacks. Resilience is divided into four components – emotional, mental, physical and spiritual. Each component is critical for developing resilient performers. This is imperative if you are to thrive rather than simply survive in a culture, which increasingly expects you to deliver more whilst spending less.

"Success, I realised, is to be measured not so much by the position that one has reached in life as by the obstacles which had to be overcome while trying to succeed. So when you are having one of your own dark and desperate days, remember, NEVER give up!"

Inspiring Women's Words of Wisdom

1. Balance

"In hindsight I was taking on too much. My childcare arrangements were not ideal: my children went to another home each day and I would have to pack everything and prepare each morning. I had a new-born and each lunchtime I would have to go home to feed him. By working so hard I thought the world around me would honour me, as I struggled with my heavy bags on my shoulders and my lists of things I had to do each day. I expected that I could do it all; so I never asked for help. I would see this as a weakness. I was barely surviving and I was my own last priority. I realised that I needed to become my primary priority in order to be stronger and give in abundance to others."

2. Be Compassionate to Ourselves and Others

"We load ourselves with guilt. When we're at home, we're feeling guilty about our work. When we're at work, then we're feeling guilty about our home. We need to make a choice and stick with it. Don't judge ourselves so harshly and, furthermore, don't judge anyone else for the choices that they make too. We just have to remember that everyone has got it tough. If we look at it through that lens then maybe we will be far more supportive and far less critical of others. We owe it to women to help them."

3. Prioritise and Outsource

"I notice that the women who succeed are driven and perfectionists. They want to do things well, 100% right. That's physically demanding. I saw a presentation once, where the speaker said we need to, 'outsource everything that's not important to you, otherwise you will have zero time for you'. I blended a nanny with after-school clubs. I wished I'd had the nanny full time from the start. I still have one now. You can't display management and leadership in every sphere."

4. Time for Reflection and Recovery

"Reflection is really an amalgamation of actions; so you need to look beyond reflection. In yoga what happens is you go through a yoga class and at the end there is a relaxation and reflection moment. The whole point of physical action in yoga is to get you to the point where you can reflect on the action that you've taken and take you to a higher state of awareness. Reflection shouldn't be an impediment, or an excuse not to act. It should be amalgamating the action you have just taken and reflecting on what the next action is that you are going to take."

5. Perspective

"I was taught as a young girl some wise words by my very old Malaysian grandmother, 'Before you are judgemental about someone else, walk a mile in their shoes. See it from their perspective. Otherwise you will become nasty, twisted and embittered. That is not good for your health.' I have tried to apply her wisdom as I have struggled in business. It is not easy to step back and see other's perspective. When I do it is very liberating and helps me get an outcome we both feel good about."

6. Know Your Body's Needs

"You have to keep yourself healthy. You need to be really firing on all cylinders for big leadership jobs. People might think they are cut out for it, but they're not. You have a little inner voice that says actually you have reached a level where you feel you can contribute, but you're not so over-stretched that you are creating anxiety in your team. I honestly think most people have this inner voice and know."

7. Time for Meditation

"In my darkest hours, it felt like everything was closing in on me. I got quite depressed by other people's expectations of me and felt I was letting them down. I was always wired up and my brain never seemed to turn off. It raced from one self-imagined drama to another – some were real. I just couldn't pull up from my nosedive to failure. Then my coach taught me to use mindfulness and meditation. At first I really couldn't focus – my mind was racing off, jumping around. Eventually mindfulness became my saviour. I calmed the noise like a whirlpool transforming into a still calm pond. Ok there were some rocks thrown in the pond every now and again! Now I am not perfect, or do mediation practice daily (as I know is best if I were to) but it has saved my sanity, my job and my relationship."

8. Fitness for Life

"Earlier in my life fitness was part of my weekly activities. I felt so energised and vibrant. Then for about 10 years it just slipped away with the family and children. I had a wakeup call when my best friend got cancer. It spurred me to look after my body better. I still have fun, yet think carefully about the food and drink I cram into myself. I also do about two fitness classes each week. That has really helped reenergise me. I suppose I also sleep deeper and wake more refreshed."

9.   Don't Put Yourself at the Back of the Queue

"As a woman I see myself as a natural carer – I enjoy helping people and, so, leading and developing others is part of who I am. It's in my DNA. I just must remember that I need to give leadership to myself and not forget the 'me' in all the 'them'. I used to serve everyone else first and myself last. Not anymore – it's not selfish, just wise. On a recent flight the safety video reminded me that in a sudden loss of cabin pressure, as parents we have to put the oxygen mask on our own face first, before then doing the same for our baby."

10. Time for a Break?

"You have to take time for breaks and holidays, in order to keep operating in my line of work at the level of high performance that they call for. At first I just kept going and going. I suppose after 12 months without a proper holiday, I had a bit of a break down – I should have seen a doctor on reflection. Now I always take my full holiday entitlement and especially two weeks in the summer. My PA knows I won't have my Blackberry with me and so does my Deputy. She knows I trust her to make the decisions when I'm away. She doesn't do it exactly the way I would always have done, but it is good enough. She also feels empowered and good about herself. Also, it means I come back refreshed and she can then take a break too."

Chapter Reflection:
Cultivating Wellbeing

In your leadership

- How do you create a healthy work environment for those you lead?
- How creative are you in building sufficient trust and flexibility, which respects the new world of work?
- If you are caught up in traditional ways and structures of working, how can you challenge the status quo?
- When managing your talent, how can you factor in their career development for the longer term?

For you

- How can you work with your family/relationships to agree what's most important?
- How do you set boundaries and what can be outsourced?
- What responsibilities can you delegate?
- When do you create "me time"?
- When can you look at your diary and plan (in full) holidays for the next 12 months?

Chapter 8
IQ: Cognitive Intelligence and Wisdom

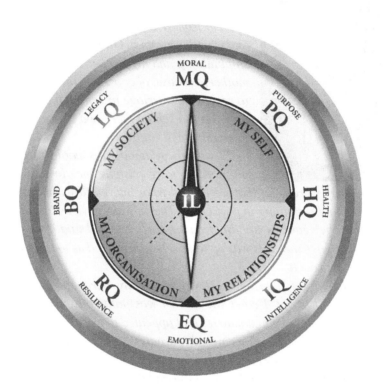

"Inspiring leadership is about working closely with your team to deliver a really great result. Of course, you can be friends, however, you also need to create value for the organisation. Gaining a variety of experiences means you get a greater sense of what's going on which helps people to think differently, innovate and make great decisions."

Wang Le
Programme Director, NGO – China

Dame Anne Pringle
Diplomat, Foreign and Commonwealth Office

"I'm from a very large family of six children and we all grew up in Glasgow. My father was in shipbuilding and my mother was a stay-at-home mother, because, of course, in those days you had to resign on marriage to bring up a big family. I also went to school there and I then left to go to university at St Andrews.

"I was a workaholic at school. It wasn't that my parents were pushing me. In fact, very far from it. They were keen that we all did what interested us and they never pushed us to do anything in particular. They always gave us lots of freedom of choice. They gave us stability from an early age and said if we wanted to do certain things then this was up to us. They just urged us to think about the risks and approach.

"I had a great upbringing. I worked really hard and found I liked languages and travel. I can't say at 16 I was politically aware, so it was more the idea of living in countries that appealed to me; the idea of living in countries rather than just touring. My parents were very supportive but left it up to me to choose but were delighted when I chose to go to university. All of the family have gone on to do successful and different things overseas, which is a testament to my parents being great parents. They got the balance right between exercising responsibility and allowing us to be independent, which they taught to us from very early on.

"From university, I went straight into the Foreign Office, which is where I have spent the last 35 years of my life. It was not really my intention to stay so long with one employer but the Foreign Office is a fabulous place, fascinating and challenging. So you get sucked into it and it's hard to leave. Why did I choose this career? It was probably the interest, the challenge, the travel and the sense that you can make an impact in the world, make it safer and better. This deep sense of commitment is shared by many diplomats. Eventually however, the frequent moves can be tiring. There are also real challenges for running a career and having a family if you're in the Foreign Office, especially if your spouse is as ambitious as you are.

"I met my husband when we were both working in California. He's a lawyer by background and was working in the oil & gas industry, based in California but mainly going to Alaska. I was doing a trade and investment job there early on in my career. We spent very happy years in California, thought about staying. However we were both very ambitious, and weren't ready for this yet. We married in 1987, quite late, as we were both in our early 30s. This was the big period of challenge for us as we both had our own careers and were suddenly faced with Foreign Office postings. For my generation, and also actually the Foreign Office, this remains the big issue really. Having seen my mother do the motherhood role extremely well, I could, I suppose, have had that sort of life but I didn't want this for me and I couldn't see a way to balance it actually with my job. Twenty years on, of course women are now balancing motherhood and work better and the Foreign Office has evolved and become far more receptive to holding onto its talent, to developing workplace schemes to help with work-life balance, particularly in the UK, with flexible working patterns. All the things that help you to run your family life and have a career. None of this was available when I joined. But you still face a crunch point when you go overseas about what happens with your spouse.

"My husband and I both determined early on that we were going to pursue our careers. So there was no argument and, in fact, we have a fabulous relationship. Early on we tried to arrange the perfect solution, to get assigned to the same place. We didn't manage that then and settled for being not too far away in terms of travelling by train or plane. I believe that you have to determine your parameters. What worked for us was not missing a weekend together. At one point he went to Singapore and I thought about taking a year out to join him. It's a wonderful place. However, it was filled with young mothers and kids. With the best will in the world you need to accept what your scene is. This was not for me. Even if I had completed a university qualification I would have been bored and I love my job. So we did the 12 hour flights; fortunately it was only for 18 months until my husband returned to London for a role with a major law firm. I always negotiated with the Foreign Office and there were only certain postings that I would bid for. If I was not lucky enough to get them then I would not have been 'postable' overseas and this would have been a crunch point for me. However, it always worked out.

"When I was posted as Ambassador for Moscow, my husband's employer was able to move him there with me. Of course, by then, various things had changed. Technology was so much better and it really didn't matter where he sat. In the end, what is achievable in the 21st century wouldn't have been achievable for us when we started out. We have been fortunate that, as I've moved up the ladder, the culture in the office has changed. Also, the determination to keep women and technology and travel has moved with the times. We've had fabulous careers with great fun along the way and it's worked for us. If you have a Foreign Office career then you really have difficult choices to make. It's more normal for men to have their spouses travel with them. It's less true for the women. You often see women Ambassadors who are unaccompanied. Their men have careers that they are not willing to give up. Successful women, in my experience, tend to have ambitious spouses.

"I have never honestly had dark moments in my life. We're both very positive people. I have had testing times, for example, Singapore, which is something that you don't do lightly. Again, we had a lot of fun. My view is that it's all down to your attitude. If you really want something to work, whether it's your career or relationship, you will make it work. Anyone is going to have loads of challenges put their way. For some people it sinks them. It has a lot to do with your determination. We were very clear about our needs and that we wanted to be together as much as possible. If you're clear and honest about this and you're both determined then you can work this through.

"When I started in the office as a junior, they didn't care as much. It was more about moving me from job to job. They didn't start taking me seriously until I got to first secretary level (middle ranking) when they realised that I was good and I suddenly came onto their radar screens. They knew I liked a challenge, that I worked hard and that I had no children. They needed me to work really hard, so I basically got more and more challenging jobs.

"I was looking at all of my old HR documentation over the last 30 years, and in terms of mapping my career, I always said "here are the jobs that I would be interested in next and here are the ones that wouldn't work for me". It was clear I always tried to steer my career in a way that suited my personal circumstances and gave me sufficient challenge.

"You have to push yourself forward. I have to say when I see really pushy

women, or men for that matter, I don't like them. Pushing yourself and being pushy are different. You have to get noticed and be prepared to fail and pick yourself up again. You have to be prepared to do the tough jobs. You will inevitably make mistakes but you've got to be prepared to take risks in order to grow. I always liked having challenging new jobs where in the first week you think 'how am I going to do this?' and I liked this feeling because I knew I was pushing the boundaries. I always said I would leave when I recognised that I'd reached my level, when I felt I had too much responsibility, and the truth is I never felt that. So I just kept going.

"You need to be able to be honest with yourself. Not everyone is cut out for a leadership role in life. It's hard, it requires huge commitment and determination. You can't just switch off from it.

"Leading other people is always hard. In Moscow we had all staff meetings. They hadn't happened before I arrived but you need to talk to people face to face and crunch through the issues that are bothering them. You need to do this honestly and openly. For me, leadership is about setting up structures to get feedback loops. If people are not speaking to you honestly, you need to identify members of the team who are courageous enough to tell it like it is. Being visible, walking the floor and having clear structures and objectives so we all know what we're working to are important.

"It's also about tackling performance and not letting it slide, doing the tough stuff and taking the hard decisions that no-one wants to take. On a personal level, I didn't work the 'leadership image' very much. I like to build a team and a rapport with people, to understand what makes people tick and when they are below par.

"There isn't a leadership recipe, people do it how they do it. People say I'm a 'natural born leader', but I think what they mean to say is that I'm a natural born bossy person! I do prefer to lead than be led, I'm very happy to take risks, and I love to bring a team on to success and bring people on who have huge potential but may be a bit shy coming forward. I love doing all of this and get a real buzz out of it. Leadership is a whole bunch of things really.

"I had some great role models, mainly men. There were a couple of women but they weren't role models for me. I also had a couple of good mentors. I had a senior adviser who always looked out for me at various

junctures when I was struggling to get my next job. They made sure that I was in the frame and that I was taken seriously, even just getting to be considered. Above all, I loved my job and I actually knew that I was good at it.

"The Foreign Office for a girl from Glasgow, was daunting. Even little things: people with double-barrelled names were just not commonplace for me or even part of my background. Also, plummy self-confident men who would say 'black is white and you'd better believe it'. It took me a couple of years to get behind that and say 'actually you're talking a load of bull!' That was a real eureka moment.

"When you're clear on your position it really boosts your confidence. You think what really matters is: do you know your job and have you got all the skills you need? I had the leadership and passion. It's not something that you need to shout about as I thought it would be self-evident to people. Although here I am saying people need to push themselves forward, actually I never did - it just worked for me.

"There's a saying, 'behind every successful man, there's a great woman'. It's the same for women leaders. You need a great relationship where your partner is encouraging you to succeed. It makes a huge difference. So all of this kept me sane. I always had people in my team who were prepared to be honest with me so I could adjust my style or behaviour if it wasn't hitting the mark. I have had to flex my style around people. You have to be conscious of your impact.

"A lot of people asked me whether I found it difficult working in Russia because of the male culture and there are very few high profile women in the Russian diplomat service or politics. I didn't find it a problem, however, as Russians are happy to deal with you if you are confident and know your stuff and tread carefully. They will very quickly intimidate you if you are on weak ground. So you really have to be up to the mark. Why wouldn't you be?

"It is a truism that you have to be true to yourself and really honest about what you want in life. If work-life balance is important, if bringing up your family is important, how do you wish to balance that that and have a spectacular career? It's very hard to juggle. You see a lot of women doing it these days and it's challenging. You have to compromise. So you must know what you really want in life. You need to know what works for you and the bits of your life that are most important and these things change over time.

It's not static."

Definition of IQ: Cognitive Intelligence and Wisdom

IQ is a measure of cognitive intelligence, determined by a standardised test. IQ brings with it a long-withstanding history and debate of what it means, therefore it offers a multiple definitions rather than a single and agreed definition. Traditional psychology has led us to believe that IQ is set by the time we reach a certain age. General consensus was that the brain was relatively unchangeable, after early development, approximately by the age of 18. That viewpoint is highly restrictive, and this is causing a skewed view and labelling of intellectual capability, when there are other aspects which are not fully appreciated. We have also experienced first-hand with our clients, that high IQ, in isolation, is insufficient to make someone an inspiring leader. With the evolving neuroscientific research, we know that, through our experiences, we can establish new neural connections, which enable us to develop our knowledge and wisdom. Connections within the brain are constantly being created, or removed, largely based on how those neural connections are utilised. Evidence shows that the birth of new brain cells (neurogenesis) occur, even when we are much older. Based on these new insights, and our own experiences of testing and developing talent, we have created our own definition of IQ in the context of the Inspiring Leadership model. It is crucial that we include the aspects of wisdom and judgement and not just cognitive intelligence. Therefore, we define IQ as:

> *'**Cognitive intelligence** and **wisdom**. It is the mental capacity and agility to learn, leverage and promote new knowledge, make the complex simple and apply reasoning for wise judgments to solve problems and make good decisions.'*

Wisdom is our ability to apply discernment, between what is the right and wrong thing to do, under any given circumstances. This involves our understanding of a variety of things such as situations, people and context. It is based on our willingness and ability to apply perceptions, judgments and reasoning to make a decision, or take action. In turn, we must hold strong to our convictions. There is no point being wise if we then internalise this wisdom and hold back, for whatever reason, from sharing it with others! Submissive compliance of our past has been a major cause of today's crises.

In Nancy Kline's book, *More Time to Think*, she observes how we live in an 'epidemic of obedience'. As we tap into our wisdom, we then need to be courageous. The term 'courageous' comes up a lot in this book. For courage is often the thing that holds us back from making choices, being honest in our views, or from aiming high. Courage has the power to help us realise our full potential. As leaders, wisdom is absolutely critical as we have been hired for our ability to think for ourselves, not just to lead. We are the final decision makers within our own sphere of influence. At the end of the day, as the saying goes, 'the buck stops with us'. With such significant responsibility placed upon a leader, I would want to know, 'who is doing the thinking around here?' It is our duty as inspiring leaders to always create the space. We must seize vital moments that encourage our best thinking and then find our voice and the appropriate platform to air our wisdom and experience.

Carol Nicholls CBE is a highly acknowledged, successful head teacher at an all-girls college. Carol shared with me, *"If you say to your daughter, what do you think about something and they respond with, "I don't know", then it's not enough. You need to tackle it. They need to be able to have thoughts and opinions. We need to encourage this. The very first thing the girls must do is learning to think for themselves. At 16 years old, their cockiness and brashness wanes. They need to find other ways to communicate and we need to encourage them to take responsibility. We also need to provide the safety net behind them to support their confidence. As a parent, it's about creating the richness and creativity that family life can offer. Do you know your daughter's thinking? She is her own person and you need to nurture this. And when they say, 'what if I'm wrong?' then we need to say, 'So what, what will happen?' If it doesn't matter, then as long as you adhere to some basic principles, then that's okay. It is important to always help them think about, 'what can you can do to better yourself?' Encourage them to think about what they need to do to make themselves heard. We sometimes worry too much about what other people think. In organisations, I am concerned that we discourage thinking."*

This conversation with Carol has fundamentally shifted my own approach to communicating with Alanadh, my daughter, who is clearly growing up into a highly capable, intelligent young woman with a strong mind and an even stronger will. It's easy to forget to treat our children as potential thinking peers, as adults who can do great thinking, in their own right. This attitude to encourage *courageous thinking* will serve them well, long into their careers.

There is a wonderful saying, *'Experience is mandatory, yet learning is optional'.* IQ is not just about gaining lots of experiences. Critically, it is our personal *learning* that we build, as a result of these experiences. In our impatience to grow our careers, deliver great work, or drive results, we forget to feel more enriched by our journey and grow our own personal leadership as a result. This is particularly challenging, when dealing with the Millennial Generation (Gen Y), for example. For them the expectations of the workplace are significant - with short attention spans, considerable ambition and a desire for immediacy.

The quality of our experiences, plus our learning, is essential to future long-term career success. So, it is not the tick-box exercise for our CVs, it is the depth and breadth of learning that we create for ourselves. As Isabelle shared in PQ, the true gift is the journey up through the mountains, rather than just reaching the summit.

One inspiring leader shared how she was always very thoughtful about her career path. When others on her graduate programme were eager to move rapidly, she stayed, in order to get grounded experience and get the right foundation in place. She believed that would help her career later on. Her contemporaries became individual contributors and analysts, whilst she was leading a team of 22 people and managing a P&L line (profit and loss). She says, "*I have always been guided by the opportunity to learn, and by what I'm passionate about. I place a conscious lens on my career, and, when I'm not sure about something, then I seek advice. Who cares if you're at a lower level at the time, if you are getting to the heart of the business and accumulating the most challenging experiences? I also believe the major learning that you get is from your mistakes and this generally becomes visible when you've been in your role for about three years.*"

In essence, it is in the act of establishing a *journey of learning* that we enhance our knowledge, understanding and leadership. We should also maintain sufficient time in a role, in order to accumulate wisdom, make a positive impact and drive value. This also applies to our teams and organisation. As we work at pace, we must find mechanisms to reflect and learn about our strengths and achievements, as well as learn from our mistakes. True learning can only be achieved when it takes place in a safe environment, free from judgment and criticism. This means that we open ourselves up to the full potential of our learning and do not close down our defences to deflect potential 'threats'.

The IQ component is also about us *truly listening* to our internal thinking, so we can tap into our full potential. Our greatest successes often come from the inspiration that's created through our own internal thought processes. Yet, we are often too busy, manic or even afraid to listen! Many of my interviewees describe how their belief system affected their ability to think effectively in any given situation. This was whether giving presentations, influencing the board, asking for something that they wanted, or in promoting themselves. Our experience can be either a place of heaven or a place of hell – it all depends on our mind and how we think about it.

We know from Chapter 4: The Neuroscience Behind Inspiring Leadership and Chapter 7: HQ - Health and Wellbeing, that if our amygdala is constantly on alert or we are stressed, then this affects the quality of our thinking and, in turn, our ability to impact others. So, 'listening' is an art form in which we find power from our internal dialogue. We are seeking wisdom, based in reality, rather than thoughts tinted and hindered with self-limiting beliefs such as, 'I can't', or 'I'm not'. This sense of clarity is the true test of wisdom and intelligence.

True success comes from nurturing a strong *self-awareness and control* of our emotional reactions, when we are making choices. This does not mean we fail to utilise our feelings to help us make informed and intelligent decisions, quite the contrary. However, it does require us to understand specifically how these feelings influence our thinking processes.

In our IQ definition, we also include the *promotion of knowledge and wisdom*. In a complex, knowledge-based era, purely relying on our own talents and intellect are not enough. We must also listen to and promote the wisdom of others. We should not be blinded by our own, or others ego-based drivers causing ignorance, arrogance, or biases.

The truth is that the level and quality of our achievements and success is based on the quality of our own thinking that we do first. Again, in the (slowly) changing structures of our organisations, heavily influenced by the enhancement in technologies and social media, we must enable leaders to effectively network to share knowledge and collaborate. Technology won't solve this issue entirely, so our solutions must have the human touch.

Self-control is an important component when making *wise judgments*. By applying it, we are able to over-ride our own impulsiveness and automatic habitual responses.

By making the subconscious conscious, we become aware of our emotional attachment to our impulsive choices. For example, we are impatient with rules, attitudes and our desire for immediate gratification. We can manage this by intervening with self-regulation in order to adapt and respond in constructive and positive ways.

In work we have experienced that what marks out the most successful leaders is the ability to operate at 'high tempo'. They can move quickly from one thing to doing something else, whilst maintaining momentum and drive. Such tempo comprises *agility* and *pace,* something which is essential in business today.

Many of the leaders I interviewed described how we are not alone in our efforts. We must not be afraid to ask for help. Knowing this and understanding that we are resourceful and have extensive support available to us, will help us to be successfully agile and make sense of the complexities surrounding us.

Of course, the effective application of cognitive intelligence and wisdom is the true measure of success. In utilising the information and resources available to us, we must *take the initiative* and drive to action. This helps us to create positive progress and add true value.

Through our creative and cognitive processing, we can affect change and make a difference by making wise decisions.

My mother has always been vibrant. However, at 69 years old, she admits that, over the last few years, she is holding back on her life ever since she lost her soul-mate, in fact. She always gives the advice, *"Get out there and give life a good shake"* to others, and yet, she has stopped doing this for herself. She recognises this issue and with each year that arrives, she says, *"This year I'm going to..."* which is quickly followed by, *"you know, I think you need to carve, I was going to, but then it was too late on my tombstone."*

Let's be clear: Even when we don't make a decision, or we procrastinate, this in itself is a decision. Only when we do that, then our destiny is being shaped *for* us, rather than *by* us. Surely we may want a little more control over this? It is here that we take responsibility and accountability for affecting and shaping our own destiny.

In PQ I highlighted the importance of meaning and purpose and there is a wise saying that, *'If you don't make a plan for your own life, then you will end up in someone else's plan. And guess what they have planned for you? Not very much! Failing to plan is planning to fail. Make a decision and take more control of your life.'*

Paradoxically, we need to be sufficiently flexible, with highly attuned antennae to grasp potential opportunities that may alter our course. Inspiring leaders have the ideal blend of both and found that opportunities arise from the most unexpected places.

The ability to think well requires a source of *energy*. When we think, we deplete our *energy resources.* Consequently we must remember to refuel our tank. I often found that I would do this through sugar highs and the caffeine rush that would come with having coffees and chocolate for mid-afternoon snacks at work. Whilst the spike of glucose and caffeine has been a helpful intervention on many an occasion, it is of course just that. A spike.

Back to HQ health and wellbeing: what we put into our body and how we exercise it impacts the functioning of our brain and our mental processing.

The Consequences of Lack of IQ

Intellectual firepower, technical expertise and knowledge are often the stuff that makes us successful early on in our careers. In traditional leadership philosophy, knowledge is power. Therein lies the difference between that of *abundance* and that of *scarcity*. Some people get promoted into leadership roles, yet mistakenly still aim to withhold information. They believe it to give them an edge on their colleagues. Such leaders incorrectly believe that by sharing an idea, they then lose power and control. It actually makes them more closed and less trustworthy. In highly competitive working environment, it becomes very difficult to create a culture of collaboration and knowledge sharing. This is the philosophy of scarcity. This rivalry over the distribution of power and misguided attempts to hold on to knowledge and information means that they are blocking progress.

This does not fit with the 21st century model of leadership, one that has established the new power principle that favours the collective over individual leadership. This latter does not encourage the promotion of innovation or creativity nor does it encourage others to achieve their full potential.

All too often, we see leaders who do not support the growth of others. The saying is very true, 'what got you here won't get you there' and they need to move from scarcity to abundance to really inspire leadership, rather than manage by manipulation and withholding. I have often seen the ineffective behaviours of leaders where they have established structures and boundaries that guarantee power.

One inspiring leader shared a low point in her career, *"I remember when I was hired into a senior level position. Everyone kept going to my colleague, who did my job before me, and asking for advice. I kept getting side-lined and was treated like the junior person. It was hugely frustrating to be in this position, as I wasn't being part of the decision. I went home and started to cry, I was so frustrated and angry. My husband, who is so often the voice of wisdom, said to me 'Crack through this and solve the problem for yourself and then others will breakthrough too'. I went back in, diagnosed the problem and created the solution. Sure enough, the breakthrough did come."*

Bureaucracy and politics within our businesses ensure that the odds are stacked in favour of ***power structures***, reducing the potential for growth, risk-taking and collaboration. I recall working with one CEO and business entrepreneur, who, in fear of losing power, would resort to micro-management. In an effort to keep the investors and CFO at arm's-length, she set up team meetings that would require her presence, but discourage cross-team knowledge-sharing. This way she became the gate-keeper, using tactics to hold those with power at bay. Unfortunately, this meant that her time was being consumed by business operations. Instead of working *on* the business, she was working too far *in* the business. One could be forgiven for forgetting that she actually was the CEO.

Another power-play tactic used by *expiring leaders* is that of aggressive behaviours, intimidation and bullying. No one will dare to challenge their ideas and thinking out of fear or negative consequences. There is no *trusted adviser, or confidante* to have the courage to whisper in his or her ear, 'Emperor, you have no clothes'. I have seen this constantly throughout my career and heard many examples in my interviews with leaders. In toxic, bullying environments, then people stop offering up ideas, hold back from giving honest feedback and even lose their voice. Tragically this was just at the crucial moment when their contribution was needed the most.

Fear of relinquishing 'power' leads to the other issue of retaining too much control, not letting go, or not stepping up to becoming a true leader; that is *capacity*. It becomes harder for people to look at us and say, 'This person has the capacity and is ready for a bigger leadership positions' if we cannot delegate and show that we are ready.

This short-term attitude of jealously guarding your power is not serving your longer-term career prospects. Alternatively, as perfectionists we claw back work that's 'not good enough', in our eyes. In our eagerness to show our willingness to work hard, we take on other people's metaphorical 'monkeys' (their difficult problems) and, before we know it, then we're running a zoo full of monkeys! At this point we are so stressed, that we are not only not thinking well, but we are also limiting our potential to progress.

One inspiring leader said to me the antidote to this is, *"I aspire to be respected as a leader by growing other leaders. By delegating, empowering and coaching others, I deliberately aim to make myself redundant. In that way I can be metaphorically on the balcony and not on the dance floor. I therefore create time to stop and really think for myself about the big strategic issues. I focus on where I know I can add value. I am paid a lot of money to inspire leadership and answer just three questions a year. The skill is to choose specifically what those three questions are, answer them correctly and so add real value by delivering on them."*

Now there's also a ***biological implication*** when our identity and egos demand a sense of power and control; the sense of status produces increased dopamine and testosterone. Whilst someone is promoted in the status stakes, someone of course must be 'demoted'. This is less of an issue when we are included and part of the 'in-group', where a sense of status exists in some form, even when we are not the actual leader. Remember power can be derived in a number of ways, including: leadership, ownership, knowledge, intellect, extent of followers, social status, or even being the only woman in the executive team or 'the queen bee'. However, when we are excluded and part of the 'out-group', or in the minority, this can have a detrimental effect. Then the experience can produce the same emotional reaction as pain and also responses such as 'fight, flight, freeze' (amygdala hijack) and hormonal release (adrenaline, cortisol).

In our leadership, it would be interesting to self-assess exactly what we are experiencing – low or high status – and the resulting implications and impact on us. I've experienced going to networking events where a male colleague and I have both noticed that I have been excluded, almost to the point of being blanked. Unfortunately, in all instances this has been by women. It used to anger and upset me, but now it only serves as a source of humour, in a quiet moment of reflection after the event. It is disappointing how, as women, we continue to elevate the men to power positions, and use dismissive tactics to purposefully disempower women. Both men and women must play their part by encouraging inclusion and treating people equally and respectfully. If we operate on the principle of *abundance* and apply the ethic of *compassion*, then we will actively encourage the growth and development of others. By being abundant, we advocate collaborative working and valuing everyone's ability to think for themselves and contribute.

It is also important in our leadership to get the right amount of balanced focus on *strategy vs. delivery*. I have found in my work with many businesses that you often get a greater emphasis on one, or the other, and struggle to get the balance between both.

Naomi Eisenstadt CB is a highly inspirational leader, which is combined with a wonderful humility. Her highly intelligent strategies for making a positive difference for disadvantaged families and groups whilst the Director of Sure Start and Director of the Social Exclusion Taskforce have delivered visible results. Naomi shared with me how she believes that we, "...*often over-value strategic intelligence and under-value tactics.*" Using our intellect to create a strategy can be highly appealing, even the initial momentum for change. However, new initiatives and leadership mean that many change efforts lose momentum and are even dropped. When it comes to over-emphasis on delivery and tactics, this is often where technical experts and professionals (in particular, for example, HR) can metaphorically 'get deep into their opposing trenches, fighting the battles', rather than comfortably taking their seats at the leadership table to shape and influence strategic direction.

Naomi shared with me, *"One of the things I learned when trying to work other organisations is the importance of having a shared understanding of what they are trying to do and what we're trying to do and align goals. I remember interviewing someone for a civil service promotion and asked them, 'why was cross-governmental working so difficult?' and the answer was, 'they don't understand what we're trying to do'. For me that was the wrong answer. The answer should have been, 'how do we understand what they're trying to do, so that we can align better?' If you try to solve problems, always by assuming that the other person, with whom you're trying to solve the problem, doesn't understand your goals, or is stupid, then you're not going to get very far. I always try to understand why someone would think that way and then work together to build consensus, without compromising on the core values. It's really hard, but that's the task."*

An insular focus, working in silos and the lack of alignment fail to realise the full potential of the end-to-end value chain and leverage the entire intellectual capital available. Yet, in a competitive environment, where we are encouraged to 'promote' ourselves and where bonuses are based on our individual ranking and comparative performance, it brings out the most basic, self-preservation instincts. This detracts from a healthy team spirit. Our views become blinkered, as we see our own efforts as applaud-able and those of others as falling short of our own 'high expectations'. These judgments and biases are very common in business, even though we try to rationalise them, with very plausible reasons. The full firepower that exists within any organisation is that of the *collective team,* rather than of the single lone ranger.

In Jonathan Bowman-Perks' book, *Inspiring Leadership,* he creates the analogy of the 'monkeys'. These monkeys represent chunks of work. He states, "*I willingly took every monkey that people gave me. I then had a veritable zoo and was too overloaded to think straight. I hated the situation... I thought of asking to be posted to another much easier and lower profile job. Essentially I was considering resigning from that job.*"

We know from research that women, in particular, take on far too many monkeys! We say 'yes' to many things and then start to feel a sense of failure when we cannot manage it all. We feel burdened by the choices we make and yet struggle to take the simple, yet crucial step to recalibrate and reorganise. It is hard to change our behaviour, and consequently, we become the go-to person and the one who always says 'yes'. If we want to be successful in our leadership, we need to learn to say *'no'.* We benefit by creating some personal boundaries for ourselves and others.

This means we also need to learn to *delegate.* Not just the dull, dirty, unpleasant and boring work that we're trying to get rid of, but, more inspiringly, by delegating the more sexy and interesting pieces of work too. This is not about passing on our monkeys to others! Rather it is about freeing up our own agenda, so we can also determine the pieces of work that are going to help grow and develop us as strategic leaders. Our work then becomes of greater value to ourselves and to the organisation. If we have zero spare capacity and are 'maxed out', then this is a harder task.

But here comes the other challenge. We also have *high expectations* of others and ourselves. So to whom do we delegate? Too often we delegate and then take the task back, frustrated when it's not delivered exactly to our high expectations. An essential part of leadership is to empower our team. If they don't have the right skills, then we need to coach them and support them. In my interviews with women who have house-husbands, they often talk about how the husbands don't quite manage the house the same way that they would. However, they have had to learn to let go of this. They have had to manage their thinking about their own standards, or approaches and let go or have conversations about ownership.

Often in our pursuit of *the next big role*, we forget to ask ourselves is this role right, both for me and for the organisation?

Fedelma Good shared, *"I'm now in the world of Marketing and Introduced to the Direct Marketing Association. I was invited on to the Data Council and was subsequently elected to the board. I put myself forward and was elected as Board Deputy Chair. I believed the principle of the Deputy Chair always moving onto the chair's role was not as it should be. I felt I could change the principle and the Deputy Chair role was the one I was right for. I believe that the move is also not always about the step beyond; you may just be the person supporting. I knew that the Chair position didn't interest me, for example. Just because it has always happened, for example, that the Deputy Chair got the Chair role I don't believe this to be the right thing. I felt I was there to support the Chair. I feel you don't always have to be the 'top dog'. Just hiring someone because it appears that they're next in line is a load of baloney and may not necessarily be the right thing. I'm clear about, 'this is what I am, I don't enjoy it when the focus is on me. This is not my kind of leadership. I'm truly not comfortable and don't enjoy this'. It's okay to say that and people should feel comfortable with this too."*

Being really clear about what we're great at and passionate about is crucial to navigating our careers. Also, we should be honest with ourselves when we are unsuited to a role and are the 'round peg in the square hole', then actively do something about it! Many leaders I've interviewed spoke about occasions like these and that consequently they have not been at their best. Know your limitations.

Paradoxically, we also hold ourselves back from opportunities to grow and *experience new challenges*, for fear of failure and through lack of confidence. I believe that we are more powerful as humans, yet we often hold ourselves back from unleashing this. Self-imposed limitations are mainly based on assumptions rather than reality. This is often because of our own attitudes and dialogue – both internal and external. Maybe there are stored memories (in the hippocampus of our brain) that are defining who we believe we are today? In my research I have found that we often create an emotional hook linked to our past, to our education, our wealth, our career success and, especially, our failures. When these form our inner dialogue for who we are, or aren't, they limit us. Our internal self-critique is like a 'restrictor/governor on a car', one that constrains us below an artificially imposed maximum performance.

Whatever the reason, we must break down our assumptions and fears. Try asking ourselves questions like, 'If we knew we could do this, how would we do it?' Or ask ourselves, 'If we knew we couldn't fail, then how much could we achieve and how good would we feel?' Knowledge can always be gained, whether it is through training, mentoring, or coaching. Yet we do not leverage the resources available to us, and, instead, our independent streak holds us back. We are far more resourceful than we ever realise. By naming our problem, or concern, we are able to think through to create solutions. Through appreciation and gratitude for what we already have, we can value our strengths and this belief has the potential for creating seismic shifts in our performance and happiness. We create the *positive philosophical choice* to believe in the best in others and ourselves in order to step towards success, rather than step away from opportunities. And, if we are not sure, then there are plenty of people around who are knowledgeable and talented enough to help. If only we would ask...

Of course, we all make *mistakes*. As painful, or embarrassing, as it may feel at the time, mistakes provide us with the greatest catalyst for our learning. However, fear based cultures are preventing people from being at their finest, or working to their full potential. These intimidating cultures prevent us from being courageous in our risk taking, for fear of the subsequent negative consequences. Our very societal underpinning has become one of critique, *judgment* and intolerance.

Social media has become the international platform for our views. Sacrificial lambs become our target for venting our own unhappiness and discontent, whether it is societal, in our communities, our organisations, our teams, or even our own families. Women judge other women both for their career ambitions, or their lack of career ambition. We often talk about ourselves in terms of our *intent* and others in terms of their *actions*. We turn heroes into zeroes, and vice versa, at the blink of an eye. We look to leaders in authority and criticise them personally for what's happening, rather than appreciating them for who they are (particularly when it's not in our favour). Those leaders in Government epitomise this in its most visible form, both in our critical and jaundiced views of them and their judgemental behaviours towards each other.

This has the dangerous whiff of hypocrisy and can make us fickle and highly subjective!

We are creating a society where the threat response centres of everyone's brains are in danger of being on constant high alert. Indeed cynics might observe that it is in the best interests of parts of Government, such as the military, emergency service and security services, to keep us in a state of continual anxiety and fear. In that atmosphere of negative provocation, they can justify and sustain their status and funding.

The challenge here is: how do we start to look at each other through an alternative lens? How do we intervene and think differently? This requires a deep awareness of ourselves so we can break our recurring negative mental processing and suspend those unhealthy judgements. If we believed that everyone's intent is good, how would this change our thinking? Only then can we see the best in others and also help to facilitate them bringing out the best in themselves.

Now of course, having sound judgement and being discerning is equally important. We must be able to make wise judgements about people and business. *Pattern recognition* is a complex process that integrates information from at least thirty different parts of the brain. Faced with a new situation, we make assumptions based on prior experiences and judgments. Thus a chess master can assess a chess game and choose a high-quality move, by drawing on patterns they have seen before. But pattern recognition can also mislead us. When we're dealing with seemingly familiar situations, our brains can cause us to think we understand them when actually we don't. We have seen highly intelligent leaders make some crazy mistakes and errors in judgment. What helps with discernment is not just our own wisdom, but other's diverse wisdom too. However, we continue to hire people in our own likeness. I'm not talking physically, although that happens with surprising frequency! We hire in our mirror image, in terms of our leadership style and attitudes. We are in fact unconsciously creating our own in-groups because this gives us a level of comfort and connectivity.

In a world of open economies, free markets, lowered trade barriers and a frantic spread of information through technology, virtually every business has become far more brutally competitive. For us to be *truly discerning* and *wise,* then we must be able to leverage the full intellectual capability of the *diverse team* that we have around us. There has been significant research and publications about how leaders fail and derail themselves. We have also done a lot of psychometric feedback and coaching with leaders to understand their strengths and subsequent derailers. Failure has been linked to:

1. **Poor strategic direction** – due to either our parochial thinking or our 'power hungry' egos.
2. **Lack of execution** - linked to lack of leadership. One leader said, 'we hire for intellect and fire for lack of emotional intelligence'.

There is a great book called, *Why CEO's Fail: The 11 Behaviours That Can Derail Your Climb to the Top and How to Manage Them*, by Dotlich and Cairo. This captures the essence of these issues and how to manage them. The overplayed characteristics which can lead to derailing are:

1. **Arrogance** - you're right, everyone else is wrong.
2. **Melodrama** – the need to be the centre of attention.
3. **Volatility** - mood swings.
4. **Excessive Caution** – fear of making decisions.
5. **Habitual Distrust** - focus on the negatives.
6. **Aloofness** - disengaged and disconnected.
7. **Mischievousness** - rules are made to be broken.
8. **Eccentricity** - being different just for the sake of it.
9. **Passive Resistance** - what you say is not what you really believe.

10. **Perfectionism** - getting the little things right and yet the big things wrong.
11. **Eagerness to Please** - try to win the popularity contest.

Now, the question is, who do you consider to be your 'first' and 'second' team? We often believe that our own team, which we lead, is our first and most important team. We see ourselves as being just a 'member' of the team above. We may view the needs of the team above us as an irritating, but necessary, distraction. We look after and protect our own team, and yet get frustrated with the team above when it comes into conflict with 'our team'. We may even air these frustrations. We may equally take pride in being the rebellious maverick, giving ourselves 'hero' status. We resort to the tactics of the 'organisational terrorist' fighting against authority and control. The revolution occurs underground, in the corridors, in the meetings. We criticise the team above in the misconceived 'privacy' of our own team meetings. Whilst thinking such disloyal behaviour to be cool and gaining us popularity with our own team, it actually loses us their trust and respect. They will rightly wonder, 'If our leader says that about their team above, then what might they say about us, when we are not in the room?'

I have seen this many times in my career and it's disheartening and actually ends up affecting not just the reputation of the leader, but the team as a whole. As leaders, we must consider that our 'first team' is the one that is the next level up. The 'second team' is the team we lead. We have a responsibility to contribute to our first team, and be a genuinely active member, rather than seeing it as a distraction or inconvenient interruption to our own leadership.

Building a metaphorical *Army of Giants* around us is essential to success; these people have specific skills that make them a few inches taller than us. We must then value the intellectual, emotional and social capital that a diverse team brings. Research shows that aggressively dominant people have been proven to be poor at determining the value of social learning. They equally don't incorporate this well into their own wisdom and the decisions that they make. Social learning requires performance-enhancing behaviours, those that occur as a result of group-based equality.

Have you ever noticed how it feels when you have a completely different 'type' of person in the team? We've all seen this often. It's illustrated in particular when you consider the functions (for example: HR, Legal, Marketing and Finance) working with the business (Operations). We like to bring in experts for advice. However, we then fail to listen to their expertise, instead, getting frustrated when the advice challenges our own views and needs. Issues of diverse thinking become the greatest source of conflict, rather than being seen and utilised as the greatest source of wisdom. Our in-groups get tighter as we 'protect our own' and play the part of the organisational terrorist and, so, undermining the external force.

By truly valuing difference and turning potential points of conflict and friction into healthy debate and discussion, we can work towards a win-win scenario where both sides get a successful outcome. This means letting go of our over-inflated egos and personal agendas, which may be self-serving, rather than serving our business needs

One of my biggest concerns for this component, is that in tough times the first place to get cut back and downsized is HR. I'm not talking about the basic, transactional HR. This is about the *investment in leadership*. In efforts to cut costs and demonstrate efficiency, mediocre interventions are offered for our executives. I've seen this consistently in the field of coaching, where the investment has been reduced so much that the most talented coaches are walking away from assignments. Instead they are going to organisations where their talents and contributions are recognised and more valued.

Training courses and developmental experiences get shelved, until 'better times'. The fact is that it's in the toughest times that leaders need the most intellectual stimulation and support. How we treat people in the tough times may not reflect immediately in any movement, but this will undoubtedly shift with the changing economic climate. I spoke to one leader who recalls a conversation with a Partner, when one consultancy firm acquired another. The Partner said that the acquiring firm had stopped all development to make even more money and his advice was, "*when any firm stops investing in developing you as leaders, then get out and run for the hills!*" Not surprisingly, a lot of the best consultants left in the three years following the acquisition.

You will know from my earlier chapters that, whilst I believe data and insight is important, it is not the final answer. My frustration comes with the *stereotyping* that now occurs, in particular, between women and men. Many statements that are made are stated as true, and they lodge themselves as facts deep in our psyche: 'the research says X, therefore it must be so'. One inspiring leader described how she was asked to change everything that she had learned in terms of how to be successful as a leader, and become 'more feminine', in order to succeed in her role. I believe there are a number of issues here. Labelling means it's hard to break through biases. We fail to value individual differences, by only seeing men and women as fundamentally different. Our expectations for how we are and how we should be behaving then make us judged. We start to think ourselves in normative terms and align to these social constraints. I have a chapter on research in this book, however it is provided for you as a source of insight only. It does not and cannot define us as individuals.

How can IQ help you as a Leader?

Helen Sachdev is a talented, highly successful leader at the same time as being a great Mum. In our interview, she described how, *"I didn't do well in terms of my 'A' levels. My Dad saw an advert for an alternative education route, which was a new sandwich degree being set up in Manchester. It offered a one year stint in business and, having reviewed the options in the UK, I got together with a friend, and we got on with organising a placement in the US. I was told by a tutor that I had to take one of the placements offered in the UK, but I challenged him and asked, 'if you were me, what would you do?' He laughed and could only concede.*

"I guess that's my first really memorable experience of challenging authority and winning through. The rewards of living and working in Boston, MA, were definitely worth the risk of challenging the accepted view. Since then, I've been told many times there are things I can't do or there's no point doing. I've come to recognise that these moments are often pivotal decision

points in terms of what happens next in my career and my life. I've learnt to take risks at these critical moments, to be honest and to not keep my head down.

"I also recognise it's important to stay true to my values but it's also important to balance this against the need to be invited into the heart of the organisation where decision making takes place. Adapting my behaviour has been an important aspect of me being given permission to 'earn my seat at the table'. I've found it's important to recognise and adapt to the dominant culture - real change is only really achievable if you are working in partnership with the establishment, as well as challenging it. Things don't always go the right way and, at these times, it's helpful to slow down and challenge blockers to understand what are our excuses and what is reality. This has been the basis for my attitude. Early in my career, I would take on roles and opportunities, even if I didn't know exactly how I would deliver them. I had the benefits of a lot of theory and applied textbook management that I had been exposed to early in my career, and actively looked for opportunities to put theory into practice.

"After I had been working in Sainsbury's for 14 years, I wanted to move on. I'd never applied for a job or even written a CV. So in recognition of this, I searched out and used up my own cash and holiday allowance to go through a 1-week condensed training programme to help me gain the necessary skills. I believe I would not have got my next step out and up without this investment.

"It's also about knowing when to ask for things; the timing is crucial. I think the best time to ask for what you really want, whether it is resource, or some flexibility in how you choose to work, is when you are performing at your best, and when people really want you. This is often at the point that you are being offered a new role. Rather than being just grateful to be asked to do this exciting thing, think what support you need to be successful, go in super-confident and ask for it. I have also learnt that you need to choose your battles, to sense at what point you should let things pass, and in contrast, when it's the right time to call it out. I found the coaching I was provided helped me to notice the signals and manage this much more effectively."

In all of my interviews and research, there has been no consistent theme in terms of inspiring leaders' backgrounds. They haven't all been through private education and have degrees from top universities, born into privileged backgrounds, have wealth and stature. In some cases it's quite the contrary. Stylistically, they are also very different in their approach to how they led.

There is no real compromise on authenticity to fit in a 'man's world' only collaboration. What was clear is that their success, like Helen's, is *compounded by their spirit*. They all have an energy and fire within, which is so fierce that it outweighs their inner-voice, overcoming the internal critic that usually holds others back from achieving their goals. Interestingly, I found in my research that those who come from some of the most challenging backgrounds have a determination and resilience that drives them through. At times, however, there is a deeply independent streak; creating a sense of control over their own destiny, without reliance on others. For them, it is a harder task to ask for help.

In the early part of their careers there have been times when these inspiring leaders had met with others who excluded them, acted in the superior way, or made them feel slightly inadequate. They learnt the hard way that when we elevate the status of others, then we disempower ourselves. They became more successful when they interrupted their internal critic, which had prevented them from achieving their full potential.

If we consider that our main focus is – *to be everything that we possibly can be* – then we can aim to achieve our full potential as inspiring leaders. This means making the *positive philosophical choice*: taking a view that I'm intelligent, worthy and talented and my team are too. This is a far more healthy and empowering view of human behaviour, rather than others such as a negative view of human behaviour which might view everybody as: selfish, greedy, nasty, dishonest and out to get you. Sometimes we may believe that critical decisions and choices are outside of our control. This is particularly relevant when major change and career choices need to be balanced alongside family choices.

In our containment-based responses, much of this is underpinned by *assumptions*. We often make untrue limiting assumptions, which we live as true.

Identifying, unravelling and eliminating such dangerous assumptions is what helps us move on in our lives to become more inspiring leaders of others.

By breaking down our assumptions about what can and can't work, and being creative in our options, we then may actually come up with better solutions to suit both worlds.

We become far more powerful when we manage our *internal dialogue* so that we move beyond *self-limiting beliefs* to opening up our minds and believing in others and ourselves. We then open up our full mental capacity to think through our issues in a logical and structured way.

I find Rudyard Kipling's poem helpful in this context:

> *I keep six honest serving-men:*
> *(They taught me all I knew)*
> *Their names are What and Where*
> *And When And How and Why and Who.*
> *I send them over land and sea,*
> *I send them east and west;*
> *But after they have worked for me,*
> *I give them all a rest.*

Knowing we are resourceful and have unlimited resources available to us, particularly in the era of cutting-edge technology, we just need to draw on our courage to take more risks in our careers and our lives. So *ask* for what you need of the organisation, family, spouse and society.

This does not mean that everything will be seamless, by any means. In Lisa Lockwood's book, *Reinventing You*, she shares, *"...does not mean everything is perfect being happy, or joyful, does not mean that everything is perfect. It means you have decided to look beyond imperfections in your environment and shift your focus to all that is good, or what could be good."*

This is about having the *confidence* and knowing that we are aiming for everything that we can and want to be, and that we have everything at our fingertips to help us get there. When *blips* occur, they are just that. Blips.

They are moments in time and we need to ask ourselves, 'Will this matter in one month, in one year, or in ten years from now?' The blips are not to be feared, but embraced as fantastic opportunities from which we can learn and grow even more. This can be the greatest catalyst to our development and careers, if only we choose to embrace it.

Of course there are the *externally imposed limitations* put in place by others. People told Isabelle Santoire she could never be a professional Mountain Guide. People told Lisa Lockwood she would never make it on the SWAT team and when Latha Caleb's father expected her to work in the family business, she forged his signature so she could overcome his constraints and become educated. The list goes on. Yet, each of these women has been successful, despite the 'advice' they've had, not because of it. Now, that's not to say that we should not listen to the words of advice from those around us. When people said *'Leigh, you will never make it as a singer; stick with the day job'*, a message subsequently reinforced by my howling dog, I realised that maybe they were right!

We've seen many leaders derail and often they have ignored the wisdom of their teams and the needs of their business. In our hyper-busyness, we encourage fast decisions and expect best thinking. Inspiring Leadership is about creating a safe environment that encourages the best possible thinking. It also encourages true listening, which culminates in a decision, or action that helps our business become more successful. The greatest thinking does not come from immediacy, which is influenced by our internal thought patterns and lacks creativity. This requires us to effectively *oscillate between reflection and pace*. Reflection is for our best thinking, whilst pace is to get things done!

In our Masterclasses on 'Effective Meetings', we facilitate an observation session, before we move into team coaching (some of our tools are shared in Chapter 14: Tools, Techniques and Resources). Meetings have become a major constraint in businesses. Whether it's too many meetings, too many people at the meetings, too much communication and not enough decision-making, too many people dominating and too few contributing. Does any of this sound familiar?

As inspiring leaders, we have the opportunity to work far more intelligently. We have the power and influence to restructure the way that we all work, in order to make the time we spend at work add more value. We also need to have greater consideration for the complexity of teams in a virtually connected world. *If the quality of our decisions is highly dependent on the quality of our thinking (Nancy Kline),* then as inspiring leaders we must consider how we work together virtually more effectively. We must be able to create thinking enhancing behaviours and approaches, rather than thinking inhibiting ones.

'Everything should be as simple as possible and no simpler.' In the complexity of business we require a few, clear and focused objectives. We must avoid swamping our people with far too much change initiatives and running the risk of diluted or zero delivery. Instead we need to decide and commit to what we need to focus on: the *vital few.* To realise the power of a single decision, we also need to make it public. I have seen on numerous occasions how HR have had a strategy, but then never found the courage to take this fully to the business. Knowing there were contentious issues, there was not sufficient confidence to advise and collaborate with the business. Making a decision and communicating it, so that the other person clearly understands it, means that it has the best possible chance to become reality.

By knowing what we're not just good at, but great at, then we can leverage this to our full advantage. In leadership, the whole benefit of having an amazing team is that they can help to complement each other and fill in the gaps in our own knowledge and experience.

Self-awareness comes up a lot in this book, but interestingly, it's often the underpinning issue that causes us to derail. This is essential for managing talented people and particular the impatient Millennials (GenY).

Annalisa Bicknell describes how, *"...with all the experiences you have in your life you become a bit more relaxed and more mature; more confident in your ability, so you don't have to fight every battle. You can take things step by step; you don't need to change the world in seven days. I have learned over time to be more patient - more patient with myself, but also more patient with the people around me."*

I advocate transparent cultures that support people when they make mistakes. However, what is foolish is to allow repeated mistakes, caused by ignorance and insufficient reflection, when investment could have been made in terms of time and development to prevent it.

We must also be able to help individuals realise their full potential. This means giving *just-in-time feedback* and not to wait for the performance management process at midyear or the end of the year. By then it's far too late. We must spot and recognise when people are doing well, and they will want to do more. It helps to approach each difficult conversation with a combination of two things: compassion and courage. At times, this feedback may also need to be reinforcing, even in the face of adversity.

Helen Sachdev's father was very influential in his support of her, *"When I've been in a scrape, there's always been someone in the background pitching for me. My Dad never said very much, but when he did it was always something very valuable and really mattered to me. When things would go wrong and I would knock against authority he would say to me, 'You were always really feisty, better to be like that and challenging rather than just be the wall-flower'. He saw my strengths in me and boosted my confidence."*

In my own story, by being open to *experiences*, I was then presented with an opportunity that actually turned out to be life changing in terms of my career and home. I was working in the finance sector reviewing the talent strategy for the organisation. When a colleague was leaving the organisation, then an opportunity arose to assess, select and manage the executive coaches. It was a significant strategic project.

Fortunately I had sufficient capacity, so I put my hat in the ring. As an area that was suffering from high costs and little alignment, I intuitively knew that this was an amazing opportunity. It not only became one of the most high profile internal pieces of work in the firm, but also transformational in terms of leadership development. It received significant external recognition, at a time when the coaching market was saturated and unregulated. It resulted in me working with the best coaches in the world and the top leaders of our organisation. When I left to set up my own business, I brought this experience with me and it became a key component to the Clareo Potential Operating Model that we use today.

By having truly diverse teams and building an *'Army of Giants'* around us, we are then able to increase our intellectual firepower and overall group wisdom. If only we would listen.

Shola Awolesi shared with me, *"I am the fourth-born of five children, three brothers and one sister. I come from a middle-class Nigerian family. I've had a mixed background, having grown up in the UK until I was ten years old. Then I went to Nigeria for a further ten years, where I completed my secondary education.*

"My role model was my mother; she was a strong and inspiring leader of the community with a passion for women's issues, particularly in Nigeria. She was a businesswoman and entrepreneur.

"My Dad was a more gentle, quiet leader and we have a very democratic home. He lost both parents at a young age and it was through the support of the community that he was able to study.

"Going back to Nigeria to give back into the community was very important and I learnt first-hand for him about the importance of giving back. So I had the best of both worlds with both of my parents. The differences were between having a lot to then suddenly not having a lot. We were rebuilding block by block and this has made me highly adaptable to many unusual situations. I feel really blessed and fortunate about giving back. My background plays a huge part in this.

"We all had a voice on major decisions and so this feels comfortable for me. We have an interesting family, with strong individuals who are quite independent and with time we have learnt to be more interdependent: when we need to do stuff together then we do. This is how we differ from more traditional Nigerian families; as it's less hierarchical, I find I'm the reluctant leader. Titles don't sit well for me.

"When I find myself in leadership positions, then I take on more of a proactive role; this is just what I do. If there's something that needs to get done, then let's just get on and do it. I only started to feel more comfortable with leadership when I attended an Ashridge leadership programme, which gave me an opportunity to reflect on my own experiences and influences in

leadership and helped me to understand my own leadership journey.

"Coming from a Christian background, I'm very values driven. This ties into the choices about the jobs that I have taken on. I believe in doing something that has a particular purpose and making a real difference. I do believe in getting things done."

It's important to have people around us who we can totally trust. Who are committed to, and share, our vision, but offer different perspectives. Creating feedback loops and having honest conversations means that people will say some quite frank things to us. Understanding others' perceptions and getting to the truth is essential. Rather than seeing feedback as a form of Trojan horse with hidden intentions involving personal attacks, instead we would be better to accept it as a gift.

Sayyeda Salam shared her own experience, *"Learning to work in a cross cultural environment can be really tough. One night I felt close to tears. I had to keep fighting through. I was so frustrated because I had a terrible boss. I remember thinking a lot about the team and the wider situation. I decided to take a more mature approach and booked in time with the director. I said how we needed to 'up our game'. These are the ways I think we can do it. It was very much about recognising the problem from a wider perspective and not just my own perception. It gave me the confidence to feel comfortable with leadership."*

Firstly, we will benefit from intervening more to support and develop people at key *induction points*. For example, bringing on board new people into the team, bringing together a new and diverse team, or promoting a leader into a new position.

This is not the typical induction in terms of policy and process. This is about helping people for the first few months, so they can integrate well and build effective and influential relationships. It addresses the cultural context, politics and behaviours that exist to give new people the best possible start. Where I have seen this work at its best is in organisations where the induction starts long before the individual joins. As we heard in her story, Sayyeda also took responsibility and so, instead of bringing the issue to leadership, she brought thought through observations and solutions. She 'spoke her truth' and held the *courageous conversation* that needed to be had.

She took responsibility for shaping her own destiny, as well as that of the organisation.

Jane Parry shared with me, *"Through my entire career I have received a massive amount of training and personal development support. I went on a women's only 'career skills development programme' for junior managers as there were not enough women in senior management roles at the time. I vividly remember the advice. These practical tips were crucial in terms of how to successfully hold down a job. I've had lots of different opportunities to do lots of different aspects of business. By staying in a role for a sufficient period of time you get to really understand the business, and by moving to new roles, you get a deeper awareness of different disciplines.*

"At one point I took on a role as a business analyst - I wasn't much good at it and I didn't really enjoy it. But this is crucial in terms of fast tracking your career development because you take away two core lessons: the first is how to identify and leverage your skills and strengths, and the second is a greater self-awareness of what you do and don't want in your career. I felt the culture had changed to hard, transactional based management that was dismissive of people that had been there a long time. It didn't fit for me so I spent a year proactively managing my exit from the business.

"I received a new job offer and felt in control - I felt I had made the right decision for me and my career. Subsequently, I was head-hunted by Duncan Lawrie Private Bank, which gave me the remit to decide what we should do to grow the business. After my six-month probation period, I became the first woman to be appointed to the UK Board. What's great about my current boss is that he has hired me to do a job that he trusts me to get on with. This is so unlike some of my previous experiences, where the culture seemed internally focussed and all about how to stop you."

At a personal level, *professionalising ourselves* through education and experiences is important. The benefits are broader than this though, it helps us to develop our wisdom and liberates our thinking. In our leadership it is not about the 'what' we are doing, but 'why' we are doing it. What is the rationale and purpose for pursuing different forms of development? We need to ask, "Is it needed? Is this the most valuable thing that we can do to enhance our leadership?"

As humans we require *intellectual stimulation.* The more we educate ourselves, the more we create new neural pathways and connections. In Robert Holden's book, *Success Intelligence*, he describes the difference between superior and inferior goal setting. He notes how often leaders focus on achievement based goals, rather than purpose based goals. They get a sense of achievement from doing, rather than being. Robert states, "Wisdom is Not an MBA" and so we should be cautious about the professional labels we are searching for, versus the quality of experiences that will truly support our career trajectory.

As an inspiring leader, it is important for us to also earn trust. There is a saying, 'people are not prepared to understand you, until they have at first been understood by you'. To learn about people's needs, motivations, concerns, we must be sincerely interested in them and *ask questions* from a position of curiosity and *not knowing.*

We then need to *listen, intently,* to what they have to say, so we are exquisitely attuned. This means suspending our own thoughts, perspectives and judgements. This is harder than it seems. Often, we listen only to wait for the pause – the intake of breath, so that we can jump in and offer our own opinions and advice.

The question is, whose agenda are we really listening to? Like a muscle, this takes a little bit of practice to build up and sustain. The results are powerful though as, right at the very core of our biology, we are releasing oxytocin, which is the relationship building, or love hormone.

Building trust in this way requires us to let go of our egos and tap into our humility as leaders.

Intellectual Stimulation and Learning

"Everyone you meet and everything you do has something to teach you; if only you would really observe and listen."

\- Jonathan Bowman-Perks MBE, Executive Coach and Author

Laura Birrell works at the BBC and shared with me, *"I have spent time building my experience and then moving up, rather than just being promoted, before doing a job brilliantly. I have climbed my way up. My career trajectory has been matched by my momentum. I wouldn't be here if that hadn't happened. You need to focus on your potential and not time. Have balanced growth spurts. After six months as an HR Business Partner, I was managing two board members and 600 people. It's been so exhilarating and my boss has put her trust in me. She's taken big risks with me and never stifled me. When you enjoy something so much, then it's easy to just come here and stagnate; never necessarily leaving. However, I feel I'm on a crusade and so I raise the bar for myself each year, getting better at what I do and continually growing."*

Many organisations apply the 70:20:10 approach to personal development, which is based on significant research by Morgan McCall and his colleagues working at the Centre for Creative Leadership (CCL):

- *70% from on the job experience.* Consider how you can gain depth and breadth; work in challenging environments such as turnarounds, managing profit and loss accounts, leading international teams.
- *20% from people.* In particular from the boss. This can be in the form of mentoring/reverse mentoring, coaching, advocacy, role models, networks and feedback.
- *10% from courses and reading.* Courses can provide us with the input and tools to transfer back into work, and so cannot be underestimated. Just a little cautionary note - endless attainment of professional courses and qualifications may not directly translate into career success. It is a surprising truth that the average person in the UK and US reads on average only one non-fiction book per year. So if you were to read three

books on just one specific topic, then you can quickly become a comparative expert!

There is more information about specific interventions in the Tools, Techniques and Resources chapter. The most essential and under-utilised opportunity is in the true development of leadership and the future talent pipeline at a deeply personal level. Whilst training programmes are important for awareness, the real shift occurs through embedding habitual learning. Our learning memory is significantly influenced by the context we create for the learning experience. Many relationships that are valid in one context may not be valid in another. The brain does account for some of this by learning the context. However, this is often why much of the training that we provide doesn't quite create the behavioural change that we anticipate.

Goals involve a powerful combination of motivation, attention and emotion. *Goal based learning* therefore promotes a feeling of reward and significantly increases the effectiveness of learning. We're not quite sure how (scientifically), but attention and emotion can alter the routing of neural networks on a millisecond-by-millisecond basis. Goal based learning causes the release of the neuromodulator dopamine. However, there must be predictive validity between the learning and the outcome, otherwise behavioural change does not take place.

We have seen the most transformational change occur in our coaching, when it has occurred through *blended learning* which includes, for example: analysis and feedback, team coaching in the meeting environment, or business related project work. This creates different contexts and opportunities to reinforce and embed the learning more effectively.

This is particularly important for *un-learning* behaviours. So, when you have a learning opportunity for you or your team consider how this can be reinforced through goals and repetition. The neural synaptic connections in our brain have particular strengths, so when neurons are repeatedly activated the (synaptic) strength of the connection between them increases. Through repetition, or 'habit learning' this causes new synapses to form. As the saying goes, 'neurons that fire together, wire together'.

So what does all this mean? If we get the context and learning opportunities right, then we have every chance at successfully creating behavioural and cultural change.

Olivia Byrne
General Manager, Exclusive Eccleston
Square Hotel, London

Having graduated from Ecole Hotelière de Lausanne, Olivia was only 23 years old when she followed in her father's footsteps to become an hotelier. In 2011, they opened the exclusive, boutique Eccleston Square Hotel (previously a budget hotel) in the heart of the city of London. At 25 years old, Olivia became General Manager. I was in full admiration of Olivia, not just because of her astonishing achievements, but of her combination of intellectual capability, wisdom, vision and leadership. She has worked hard on creating a unique design, setting it apart from others.

"I am French-English and therefore bi-lingual. I went to boarding school in Switzerland and have grown up in an international environment. My father was an hotelier, owning two hotels in Paris. I grew up hearing stories about his work. From the age of 11, I helped out at the hotels. I realised it was in my blood, like my father, and I had a clear sense of direction. My father sold his hotels 10 years ago. We had the idea to create a family business and pass on knowledge to the next generation. I have never felt pushed; it was always my decision. My Mum owns her own publishing company in France. When I was small, my parents worked extremely hard and never gave up. They wouldn't panic. They would stay cool and always find a solution and a way through.

"When I decided what I wanted to do, I looked all over the world for a hotel. I loved Miami, but it didn't make sense for me as the environment and mentality there was very different. With my parents being based in Europe, then it would have been tough for me there too. We saw the London hotel as a strong long-term investment opportunity. It used to be a budget hotel and we wanted to change it into something far more exclusive. When I graduated

I came straight to the hotel. We employed a General Manager and we were very lean about running the business. Much as we tried to bring out the best in everyone we took on form the budget hotel, sadly we had to let go of all of the existing hotel staff. We also ended up having to let go of the General Manager in the end. I ended up managing the hotel, which we hadn't expected so quickly. As a family business we had invested money, emotion and a lot of passion into the business.

"It was very tough in the beginning. It was hard to monitor the performance. With the delays that occurred, then we ended up opening the hotel three months later than originally scheduled. It was a further three months after opening that I realised nothing had been organised. It was such a tough environment and we had to start making people redundant department by department. The shift from Budget to Boutique Hotel was significant; it needed people with a real passion like us for exceptional customer service. We networked with people from around the hotel businesses and recruited based on reputation and put some stability in place.

"The toughest part was in that first few months of opening. We had absolutely no reception staff. It felt like there was no light at the end of the tunnel. So we brought in a management company to support, as we just needed to get the big decisions made and start to create value again. I often did draw on my gut feeling, as my father advised me. Whether I was the correct thing or not, I realised I just had to let things go and make the decision. Changing the hotel meant we faced 'mutiny' at one point and so it was great that I had support. Staff were handling things in an immature way. It was very emotional at the beginning. I knew then that I had to be the bigger person and use my back-up and support. I found my voice and said what I thought. Actually, I said what I believed in passionately. It was an unpleasant time and it was a shame we had to make so many people redundant. I felt very vulnerable at various times throughout the experience.

"James, my brother, arrived to support me six months later. We are a small family company and entrepreneurial and so it's been great to have James here for emotional back up. It's really great to have someone to talk to that you can trust and strategise with, testing things with when I'm not too sure. Once my brother arrived we found that the support of the management

company was no longer needed. I've learned it's about having the right types of people and support available to you at the right times.

"It's been such a learning curve. I used to lack confidence, but now I'm very much part of and leading the team. Sometimes I am a bit of a control freak. If the team do great work then I make the effort to praise and reward so they know that they are doing a good job. It can be very tough to be honest when you are so close to something, and I don't want to hurt people. I also understand though that it's our business. So we put our hours and hard effort in, the same as everyone else. Some people can't handle this type of environment so it's crucial that we find the right people as it makes such a big difference.

"We have a super-cool team, very high energy, passionate and hard working. Other hotels have hierarchical structures and lots of staff. Whereas we offer something very different here; we have a flat structure that allows everyone to get fully involved. We have a real team approach and encourage ideas generation. It's strange how some people fit and then some people don't. With this hotel, we have created a unique experience. It's important that everyone goes the extra mile, get involved in other tasks and they are willing to support each other. Our relationship with our staff is like an extension of the family. It's less about being the boss and more about keeping the trust.

"My advice now through all of this is to listen to your gut instinct, which comes with experience. You may not be able to quite quantify something, but you can smell it, sense it. Sometimes I make mistakes. It's all an important part of management. You need to rely on other people's opinions a lot and know that, as an entrepreneur or leader, you have to make a lot of decisions. For a business to grow at pace with immediate results, sometimes this means making tough decisions early on. Some people are too afraid of making decisions and hurting their employees' feelings. As I can be very emotional and passionate about what I do, I've learned not to take things to heart too much. I do find it's very hard for me to change my mind once it's made up and so I think it's always important to have a trusted confidante.

"My days are crazy and people don't quite understand my work-life. Theirs is very different. They are all working very hard and are very career *focused. For me my passion is my business and so outside of work is the area that I don't get much time for at the moment.*

"When it comes to women, I feel that some women have regressed a bit. I see really educated women. They base their lives around boyfriend, marriage and family and they get 'stuck' in their work. They no longer seem to have the fire in their belly. At 25, it feels so young and I feel we change so much. We need to take the time to takes some risks and grow, in particular if we are not happy. I look at some of my friends who are already acting like a married couple. I have been very lucky with my opportunity; I realise this. I see that big corporates can be very tough environments and I see how this impacts on the confidence.

"I believe that experience is everything. Books and academia are just not the same. This is a people business and so you need to understand more about what people think. That means first-hand experience of dealing with people in challenging situations.

"My legacy is the success of our hotel business. I want people to come to this hotel and say 'wow' and have something that they've never experienced before. I want to make my Dad proud and provide a future for our family, maybe one day for our children. It's not about ego; this is last. It's all for the hotel. It may seem a bit selfish, but at this point I love what I do and this is shaping me as a person. I have some great days and some bad days. I love my sports and am naturally sporty. I could never switch off from work and I find that it helps the brain when I'm thinking about it. James and I always talk about our work! We've had to fight hard for this business. We do not have lots of money and we have to fight for every penny. We have a budget like everyone else. If this hotel fails, then we fail."

Inspiring Women Leaders' Words of Wisdom

1. Building Self Awareness

"Some people say leaders are born, but that's not true. Yes, you may have innate skills. But it's important to develop 'self', understand your weaknesses and your strengths. Have trusted confidantes and seek feedback. It's important to not be defensive, but just see every opportunity as one where you can learn."

2. Trusted Advisors

"It's hard to say there's a single, particular role model out there. I've had great advice from various people along the way. For example, I have been told by one person, 'you have to make up your own mind' at the age of 24 when I was asking what to do. I remember speaking to my father who said, 'little girls grow up talking about wanting to get married and maybe do some career. You may not have thought about this, but boys grow up thinking they want to do something and maybe they'll get married. I'm just telling you this because I think you should go whichever way you want'."

3. Self-Belief

"I was an expert in recruitment. I would get a terrible blush and nervous rash around my neck and would put a scarf on to cover it. A business partner once said to me, 'I know you find this difficult, I have faith in you and genuinely want your input'. You need to have faith in your own ability."

4. Role Models and Mentors

"I was given a mentor who was 10 years my senior. She was given the role, but clearly didn't enjoy, or value it. She was part of the feminist era and the only woman in the business at a senior position. She clearly had to fight to get to where she was and had the attitude that, if she fought hard then others should do so too. This was not the kind of role model that I looked to. In this era there were no real female role models that were balancing work and home and helping other women. When it comes to role models, I can admire people and take fragments of their careers and success. I think this is important, and not to try to imitate them, because we must be authentic."

5. Coaching Others

"It's important to delegate, and provide the necessary support. I understand the difference between delegation and abdication. Making it happen was all very exciting. Seeing others grow as a result, is even more exciting. It is important as leaders to take responsibility for coaching and growing the pipeline of talent, so that others can thrive."

6. Experiences

"I've done many different things in my career, so the diversity has given me the breadth and I haven't become linear, or parochial. This happens too often and, also, often too soon. Gaining lots of experiences is not just helpful for developing our careers, but also developing us as people. There is so much support available to us now and so I think we can get adventurous."

7. Confidence in Career Navigation

"I've always been an adventurer. I was an ex-pat child and also independent as I was an only child, so I always knew how to socialise. I approach my career with an element of pragmatism and like a challenge; so I have always been curious about giving new things a go. I would often take side-ways moves in order to move up. I have found the more you challenge yourself, do new things and achieve, then the more your self-confidence grows. I recognise there were many times I didn't have a bloody clue, but I was confident enough to go and get the answer."

8. Safe Environment for Mistakes

"It's important how you treat people in their first failure. We need more help when the first mistake is made."

9. Know Your Potential

"It is important not to let potential stay dormant and talents remain undeveloped through fear, leisure, or complacency. It's living half a life and results in lethargy and un-fulfilment. Drawing on your personal power and capacity to continuously learn is crucial to progressing as a leader. I recall times when I have stepped away from opportunities, for fear of failure, and later regretted that. There have been times when I have ventured into the unknown, and also fallen flat on my face. I've learned a lot along the way. There have been times when I've embraced opportunities with both hands and it's proven to be some of my best experiences."

10. Build an Army of Giants

"I quickly learned early on that, if I want to be a good leader, then I need to surround myself by people ten times better than me. It can only happen if you support and respect their skills and knowledge. I often say that 'I am the driver, you are the wheels, tools and knowledge. I don't have what you have and I need you in the team'. I'm not a specialist and don't know everything; I'm not a subject matter expert."

11. Stretch Yourself

"You need to have the confidence to put yourself forward. You are more adaptable and flexible than you realise. Do stretch yourself, you'll find a way to manage things. You are more than any of your self-imposed limitations."

12. Time to Think

"My travel to and from work takes me two hours. This isn't wasted time though. It provides me with a great opportunity to let my brain run around, to think things through. It's also real 'downtime' between home and work."

13. Development and Behavioural Change

"When I interview people I ask, 'What have you changed, based on the most recent feedback you've received?' It's crucial to leadership skills to be perceptive and respond to feedback."

14. Breadth of Language

"There is research on the number of words, diverse vocabulary and complexity of language that children are exposed to. Virtually all other success on the social class gradient is about being articulate. So, there's a massive disadvantage from very early on.

There is a discourse at the moment about feckless parenting, it's not that this doesn't exist, but there are other factors in play that make this stuff very hard to shift on a population basis. It's also about the ratio of praise to criticism here. Everything I learn makes me realise how hard it is to shift this stuff. "

15. Embracing Opportunity

"If I reflect back, I think I would have been less serious and intense. Because I've felt the need to protect myself, I haven't opened up as much as maybe I could have. I think I could have relaxed a bit more and taken things as they came, but that just didn't happen at the time. So I really suggest for others to embrace opportunities and be open to the learning, and not to fear, or hold back from it."

16. New Cultures, New Worlds, New Wisdom

"I have been an international person from the beginning. My mother is British and my father is Norwegian and they were both in the air force, which is how they met, so I have a military background. I grew up in a third country, which was Belgium. I had three languages, which I spoke every day and I grew up in a very multicultural environment. When you grow up in this sort of environment you develop a greater understanding of the differences in people. I learnt to be respectful of those differences, because they are all great and one should enjoy them. Therefore I wanted to have a life, which was international and wanted to continue that. My upbringing was quite hard: we travelled and it involved different languages, and having to grow up and learn everything a child had to learn in life, yet in three different languages, was difficult."

17. Formalised Training for Confidence Building

"There was a real lack of management role models and management training in my early career. I believed this was a crucial part of applying intellectual rigour and analysis to validate, or challenge my intuition as a manager. I took the responsibility for learning into my own hands. I started going to the library to learn from books on management to give me some frames of reference for my work. I found it easy to emulate what to do and what not to do; I just needed the framework to support me and give confidence."

18. Career Transitions

"In big companies there are some glass ceilings, and I don't mean gender wise. Here there are two really big steps and transitional points. This is where someone has been the technical expert, the executor and the implementer of a very high order. They then transit to the person who sets the strategy, who shapes things, who just by a nudge on the tiller, who by extreme sophistication and subtlety can just encourage things along. Preparing someone for this and knowing when they're ready is quite difficult to judge. You need to know if they have the appetite and whether they want it. How realistic are they in knowing what the job is going to be like? Then you look at the risk factors for example, asking, 'What has she shown me about herself and her ability to take on new challenges?' You also need to know how she can extrapolate that into the likelihood of success in stepping forward into this role. I evaluate all of these things very confidently."

19. Effective Delegation

"You need to get work done through others. You can't be all over people like a rash; you need to give people enough space to do their thing and be supportive. You have to go in like a helicopter and at the right points swoop in and then soar, backing off. You can't just hover. I had found this when I was working for a female leader in the finance sector. She was scrupulous about detail, and so I would be up all night working, whilst she would be texting me."

20. Understanding Local Challenges with a Global Perspective

"I've travelled around the world over the years, working in some of the most unlikely places and having some of the most unusual experiences. This included travelling to parts of the world where I've been escorted in armoured controlled vehicles. It's so important to me that, when I have employees in these places, I know more about the challenges that they are experiencing on the ground. I do believe that organisations in our country struggle with perspective. We have many long term serving employees that have never experienced this. It is so difficult for them to conceptualise because they don't even travel, or stretch themselves outside of their own area."

21. Asking Stupid Questions

"I believe that there's no such thing as a stupid question, when you are seeking to create better understanding. So I used to model asking the 'stupid' question all the time, because I wanted people to have the courage to ask too. It's not stupid when we know the answer."

22. Learning and Letting Go of Mistakes

"What I do know about myself is that I'm my own worst critic, my mistakes stay with me far longer than they should do."

Chapter Reflection: Cognitive Intelligence and Wisdom

Myself:
- What do I want to achieve in my career and life?
- How do I keep continuously stretch myself, keep myself relevant and continue to develop my learning and wisdom?
- How can I create the right balance between time to think, time to innovate and time to take action?
- How can I manage risks, whilst taking more of them?
- What resources do I need to put in place to increase my chances of taking courageous steps and achieving greater success?
- How do I create more breadth and depth to my learning and experiences?
- What am I assuming that is stopping me from moving forward?
- What is the liberating thought and action?

My Organisation:
- What structure and responsibilities do I put in place that help people thrive?
- How do I create a positive environment that gets the best thinking from people?
- What cultural limitations are holding back our ability to create greater diversity across all levels of leadership?
- How do we treat people and manage our mistakes?
- How can we get the most out of our investment in people?
- How can I create a trusted environment that encourages and values everyone's contribution?
- What are we assuming that is stopping us from moving forward?
- What is the liberating thought and action?

Chapter 9
EQ: Emotional and Social Competence

Contributing Author: Dr. Reuven Bar-On

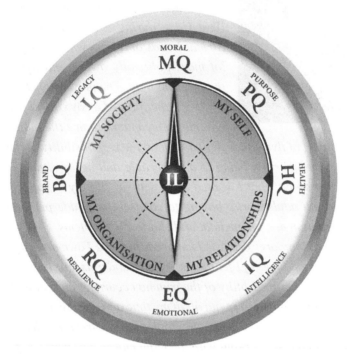

"A whole life can change when you meet someone or open your heart and network up to help others. We must give selflessly and help other women more. We must do so without any expectations of wanting something in return. People often warn me of those who take advantage of this. But my response is that what is in my karma will come to me, what's not, won't. Others need to concern themselves with their own karma."

Pinky Lilani OBE,
Spice Magic & Founder & Chairman of
Women of The Future Awards

Julia Lauren Zingu
Managing Partner, Consulting,
South Africa

"I trained as a social worker at university at West Cape during a time of turmoil in South Africa. It was at a time when groups became a lot more politically aware and formed part of the freedom fight. The university closed.

"My father passed away when I was 10 years old and so my mum became the main worker. I was the eldest of five children and took on the responsibility of the family to support my mother. By being in a vulnerable and needy situation, the seed was planted about what I wanted to do with my life. By the age of 21, I was fitting into an adult world, having to counsel and guide people who were much older than me, on medical and children's problems.

"I worked in poorer crime ridden areas in Cape Town and so you have to face all the challenges of life. It took bravery and guts, but I also found I was affected by the responsibility of the trauma occurring on a daily basis.

"I decided I wanted to spend all of my time and energy in social work and working with children. I eventually took on the Director role. Helping the vulnerable and also working with the team makes me stronger. You need to develop and support those around you and be stronger as a team.

"I married a professional man at 36; he was a physicist. He later got a scholarship in New York and so we went to live in Pasadena. It was so unlike South Africa, where you live, work and die in one place and there's a lot of restriction of movement. These restrictions meant that foreigners knew more about South Africa than we did. We loved the freedom offered by moving around and so we decided we would live in different provinces.

"My husband passed away a few months ago.

"We motivated, coached and supported each other in our marriage and as parents. I'm very lucky that my husband was a very good listener. I would come home and tell the story, sometimes ranting and raving! Once I'd unleashed then he would be my voice of reason to talk through what was

happening and how to approach things. My husband was my combined partner, coach and psychologist. You need to have this sounding board in your life to understand the fears that you have.

"In work, I don't have the time to reflect on my feelings. To have this at home helped me to see things in perspective and to test the ground. At that moment you may not have the answers. Milling over things in the car, or over coffee, you then gain a better idea as to how you can solve things. I believe there is no difference between wife, professional and parent. You always need to be caring, dignified and honest. You don't just do it outside work. You also need to have balance and you need to know who you are. It is particularly important to have a balanced social and private life.

"You need to acknowledge your own learning curve. I quickly learned early on in my career that, if I wanted to be a good leader, I needed to surround myself with people ten times better than me. It can only happen if you support and respect their skills and knowledge. I often say 'I am the driver and you are the wheels; the tools and knowledge. I don't have it and I need you in the team. I'm not an expert and don't know everything.'

"When I was the Head of an international organisation in South Africa, I managed a women-only team. As I look back, I think I will never have only females at top management. The dynamics can be very explosive. If you have males as part of the top management it brings more balance in how the team handles itself.

"We deal with very emotive and explosive issues at times. In a crisis situation it is important not to panic. I always remain calm. I've become very logical and rational, which I believe helps to pull the team together. Developing skills as a leader is about listening, respecting and valuing the silent moments in the meetings. It helps you to internalise what's being said and helps others to think through their processes. Constant talk creates cloudiness and chaos.

"It's important to savour the silent moment in the meeting and discussion and not to be too eager to present solutions. You can step out of a discussion, when there's a lot to think about. You can also come back and engage in more talk.

"You are being challenged all the time. You need to be honest with

yourself and those who are questioning you. There can only be one leader. Sometimes you have people with different aspirations from you. You either create the opportunities and set boundaries, or are honest in that you may need to end the relationship, if it is not conducive to the environment. I have had the tough conversations with people. It's important to do this with respect, ensuring that the person leaves the organisation on a positive note. Bad words from people can negate all the good work that you've achieved.

"You can have clashes between the leader and subordinate, where they agree to one thing, but then go off and don't follow through. This can be very harmful to the organisation and workforce. If you have people leading in different directions, it creates utter chaos. When you take hard decisions, people won't come and tell you they appreciate what you've done. However, if you are clear about the boundaries, then people move forward. If you don't address conflicting issues, especially in the top management team, it can only be detrimental to the organisation.

"I have learned not to go into conversations with pre-conceived ideas. Instead I listen to and understand other viewpoints. Now I'm calmer, as I work through the various scenarios in preparation for key meetings. Because I'm calmer, I know I've considered options and don't have all this anxiety sitting on my chest. It makes it so much easier. When you come to a decision in the moment, your reasoning, approach and centred-ness no longer make it personal. This is especially the case if there is a personality clash. Once you reach calmness, then you look at the person through different eyes; you really create empathy for the other person.

"In South Africa, especially, we have to deal with men who can be very difficult and chauvinistic. We need to see them as the person, not as the title, or seniority. I made this decision of addressing them as a person, rather than the CEO, or high-powered individuals.

"I believe that it's not about who you are, it's about the change you can facilitate. It's being proud of the product. It's about inspiring other people. It's not about you at all. It's about your people and feeling proud about them and their development."

Definition of EQ: Emotional and Social Competence

There has been a surge in research focused on the relevance of emotions in the everyday life and the implications of emotional intelligence for leadership. This has been heavily influenced by the shift in our understanding of our brain and physiology, in particular the advances in the field of neuroscience. Emotions and feelings, as more nebulous and misunderstood, have largely been de-prioritised, or even ignored. This has been the case when emotional intelligence was compared to the cognitive intelligence based competences of analytical, problem solving and judgement – until now!

We now know that decisions and judgement are heavily influenced by both the logical calculation that comes with experience and knowledge, but also from emotions and feelings. In fact, far better decisions happen when emotions are managed effectively so they work for us and not against us.

Dr. Reuven Bar-On's model of emotional intelligence is one of the most popular and tested models of emotional intelligence (EI). He describes EI as a multifactorial and interrelated array of emotional and social competencies and skills, which help us to cope with daily demands, challenges and pressure. They determine:

1. How well we understand and express ourselves
2. How aware we are of other's feelings and help us establish cooperative interpersonal relationships
3. How effectively we manage and control emotions
4. How best to cope with the immediate situation and solve problems of the personal and interpersonal nature
5. How successful we are in generating positive emotions in order to be sufficiently self-motivated for achieving personal goals

According to Reuven, most definitions, descriptions, measures and models of emotional intelligence have included one, or more of the following key components:

- The ability to recognise and understand emotions and to express feelings
- The ability to understand how others feel and to relate with them
- The ability to manage and control emotions
- The ability to manage change, adapt and solve problems of a personal and interpersonal nature
- The ability to generate a positive mood and be self-motivated

Reuven's extensive research concluded that EI develops over time well into the 5th decade of life; and it can be improved relatively quickly through training, coaching and therapy (as long, of course, that there is sufficient self-awareness in the first place). He originally hypothesised and later provided numerous research findings demonstrating that leaders with high emotional intelligence are more effective, productive and successful in meeting the demands and pressures of their environment. Cognitive and emotional intelligence are part of the individual's overall general intelligence and both combine to create a strong predictor of successful leadership.

In the context of the Inspiring Leadership model, emotional and social competence ('EQ') is defined as *the ability to effectively understand, manage and express one's emotions and to be aware of others' feelings for the purpose of establishing and maintaining healthy interpersonal relationships'*. Simply put, this is having emotions work for us and not against us.

Understanding Emotions

Understanding emotions is, first and foremost, about emotional self-awareness and the ability to decipher emotions, body language, pictures, voices, and cultural artefacts. This requires us to pay attention to what's happening around us and, at the same time, within us. When working with leaders, I have asked them to step outside of their office and slowly take a 360 view of what's happening around them. Or, I ask them to hold back in their meetings and just pay attention. They are often surprised with what they notice about individuals, the energy and the interactions. Awareness and interpretation is complemented by the skill of *intuition*. Intuition is often misinterpreted as being intangible. However, it is actually mostly linked to past experiences that have been stored in the long-term memory (the hippocampus) and held deep in our subconscious. Frequently described as the gut instinct, many leaders cite their intuition (when combined with judgment) as being an invaluable asset to their leadership.

In *Educating People to be Emotionally Intelligent*, Bechara, Damasio and Bar-On describe how our *'emotions begin with the perception of an emotionally competent stimulus...which enters our brain's sensory processing systems.'* The presence of the stimulus is made available to emotion-triggering sites in the amygdala and the prefrontal cortex. These can either be in our immediate environment, or through recognition from our memory. The object of our stimulus and our, subsequently, elicited emotional reactions travel within nanoseconds along our neural connections. Primary emotional inducers are automatic and immediate. Secondary inducers link to memories and thoughts and are, therefore, more gradual.

Either can be pleasant or aversive in nature, dependent on our perceptions. These emotions then translate into feelings. Emotions trigger biological changes in our body and our brain state, some visible to the external observer. However, mostly aren't visible, for example: increased heart rate, muscle contraction, the 'amygdala hijack' and so forth.

We've also all experienced or witnessed external signs of emotional expression, for example: posture, skin colour, tonality, and facial expression. Noticing the stimulus and patterns that trigger different emotions, as well as interrupting or redefining them, is an essential skill in leadership.

Managing and Expressing Our Emotions

Managing and *expressing* our emotions and the ability to be aware of others' feelings are based on the quality of our interpretation in the first place. Often we hear phrases like we need to 'stop and think' more. Whereas actually we need to stop and think and *feel* more in order to be an inspiring leader.

As described in the chapter on PQ: Purpose and Meaning, how people feel about things is essential. Whilst the neo-cortex is responsible for the rational thought, it is the emotion that lies in the limbic system that establishes resonance between two entities. Our highly connected world is based on the quality of the relationships and our feelings influence human behaviour. It is their emotional connection that makes people buy into us, be led by us and buy from us.

We only have to look at major brands such as Apple, Virgin and even the Royal Family to see how emotions lead people to buy into what such brands stand for. Alternatively, leaders such as Nelson Mandela and Mother Theresa have moved and influenced millions. People don't buy what you do; they buy why you do it. Through effective and authentic expression of emotion, we can create the compelling story that generates limbic resonance. People vote for (or don't vote for) advocate leaders. Customers and clients purchase from organisations; people stay loyal to organisations, communities and relationships. Leadership success and failure is more determined by factors of emotion and emotional intelligence.

The emotionally intelligent leader is attuned to social norms and cultural differences. *Culture* is the outcome of generations of shared patterns, wisdom and growth. It is formed out of a set of shared beliefs, values, experiences, assumptions and philosophies. With the world more globally connected, our organisational structures are complex and heavily matrixed. Our leadership platform has therefore shifted. Our 'sphere of influence' is now spanning more challenging, and often more sensitive, boundaries. Our ability to leverage relationships and understand our customers across different cultures is crucial to success. So when we talk about emotional and social intelligence, there is also a contextual setting that needs to be considered. EQ has therefore evolved into a more fluid and responsive style of leadership that understands the different sensitivities involved.

The emotionally intelligent leader can harness emotions, even negative ones, to manage them effectively towards a desired outcome. Traditionally, we recognise and promote leaders for their intellectual and cognitive capability. Disappointingly, many organisations have yet to recognise the value of the emotionally intelligent leader.

Until we re-evaluate old models of leadership and assessment methods, we will continue to hire and develop leaders based on our own bias for what we value in leadership (i.e. technical knowledge, cognitive intellect and drive). This selection process and bias often undervalues the power of emotional and social intelligence.

Since the role of the leader is to encourage, motivate and mobilise people to do great work and customers to buy their products and services, then EQ skills are crucial. Importantly, EQ is not a set of innate talents, but rather they can be learned, if the awareness and motivation is there. This is contrary to what some of the pop psychology will lead you to believe! Our brain is highly 'plastic' and so can learn these new skills with sufficient training and willingness. However, like with all development, it is far easier to have developed these skills at earlier life and career stages, rather than trying to develop emotional intelligence when an individual is already in a leadership position.

Consequences of Being Deficient in EQ

Based on Dr Reuven Bar-On's research conducted with Dr Marian Ruderman at the Center for Creative Leadership (CCL) in the US, deficiencies in EI were found to be one of the most important predictors of 'derailment' in leadership. The major contributors to derailment, based on their study, were the deficiencies in the following emotional and social competencies:

1. Emotional Self-Awareness (they couldn't see it coming)
2. Stress Tolerance (they couldn't manage stress and work under pressure)
3. Impulse Control (they lost it)
4. Flexibility (they couldn't change gears)
5. Optimism and Happiness (zero self-motivation to do anything about it)

It is crucial to also mention their positive findings on the flipside of derailment – a successful leadership. Those EI factors that contributed the most to successful leadership, based on the CCL study, were the following:

1. Self-Awareness
2. Social Responsibility (including social awareness, cooperation and teamwork)
3. Stress Tolerance
4. Impulse Control
5. Optimism and Happiness

The Impact of EQ Deficiency on Culture

Building global leadership assumes the *transferability* of the leader and their skills from one region to another. However, this is not always easily achieved and can be fraught with difficulties. These nuances have led to communication breakdowns in leadership teams, with unfortunate consequences. This highlights a key factor about emotional intelligence: EQ involves an appreciation and consideration of what others bring to the table and their respective styles, or cultures.

There is far too much emphasis in the language about our expectations of how others should be, in order to 'fit in around here'. Are the terms we use such as 'fake it', 'push forward', or 'break through' the language and attitude of the dominating culture, nation, or even leader? 'Fitting in' has an underlying issue by de-valuing diversity.

It unhealthily reinforces the existing culture that drives the behaviours in the organisation. I believe, as inspiring leaders, we must reflect on the majority attitudes and bias, where there is a form of dominance. This dominance could be in gender, culture, or styles, and we should consider how respectful we truly are of diversity. Do we lead with the prevailing dominant culture, or promote a culture of inclusion?

The Impact of EQ Deficiency in Organisations

In Clareo Potential, we managed a global programme for the Top 60 C-Suite leaders for our client, combining coaching, workshops, team events and project work. The 60 leaders were split into groups to work on the different strategic projects. The groups were mixed to create the most diverse possible gathering of leaders to support the cross-matrix relationship development and learning. Bruce Tuckman's simple four stage *forming, storming, norming, performing* model for building new teams was evident.

In the earliest stages of the programme, the biggest factors that impeded progress were the quality of leadership relationships. The primary breakdown in communication and relationships was nothing to do with the task, it was everything to do with different leader's styles. The potential for conflict came from a variety of different characters. Whether it was the abrasive individual, the decisive individual, the risk-averse individual, the dramatic individual, the emotional individual, the paternalistic, or the high ego and status driven individual – the list goes on!

There is a danger that cultural stereotypes can become our intellectual opponent. Our unconscious biases and resulting reactions convert into passive or even overt discrimination. By not understanding the cultural components of our peer groups, we are prone to ignorance and disconnect.

Emotional Self-Awareness

In my consulting business, we often use a number of psychometric, talent assessment tools and interview techniques, in order to help build greater self and mutual awareness by the individual leader. This is often as part of a top 100 or 150 talent assessment and development programme, some form of team development, or even individual one-to-one coaching.

The various tools we use reveal the bench-strength of the organisation's talent and the capability of the individual leader. These insightful tools build a foundation for *greater self-awareness* for the leader. Through our vast experience of running these assessments, there is a consistent theme of a 'leadership development need' that often has the potential to derail leaders, or hold them back. It is their need to enhance the quality of their social interaction and the ability to lead successfully through others. Some lack the emotional connection and empathy – a vital skill for leaders who want to build trust. When we are called in for executive development to deal with team performance issues and relationship conflict, then a need to build greater trust is often at the core.

The Damage Caused by Toxic Environments

An effective leader knows exactly how to motivate his or her people.

They do this without resorting to fear tactics and selecting favourites amongst their team. Unhealthy manipulation with the intention of driving greater performance, paradoxically has the reverse effect. People operating in a *fear culture,* or an *emotionally charged* environment cannot give their full selves to their jobs. Their energy is being drained and misdirected, in order to protect themselves. Their energy is also sapped by having to manage their toxic environment. Their brain's threat response centre (amygdala) is on high alert and this triggers extra cortisol to course through their body.

With a growing understanding of cognitive and social functioning, as a result of rapidly advancing research in neuroscience, we know that EQ is no longer the 'soft stuff'. It really does have a detrimental impact on our results when we get it wrong. In Dr. Reuven Bar-On's research, whilst women were more aware of emotions, men were more equipped to manage theirs. From the work that we do in Clareo Potential, to assess and develop top leaders, self-awareness, empathy and the ability to manage emotions are some of the top development areas for leaders. As leaders we need to leverage and balance all three of these important aspects of emotional and social competence.

Another key development area that comes up is the leader's ability to maintain composure, when under pressure. Lack of composure, whether it comes in form of shouting, confidence loss, or passive aggression, sends a strong message to others that we have lost control. Others will perceive that we are not strong or experienced enough to handle more difficult and challenging situations. In 360 interviews and feedback, it is ineffective emotional management that causes some of the greatest conflicts between leaders. Once specific relationships are fundamentally flawed and broken, it is hard to rebuild the trust that is needed to work effectively together.

Dr. Reuven Bar-On notes that deficiencies in emotional and social intelligence correlate with a lack of success and can lead to 'derailment', which is a leader's worse nightmare! He emphasises that the problems leaders have in coping with one's environment are common among those who are deficient in the following competencies: problem-solving, reality-testing, stress management, and impulse control.

Here's an interesting paradox. Traditional organisations ask leaders to be

296

authentic and bring their 'whole selves' to work, yet they want those very same leaders to leave their emotions at the front door. All leaders and executives work in extremely tough and challenging environments, and yet we try to *contain their expression* of feelings. Traditionally, revealing emotions has been seen as a weakness in the leader. However, we are now in an era of leadership where past rules and taboos are no longer relevant. Our feelings must find an outlet in some way, as suppression of these emotions can be detrimental to our health and wellbeing.

An important skill in our leadership toolkit is finding emotional outlets in a constructive and healthy way. This is far preferable, rather than through expression in the form of outbursts (perceived as out of control), or containment (perceived as withdrawn and unapproachable), each being equally damaging. Many leaders' reputations are affected by the way they manage their own and others' emotions and feelings. At an extreme, it limits their potential within organisations. It's not expected that we block out difficult thoughts, or emotions. However, inspirational leaders are <u>mindful</u> of their inner experiences, but do not get caught up in the internal melodrama!

EQ and Vulnerability

One inspiring leader shared how, at one point she was very keen to have the responsibility for running a large Profit and Loss account for the business. At the same time was keen to have another baby in the future. She told me, *"I saw a job which gave me the experience and promotion I wanted. However, my boss's boss did not want me to go. I knew I wanted the P&L experience before I went on maternity leave, however, I'd not explained the real reasons for the urgency. It came to a showdown at which point I said to him, 'isn't it obvious that I want another baby?' He sat me down to talk it through. It was a hard conversation as it required courage and I admired him because he wasn't at all embarrassed. I found that by being open and transparent, it empowered both of us as leaders to have better and more productive conversations. Although he made no promises, he saw it as important and was willing to work with me to help me. When I returned, he stuck by his commitment and helped make it happen."*

Being vulnerable and transparent was the 'tipping point' for their conversation and everything then shifted. This inspiring leader put all of her faith in her boss, particularly given how hard it can be to make promises for the future in a changing organisation. True to his word, when she returned, he helped her to secure the new role that she wanted. It doesn't always serve us to hold back from the real conversation with those that can help and influence our career, even though it may be personal. The fact is, as women, there is another factor at play. Leaders must be able to have the open dialogue that combines the personal and work aspects. When we do have these courageous career conversations, we must take a longer perspective of our career and organisation. As with any strategy, we should not just focus on the short term need. This is effective career management and development, with inspiring leaders acting as the enablers and facilitators.

I recall in my earlier career as a leader, I fundamentally believed in *'wearing my heart on my sleeve'*. I optimistically anchored myself in the belief that there wasn't enough authenticity in business and, by sharing all of me, then this would help me to build relationships and trust. However, my approach and behaviours were based on my naivety and inexperience. In an effort to make me seem more 'human', by sharing when I got it wrong, I made myself too exposed and shared too much. Unwittingly I created a different type of image to the one that I was hoping for - to be seen as an authentic leader that people felt confident in following and going to when in need.

Moderating between strength and vulnerability, emotion and logic, support and empowerment, is the true power of the inspiring leader. For me, it took some tough feedback from my boss and some subsequent coaching, which enabled me to re-adjust. Again, this is neither suppression, nor over-expression; instead it was learning the most appropriate and effective management and expression of emotion.

EQ and Tribal Behaviours

Research suggests that the 'natural' creation of 'in-groups' and 'out-groups' are directly correlated with levels of self-regard. By being part of an in-group, participants 'like themselves' and have a more positive impression of others in the in-group, potentially resulting in greater self-esteem. They feel special, are relieved to have been selected to be part of something elite and rather exclusive. It is natural to feel proud to be part of a high performing team. Ironically, in creating a strong sense of 'us', we have to demonise our 'them', as opponents to be ridiculed, compared with and competed against.

The resulting implications for those not selected to be part of the in-group, is that, by implication, they are now in the out-group. The impact is that this causes an erosion of the self-esteem of those excluded from the in-group and reinforces intra-group biases. Of course, the compelling arguments for equality, or gender parity are reinforced by these insights about dominant groups and decision-making. It is difficult to achieve the desired change. This is especially the case since there is often a lack of awareness of the subtleties in either our own conscious or sub-conscious bias. This ripples through our entire people management processes.

EQ in Managing Fears and Insecurities

As humans, we are intelligent, powerful and imaginative. However, we can limit ourselves based on our attitudes reinforced by our internal and external dialogue. Appreciation and gratitude has the potential for creating positive seismic shifts. We often work with leaders who are struggling, not because they have unwelcome thoughts and feelings, but because they anchor themselves on the *inner dialogue and resulting self-limiting beliefs*. They suffer because of their over dominant internal voice of the critic or judge. This narrative erodes at our self-belief.

Jaz Rabadia, a young, highly capable up and coming leader described to me, *"I felt like an imposter inside, but people said 'We don't see you like that. We see you as an energy manager who's climbing the ranks'. It's really hard, because I ask myself, 'How did I do it?' I don't always feel confident inside, even though no-one experiences that."*

This is a self-perpetuating problem. The energy that is demanded by this 'voice' to manage emotions, feelings and anxieties actually draws vital resources away from our brain's cognitive processes. In other words we stop thinking clearly. We procrastinate, become indecisive and limit our creativity around our options and how best to leverage our resources. Each time we give power to our self-limiting beliefs, we are also creating a new 'record' for our long-term memory, stored in the hippocampus of our brain. So, it does not become a one-off experience, but rather a growing, perpetuating destructive self-concept. Limited self-belief has a ripple effect on an individual's happiness and optimism.

Our insecurities, our assumptions and our fears hold us back from building effective relationships and achieving our full potential. In the book, *The Tools*, Phil Stutz and Barry Michels recommend a simple approach to handling a fear or an anxiety. Step 1 is to say 'Bring it on!' Step 2 is to say, 'I like fear'. In Step 3 you say to yourself 'I like fear; because fear sets me free!' Another equally helpful book is called, *Feel the Fear and Do It Anyway*, by Susan Jeffers.

By taking the courageous step of facing and dealing with our fears, we move from avoidance to taking control. We know that we are resourceful, and so we can use these skills to set us up for success or failure. And, if we get it wrong, which often as humans (and not robots) we do, we need to turn it into a powerful learning opportunity. We should definitely not beat ourselves up about our failures. The danger is our destructive self-perceptions turn bad experience into a script: *'This is who we are'*. They become our identity. This is an act of serious self-denial. They are not the full-representation of who we are and yet become the context for our self-definition.

These emotions are also hungry ones, which like to be fed and they can be pretty exhausting! Therefore, we need to separate our experiences and our identity, forming a new language for each. It's the difference between saying, 'I experienced a failure' and saying, 'I am a failure'. Whatever we identify with, we attract more of. I myself have often created an identity around my experiences. I have always loved the work that I have done to develop talent, but when I first set up my business I would have to 'sell'. I would tell myself (and others) that 'I'm not good at selling', or, 'I don't like selling'. When I didn't win a piece of business, then I would build this into my story by saying, 'see, I told you that I'm not good at selling'.

Of course, it became self-fulfilling and the vicious cycle started. At one point I hated selling what I did in my business so much, that I almost chucked it all in and went back into working for a big corporate. Reframing and altering the language I use, with an added dose of realism, has helped me to refocus and leverage my strengths. I have detached the negative emotions and self-limiting beliefs to re-engage with my own identity and drive my vision for the business forward.

In her beautifully clear book, *Time to Think*, Nancy Kline refers to the *positive philosophical choice'*. This is based on adopting the view that, by nature, human beings are intelligent, multi-faceted, powerful, imaginative and loving and so are able to think through any situation. Behaviours to the contrary are as a result of assumptions generated by our experiences, conditions and attitudes. I believe that, rather than anchoring ourselves to our own, or others' imposed limitations, we can leverage our strengths and our capacity for resourcefulness. We have the freedom to empower ourselves to address the issues we face, to be authentic and to create *'positive forward motion'*.

EQ and Impulse Control

Another factor of emotional and social intelligence is *'impulse control'*. An area I personally struggle with every time I look at the dessert menu, or go shopping with my daughter, Alanadh! Low impulse control can emerge in a number of ways, for example, lack of emotions management and expression resulting in angry outbursts, or speedy decisions affecting the business, or even the end customer. This may be as a result of our impatience to make things happen without due-diligence and consultation.

Bias and Stereotypes

With regards to the women's agenda, I believe there are some growing issues for second-generation gender bias. We are becoming heavily influenced by the 'stated' stereotype. The characterisation of groups is becoming the definitive narrative that informs our bias. For example, 'Women show more empathy and have greater ethics' and 'men are more driven and show their emotion through aggression'. Whilst research provides us with valuable insight, it is not the final piece in the jigsaw; this final piece is actually the individual person – the one that is seated in front of you.

The language that is used is creating divisive results. In order for women to succeed, it is not, and cannot be, about the 'them and us'. As quickly as women are responding to the environment and developing their leadership capability, men are too. In my research and interviews, what has been clear is there are many male leaders with emotional intelligence, empathy and high integrity. So it disturbs me when people use language that suggests otherwise, or creates a skewed view. In a new and evolving era of leadership and society, we need to be challenging old taboos and stereotypes.

Presence, Appreciation and Respect

In *Inspiring Leadership*, Jonathan Bowman-Perks MBE, describes how, *'the lack of attention, care, or interest in another person is symptomatic of the absence of presence'*. Leaders who lack presence struggle to make connections with their stakeholders in a number of ways: in presentations, team meetings, public relations and media. I recall a time when I was introduced to a prominent political leader of the opposition at a conference. He looked straight through me, unable to make eye contact, whilst he limply shook my hand and with some apathetic greeting that was robotic, rather than genuine. He was obviously completely disinterested; it did not even occur to him to ask a single question. At first I took this personally, asking myself *'what had I done wrong in the introductions?'* Then, I noticed he repeated this pattern with others, until of course there was a photograph opportunity and the energy shifted. The powerful decision that we make when we take on positions of leadership brings with it significant responsibility. A responsibility for the people you lead and the people who are impacted by your leadership. This fundamentally means that 'the people' are your No.1 agenda item.

The shadow that the top leader casts permeates and dominates our organisations. It drives the majority of the behaviours of our followers, both healthy and unhealthy. People look at who's currently in charge, and extrapolate that the style of the people in leadership positions is the actual preferred style of leadership. Yet everyone has shortcomings and we should be wary of imitating others. Judy Garland said, *"Always be a first rate version of yourself and not a second rate version of someone else."* It's more authentic and trustworthy too.

Emotions can be either our greatest asset, or our biggest adversary. Dr Reuven Bar-On's famous one-liner in defining emotional intelligence is '*the ability to have your emotions work for you and not against you*'.

If we think we are going to get upset about something, then we are most likely to do so. Our dominant thoughts culminate in a self-fulfilling prophecy. Our emotions either create an upward trajectory of confidence, or a downward spiral into low self-regard. *Noticing* our emotions and what's going on for us, followed by *intervening*, so as to *choose* which route we take is completely within our own power. We always have choice in how we respond. As leaders we must manage our emotions effectively, when things don't quite go the way we had hoped. This is the emotional and social maturity of true inspiring leaders.

Organisational Terrorists

There are also times in our leadership lives, where we come across *organisational terrorists*. These are the sorts of people who, no matter what we do to try to engage them, decide that their relationship with the business has already broken down beyond repair. They have quit the organisation, but remain. They draw a salary and do just enough to keep out of sight, from where they can snipe at leaders and 'the system'; both which they love to hate. Unfortunately, their behaviours can be a significant drain on the rest of the team. This becomes extremely tough, as inspiring leaders we believe that we should be able to turn around any and every situation and person. So we stick with the situation for too long, working hard to turn things around and work with these behaviours.

Our amygdala response to the 'threat' is that our own leadership performance can be affected. Organisational terrorists drain huge quantities of energy. This is not just by the time spent with them, but also cognitively and emotionally, as we try to create solutions for how we can manage them and help the team live with their negativity. Some leaders even avoid having the courageous conversation. Instead they quietly move the 'problem', or even promote them, so you find the same 'organisational terrorist'" keeps popping up in different places in the business.

In the short term, it's easier clearly to move the person who is the issue, rather than having to deal with the conflict and consequences. There are times in our leadership when we need to accept that there are some areas we cannot influence and take the courageous step to managing the situation effectively. Sometimes we are challenged and our immediate responses can cause adverse reactions. We've all had them. But acknowledging, reflecting and noticing where things went wrong and how things could be handled differently is the best learning any leader can get in their career.

No-one knows this better than **Liz Satow**, who recalled an experience from her earlier career:

"I had a horrible professional experience where there was a complete breakdown in a relationship with the head of the office. I lost all trust in him and ended up resigning. Leaving the country and the job that I loved, I was broken, wounded and very angry.

"In order to move on I realised I had to first forgive him and that took me ages to do.

"It was humbling and spiritual process. I did a lot of meditating and praying about it and had to be honest about my own feelings. Every time I started feeling and sensing that maybe much of what was bothering me was because I have the same 'seed', as he did, in my own heart. I may not have done what that manager had done, yet I've seen the seed of it in myself at different points. It was such a humbling experience.

"I realised that actually I was no better than him. It was awful to confront this realisation, because I had put all of the blame on him. I had looked at him one-dimensionally. Over time I realised that I hadn't behaved at all well myself. We were each responsible for our own behaviour. This was a reflective process and quite a wake-up call. I still think about how I could have done things very differently and maybe changed the relationship in a positive way.

"I remember I used to think, 'when I am leading I am never going to be like him'.

"But that's not enough. You need to see and chase the positive aspects of

another leader, whilst being open to people pointing out your own weaknesses. You need those trusted advisors, people who will tell you the truth about your behaviour. This was an early formative experience in terms of changing and improving my leadership style."

Emotional and social competence, or a deficiency of it, has the power to change the shape of the organisation and its talent profile. We know from the Gallup research that *'People join great organisations; yet they leave poor managers'*. It is the managers/leaders who have the greatest impact on employee engagement and this is consistently shown in all the research in our client's firms. The question is, do you want to attract and retain great people, or do you want to be the leader that disengages, or drives your people away?

How Can EQ Help You as a Leader?

Liz Satow went on to say, *"I was told by one person, 'You talk to me like I was anyone else, I didn't realise you were the response manager. You didn't talk down to me, like others normally do.' When he found out who I was, then he got nervous, however, he got used to my respectful approach. So, being respectful to everyone is really important cross-culturally. Especially in places where there's hierarchy. Sometimes I have struggled with this as a woman; particularly as a woman growing up in India. I don't like being talked down to. You can try to exploit the hierarchy and say this is my role, I don't care if I'm a woman. But it's not who I am. In the long run it's not effective. Pulling rank for me is rare; I've done it twice in my career. I come in and try to be me in that role. I aspire to be as effective as possible in that role - as myself.*

"I think in parts of Africa it's been a challenge, as I've been a manager for different disasters there. I'm not very big physically, I'm single and young and that makes a difference. When I arrived at Swaziland in 2008, they'd just changed the law the previous year to say that women were no longer minors. So for example, women couldn't open a bank account, without a father, or husband's signature and domestic violence was a huge issue there. I've had people say, 'Who's this girl that's trying to make decisions?' All these things about being a mother, married, older - they are all symbols and a status.

Without those it's much more of a challenge to get the respect that the position might require.

"I've been fortunate that I've always had a few members of the team who took me seriously and so I've always had back-up. For example, I had an ex-military man on my team, who had had far more disaster response experience than I had. Yet, he would always turn to people and say, 'this is my boss and it's her decision in the end'. I don't know if he noticed he was doing it. I saw that he did that much more when there were men around. It was never in a patronising way, it was always respectful. He'd say what he thought, but then acknowledge it was my decision. So, I've had help. Some times I've had to sit down and talk through how things needed to work. Whilst at other times I've been much harder than I've wanted to be.

"That last strategy is a double-edged sword, because you can push people into a place of heavy resistance if they're really against it. I've tried different tactics: from one-to-one meetings through to very public decisions. Because the authority is recognised, it must be accepted and respected. There are different ways of doing it. My tendency and preference is to win people over. There were times when I tried to mow people down. However, as I've got older and gained more of a wiser and wider perspective, I have now seen how this is counter-productive and ineffective."

People are inspired to work for leaders that treat them with respect and genuinely understand their talents, strengths and needs.

Throughout the research, leaders consistently cited treating people with respect and as equals as the key attribute to building successful relationships. Emotional and social competence helps us to cope with life's pressures and demands more easily. This is because with high EQ we are able to build a strong foundation of engagement around us. When I have asked for feedback on the leaders that have been interviewed for the book, I often heard stories like, *"They talk to me as if we are on the same level"*, or *"They were sincerely interested in my thoughts and ideas."* Often this is unique to the individual. It requires each leader to be connected, at a very personal level, with their people, or stakeholders. This is where we get the honest feedback, the best thinking and an amazing energy for collaborative working and knowledge sharing.

Effective Decisions

A leader's primary role is to make effective decisions. Our brains have developed a series of intricate neural connections, shaped by years of experiences. The emotional hooks that we have stored in our memories re-play in our behaviours today. These subsequently form triggers, which we can choose to ignore, or respond to. When our emotions take over, then it becomes more difficult for us to apply logic, reasoning and thought. The emotional pull can overpower our reason. We think we understand certain situations, when actually we are filled with pre-conceived ideas, biased-fuelled perspectives and assumption-based misinterpretations. By being more self-aware, better at managing our emotional reactions and choosing how to intervene, then we can slow down our impulse and wisely respond in the moment.

Each interaction that we have has the power to influence; for better or for worse. When we *truly* listen to encourage others' thinking, or make a decision, then we alter our relationships and our destiny.

The complexity of leadership today therefore requires us to move out of our comfort zones of 'sharing' technical knowledge and expertise. We need more tools in our mental kit bag for influencing and persuading people. In that way we can both cognitively and emotional connect with others and they with those they seek to support.

People need to feel heard, understood and empowered. They need to feel good about being led by you, buying from you and partnering with you. The art of listening in order to seek to understand means that you are able to enthuse and inspire those around you.

Today's mixed generation of employees want to feel they are contributing, feeling empowered and truly making a difference. Gone are the days of the 'industrial' style leadership. The skills and components of emotional and social competence (EQ) have become an essential part of leadership. Altering perspectives helps us to become more creative with our options as leaders.

Jackie Uhi described her experience of working: *"I moved from Australia to Asia which was a completely new frontier working with an all-male,*

Islamic executive board. There was no real chance to network as the main networking took place when the men were at the mosque. This was just the way that it was and I had to adjust. This experience really helped me to build further resilience. I had to operate in an environment where I needed to influence senior leaders, in order to get a good outcome. This was what I did successfully. So I don't really believe this pressure that you need to 'go for drinks with the boys'. We keep asking women to do what men do."

We must be able to play the bigger game and see more than one option for building relationships, navigating the network, or managing our career. If we always look for the barriers and the symbols of 'injustice' and see them as frustrations then the resulting emotions, whether resentment, anger, or frustration, will only eat away at us. If, instead, we see them as opportunities, then we open our hearts and minds to being positively focused, resourceful and pragmatic. Lisa Lockwood shared with me, *"I believe that there is nothing that you can't do successfully, if you master your emotions."*

EQ as part of Multiple Intelligences

This becomes apparent in the assessment work that we do with top leaders in organisations. The combination of cognitive, emotional and social competence has become the non-negotiable for most leadership positions today. By giving attention to and developing both IQ & EQ 'muscles', then you are able to set yourself apart as an *'extra-ordinary leader'*. The problem often occurs when leaders struggle to let go of their need for power and control, relying purely on their knowledge and intellect. Leadership, however, requires achieving results through other's willing participation. You need people to willingly give their discretionary life energy to help you deliver successfully.

This approach would be even more robust and effective for leadership performance, and most other aspects of human behaviour and performance, if we expanded this mix to include:

1. Cognitive intelligence
2. Emotional-social competence
3. Moral integrity

4. Purpose and meaning

5. Resilience

Then we would have one of the best approaches to leadership selection and development yet designed.

I recall a conference event that we organised, where one of the leaders was talking about his leadership style. He shared, *"I know I am not necessarily the most intelligent person in the room. I do not feel threatened by this, because that's not what I necessarily bring. I know my core leadership strength is to engage and motivate people, bringing the best team together to deliver success."*

This starts with us! *Passion→ motivation→ engagement* is the fuel we need to move things forward with the best development programmes. Without it, all of the work we put into selecting, developing and promoting the prospective high (and inspiring) performers is a waste of our time, energy and efforts.

Overcoming the Imposter Syndrome

I have found throughout my research that many leaders are 'blocked' by their *imposter syndrome*. This syndrome is based on a fear that they are not good enough and will be found out as a fraud and imposter. Their 'inner gremlin' says negative things like, '*I am not good enough*', or '*they've had a better education than me, so they must be more intelligent*' or, '*I don't know what I'm doing*'. We must be aware of our strengths and weaknesses; we must reframe our internal dialogue and only then can we be fully authentic. The fact is, the majority of us – men and women – are all thinking and worrying about the same things!

As a wise client once said, *"If we worry what other people think about us, then we would be surprised how little they do!"*

A great skill to off-set the imposter syndrome is to surround ourselves with a strong and trusted team, and then we can leverage its full capability. Whilst it is useful for us to have the level of awareness of our limitations, it's important that the 'gremlin' within doesn't get creative with the limitations that we have. Too much self-criticism can paralyse us into inaction.

Listening So Others Feel Heard

Peter Burditt is an exemplar in the way that he treats people: consistently, with kindness and interest. It's made him one of the most inspirational and effective leaders that I have ever had the privilege to work with. His approach is, *'Everyone has got something interesting to teach us, if only we would **truly listen** to them.'* Then we can consider ourselves inspiring to others because we show, genuinely, that we care. I think we have all been in poor meetings - those where people talk over each other. In such dire meetings, the quieter contributions of the introverts are often ignored, or lose the full impact of their influence. Such meetings become elongated, merely providing opportunities for the loudest to download and to have endless debates without incisive decisions.

As described so eloquently by Nancy Kline, "*...most people think that listening is linear. They think that listening is lined up, waiting to speak*".

This reminds me of back home in Ireland. We love our 'hyper-chat'. We would have conversations until the early hours of the morning about everything and anything. We would be patiently waiting for the other person's in-breath, or pause so we could jump in with our thoughts and the next story. When the in-breath didn't arrive, then we would talk over people, just to get the opportunity to speak.

Since then I have learnt the techniques of truly listening and paying attention to the person in front of me. Consequently, the quality of my relationships have fundamentally shifted for the better. People feel heard. Nancy Kline describes how, "*...the attention of this calibre is exactly the thing that saves time, even generates time. This is because truly good independent thinking emerges. It is not hammered, or sculpted.*"

By facilitating the power of someone's own thinking, so that it is uninterrupted, or uncontaminated with our own perspectives, then we unleash enhanced creativity and greater possibilities.

Sayyeda Salam shared her style of leadership with me, "*I want to create an environment where people feel valued and heard. Being in charge of the whole team, I've spent a lot of time listening, hearing what people have to say. I use these insights to integrate into the work we do. I believe it is* *essential to contract together as a team. When we would meet together, then we would originally talk about what was going well for ourselves. However, I realised that people were reticent about this. Now, instead of sharing our own successes, we talk about the great achievements that we're really proud of in other people."*

As leaders we sometimes mistakenly feel we need to be the experts. If we're not instructing, then it feels like we are not being productive. Inspirational leadership, however, empowers our teams, realising the full power of the diverse talents and ideas contained within them.

The great news is that we are not stuck with our level of emotional and social competence. Through focused development and interventions, we are able to create new neural pathways. This is known as brain plasticity. Starting with enhancing our self-awareness this helps us to make the shifts.

This means we just need to be ready for the feedback! There are some great tools to help build greater self-awareness like the IL-i^{TM}, EQ-i and 360 feedback. Granted it can sometimes a bit tough to hear frank feedback, but a necessary insight for us to take positive action and move forward.

Stephen Covey used to say, *"Seek first to understand and then to be understood."* In other words we are not **prepared** to understand, until we have at first been heard. By approaching each difficult conversation with a combination of two things – compassion and courage – then we can create positive forward motion. If we enter these conversations with limiting assumptions and attitudes, such as with judgment, bias, fear, ego, then it is virtually impossible to achieve a positive outcome. This is an act of compassion; helping to build trust.

As leaders and experts we are often the 'trusted partner' in the business. Once we have built a level of trust, then we are able to truly influence and have the courageous conversation over poor behaviours, or under-performance and issues of conflict.

Our ability to 'self-coach in the moment' is an important skill, which requires heightened levels of awareness. Sometimes we'll make mistakes and bad judgements - we all do. The maturity of our response and how we work through this is the important issue. Some say that *'there's no going back once a bridge is burned".* I can understand the sentiment, however, it really isn't the reality. We think our mistakes will haunt us; that one bad argument will mean the relationship can never be recovered, that the mistake will remain a black mark on our record. The fact is that if we take the courageous step and tackle the issue within a relationship, rather than avoiding it, then we will move things forward.

Appreciation and Catching People Doing Things Right

As leaders, we often focus on the areas that require improving. We look for the errors and take pride in spotting the issues. We are constantly looking for opportunities to make things better, drive change and launch new initiatives. We also live in a high performance culture where 'giving feedback' is prevalent. So we have naturally become hyper-critical and judgemental of ourselves and others.

However, we all need to feel appreciated. It is essential. Not just at an emotional level, but we also know now this is true at a neurobiological level too. Appreciation and gratitude affects the flow of blood to our brains and releases the 'feel good factor' hormone, dopamine. How incredible is that? That such a simple thing as appreciation has the ability to positively influence our own and others' thoughts and emotions. With something so powerful, it is then essential that we are able to alter our inner and outer dialogue.

As leaders we need to take the time to share and celebrate our successes. Not just the big ones, but the small ones too. We need to 'catch people doing things right', and in the moment wherever we can. But if this is not possible, then we can't afford to let the opportunity slip by unrecognised. Nancy Kline recommends a minimum ratio of at least 5:1 - of 5 amounts of appreciation to every one piece of constructive feedback. In giving our appreciation of a colleague we need to be 'succinct, sincere and specific'.

EQ and Moments of Truth

Organisations with far-flung networks of frontline employees have devoted huge efforts and investment in efforts to attract and retain customers. Creating a deep, emotional connection with customers transforms them into committed followers and purchasers of the brand. Remember, emotions drive behaviour. *Moments of Truth* are the touch-points and interactions between the customer and our frontline. With 'switching' now made so easy and a high amount of emotional energy and expectations invested into the outcome, the exceptional handling of these moments are essential to continued loyalty. Hiring people with emotional and social intelligence is also an important thing for business brand and reputation, particular in the service industry. I see how organisations at times struggle with this and resort to scripting the customer experience, in turn removing the authenticity and responsiveness required in different situations. I've found these clinical 'moments' occur frequently and it has resulted in my own choices to switch suppliers: phones, banks, energy, shops, restaurants etc.

We were recently travelling on a Virgin airlines flight. At almost 40 years old, it was actually my first time travelling with them. On the flight, we met a young flight attendant, Simone Roberts. Clearly efficient in the work that she does, Simone also knew how to connect with people and make them feel great. It wasn't the well-rehearsed 'serving the customer'. It came from a different place; from within her. She *loved* her customers. So, Simone would strike up a conversation with people in a fun and engaging way. She exuded energy and passion for her work. She even recognised us on our return journey and connected again. By the way, with our limited funds, this was not because we were travelling business or 1st class. Quite the contrary, we were so far down the back of the plane that we could pretty much help ourselves to our own beverages - from our seats! However, we definitely had the 1st class service. Unfortunately, without the champagne and caviar!

The next week, we were travelling to Vienna on business with our regular carrier; we were back to the normality of the transaction customer service. These moments of truth were so strong, that I felt compelled to mention it in the book. And, as we look to booking our next holiday and launching the book, I know which website I will be going to in order to make the bookings! There is a wealth of research and studies about what influences purchasing choices reinforcing the importance of moments of truth. We must remember, however, that transactional customer experiences do not come from the heart. Nor are they responsive and sufficiently flexible to connect with customers, creating the spark. It starts with passionate people who are emotionally and socially intelligent.

Finally, we have heard a few times how we, both male and female leaders, need to support each other. Instead of competing with each other, we need to find ways to facilitate greater collaboration and act as champions for each other. Our internal competition means that there will always be a loser. Through working together and communicating towards a win-win outcome, we have far more potential to succeed and be happy, whilst doing so. Inspirational leadership involves positively role-modelling excellence.

Pinky Lilani espouses emotional and social competence in its most abundant form. Pinky says, *"The greatest human craving is to be appreciated. I believe that you have not lived the perfect day until you do something for someone who cannot repay you. I believe in the goodness of people, and there are few that want to take from you and run. Everywhere I look I see what can be done. It all becomes so easy when you really believe this. In terms of collaboration, I cannot do it all myself and I like to bring people in to support and help them to shine. They never forget this. The richness of life is there for anyone to grasp hold of. It's not about money and we cannot judge others based on the money they make or their education. I believe you need to be passionate and love what you do, true to yourself and add value."* People are more committed and willing to go the extra mile for leaders who they admire.

Principles and Behaviours

In summary, emotional and social competence is about the awareness, understanding and management of our emotions and the expression of our feelings. It requires and contributes to a more sophisticated level of leadership, because we not only need to be in tune with our own feelings and emotional responses, but also in tune with those of others.

The management and expression of these emotions and feelings are extremely powerful in building trust and empathy, yet we need to apply this in the context of any given situation. We need to be responsive to the diverse needs and cultures that we are working with. It is important to recognise as humans we are aware of (1) our emotions *followed* by (2) feelings. This is because primitive emotions are physiological and begin at the peripheral and sub-cortical level (limbic) and *then* are cortically 'translated' into feelings (which represent our understanding of emotions). According to Prof Antonio Damasio, feelings are 'second-order emotions'.

Composition – the composition of the leadership team requires careful thought. Building diverse thoughts, styles, cultures and skills is very powerful, as we know from research. Yet, new and diverse teams need to be supported with the right development strategies to help the transition. A high level of awareness of our own cultural profile and that of our team is essential to success.

Attention – By being completely interested in our people, their lives, their passions, their hopes and aspirations, then we can bring out their very best performance. When you are with them, be completely with them. Be present, avoid the distraction of emails, phone calls and even our own internal noise, since these show little respect for others. The power of attention is that it gives the clear message to the people we lead that we care about them and trust them – we value their thinking. They in turn will see us as more trustworthy, particularly if they see us as being attentive of them and their needs. The other form of attention is that which we pay to ourselves. We need to be curious and aware of what is going on inside and around us, paying attention with a peculiar intensity in order to notice our emotions and feelings, so that we can intervene and manage our patterns (memory) and subsequent expression.

Appreciation – Go out there and catch people doing things *right*. They're so used to people being hyper-critical and pointing out their faults and shortcomings. We will put ourselves in the top 10% of inspiring leaders around the world, if we authentically practice appreciation. This requires us to be sincere, specific and succinct in our comments of appreciation. Appreciation can be of an individual, or the performance of our team. This has been proven to have biological benefits and improve the individual performance of a team by 20-30%.

Celebration – It's really important to acknowledge our successes along the way, both as individuals and teams. When we review our performance, if we are highly self-critical then we look for our failures and how 'we can do better next time'. Our successes correlate with our core strengths and so, if we tap into them, can leverage the full potential contained within. It is the virtuous circle: we look for what's going well, celebrate success, we enjoy the sense of achievement, therefore we perfect what we do and get even better at it. Through the laws of attraction we build on great results!

Collaboration – In a competitive environment, it is easy to get caught up in our own team, or individual silo. The danger is that we see life as a win-lose, zero sum game fearing that if others do well, then it has detrimental effects for our career and us. If we are far too competitive then, '*we may win the battle, but lose the war*', creating life-long enemies and a reputation for being too self-serving. As inspiring leaders, championing a cause, or an individual, we can share abundantly through supporting others to succeed. Then we can leave a positive and lasting legacy.

Self-Belief – If we are to feel unburdened by our insecurities, fears, egos, or limiting assumptions, we must become centred and grounded in reality. This means being able to separate our *experiences* from our own sense of *identity*. By understanding our patterns, and stories we tell ourselves, we can intervene. The challenge with tackling issues of self-belief with 'fake it to make it' interventions, can often reinforce the feelings of being a fraud and inauthentic. By intervening in our thoughts and emotions, we can reframe a potentially negative situation. Instead we can create a greater sense of reality and let go of the attachment to unhelpful emotions.

Kim Morrish
Entrepreneur and Director of Ground Control

"I grew up in a family of 'beauty queens' in a small university town in Virginia. My mom pushed my sisters and me academically to gain entry to the best university possible, and grounded us for six weeks if grades ever fell. My father encouraged us to work and have our own money from an early age. By the time I was 12, I was hooked on the immediate satisfaction of 'working for tips' by selling cokes in the stands during big university football matches and pocketing up

to £70 in three hours. Keep in mind this was the late 1970s and I was 13 years old - this was a lot of money!

"When I graduated from university 25 years ago, I had one clear ambition: make a positive difference in the world. This ambition took root at the University of Virginia, where I studied International Relations, and grew into my aspirations to join the US Foreign Service. I subsequently worked in international development for several years before pursuing an MBA. I understood the exceptional gift an education has in this world. I took two years of leave without pay to gain formal, commercial management training at the Darden School of Management.

"With my newly acquired MBA, and all the associated student loan debt, I returned to the US Foreign Service to run development projects in Bolivia. At the time, the country was the second poorest nation in the Western Hemisphere. I extended my time there for a third year to continue working in microfinance which provided sustainable, affordable access to banking services to small and micro businesses.

"I look back often at the quality of the people serving in the Foreign Service - their experience, ethics, drive and commitment. Who you spend time with, especially early in your career, influences your outlook and habits. **"Working with people who will positively shape you is vitally important.** My career progression required a move back to Washington, where passion is often stifled by bureaucracy. The German firm IPC GmbH, which specialised in setting up microcredit banks around the world and was considered top in class, recruited me there. The Managing Director and owner, Claus Peter Zietinger, invited me to join them to launch their US subsidiary in Washington D.C. to recruit US graduates for their international projects.

"I've always loved the motto: Be brave and take risks. I jumped at the chance to take a more direct role in project implementation and to lead a "start up." It was truly my dream job – a leadership role in a commercial enterprise that made a positive impact on people with very limited opportunities or access. I was in charge of everything from launching operations, to branding, marketing, recruiting US staff, business development, and setting up our financial controls to qualify to work as a US

Government Contractor. After working in projects in Haiti and Bosnia, I led a project in Jamaica where all the indigenous banks had failed. We tried to save a small business loan programme. There I met my future husband, Simon, who was also consulting on the banking crisis and unexpectedly became pregnant with our first child.

"When the world around you changes, evolve or perish! Working in these very challenging economies with unpredictable conditions and a baby on the way was not a viable option. I had spent six great years overseas, in work which inspired me. Having recently left the security of the US Foreign Service, I was a bit out on a limb with a baby on the way and a career that required constant overseas travel.

"After selling our internet-based business How-Smart, we moved to Boston so Simon could pursue an MBA. We had 18 months in the US before returning to London. This scenario, with a one year old baby, is not conducive to great career progression. However, I have always believed that you have to thrive wherever you find yourself and I managed to secure a role with Harvard Business School Interactive for the short time we were there, which also allowed me to enjoy time with our daughter. Unlike my two years of 'boot camp' during my MBA programme at Darden, I was now in this amazing learning environment where I could build connections and expand my mind without the constant demands of academic preparation.

"It's important to know where you want to go, but to also have a plan. When you're trying to buy a business, especially as a buy-in team without prior industry experience, you need a compelling and comprehensive plan to convince the seller to sell to you and to raise financing to pull the deal together.

"We were able to raise a total of £10 million from Bank of Scotland, a vendor's loan, getting the directors of the business to mortgage their homes and invest with us, to scrape up every bit of capital we could manage through mortgaging ourselves to the hilt, and then getting friends and family to invest £10k each to make up the shortfall. With only £440k of our own money (which was all leveraged by increasing the mortgages on a couple properties we owned), we took majority control of this company with £8 million of turnover that carried out commercial landscaping throughout the

UK. As an aside, neither Simon nor I had any prior experience in that industry. To reinforce that fact, my dad told me he wrote off his entire £5k investment when he watched Simon do a hatch job in mowing his lawn during one of our visits.

"When we bought Ground Control, we had 18 professional staff members, 50 operatives cutting grass and about 40 subcontractors. Today, we've grown the business from £8 million to over £75 million in turnover, 550 employees and 400 subcontractors employing over 1500 people. We maintain over 31,000 commercial sites throughout the UK for some of the biggest and best known companies, including Tesco, Sainsbury's, Royal Mail, MoD, BP, United Utilities, Thames Water, and the Tower of London.

"My role has evolved from selling and recruiting to a focus on our people. Along with strategy, I focus on resourcing and retaining our best people and helping them develop to reach their potential.

"The original business of all white, male, English managers and directors has evolved to include three female directors, a multicultural and diverse staff across all levels of responsibility, pretty much all of whom are 'fun at parties' and contribute greatly to the entrepreneurial culture of our business. Every employee has share options, and the entire senior team having significant shares in the business as well. The original directors who mortgaged their homes to invest with us have all taken significant profit sharing over the past couple years, and we've paid out over £1 million to 64 other employees through profit sharing.

"Along with growing the business significantly over nine years, we've also doubled the size of our family to four children to include Savannah and Leo, now ranging in age from five to fourteen.

"There are few career paths that allow you to achieve all of your dreams, write your own rule book, and put you squarely in charge of your success or failure. I've worked in a wide variety of cultures and countries where my gender, age and skin colour mattered. I've seen the challenges of trying to balance a family with career aspirations and how much is sacrificed on both fronts in compromises. It's not always fun to play a game where someone else has written the rules and the cards are stacked against you.

"I love that I can wake up every day and focus on making a positive

319

impact on the people in our business - from the small to the enormous. It's a joy to work closely with an amazingly dedicated team who share the same vision and passion for building our business and to ensure it's a great place to work. Don't get me wrong – it's not without its sleepless nights, months and years and sometimes this can be extremely tough!

"However, owning and managing one's own business is tremendously fulfilling and rewarding. I've been able to drive what I truly believe is 'a level playing field' for our employees, a commitment to family friendly policies with 20% of our female staff flexibly working, along with driving significant corporate social responsibility giving.

"I recently read Sheryl Sandberg's book, Lean In. *Immediately, I bought 12 copies for the female managers of our business, the Managing Director we recruited a couple years back and my husband. I'm thrilled that we now have six female senior leaders in our business. The world we live in, even in the business I have worked so hard to shape, is not always an equal place for men and women. A lot remains to be done here, and with two daughters and 100 female professional staff, I am working hard to address this.*

"I believe you can have it all, but not necessarily at the same time. I know how lucky I am to have had a career with a social mission for six years where I really felt that in some way my work was creating opportunities for the disadvantaged. Driving a business where 'caring for our environment' (our tag line) and supporting our employees charitable fundraising has been tremendously rewarding. Buying and growing a business to £75 million in turnover and generating significant wealth for ourselves and our team has been a lot of fun.

"Building an extraordinary team of people who inspire me with their innovation and dedication every day is my greatest satisfaction. Whatever you think your competitive advantage is, or your unique selling proposition, your ability to find and keep outstanding people will be your greatest asset – professionally and personally.

"Of all the challenges, heartbreaks, successes and joys my life to date, by far the most amazing achievement has been my partnership with my husband and being a mother to my four wonderful children.

"Thanks to the amazing team we've built, I've been able to step away from

Operations and have more time to focus on my kids and shaping the way they view the world. Whether this has been during two maternity leaves, when the kids are off school for holidays, or when they've simply needed and deserved more time from me.

"All four of the children are likewise supportive and understanding (mostly) when business demands an excessive amount of my time and attention.

"My advice to others would be:

- *Know where you want to go – 'If you follow your dreams, the world conspires to help you'.*
- *Have the confidence to be brave – this is missing for women.*
- *Have the courage to say when something's not right and stand up for your beliefs.*
- *Surround yourself with the very best people - from whom you marry to the people you work with. It makes all the difference.*
- *Train to be a leader and not a cog in a wheel.*
- *Believe you can have it all; it just may not be at the same time."*

Inspiring Women Leaders' Words of Wisdom

1. Building Cultural Awareness

"We loved the freedom offered by moving around. Restrictions meant that foreigners knew more about South Africa than we did. We decided we would live in different provinces. Strong leadership is about adaptability and to understand various cultures. The leader I am today is based upon these experiences. To be a global leader, you need to understand customs and cultures and how people relate to one another. I engaged coaches to support the cross-cultural working. This meant they would leave issues outside of the boardroom, so we can focus on the issues at hand."

2. Influencing the Outcome

"Each interaction that we have and each decision we take has the power to influence our relationships and our destiny – for better or for worse. To be an inspiring leader we must positively impact both, this often requires us to call on our courage."

3. Working Towards a Win-Win

"Be clear about some principles you are willing to negotiate on, what you are willing to give up and what you won't give up. Is it a win-win situation, or will there be a loser? And is that really the outcome you want? By keeping the end result in mind, it helps you to approach a negotiation with a success attitude."

4. Manage the Clashes

"One leader found me difficult and he felt I was "rude". I realised then that I needed to adopt different manner of styles to suit different needs. We both had the same goal so, instead of fighting it, we worked on how could we get to the endpoint."

5. Support Network

"I love working and feel energised when I go into the office. I have incredible support in my husband, and I couldn't handle the emotional equilibrium without him. He cooks dinner and gets stuck into helping out. I couldn't do my job, unless he was so supportive. When we have kids, I really want to continue working. By being clear on your relationship and equality in the home, it is really important to success."

6. Fruitful Relationships

"Even in a conversation with someone whose values and outlook are different, I always want the outcome to be fruitful. The resource that I use is the intelligence of my heart. When I create quietness inside, I control my breathing and allow a response from a place of compassion. Then, hey presto, something really works!"

7. Management versus Leadership

"When younger people want promotion, they talk about the structure and systems. The biggest challenge is managing people. It's working with lots of different individuals, in different departments. If you get this bit right, then everything else will fall into place. There are few people that can get the very best out of others."

8. Managing Emotions

"One thing I've learned is that you don't always have to address emotion. I always felt if someone was emotional, then you need to respond to that emotion. Whereas, I've since learned that it's sometimes much better to bypass the emotion and talk about the facts.

As someone who's emotionally aware of what's going on around me, it can be quite difficult to step back. But it's important to say that I'm not going to take on their emotion. Instead I will try to address whatever problem they are raising."

9. Get Feedback

"I was too brash, harsh and direct and described as the nightmare woman. I had to change my style and listen to the team. They gave great feedback. I noticed how lost you can be when you join. You need someone to tell you things are wrong. My husband would say, 'You need to stop turning into a bloke by wanting to fit in and be noticed.' I got a great coach to support me with understanding my authentic style and changing my behaviours."

10. Working On Your Terms

"There is a distinct lack of role models who resonate with me. I don't want to work stupid hours, or to sacrifice what's most important. My advice to others is: be smart about job choices and ask for what you need. It's okay to negotiate to meet your terms, whilst understanding the business needs, and be happy, rather than strive to fit someone else's standards and ways of working."

11. Being Confident in Your Authentic Self

"Identifying what is truly authentic is one of the core issues of the workplace today. We are so economically driven; it's all about keeping the job. We suffer for that. So much potential is lost for businesses and individuals. I found by being authentic and myself and answering with honesty, that it boosted my confidence and credibility."

12. Be a Role Model

"My concern is that there are a lot of senior women spouting off what we need to do and are presented as 'role models'. There are junior women who then look up to these women and learn from them. This whole cycle means that we are not living true to our integrity. I find I hit the curb and fall in a ditch, when I'm expected to be different to who I am. It's so counterintuitive. I find I go against this and get disengaged. You have to do what's natural to you and so be inspiring to others."

13. Believe in Your Team

"Our CEO gives you the confidence and space which makes you believe in yourself. He saw it in others too and he saw this within his team, which was vital. It means the team doesn't fall apart. He helped us make a step change in what we achieved because we had the confidence to move forward. I've found too many leaders tend to chip away at your confidence."

14. In Service of Your Team

"Someone once asked me, 'Having achieved outstanding school inspection results several times, what do you think about your management and leadership and what made you so successful?' I told him that I tend to lead from behind. I had never really thought, or reflected as to why. With women they tend to be like that. "

15. Make Time to Be A Leader

"In terms of my people, one-to-one meetings are always the last thing that I ever sacrifice from my diary. That is because I see how crucial they are. Our employees need to believe that they are truly important. A real leader focuses on their people, their needs and performance. Leadership is a big responsibility in enabling the performance of people and the task itself. It is as if the activities of leadership are the bi-products of the activities of the task. It's important to get the balance between driving stuff through and just 'being' with people. Ask yourself, where can I make time to be a leader?"

Chapter Reflection:
EQ Self-Reflection

Take time to reflect on the following questions for yourself your team and your organisation:

Myself
- How emotionally self-aware do you think you are?
- What are the recurring patterns and internal dialogue that are helping you?
- What are the recurring patterns and internal dialogue that are hindering you?
- How good are you at managing your emotions once you've identified them?
- When you are emotionally upset (the amygdala hijack) how do you intervene and get yourself back to a good place for damage limitation?

My Team
- What do other people say about your level of self-awareness and emotion management?
- How successful are you in using emotional expression to build empathy, trust and a compelling story for others?
- How good are you at managing your impulse control?
- When working with diverse teams, how respectful and responsive are you to the different styles and needs?

My Organisation
- How do you look for emotionally intelligent leaders?
- How do you encourage and promote truly diverse teams?
- How do you create interventions to support the performance of new and diverse teams?
- How do you create a culture of trust and openness, where emotional expression is valued?

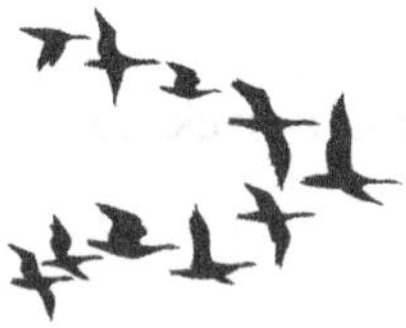

Chapter 10
RQ: Resilience

Contributing Authors: Dr. Donald Bosch et al, Headington Institute

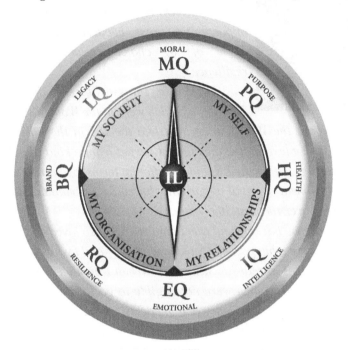

"Having committed 13 years as one of the longest serving woman in government, resilience was essential to my own leadership. I believe that success is not a zero sum game. You need to build your team and share the successes with them. Strong leadership is the expression of a coalition of values such as having greater meaning and purpose. Building consensus creates a position of strength. Don't be surprised by the loneliness of leadership and believe in who you are. You need to press 'delete' on the impostor syndrome button. If you believe in what you do, then people will join your journey. Persevere and learn resilience."

Rt Hon Dame Tessa Jowell MP DBE
The former Secretary of State for Culture, Media & Sport
House of Commons, Westminster

Sally-Anne Airey
Ex-Wren, Executive Coach and Consultant

"Most of my life, I've felt that opportunities have come along and I've made the choices that felt right at the time. On reflection, I think that perhaps the opportunities arose, because I was open to them. Some of my choices required courage and resilience.

"For 23 years I was an officer in the Royal Navy, 10 years of which were in the Women's Royal Naval Service, before the WRNS integrated into the RN in the early 90s. My professional context shifted during that period from a kind of collegiate of women working within the RN, but on different terms to our male colleagues, to an environment of equal opportunity based on individual ability. Much has changed over the past 30+ years.

"My academic background was Linguistics. I also loved the sea – sailing and rowing were a big part of my teenage years – and I wanted to travel and use my languages in real-life situations. When I applied to join, I actually didn't realise that women were not eligible to go to sea at that time. My research had been rudimentary and my decision – as with many I've made since – was strongly heart and gut based. It was the right decision, but as I reflect on that period now, I realise that I had to learn to adapt my expectations and adjust my behaviours.

"The RN was an action-oriented environment. I think I succeeded because I worked hard, I responded to opportunities and my talents suited what was required of me. I was frequently told that I 'didn't suffer fools gladly', which I never really took as a compliment. However, that probably helped me to be highly assertive in a largely 'man's world' back then. I did well and got promoted early in my career.

"Tough demographics drove the political decision to integrate the WRNS fully into the RN in 1991. When I returned from a posting with the United States Navy in my early 30s, it was to an environment in the throes of fundamental change. I applied to transfer to a long-career commission and sea-going service (all Wrens serving at that time were given this choice). My

candidature was welcomed and the wheels set in motion. However, over the course of the following months, I began to see things differently and to shift my priorities. Integration had also brought with it the option to remain serving as a mother (just as fathers had always done).

"By now in my mid-30s, I began to feel the impact of my ticking biological clock and recognised the choice before me: between opting for a sea-going career and starting a family. This was an extremely difficult decision, but I elected to have a family, because it felt like the deeper calling. Two years later I gave birth to my twin sons. At this point I received a key, yet simple, piece of advice from my boss to 'keep your options open'. Instead of leaving the RN, I became the first officer to return to the RN from maternity leave and was subsequently promoted to senior rank.

"Courageous as this may perhaps sound, I was aware that I found it easier to go to work than to stay at home. At work I felt I was in control and could manage my environment to achieve results. Of course it was challenging to juggle both, but easier for me to do this, than commit totally to being a mum. I'm not proud of this and I admire women whose nature is more nurturing than mine was.

"Soon after my 46th birthday, I left the Navy. I'd been feeling a strong sense of misalignment for some time, both professionally and personally. During that year my husband and I divorced, I remarried, ended my career and moved abroad – to Kyiv, Ukraine – as a 'trailing spouse', with my second husband and my sons. Whereas I'd always felt pretty resilient in the face of change, during that year I felt as though my resilience depleted to a very low ebb, like a battery completely drained of its energy. I felt very vulnerable. Gradually I became aware that my sense of identity had been a function of my achievements, of my 'doing' rather than 'being'. And I really didn't know who I was.

"As a student of French, I'd been fascinated by the work of mid-20th century writers like Camus and Sartre, particularly around existentialism: the belief that individuals—not societies, or religions—are responsible for giving meaning to life and living it passionately and authentically. After years of 'giving service', filling an 'important' role, I felt as if my life's meaning had gone.

"As an antidote, I threw myself into work at my sons' international school; first on the board of governors and then as the school's business manager. However, while outwardly still assertive and capable, inwardly I was struggling mentally, physically, emotionally, and spiritually, to cope. I wanted to stop, but didn't know how to. The cost was high: a growth formed on the left lobe of my thyroid to the size of a golf ball before I even noticed it. An emergency operation luckily removed it completely and today my thyroid functions normally.

"The journey between then and now has been interesting; what I have learnt has transformed my life. The lump on my thyroid represents for me my struggle to express myself authentically, to know and be me. I was choked, blocked and stifled. In releasing myself from this struggle, I've found a quiet, peaceful inner space, from which I draw my energy and my passion for life. I've found that in focussing on this space, I feel a powerful connection to my inner being and through this to the world around me. As this connection strengthens, I'm aware that my heart is more open, my spirit more generous and my nature more compassionate.

"Now, as an executive and life coach, my fulfilment comes from helping others to become who they want to be. As a retreat coach, I encourage others to give themselves time and space to explore and reflect on their life's purpose. I'm still giving service, but without losing myself in the process. In my daily mindfulness practice, as I breathe in the restorative mountain air around us, I focus on appreciating my family and our life in our wonderful alpine home. By doing this, I know that I'm topping up my 'inner battery': my resilience. This sustains my ability, even in the face of challenge, to live a full and rewarding life."

What is Resilience (RQ)?

In a globally connected world, where the challenges are far more demanding and fast paced than ever before, we are continuously affected by change. Resilience is our combined emotional, psychical and mental capacity to cope with these stresses and catastrophes, as well as the ability to learn from these setbacks and disappointments.

The following three symbiotic circumstances determine when we need to call on our resilience. Each is interconnected, but with a different emphasis:

1. ***Crucible Moments*** – are the life, or business changing events that trigger the need for change. They can be minor, or seismic shifts, but always require attention. Jan Carlzon coined the phrase 'moments of truth' to describe these events, and they create the compelling reason and catalyst for some form of change.

2. ***Change*** – is precipitated by an event, or 'crucible moment' and directed towards an outcome. This contains the two key decision points; the initial rationale for the change and the subsequent desired end result. Change represents progress; it has a defined start and an end point. Although we know only too well that too much change can actually have a detrimental effect. This can be detrimental on us: personally, physically, emotionally and on our teams and organisations.

3. ***Transition*** - occurs in the period between, which needs to be managed through the different stages. In resilience terms, these can be the most challenging phases of our lives; coping strategies are required over a sustained period of time. The danger comes when these blips occur like a persistent murmur, ones that are easy to pass us by unnoticed, yet they build up in our sub-conscious.

Whether a crucible moment, change, or transition, we are compelled to recalibrate and re-tune ourselves back to what is essential in order to cope with the adversity.

Dr. Galen Buckwalter of the Headington Institute states, *"It's hard to measure resilience when things are going well, although good times may increase it... Resilience determines how quickly we get back to our 'steady-state' after the air has been knocked out of us, when we must push through life circumstances that challenge our very being."* Dr Buckwalter describes how we must be both 'emotionally and cognitively' engaged in order for our resilience to be fully developed and that, *"there are natural biological processes that facilitate our recovery from stress. A process called 'allostasis' attempts to get all of the physiological systems back to their steady state, after the stress response. However, numerous biological and psychological factors can interfere with allostasis. This is where resilience becomes important, because this amazing psychological characteristic facilitates the biological process of allostasis, getting our brain and body back to normal."*

The attributes of MQ, PQ and HQ are at the core of resilience. Our aptitude and capacity for being resilient relies on: a strong foundation of morality and values; a life that has meaning and purpose, and the physical and mental wellbeing that helps us to cope. If we consider situations when we have been most challenged and our strength to be resilient is also frequently undermined, those have been when any of these three components are compromised. Also the attributes of Cognitive, Emotional and Social Resilience (IQ and EQ) help us leverage all of the resources that are available to us. It lets us manage and lead through adverse times, to make wise judgements, become creative and collaborate with our support network.

Having purpose, meaning and a sense of identity, helps us to contextualise the stressors and traumas with the knowledge that at some point normality and fulfilment will return. I also believe that resilience is not just a passive reaction to life's challenges. In Daniel Pink's book *To Sell is Human*[1], he describes the importance of the salesman 'staying buoyant amidst a sea of rejection'.

RQ requires us to connect with three time periods: the *past* in order to allow us to learn; the *future* to provide direction; and the *present* to keep in tune with ourselves. We must keep a level of pragmatism and drive that leads us to our end goal. We should not be evasive, or even ignorant of the fact that life may often drift a little 'off plan'. Neither should we be too complacent and say, 'our business is successful, so why do we need to change?'

Resilience is also about clarity of focus and our proactive energy to bring things back on track. It is the art of saying 'no' (for anyone who's been on a diet will know what I mean). It is also the act of saying 'yes' to what really matters and the strength to grab life's opportunities, and knowing the benefits that result from positive change and growth. To be resilient is not being rocked by the change, but embracing the new with both hands, knowing that you have the resources and energy to see things through.

RQ is also about *how* we respond in the moment; our recovery from what life throws our way. Our family of origin is often where our journey into resilience begins.

Whether we grew up surrounded by love, support and challenge, or encountered more dysfunctional childhoods is critical. We sustain our emotional states through both our conscious and sub-conscious thoughts. Like a music archive, we take out the old familiar favourites to listen to, whether they're from a good era, or not!

Therefore, RQ requires a deep awareness of self, combined with an understanding of the past patterns and triggers that determine our emotional and physical responses. It requires us to notice our thoughts in the moment. We have to handle the complexity that comes with recurring patterns, and the subsequent stories and narratives that drive our behaviours. By detaching the narrative from the emotion and feelings that come with the experience, we are able to find sense and make alternative choices. Resilience then becomes about the positive activation of our emotional, physical and mental responses.

Viktor Frankl wrote about the fact that he had come to predict those people in the concentration camp that would be okay, and those who would not survive, *"Everything you have in life can be taken from you except one thing. Your freedom to choose how you will respond...This is what determines the quality of life we've lived."* Stress and the inability to cope can also emerge when there is an absence of hope, a greater cause that give us purpose and some sense of identity. We have to feel we are contributing and creating value in some way that feels right and is nourishing. Without this we stagnate and shrink into ourselves, limiting our full potential. However, we sometimes confuse our states of hyper-busyness with real purpose and identity. The fact is, we can sustain our resilience, but for all the wrong reasons.

RQ is about finding the optimum balance between drive and recovery and is importantly underpinned by our sense of identity for what we do today and hope for the future. It is also a balanced blend of positive attitude and emotions with a firm grounding in life's reality and unpredictability.

I must confess to making a false assumption that resilient leaders come from stable and happy backgrounds. However, it turns out that just as many come from more challenging backgrounds. During these turbulent economic times, we have seen many leaders cope, even thrive, more easily than others. Through my interviews with, and the research into, leaders around the world, resilience has proven to be a key factor that unites them in their success and differentiates them from others. The blend of attitude, resourcefulness and coping strategies that they deploy, help them to sustain their performance through the stormy weather. Their experiences, both inside and outside of work, have shaped them. Interestingly, they have not defined them. Noticeably, these leaders have a healthy level of self-esteem and are not too distracted by the internal narrative, which comes with limited self-belief.

Being clear about who you are and what you stand for is key to a healthy resilience.

An inspiring leader, wishing to remain anonymous, shared a particularly challenging experience with me, *"You need to put effort and attention into the stuff that you do. You need to be resilient and stay true to your own compass and what you really believe in. When you don't, this is when you tend to get derailed. When it all gets slightly too difficult, then we sometimes give up, instead of getting to the other side.*

"Recovery is needed when stuff's not going right; you need to give yourself time to recover. There was a point in my career when the new HR Director arrived. I was the only HR person based in the corporate centre. We had just come out of the de-merger. We had no HR processes and systems, which was a reflection of where we were at that time. As the only HR person, I was in the 'line of sight' and got the blame. I had a real bond with the organisation and wanted to be part of what the new HRD did. I wanted to achieve. So I listened carefully to the words of performance management. I then worked hard to deliver, based on what I'd heard. Although it was a rocky start, my relationships and experiences changed."

So, even with scars and battle-wounds from mistakes or crucible moments, these did not play into the narrative or drama of today, forming limitations or barriers. They only act as a source of insight that enables greater learning. In fact, it has only served to create a more powerful and 'centred' leader.

Consequences of Lack of RQ

Dr Don Bosch, Director of Clinical Services at the Headington Institute has worked in the training and development of humanitarian aid workers who operate in high-risk regions around the world. He found that resilience was at the core of sustained performance in such high stress environments. He was generous in sharing his vast research and experience in the field of resilience.

When considering RQ, I was curious about a number of key questions. For example, are there genetic components that give some people an edge simply by their birth-right? Are there childhood experiences that can make it more difficult for us to be resilient adults? Are there psychological profiles and biomarker clusters that correlate with how resilient, or not, an individual seems? Are there anatomical brain differences in the primary stress circuits of the brain that may affect resilience?

Dr. Bosch told me, *"Probably - yes to all of the above."* He went on to say, *"There are repercussions for the brain and the body, when we face situations that require resilience. When we experience an extreme trauma, or stressor, our physiology undergoes radical changes.*

"Beginning in the depths of our brain, neurotransmitters and hormones tell our body that we are undergoing some type of threat. The amygdala, strategically positioned to evaluate whether we are in any danger, operates without our conscious awareness. However, it can have a powerful effect on our entire physical and mental well-being. Throughout our lifetime it collects and stores the sights, sounds, smells that have been connected to dangerous, or threatening situations. It also comes preloaded with some danger situations, passed on over the millennium from our ancestors. When the amygdala senses danger, then it reacts in a big way. It sends out the message for a massive change in our bodily functioning. Our heart beats faster, our lungs suck in more air to feed oxygen to our muscles to prepare to fight, or to run. We feel apprehension and fear.

"The adrenal glands get the message and flood our entire body with stress hormones. These hormones affect all bodily systems, such as the

cardiovascular, digestive, immune, metabolic, inflammatory, renal, etc. Needless to say, stress has a huge impact on our brain. To put it in general terms, stress hormones accesses the parts of our brain where our memories are stored and think in ways that are unique to you. If these hormones and chemicals go uncontrolled, they shut down our ability to make good decisions, or think about anything other than the immediate threat. If our system stays on high alert, we end up with a brain that isn't thinking clearly and every physiological system on overload.

"Resilience is a discipline. The research indicates that over time, with exposure to overly stressful situations, our amygdala (the alarm bell or 'freak-out' centre) grows denser, or bigger! Your prefrontal cortex and hippocampus get damaged and essentially shrink from the same experiences. Think of the hippocampus as a kind of shock absorber for the amygdala. When the amygdala freaks and sends out the screaming message for flight or fight, the hippocampus tries to provide context appraisal and question whether such a massive response is necessary. So, what happens if our hippocampus starts to limp and not function well? Exactly! You'll start reacting to every bump in the road, with an all hands on deck alarm, which is not a good thing. Over time you will most likely find yourself dealing with depression, post-traumatic stress, anxiety and other resilience eroding issues."

In Monica Singer's story, she shared how her doctor challenged her about her work. He sensed she worked as if the 'lion was always chasing her', as she was always running and on guard. How many of us have similar work ethics? The implications for Monica were potentially fatal; she has been forced to re-configure her life. When we become manic, anxious and stressed, particularly over sustained periods, then it takes its toll. Our performance and health can be adversely affected. It becomes harder to maintain a positive attitude and energy to leverage our talents and to live life in abundance. Rosenbloom & William describe the experience of trauma in that, *"...it can be like having stared directly at the sun. Even after you look away, the glare seems everywhere and prevents you from seeing things clearly."* As a leader, our anxiety-fuelled hyper-busyness also sends a signal to our people. We value long hours, putting our all into our work, in efforts to keep the metaphorical lions at bay.

Without thinking things through, we can at times expect a lot from our children in terms of resilience.

One inspiring leader recollected a deeply personal story from her early childhood: *"When I was 7 years old, I was 5' 5" tall. By the time I was 10, I was 5' 8". Great Ormond Street hospital predicted that I would be a giant. I saw all the other children being small and cute, but I wasn't any of these. Some teachers can say cruel things for example, "I couldn't be the fairy, but I could be the tall witch". I really loved tap dancing and so I auditioned for the school's dance, 'A Little Mouse with Clogs On'.*

"I didn't get through the selection, not even a background mouse! When I asked why, I was told I was too tall and didn't fit in. I thought I'd wet myself with fear, but I knocked on the headmistress' door and said that it seemed unfair. They created a special part for me. It made me focused and determined to stand up for what I believe in. Years later, when my dearest friend died, at the age of 36, it made me realise I had bucketful's of resilience."

Sometimes our own judgements and bias can, unintentionally, be to our detriment. Exclusion is very tough, no matter what age we are. By not challenging pre-conceived ideas, about how things should work, or adhering to 'imposed rules' that are founded in fantasy, then we will miss out on opportunities to draw from a broader talent pool. Whether it's women into leadership, or tall mice into the dance theatre! Being conscious of our attitudes, behaviours and biases is important in any of our leadership roles. This is the case, whether in education, politics, business, or even in our relationships.

One inspiring leader told me of her deep and very personal experience, *"I can get anxious about things in general, so I've worked hard not to let people see this. My Mum was always a very anxious person. So I stopped questioning it. I would make an excuse for my anxiety, that it was passed on from my Mum. I thought it to be inherently me. It's strange the assumptions I was making: thinking it was about who I was, rather than looking at what I can change. We can all have a victim mentality, men, or women. It is easy for our learning and patterns from our past to seep through into our work and relationships in the present."*

I often hear my clients being defined by their past, and they will tell me, 'I've never been good at presenting', or 'I don't like selling', or 'I hate conflict situations'. These then become our symbols of pain, or weakness, and we must avoid situations that make us feel this way. In our shame, we look externally for sources of validation and approval. The issue is that no amount of validation from others can make us feel worthy under these circumstances.

I was coaching Lucy, a leader who had a particularly challenging relationship with her direct report. She's undoubtedly a highly intelligent, passionate and collaborative leader whose primary focus was on making relationships work. They tried hard to turn the relationship around, but really struggled to do so. The direct report took opportunities to complain about Lucy at every opportunity. Lucy started to dread going into work each day, fearing the potential conflict that would ensue. She started to develop a new language for her leadership, the gremlin on her shoulder telling her that not only was she not a good leader, but now everyone else felt so too. She felt her *'reputation in this business was destroyed'*. Feeling unsupported and persecuted, she had lost faith in her ability to be a strong inspiring leader. When we met for the first time, she'd decided that she'd had enough of the corporate world and leadership positions. The surface decision hid the underlying trauma and pain that had occurred, limiting her belief in her abilities and impeding her performance.

We often set ourselves up for failure just by our own inner dialogue. We then sub-consciously escalate the problem, making it far more significant than it actually is. These obstructive 'gremlins' only serve to impede our full potential. They anchor themselves in our own personally created 'comfort zone', pulling us back from the possibility of stretching ourselves, for fear of failure. If our internal frame of reference is that 'we are not good enough', then conflict becomes the battlefield and resilience is the skill we rely on to get through.

Steven Karpman's 'Drama Triangle' which is used in Transactional Analysis (TA) describes 3 types of relationship; the *Rescuer*, *Persecutor* and *Victim*. It is possible for us to become the *Victim*: overwhelmed, helpless and believing that things aren't happening for us in the way that we'd hoped. The

Persecutor, on the other hand, can be very critical and often filled with anger and blame. Finally, the *Rescuer* is very sensitive to the needs of others and with their radar picking up other's emotions, spends most of their time on hyper-alert, ever-ready to do what others want. The interplay between two people in a Drama Triangle, where one, for example, plays the victim and the other one plays the rescuer leads to a psychological 'game'. At the end of the game is the 'switch' where one turns on the other person to become a *persecutor.* The result is that both people in the interaction feel dissatisfied with what happened.

To illustrate the problems of a Drama Triangle, let me share the story of one of my clients, let's call her Claire. She got a real sense of fulfilment and satisfaction from helping other people. The problem was that she took this to an extreme and either saw, or unwittingly made, other people *victims* who she needed to *rescue.* In one case she had a colleague at work, let's call him Brian, who was struggling with a personal problem. She saw him as a victim and someone she could rescue. Every time he shared an aspect of his problem, Claire would then try and offer solutions and help him solve it. However, Brian deemed none of her offers good enough. The switch came when Brian angrily shouted at her to leave him alone and *'stop being such an interfering bitch'.* He had suddenly adopted the persecutor role and the result was the both of them felt awful. Their relationship was then seriously damaged and this became part of a repeat pattern between them.

Through my research and interviews, women acknowledged times when they had adopted each of these roles and played an unfulfilling psychological game. As a result, they checked out of opportunities, instead disappearing into their caves! They recognised occasions when they remained in toxic cultures for too long, blaming the environment, or keeping their heads low. As we have to face conflict, or difficult situations, we avoid tackling the issues. This is because we fear the conversations that need to be had and the potential stress caused to others and ourselves. Whatever role we choose, it affects our energy and capacity to be resilient.

One leader shared with me, *"In hindsight I was taking on too much. My childcare arrangements were not ideal, my children went to another home each day and I would have to pack everything and prepare each morning. I had a new-born and each lunch time I would have to go home to feed him. By working so hard, I thought the world around me would honour me as a heroine, as I struggled with my heavy bags on my shoulders and my lists of things I had to do each day. I expected that I could do it all; so I never asked for help. I would see this as a weakness. I was barely surviving and I was my own last priority. I was 40 years old when I had my last child. I then moved to a more traditional COO role."*

Emotions and behaviours, such as feelings of guilt, or even being judgemental, actually zap our energy. I have a really close relationship with my Mum. However, I recall how, with the best of intent, she would persistently tell me that I was too focused on my work and not enough on my family. The challenge for each generation is the judgement that we place on each other. We frequently fail to see their lives through their eyes, rather than our own. This adds unintentional pressure to a women's ability to pursue a successful career.

Lizzie Dale is a talented an inspiring HR leader. Having grown up with both parents having equal status and working for the same law firm, she explained how she'd been shaped by a family with strong work ethics: *"My Mum was the first female law firm partner in the area. I liked the concept of psychology at work. So I pursued my MA in Occupational Psychology at Nottingham University. It was here that I found I had dyslexia. However, it didn't affect my confidence; it just made me more determined."*

Lizzie shared with me how, when she worked for a bank and her boss moved on, she ended up taking the role and working directly for the Group Human Resources Director (HRD). It gave her really great visibility and was very stretching. It was Lizzie's first year off the graduate scheme and she was already in a high profile position looking after a client base; the experience couldn't be under-estimated. She described how, *"The experience provided an accelerated start to my career but the culture was challenging with long hours and our HRD demanding her 'pound of flesh'. There were some nights during certain annual cycles, such as pay-reviews, when the team wouldn't even go home, pulling in all-nighters. It was the sort of culture where you couldn't show signs of weakness and had to leave your home life at the door. I strongly believe that you don't get the best out of people this way."*

She continued, *"Going to my new role at the BBC was one of the biggest shifts. I had to adapt by becoming a lot warmer. At the bank, I was so highly strung and had to put on a different face to fit in. Whereas, when I was at the BBC, I rediscovered how to be my authentic self again. It's such a relaxed and collaborative place – I used to leave work with a skip in my step. I was contacted for a speculative role, which would have been a step back. I pushed back, and I was so pleased I did. They found another far more suitable opportunity for me as Head of Talent. I believed in myself enough to negotiate for something better."*

If we work in, or lead others in, toxic environments, we break down trust, loyalty and limit the full capability of our teams. This kind of fear culture keeps people on constant alert. Of course, this releases stress hormones, such as cortisol and adrenaline, negatively affecting the pre-frontal cortex. As we now know, this impedes the quality of our thinking and decisions. We burn people out, disengage people and if they don't drop first, they end up leaving.

Worse still they may 'quit but stay' and so we end up paying people who are not really fully present, or committed to the organisation; they are just complying. It is essential, with so few female role models around us, that we take personal responsibility for leading well. This responsibility is not just for ourselves, or even those we lead, but also for the wider agenda that demonstrates women, too, can be inspiring leaders. We cannot let ourselves down. Finally, with resilience comes an inner confidence to proactively have the tough conversations. Equally it is important to say 'no' or to negotiate for the opportunities and rewards that we deserve. How often do we avoid conversations, which subsequently eat away at us, since our voice is not heard?

Of course, there is also the issue of having too much resilience. With too much resilience we end up staying in a toxic environment, a toxic workplace, a toxic team and even a toxic relationship. We mistakenly do this, because we tell ourselves we must persevere and be strong. We even create stories to help us rationalise why we do so. It's important to realise that we always have the choice. We have the choice to change the way we think about ourselves. We are fully capable of fresh and different ideas about ourselves and to generate new alternative paths. Prolonged and sustained periods in these environments can consume us with 'toxins'. These come in the form of:

fear, anger, dissatisfaction, intolerance, impatience, pain, disillusionment and depression.

These 'toxins' then seep through into our leadership, slowly at first. It is something to be aware of, and also addressed, when it's not working for us or other people. Proactively dealing with these situations means that we are taking the power into our own hands, and not giving away our power to others.

How Can RQ Help You as a Leader?

Helen Sachdev shared, *"I was offered a great director role with a new organisation. At the time, I had young children and an unsupportive partner. It was a big step up, but I felt ready to take it on. I didn't realise it at the time, but it also gave me the freedom to get out of my situation with my partner in a way that left me financially independent.*

"The organisation was not known for taking people on from the outside and the bar was set high. Where I had always been the golden girl, I was now working in a tough, masculine culture. Everyone knew each other, and everything was high pace and high work volume. I took on quite a broken department at the time.

"It took a lot of strength to build a team up that had been battered and rubbished by other parts of the business. I would say at the time, I was more in the team than part of the leadership team. I wanted to structure things to make them better and help them to work effectively. I felt if I could get 'my own house' in order first, then I could focus on what my role was within the leadership team.

"It was a really stressful period. I was the only female on the Leadership Team, apart from Human Resources, which was more of a support role. Now that I was a single parent, I knew I had to be very strong for the family. I just needed to get through the work. So, I did long hours taking heaps home with me at the weekend.

"Whilst my daughter and son were at Pony Club, I would watch and work at the same time. It was incredibly difficult, so I negotiated and laid out some boundaries for my work - the working week belonged to the business and my weekend was my own.

"I didn't always achieve this neat separation, but having stated the boundary, it was then easier to come back to that agreement if I started to get calls over the weekend, for example. Every time I felt I had cracked it and found some capacity, I was given more responsibility. I got quicker at learning. I was given a coach at the time but I didn't get it as I felt it was performance-based, and there were breaches in confidence which caused trust issues. Eventually, however, I learnt how to do the work effectively and how to make stuff happen.

"Reflecting back, it was so hard, the pace was brutal, just getting through each day was so tough. I needed so much preparation and planning. Looking back, I'm not sure how I could have done it any better. I needed to be resilient, as I wanted the children to have a certain kind of life, and I wanted them to have quality choices available to them.

"My Nanny was a rock – she was my 'pseudo partner'. She stayed through everything, providing continuity and calm. She organised everything so it was as boring as possible, in other words no great dramas! It gave the kids routine. I believe the sacrifice was worth it. My focus for the first 3-4 years was just work, and anything else that was left of me was purely for the kids."

Regardless of the hand you were dealt in life, you can do something to improve your resilience. The emphasis here is, 'take personal accountability and take action'. Resilience is not a passive sport! The more passive you are, the more you are likely to become stuck with that original 'life script' and a potentially sad and victim-like story of how your life will play out.

Resilient people have the confidence to handle difficult situations, people and environments. They have the tenacity to bounce back from minor hassles and major crises. Those with high levels of resilience have an internal, rather than external, locus of control. They feel they are more in control of their life rather than external factors in life controlling them. They are able to reframe adverse situations in an optimistic way. They therefore don't see things (as pessimists do) in a way that feels personal, permanent and pervasive.

Those with high levels of RQ have optimism, a freedom from anxiety, take personal responsibility, and are open and adaptable. They consequently recover from life's problems, learn from them and take action.

Resilience is not fixed; it fluctuates, dependent your experiences and how you handle them. We all respond to different triggers in different ways and being aware of these triggers, will help you to centre yourself as a leader. The great news is that we can develop our resilience through how we find our truth, cut through our fears and master the art of reframing.

When **Rhiannon White** shared her story, I was impressed by her resilience in the face of adversity:

"I was working for the New Zealand National Party in the combined marketing and communications unit. The Party had been in Opposition for many years and, with a new, inspirational leader, things were on the up. It was an exciting place to be. Then, in the run up to the elections, I made a serious mistake.

"The new leader was a very impressive man, but not very well known as he was relatively new to politics. We had to help people understand more about who he was and what he stood for. So we created a short film about him, where he came from and his vision for the country. It was a cracking story and great project. I was really proud of the film and it was doing really well – lots of positive media coverage and high view numbers online. But shortly after it was released, we were challenged about the music in the film.

"It was an original piece that we'd had commissioned for the film but it was alleged that it was too similar to another well-known piece of music. It became front-page news. It didn't matter that the music was original, it was the appearance that mattered and it was the kind of detail that shouldn't have been overlooked, that I shouldn't have overlooked. The Leader had to publicly retract the campaign.

"I felt physically ill. As the senior person on the project, I knew I had to take responsibility. I took deep breath and I went to the Chief of Staff. I asked him, 'Do I need to resign?' to which he responded, 'Don't be so melodramatic!' Although clearly annoyed, he was calm and nothing could ruffle his feathers.

"I hid away in my office for a week though! And I barely slept for the next three nights. The rest of the team were really upset and I expected them to lay into me – this wasn't the kind of distraction we could afford and I was so ashamed as I felt I had let the team down. However, they were incredibly

supportive. Some of the senior politicians, who had been through worse, would clap me on the back and say, 'now you know what it's like for us, you'll be fine, you'll pull through it'. For a long time though, every time someone came up to me to talk about it, I would die inside.

"Over time it got easier. The team never judged me and we got on even better as a result of what had happened; in fact if anything it gave me more credibility. In a leadership, or decision-making position, we put our necks on the line and sometimes we just get it wrong. I learned that by owning up to the mistake publicly, that it turned out to be transformational. It's amazing when you own the cock-up and admit it, how people will want to reach out to you and support you. Working in politics can be a really harsh place and so I never anticipated the amazing support, it meant the world to me."

Rhiannon highlighted a key component of RQ. Clearly she was a leader with high integrity as she took ownership for her error, despite the fact that she was afraid of the potential consequences. To her surprise, her combined vulnerability and leadership accountability resulted in a deeper level of trust amongst the team. This was something that she had not anticipated. This is a crucial component of Inspiring Leadership: the ability to be transparent and honest, even if there are some adverse effects.

This is not always the case and often, in fear-based cultures, many leaders have fallen foul of self-preservation, playing dodge-ball defence tactics. It is a brave and courageous act of leadership to speak the truth. Being vulnerable allows for authenticity and connection with others. As an inspiring leader, there is, of course, a time and place for vulnerability and also a way of sharing our vulnerability.

When we are leading people we can't always do that. We have got to find a way to lead and inspire others. Psychodramas and fire fighting are the wrong way, as they keep our team on hyper-alert and give the pretty accurate perception that we are out of control. It's about finding a level of authenticity and transparency, combined with emotional control.

RQ presents a paradox. On the one hand, emotional, physical and psychological resilience are crucial for any leader. It helps us to be adaptive and solution focused in tough, or even threatening, situations. Yet on the other hand, the development of the RQ muscle also means that things, like our hyper-busyness, toxic cultures, or manic societal standards and customs have become the new norm. We become desensitised to what's really happening.

How many times have you heard things like 'It's just the way he is' to make excuses for someone's behaviours. Another cop out is that, 'it's always been like this' to justify toxic cultures. I've seen leaders playing the 'fire-fighter' putting out the fires. If they don't find them, then they create them. Asking your people to be resilient, for the sake of accepted norms, is unsustainable. So it is the role of the inspiring leader to have their finger on the pulse. We must challenge these norms when they are to the detriment of our employees. In our leadership, it is important we also don't get caught up in other people's dramas.

Resilience is a mind-set where we are not fazed by the big obstacles that come our way. Instead we should adopt the attitude to ask, 'How can we work together and overcome this in different ways, in order to achieve a better outcome?' Managing setbacks and adversity, in a constructive and creative way, is a fulfilling process for changing our perspectives and understanding.

Lady Susan Rice shared with me, "*When the going gets tough, the tough get going! When there are hurdles and obstacles, that's when I really sit up and get into gear. I have a good deal of patience and will stay with things, until I get there. I particularly do this in order to master something. If there's a big obstacle, then you have to work through solutions to get there. Importantly, you have to work with people; always.*

"*I had a huge issue with a project, which was outside of our control. However the consequences were extremely serious, for me personally as the leader, as well as the business. I sat with a few of the brightest people. There was almost a sense of mourning. Everyone started out at the meeting suggesting that we just give up. However, I asked the team what we could do. We broke the issue down into the individual parts. Then we came up with solutions that helped us to see it through. This wasn't enough; we worked through the fog in order to solve things. It's about the questions that get people to think about things in different way. This for me is resilience, seeing it through.*"

Resilience helps with our fight, flight, or freeze mental responses to perceived threats. This certainly could have happened in this case. However, Susan is a resilient leader, who doesn't give up so easily! Her positive attitude for forward motion and problem solving means her team doesn't get caught up in victim mode, but, instead, starts to collaborate and becomes creative to develop a better outcome.

Of course, there is also the perception of the event, or experience that affects our ability to deal with it. If we believe that we are doomed to failure, or to suffer indefinitely, then this perception has the danger of becoming our reality. As inspiring leaders, we can instead use these crucible moments as a springboard for opportunity to unleash our best qualities! By looking at the issue, through a different lens, we then adjust our physical, emotional and mental state. This in turn allows us to think more creatively and respond with positive forward motion. This skill helps us to be even more effective and trusted leaders, as we create an alternative perspective for those we lead, or have relationships with.

When I spoke to many of the women who work for NGOs around the world, in war zones or disaster relief areas, I was moved by the intensity of their leadership experiences. For me, this put everything into perspective. It highlighted the different context and impact of our leadership.

Liz Satow shared, "*After the earthquake, I was posted to Haiti. It's like you're running on adrenaline. We had a massive team in a really challenging environment. Afterwards we were all completely exhausted. Then the Pakistan floods happened a few months later. Because I speak Urdu, I was often asked to go to Pakistan.*

"*The time I went before, the Taliban were blowing up girls' schools and there were bombs going off, it was very hair-raising. Our staff were terrified. The Taliban were sending distressing pictures, via mobile phones. We were getting threats. It was intense. I'd said I wasn't going to go back there, because I was furious about what was happening and the apparent silence of the population.*

"*Then my manager asked me to go back, as they needed me. Before I travelled back I was having the most awful nightmares. However, when I returned it was an absolutely fantastic experience.*"

It made me personally realise that if these women can make such courageous choices, in the face of adversity and conflict, how much easier it is for many of us to face our own day-to-day dilemmas. Putting things into perspective and context is essential. By asking ourselves, '*Will this really matter 1month, 1 year, or 10 years down the line?*' can really help.

Something phenomenal occurs in the times of our greatest adversity. One leader said to me, *"With all of the explosions and crime in Africa, we are resilient and pull together. We come together as a network. We come together as a country. We work together to understand how we manage the stress and understand leadership."*

This is not unique. When there is conflict, terror, economic meltdowns, natural disasters and man-made disasters, then a common denominating factor unfolds. Leaders begin to visibly lead and people become more collaborative. Suddenly there is a sense of unity and focus; more than ever before! We are urged to reach out from our own worlds to create greater social resilience.

Our compassion and our commitment for creating better futures form strong communities. Great leaders become very visible when they truly step-up into their leadership positions and they create a compelling vision for the future. Consequently, a greater energy permeates through our relationships and we become more determined. I experienced this for myself, when I worked in the airline industry. I experienced this when the suicide attacks of 9/11 happened, followed by a harrowing plane accident a few short weeks later.

All of us would prefer not to need the catalyst of crises and trauma in order to unearth these inspiring leadership behaviours. I wonder how we can achieve similar levels of leadership and 'community' in normal times.

Dr. Don Botsch describes, *"We are discovering that, over time, if we are exposed to too much trauma and too many danger situations, then the hippocampus actually begins to falter and become less effective in its role. People who have been exposed to a lot... may appear to be overreacting without cause.*

"Some people, depending on their history or predisposition, can go into what is called a dissociative state, a kind of being 'checked out' from current reality state, which can explain why they may under react."

As leaders, we have become particularly experienced and adept at managing through change. We must be conscious of the impact that any change or transition is having on our teams. It is the difference between great performance on the one hand, or burnout and failure on the other.

Carol Nicholls, the Head Teacher of an all-girls' school shared her observation, *"Interestingly, I never aspired to be a Head Teacher. However, I did consciously choose to go into a girls' school, as I was fed up with girls being marginalised. If I listen to my girls, who've gone on to do great things in their lives, then they tell me - there are no obstacles that you cannot overcome. It's quite sad when other women think differently."*

We should remain true to what we value about ourselves, be confident in our strengths and our passions and determined to see these come to fruition. If we do so, then we will be living a life that is on purpose and with meaning. Often this requires a level of resilience that helps us to get through.

Principles for Resilience

The Inspiring Leadership model is about developing the integrated and centred inspiring leader. Each of the inspiring leadership principles correlate directly with resilience RQ, from MQ all the way around to EQ on the compass model, as follows:

MQ - 'Moral Resilience' - If we lead with high ethical standards, then people will trust us. If our integrity is strong and unwavering, then we will not feel compromised as a leader.

PQ - Purpose Resilience – By leading according to a compelling vision, with passion and focus, then people will be more likely to willingly give their loyalty to us. If our own life's meaning and purpose is abundantly clear, then we can find courage to pursue our dreams. We will be less likely to be distracted by the external critics, or our internal gremlins!

HQ - Health Resilience – By creating a healthy environment, then people will be able to perform at their best for us. By paying attention to our physical wellbeing, then we can find energy to sustain our own performance.

IQ - Cognitive Resilience – Leveraging our own and others' full capacity to think, particularly in turbulent times, creates the creativity, judgement and determination we need to succeed. With wisdom, sound judgement and disciplined focus, we have the willpower to see things through. Willpower acts like a muscle, it gets stronger the more we exercise it.

EQ - Emotional and Social Resilience – Leading with collaboration and drawing upon a strong support networks is powerful. We must recognise and value other people's contribution (rather than being overly judgemental and critical). This creates the energy and engagement among those around us. For us this means we are not alone, and there's no better feeling than all of us being 'in this together'.

Inspiring Women Leaders' Words of Wisdom

1. Embrace Mistakes

"Mistakes are an interesting thing. Everybody makes mistakes in business. The question is: 'Do we acknowledge them?' One of the things that I think is a big difference between the US and the UK is the US spends hardly any time acknowledging mistakes; rather we are very focused on how we are going to correct it.

"The UK instead spends a ton of time apologising for the mistake and very little time on how we are going to correct it. So what you really want to do is take the best of both those worlds. You want to acknowledge, you want to apologise, but you also want to move on and correct. And if you can get that balance right, mistakes are actually a good thing to do. This is because you take away more from mistakes than you do from everything going swimmingly. And, in fact, when everything is going swimmingly along, you then get into a mode, which in a way is good. The challenge of that is that you will actually make mistakes by doing things the same way that you have always done them."

2. Lead Through for Forward Motion

"There are a lot of tough moments. We all have them personally. Professionally, I think there are some of those things that come up where you want to just go away and crawl into a hole. You just want to be by yourself. But when you are leading people, then you always can't do that. So I think this may go back to our vulnerability. I also think that there is an independence that comes through. You've got to lead through. You've got to have the 'game face' on and you've got to be doing everything for everybody around you. You can't do that all the time. Sometimes what I have learned is that I try to be forceful and independent on my own. However, that is not always a good balance, or place to be."

3. Notice the Blocks to then Make Positive Choices and Actions

"When my marriage fell apart it had hit me hard. I was working for a tough boss who was 'as hard as nails'. I realise I was moping around a lot and I was not putting on the best face for work. He told me I had two choices: wallow in my own self-pity, or pick myself up, dust myself off and get on with my life. I realised that everyone has issues. I knew that I couldn't control what had happened. However, I could control how I moved on. I put my experience in a metaphorical box in the attic and got one with my life. I had the toughness and resilience to get through things before in my life, so I knew I could draw on those resources."

4. Adopting a More Positive Attitude

"How have I been so resilient? I have always been a positive person. That doesn't mean that I don't find things tough at times, but my positive attitude and a sense of gratitude sees me through."

5. Being Kinder to Self and Letting Go

"I think that women are suffering in silence. They carry the weight of others on their shoulders. Nothing has changed and women are fundamentally hard on themselves. They need to learn that they are not being less than what they are, by letting go of things. In fact it helps you to become who you are. Their hearts are in the right place, but there are just not enough hours in the day."

6. Keeping Perspective on What Matters

"Don't sweat the small stuff. Live in the moment, analyse yourself in the moment, but it all balances out in the long run. I always think that if I could have given advice to my younger self, then it would have been that 'it's all going to be okay'. So now I ask myself, 'Will this be important five years on from now?' "

7. Make the Unfamiliar Regularly Familiar!

"Throughout my childhood I had constant experiences of going into the unknown. Knowing that I survived gave me a great foundation for embracing change. Seeing my sisters and myself were safe and actually came out of it quite well was a positive reinforcement. So I took that responsibility very seriously. I think that it actually shaped me in a stronger way. It's frightening going into the unknown, but it was also very exciting and very eye opening. My parents also pushing me and telling me that I could do things shaped me. They would never look at my report and say, 'Oh you didn't get "A"s, that's dreadful!" It was always just about whether I had done my best. If I had, then they were happy and so was I. They always pushed us to do our best, so that we could do whatever we wanted to. I suppose that helped a lot."

8. Being Strong For Others

"In my new role as Head of HR, I found it was the steepest learning curve. I was on a huge high because it was a massive role. We have had four different Director Generals in the last six months. As a 28 year old, I was tasked with restructuring the board, within a week and a half. I found it a little terrifying. You need to be authentic, but you can't always be totally honest about what you are feeling at the time. As a leader you have to be strong for others and reveal your panic elsewhere."

9. The Timing May Not Be Here and Now

"I am a huge believer in timing. When you're feeling frustrated, you have to choose your moment. Sometimes you just can't force things through, whether it is with your husband, your kids, or your work. There are times when there is too much resistance and it's just not important enough. Then it's time to let it go."

10. Believe in Yourself, Even When Others Don't Quite Believe Yet

"Believe in yourself because it's all within your gift. There will always be naysayers out there. If you have set your goal to be popular, then that is a misguided goal. Having a purpose in your life and seeing it through is very important. If you don't have people who are naysayers, then you probably aren't doing anything worthwhile. Whereas, if you do, then that's good, because you are challenging others and making people think about things."

11. Self-Imposed Limitations

"The toughest thing I have had to overcome is my working class background. I was with well-off people at university and I wasn't hanging around them. The Graduate Programme that I joined mainly consisted of Oxford and Cambridge graduates who had been to private school. Their parents had bought them houses, whilst I was staying in a tent in someone's garden. I had zero money and was shopping in charity shops. I cringe now, as it really wasn't fashionable! My limited self-belief and comparing to others was not helping me."

12. Owning and Moving Forward From Mistakes

"I created an amazing cock-up in a conversation with a journalist, which was attributed to an anonymous source. I owned up to my mistake. I'd had some tough times with my boss, but in the moment, when I needed her to be compassionate, she was. She asked me what happened and she said, 'It's not ideal, however, here is how we are going to deal with it. We need to look forward; mistakes happen'. She chose not to tell anyone else about it, she just helped me to fix it. It really showed a level of trust and she just supported me. I feel grateful to my boss for the leadership she showed in the moment."

13. Have the Courageous Conversations

"If a team was competent, then I would trust them. One time I trusted someone who wasn't competent. Afterwards I didn't deal with his performance quickly enough. It's that whole thing of wanting to win people over and be liked. He was probably competent in a non-disaster environment. In Haiti, however, we suffered huge consequences and I still carry that responsibility for that, because I kept wanting to give him another chance. I let it go on too long; we paid a high price as a direct result."

14. Balanced Perfection

"I notice that women who succeed are drivers and perfectionists. They want to do things well at 100%. That's physically demanding. I saw a presentation once where the speaker said to 'outsource everything that's not important to you, otherwise you will have zero time for you'. I blended a nanny with after-school clubs and I wished I'd had the nanny full time from the start. I still have one now."

Lisa Lockwood
Speaker, Author and Coach (Ex-Beauty
Queen, Military, Police, SWAT,
Undercover-Agent and more!)

"I was one of seven children. I had a very strict father, who believed in corporal punishment. My six siblings all became high school dropouts. I was a real introvert; I was often found in the closet reading to myself. We were always vying for attention, because there were so many of us. I found the way to do this was to do well at school. Therefore I was seen as the 'golden child', who was put on a pedestal and congratulated. My mother

secretly entered me into a beauty pageant to compete to be Miss Illinois. However, I was too inexperienced to compete in such pageants. My family didn't have the financial income to finance evening gowns and the things that I needed for the pageants. Therefore it meant I often wasn't well groomed in pageants. We rallied a lot of local support to help out. At the pageants, I would all the time have to pretend as if I belonged, often watching and mimicking what the other contestants did. For example, I learnt how to walk a runway, or how they composed themselves.

"My hope was to gain a scholarship, by winning the pageant. However, I came 25th out of the 205 girls that competed. As a result of this, I ended up with no real further education. I then decided to enlist in the US Air Force; I wanted to venture off into the world, make something of myself. I was driven by a goal to never to live in poverty.

"I turned to the military, where I had super success! I became Airman of the quarter and then, in my last year there, Air Force wide. The Air Force is also where I got engaged to my husband. I was only 19 years old. He turned out to be an emotionally abusive alcoholic. I had to put on a brave face, going to work and doing what I could in the military. I remember I had him arrested once, but didn't press charges in the end. I was desperate to leave, but I was so scared.

"I enrolled in college and worked in a private security job in order to support myself, so I would never have to be dependent on him financially. I struggled to leave because of threats he would make. I was concerned that, if I didn't stay, he would either kill himself, me, or the next man in my life. I believed him because I had experienced his rage. Although most of my husband's abuse had been emotional, at one point this became physical.

"I decided I wanted to do the noble thing and become a crime fighter. I also knew that once I had a gun and was trained in firearms, I would feel brave enough to leave. When I became a 'rookie' in training, I told my husband I'd had enough and was going to leave him. He actually accepted this, without any incident.

"I hadn't been without a man since I was 18 but, by making this choice, all of a sudden I felt a strong sense of personal empowerment. I channelled all my efforts into being the best police officer that I could be. I took up any

chance of promotion, or training in firearms, I always threw my hat into the ring and had a go. You know, there were some opportunities that I got. However there were also some opportunities that I didn't.

"Two years on from being a rookie in training, I became a member of the SWAT team. I was an expert marksman and in firearms. I often had to deal with discrimination, because there were no other female members. This didn't hold me back.

"I broke the 'barriers' and just went for it. The team weren't too happy about this initially. I've often been asked how I did this. I realise through all of this that I had to develop a thick skin. I didn't care about the small, irrelevant stuff. At times, the very people I thought were my friends and supporters were the ones spreading these rumours about me. I repressed the rumours and just put a smile on my face. I believe that you can't let other people's opinions stop your progression. I was quickly promoted to narcotics and undercover work simultaneously. At the same time I pursued a Masters Degree.

"During my five years of undercover work, I helped infiltrate the Mafia, catch sex predators on the internet, and worked with the drug dealers and informants.

"My sexuality also became one of my most valuable professional assets in helping to catch criminals! I was able to work undercover as various characters including an exotic dancer, a stripper, a Hooters waitress and a 'crack' addict! Throughout my career in the military and the police, I remained truly focused on my work.

"Is it possible to have balance? There's never a way that everything is going to be in sync, whether it's hobbies, career, or relationships. You can't be flying high in every aspect at all times. I therefore believe that you have to focus on what is good, what is powerful and what creates success with a positive spirit.

"You need to give yourself permission to not have complete balance. You also need to be able to feel you are excelling at what you do. You have to have the ability to show up in the world being happy each day. These factors, for me, define success.

"However, despite my own professional success, I always felt like there *was something missing. I had been so focused and so career driven. However, the one missing element was a substantial relationship. A turning point for me was attending a Tony Robbins seminar. I believed, 'Who would want to date a woman on the SWAT team?' I then realized that I just needed an alpha-male that was powerful and strong enough to not feel threatened by my work and by me.*

"It was at the seminar that I realised I was worthy of love.

"I eventually found 'my someone' whom I was with for nine years with and we had three beautiful children together. Our value systems were so in sync, even down to what we ate, or our messages. However, our growth and evolution caused the dissolution of our relationship. We are still good friends though. I believe that everything happens for a reason. It all serves me in some way and there is growth through all of these experiences.

"As a successful coach, speaker and author, I'm now juggling quite a few hats and travelling the world. I believe that taking control of your life is just a decision away. I also use transformational vocabulary, believing that you never experience failure, only a new learning that helps you to also teach and inspire others.

"In my book, Reinventing You, *I talk about the keys to success, which are based on my own experiences. For example, I believe that there is nothing that you can't do successfully, if you master your emotions. Creating action plans help to take your life in new directions. I also talk about taking uncalculated risks, so say 'yes' before your brain tells you 'no'! I also believe in the law of reciprocation. By finding out and helping others, life also helps you.*

"There's an intimate place between fear and passion. It's important for you to discover your own life mission and vision. Mark Twain's quote, 'The two most important days in your life are the day you were born and the day you found out why' *really resonates with me. If you have a vision for your life by the laws of attraction it will work out for you. Finally, there is so much to be grateful for. So if you believe that all the things that happen in your life are there to serve you, then you find an appreciation for everything and that is so much to be grateful for."*

Inspiring Leadership – Building Resilience

When we are required to be resilient, there are three ways in which we are affected: Physically and Mentally / Emotionally.

Physical:

- *What activities do you incorporate into your life to keep yourself fit enough to be resilient?*
- *How do you create time to revitalise yourself and recover?*
- *If you knew that every single moment that you are not sitting you are improving the health of your lungs, heart and brain, how would we behave differently?*
- *What do you need change in your team's environment to improve resilience and effectiveness?*
- *In your organisation how can you create a higher performing, less stressful culture?*

Mental/ Emotional:

- *How can you generate a more positive mental attitude?*
- *What is your attitude towards change, setbacks and disappointments?*
- *Knowing you can choose your response, what different decisions will you now make?*
- *What are your fear triggers?*
- *As a result of your leadership style, what emotional triggers do you create in those you lead?*

Chapter 11
BQ: Brand Presence and Impact

Contributing Author: Robin Kermode

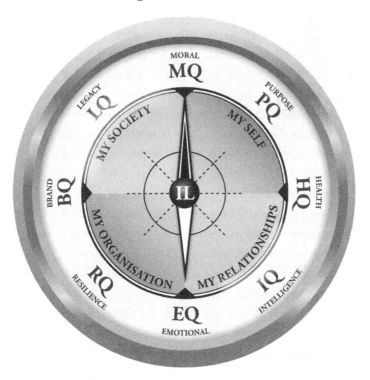

"Authenticity is really important. I am the same person at work as I am at home. I don't leave my skills at the door and just get told what to do. I would not like to do my work in a way that feels like I'm ticking boxes. You are more believable as a leader when you are just being you. I find that by sharing a bit of myself it creates a greater connection with people."

Claire Hall
HR Director (Energy Sector)

Inanch
Celebrity Hairdresser, UK Hair
Extensionist of the Year 2013

"When the Turkish invasion was launched on Cyprus in 1974, I was 1 year old. It was a very frightening time for all our family. I remember the bombs were being detonated and shootings were going on, so my parents gathered us in the middle of the night and we left. We lost everything: our home, our belongings and our money. At first we lived in tents in the Troodos Mountains of Cyprus. Then we were shipped as refugees to Ankara in Turkey. We eventually moved back on the first ships taking Turkish Cypriots back to Kyrenia in northern Cyprus, where my brother was born. This all happened over a period of four years. We then moved to the UK in 1977 to start all over again. It was extremely hard for my parents to start from zero again, which was the case for many Turkish and Greek Cypriots. But we were just grateful to be alive and well, and as they say for life in general, 'one door closes and another door opens'.

"I got my first job at the age of 13, on Saturday at a local salon in London. I enjoyed it so much, and loved dealing with clients, that I enrolled on an NVQ Level 2 in hairdressing. This is where I got introduced to a high-profile salon, when I was on day-release from college. I loved the atmosphere in a top West London salon, and was able to secure a job and soon worked my way up to the position of senior stylist. I continued my training, as I was highly ambitious and keen to progress into a supervisor position.

"Joe, my husband, left his full-time job to help me, in particular managing the business. We have worked so well together and our skills complement each other, so he's stayed on as the Sales and Marketing Director ever since. This is what makes things really work between us; he has the business acumen and I have the artistic flair and vision.

"I always dreamt of running my own salon, but was also keen to gain as much experience as possible, before I made the step. It was very risky

attempting to open a salon in London, but I was passionate about getting more out of my career. I remember my boss trying to encourage me not to do it, saying to me "The West End is full of sharks; you won't last." Thankfully I found my courage and I haven't looked back since.

"I think it's important to look to others for advice, but never permission to pursue your dreams. Sometimes it's really challenging and risky fulfilling our dreams, but you can't let your fears, or even other's fears limit your own potential. I saw a big gap in the market – for quality hair extensions. So, as a result, my vision was to turn this around and provide a high quality service, specialising in hair extensions in particular.

"The first few years were extremely tough; we never anticipated just how challenging they would be. We had an extremely tight budget and the temptation was to cut corners. This wasn't good enough for me. My vision was to create a luxury service and the very best ambience. We ended up borrowing everything against the house to finance the business. We even had to rent our house out for a couple of years and stay with my parents, so we could live as efficiently as possible. We didn't even draw a salary for our first year. Despite loyal clients and customer recommendations, it took over 18 months before we started to break even, due to the overheads of running a central London salon.

"Added to this we had also unwittingly badly timed our opening for June 2005. This was when the horrific and tragic London terrorist attacks on the underground and the buses took place quite near to us. People were too frightened to come into to London. It was a tough time. We were working every hour under the sun to make the business work.

"We couldn't have done this without our parents, who helped to look after the children. However, it caused us some challenges and they often pointed out that we needed to spend more time with the children. This is difficult, not seeing our two girls, Demi and Lema, as much as I'd like, or missing out on things like their school plays, even now. This has become easier though as the business has grown and we're fully established.

"I have a strong ethos for the salon and have the motto, 'We're only as good as our last haircut'. Our clients will always judge us based on their very last experience and the quality of service they received. Each time they

come to us, they expect the same level of inspiration and passion. 'Same again' is not our motto; we always want to share our expertise and inspire our clients with the latest styles.

"I love the variety involved in my work, for example, the editorial shoots with the models on location are very exciting. We have earned a great reputation and have worked with some high profile local and international clients, including celebrities and beauty editors. We also work with many businessmen and women to create styles that help them to appear at their best. Having a great hairstyle alters the way someone looks and really builds their confidence.

"For Joe and me, the value of giving back is really important to us, and so each year we run a charity fashion event to support Barnardo's with my cousin, Penny - the designer and founder of Pia Michi – the couture fashion label.

"Hair extensions are the biggest and fastest growing part of our business, now accounting for 60% of turnover. We've built a great reputation for applying the most natural looking hair extensions available in the world and have won a variety of awards including the Hair Awards 2013 Best Extensionist. It's always important to Joe and me to source only the best and ethically made products for our clients too.

"My top two tips for other leaders are - firstly don't give up on your dream. Have the determination to see it through. Secondly you must be prepared to take some risks; without the support of our family that would have been very hard. Knowing that we could always go back to stay with our family, if all fell through, was very reassuring."

Definition of BQ: Brand Presence and Impact

We are all aware of strong corporate brands. Visit a well-known company website, see commercials and advertising, or even the corporate behaviours and language that we hear and see via social media - what do you notice? They immediately make us feel a particular way about that company; so we know how to interact with them, or not, as the case may be. For most organisations, supplier switching has become the new norm and customers choose with their feet.

It's the same with people. Organisations are competing to have the best leadership talent. Now, more than ever before, we have sophisticated models of *performance* and *potential* and methods of finding it. In a free market, where choice prevails, many of the best opportunities often reveal themselves to us when we have a personally strong brand presence. Our reputation, or 'brand', is the accepted form of currency.

From a psychological perspective it appears that up to the age of 4 or 5 years old, much of our life is about looking outward. We seek to discover new things freely and openly. After that age we become more aware of our position in the world and carefully judge ourselves against our fellow human beings. Are we clever enough, funny enough, or attractive enough? We now spend more time being concerned about our survival and safety than we spend looking outward and learning new things. In some sense after the age of 4 or 5, it is like we lose a crucial part of ourselves.

Personal Brand is the penultimate component in the inspiring leadership model. There is a clear rationale for this position. One of the most common themes that have emerged from my research is the matter of ***authenticity***. Much of the literature that we see focuses very much on what we see, pointing to the fact that 'first impressions count'. Whilst important to understand the perceptions of others, if we lack congruence within our core, then it becomes a far more difficult path to influence others. Not an impossible path, just a tough one to navigate. I fundamentally believe that our view of talent is altering: old moulds are breaking down, forming new concepts of diversity and inclusion. Leaders who help other leaders to grow have become the new norm. This presents us with an opportunity, as greater diversity, thus authenticity, is called for.

Nikki Flanders shared, *"Leadership is about being comfortable in your own skin and bringing your whole self to work. It is not feeling that others expect you to be different. I have done this myself. I reinforce this with the women I mentor too. You need to think about your 'brand' in this way. This should not be misinterpreted. It's about not agonising over the small stuff, such as what people think about you. If you have limited self-belief then this can take you on a downward spiral. Rather, you need to think about the bigger things - the stuff that's really important."*

The true power of authenticity can only start from deep within ourselves. Our authenticity gives us the courage of our convictions, breaking down the limitations that generally occur when we are operating out of sync with this. That is why the Inspiring Leadership components are so important; they build the very foundations for who we are and what we represent:

1. **MQ: Morality and ethics** – creates integrity and brand consistency. When this is clear, it gives us strength. This helps to generate trust. Think back to the teachers you had when you were at school. Teachers without consistent boundaries have no sense of their own brand. What children (and adults) like are clear and consistent boundaries. It is difficult for child when a teacher is strict one day and lenient the next. We like to know where we stand with someone - every day.

2. **PQ: Purpose and meaning** – creates vision and passion. It's what drives us forward to take positive action. At a neurobiological level, we know that developing goals for our lives and our thirst for learning produces dopamine and even testosterone. This helps us with creating our brand authenticity.

3. **HQ: Health and wellbeing** – helps us to be centred and energetic in our leadership. We generate more energy, stamina and the resilience that helps us to perform well. This seeps through into our (internal and external) somatic, cognitive and emotional language and our behaviours.

4. **IQ: Cognitive intelligence, judgement and wisdom** – we continuously develop our wisdom whilst being discerning. What you know through your professional career and building a great track record transmits a powerful message about what you can bring to teams.

5. **EQ: Emotional and social intelligence** – builds greater brand connection that is more influential and powerful. This is about who we know. There's no point having a great track record if no one knows about us. It's also about creating followership, bringing others along with us, and helping each other.

6. **RQ: Resilience** – when we are challenged, we can stand strong and

bounce back through adversity. No leader goes through their careers and lives without bumps, scars and scrapes. The difference between the exceptional leader and the average manager is how the leader turns this into a learning opportunity. The average manager, however, lets these experiences erode their confidence and self-belief.

The Inspiring Leadership Definition of BQ is:

*"BQ starts at the greatest point of influence: for corporates, this is from the top and for us personally, it starts from within. It is the ability to be the best we can possibly be, based on our core **authentic self**, and presented in the most **positive, powerful** and **influential form**."*

We are all born unique. We are all born special. It does not make us any better, or more important than anybody else. If our brand is crystal clear to us, we will begin to radiate our brand with no mixed messages. If our brand is consistent, then our customers, colleagues and friends will know us, recommend us and love us for who we really are.

The Consequences of Lack of BQ

There is a well-known expression, 'people buy from people'. In a competitive world, this has never been truer. People don't invest in what you do; they invest in the relationship, or the experience. In the interviews with inspiring leaders, BQ is often at its most vulnerable when the first components of the inspiring leadership model have not been properly addressed.

Brand Authenticity

When there is a lack of congruence between the 'brand identity' being presented to us and what we hear, see, or experience, then we can lose trust. All too often, we focus on the physical things we can do to change and enhance our brand identity such as marketing. However, we miss the opportunity of making the investment into our people and culture. These are the 'moments of truth' that can build, or destroy our reputation. In Lesley

Everett's book, *Walking Tall*[1], she describes how, *"...companies noted for outstanding quality and service charge fees that are, on average, 9 per cent higher."* It's interesting just how often we see organisations that have well communicated values which are not integrated through their entire people processes.

There is a subtle difference in the integration, however. In efforts to control how we deliver a quality experience, many organisations have opted for tight scripting, inflexible policies and processes with endless reporting. The very thing that it sets out to achieve actually has the opposite effect. This ends up alienating the very person at the end who is expecting to receive the service. We see this all over with our schools, our hospitals, our mobile phone contracts, our banks and our shops. The list goes on. With short-term results and "big brother" monitoring our moves, this transaction-based approach limits our creativity and our time to deliver an exceptional experience.

In **Laura Birrell's** story she shared one particular experience, *"I remember when working in the financial sector, before I joined the BBC, I had learnt to totally adapt to the culture, rather than being natural. One day, I went to meet an executive coach for coffee. I asserted myself when greeting them. The coach waited until I was totally comfortable with them and then they observed, 'The Laura you presented isn't you. They'll all hate you at the BBC if you present yourself like this. Be yourself and feel confident'.*

"I thought that they would see through me and that being me just wasn't good enough. However, at the BBC I have been able to be myself, and so my confidence been built again over the last three years.

"Trying to rebuild my identity has been hard to adjust back to, as I had adapted for so long. I had to develop my emotional intelligence, as I couldn't land the message right. When I took my 'mask' off, I did so in a powerful way."

Through my research, a key area that has stood out is how people have had to 'squeeze themselves out of shape' to fit with different cultures. Adapting and stretching ourselves makes absolute sense. However, changing who we fundamentally are stops us from being able to be the best that we can be.

It is a tragic statistic that many people are unhappy in their work environments.

This deep dissatisfaction is often sub-conscious because our drive and resilience pushes us forward and we are in denial and wilfully blind. When we feel that there is a lack of congruence between on the one hand, the culture and the values of the organisation and on the other hand, our own style and beliefs, then we feel compromised as a result.

This requires expending a huge amount of physical and mental energy on a day-to-day basis. Whilst we may have the stamina and determination in the short term, the longer term implications are far more damaging. The sad truth is that the effects on our own leadership, confidence and even wellbeing last beyond the years of our tenure. At what point do we start to notice and intervene to take positive action?

I recall a conversation that I had with one of the most inspiring leaders that I've had the privilege to work for in my career, Mary Edmunds. She continues to be a key mentor and advocate for me to this day. She shared with me, *"Leigh, your authenticity goes through to your very core. Never be involved in something just because of money or career success if it goes against everything that you believe in"*. When you run your own business, this is always a dilemma and so a fundamental piece of advice acts as a reminder to stay on course. This authenticity will shine through in my own brand.

The Leadership Shadow

Poor or excellent leadership performance and behaviour is no longer contained within our teams, nor can leaders hide behind their businesses. It is very public.

With social media providing the world as the stage, our impact ripples far beyond our immediate stakeholders: such as our shareholders, executive boards and teams. We have all witnessed the shadow cast over many brands, as a result of bad decisions, unethical behaviour and much worse.

Each sector seems to have its turn too, whether it's our governments and their departments, the finance sector, the entertainment industry, energy and even NGOs.

The subsequent brand and reputational damage can last for a long time beyond our tenure, affecting customer perceptions and the employee experiences. I recall that I was working in the finance sector when the crisis first hit. In the initial stages, there was so much public anger. Consequently, we were warned to either work from home if we could, or to travel to work in casual clothes.

As leaders, we must set the tone for the organisation.

We must be mindful of the shadow that we cast and its resulting ripple effect and permutations. Toxic leadership and cultures make a huge difference, the evidence of which may not be so visible to leaders at the top of the hierarchy where the focus is often on financial results. As the saying goes, 'the fish rots from the head'.

People feel proud to work for brands that they admire and respect. Customers like to buy from brands they trust. The question is, 'How would we like our organisation to describe our own 'leadership shadow'?'

Climbing the Ladder (or gym)

As the top of the organisational pyramid becomes narrower, particularly with flattening organisational structures, the climb up the corporate ladder can certainly be a competitive one. There is a definite shift, as leaders help other leaders by reaching down and bringing others through. However, there's certainly more we can do. We still hear stories of the 'Queen Bee syndrome' and leaders who pull down those above them and stamp on the hands of those below them to prevent others passing them. We satisfy ourselves knowing that we are helping others through external opportunities, yet often we fail to support people from with our own teams and organisations. It is perceived to be easier to hold the competition at bay.

Building our talent pipeline often becomes a perceived bureaucratic HR process, rather than a leadership exercise of organic growth and development.

Whether it's feeling threatened, insecure or power-hungry, we often cloak the reality of our behaviours with what appears to be logical rationale. We have seen teams manipulated by ambitious team members lobbying for support to over-throw the incumbent leader, whilst promoting their own ability to 'do the job properly'. We have also seen how leaders hold back from giving opportunities to subordinates, just to hold people back from being visible or knowing too much. The future of leadership offers us a new paradigm for how we see others, we just need to take courage and take action to help others. So it's important that we ask ourselves, *"Are our intentions and actions purely 'me-serving', at whatever the cost, or are they 'we-serving?"*

It is completely understandable how this can happen of course. Watch *The Apprentice* on television, where people are only as good as their last project. Each week one unfortunate individual hears the words, *"You're Fired"* and is unceremoniously ejected from the team. Watching the behaviours of the teams with infighting, aggressive tactics and fear, highlights the negative implications of managing in this way.

Although an accentuated example, there are some distinct parallels with business today. Jobs are no longer for life. Competition for positions is tough. Sharp elbows are 'required' to get to the top in many cases. Finally, when we get to the top position, then of course we want to preserve that status.

Protecting ourselves to *secure* our position, by working under the radar, or not taking that next step, will never get us noticed. It can only serve to limit our full potential. And even if we think that we don't have a brand, we inevitably do. Beware - it just maybe not the kind of brand we'd hoped for ourselves!

When Norway imposed quotas for women on boards, then the negative response was that there was not enough female talent out there to achieve the targets. The fact was, there wasn't enough *visible* female talent. I was struck in my research about inspiring leadership, that there was varying levels of visibility. Yet, it's a real game-changer when you are being observed as a leader; as long as it's for the right things! As described by Arruda and Dixon in their book *Career Distinction*, *"Personal branding has gone mainstream.*

It's the most effective strategy you can use to achieve professional success and fulfilment. Once a luxury, it is now a necessity...".

Communication and Impact

When I first set up Clareo Potential, it was with the aim of helping other coaches to succeed. I had not imagined that I would soon become a coach, facilitator and speaker myself. Having worked through my vision for my future career with my own coach, I realised I too wanted to be out there delivering. There were a number of issues, however. I had been so long working *on* the business, that I had lost my nerve in terms of delivery *in* the business.

As an external speaker, my clients had very high expectations of my skill and ability. The problem was, I was so nervous I would blank before presentations and shake during them! I chose role models around me to help me determine the type of speaker I should be. Somehow this didn't quite work, and, instead of boosting my confidence, I felt less adequate. I could never achieve the high standards that I kept setting myself. There is rarely a safe learning platform to practice on. I was facing my fears of presenting to large groups, but then falling flat on my face. At least that's what I was telling myself before, during and after my speeches.

I initially engaged a specialist coach to help me with my speaking and overcome my nerves. After a number of sessions being recorded reading extracts from Shakespeare plays and poetry, practicing deepening my voice and doing the 'super-hero' pose, I was still suffering from my extreme nerves. My inner dialogue was destroying my confidence; I felt it was time to re-evaluate my career. I was invited to deliver an 'inspiring' presentation to 150 leaders from around the world. That was when Robin Kermode was recommended to me as a Personal Communication Coach.

Robin Kermode told me that on his step-daughter's bedroom wall is a poster with the slogan:

'YOU ARE BORN UNIQUE, DON'T DIE A COPY'

Authenticity was the basis for his coaching. There was no role-modelling, no Shakespearian speeches... just being authentically me. Coupled with practicing several relevant techniques and coping strategies for stress, of course! There were two fundamental shifts through this experience: first, the self-limiting belief that said I wasn't good enough and secondly, being comfortable with my unique style of delivery.

Many of us as leaders have similar challenges when presenting or communicating. Instead of dealing with this through developing our skills, we may avoid great opportunities to raise our profile. Equally we might continue on, blissfully blind to the low impact that we have on our audiences. As leaders, being able to communicate with real impact and in a compelling way is an essential part of our repertoire. However, it's an area that we tend to invest in the least. In our assessment of top talent around the world, this is the Achilles Heel for many.

Improving the clarity and power of our communication skills shifts good leaders into inspirational leaders. Whether it is with our teams, in our executive meetings, or on stage, our platforms as leaders are high exposure and, thus, influence opinions and whether someone is willing to follow you.

Whilst I've shared a couple of Robin's teachings in the 'Tools, Techniques and Resources Chapter' and more is available in his book, *Speak – So Your Audience Will Listen*, I would recommend that if this is an area of development for you, then build on this even further and bring in his expertise to support you. It makes a huge amount of difference in a very short amount of time.

Maintaining Relationships

When we are disgruntled, frustrated and disappointed with a colleague, or business, it always seeps through into the relationship. Maintaining a consistently professional brand is essential. One inspiring leader spoke of her experience protecting her brand reputation with a colleague, "*My key learning is not to burn a bridge. When I was in recruiting I really didn't agree with how one of the Senior Recruiters behaved. When I was leaving I wasn't going to say goodbye. One of my colleagues encouraged me to, telling me to swallow my pride and smile for just five minutes. When I moved to a new role in a different organisation, he actually joined the team three months later in a senior position and I was working for him!"*

There can be no such thing as a personality clash for an inspiring leader. Every relationship can be worked through, even if it's just at a professional level. The question is, what do you want people to be saying about you, when you're not in the room? Too often people burn bridges based on a set of principles and behaviours, but are actually *cutting off their nose to spite their face*!

Also, many leaders sustain relationships, when their tenure is overdue. Instead of leaving on a high with an amazing track record, they leave too soon or too late! It's important to know when the role and business is working for us and to take positive action when it isn't anymore.

How Can BQ Help You as a Leader?

People want to work for inspiring leaders, those who make a positive impact. Organisations want to hire really great talent. And, leadership can be a lot more fulfilling, when we have a strong brand and reputation. We want people to like us and work with us. We desire great opportunities that leverage our strengths and provide us with amazing experiences, so we can grow as leaders. We may even want better salaries and benefits. To do this, we must be able to compete in the market.

Our Unique Authentic Proposition (UAP)

Lady Susan Rice CBE shared with me, *"You don't have to stay in the mould, you can do things your own way. You really have to be yourself, there's nothing more important. I don't have a huge voice, for example, so I have to know this when I'm in a meeting room. I could have trained myself earlier on, however, I felt that wasn't actually me. I found other ways to adapt. I have advice about sharing some of yourself with others.*

"I remember early on in my career someone saying to me 'we don't know much about you beyond work, talk to us' and what this does is it humanises you. It creates ways of linking with people and makes you more approachable. Leading a team, you have better interactions as you're much more on the same level."

Our personal brand is our own unique promise of the value that we bring to the organisation. In a fast paced changing world, brand integrity and consistency is key.

At the same time, we must develop and grow our brand, to maintain our relevance in a fast evolving market. Understanding and working to our strengths and passions puts us in a strong position. Not only are we defining our own unique proposition, it also has the power to positively influence our psychological and emotional states.

One of my own personal challenges as a systemic thinker, is that I see the broader picture and I get excited and passionate about it. This personal learning has been crucial, as this can be harder for people to connect with. It's hard being everything to everyone and for them to understand our strengths. By presenting a clear and more focused UAP (unique authentic proposition), it becomes easier for people to engage and 'buy' from us. I have had to work hard and delve deep in order to really define what makes me, as a coach, facilitator and speaker, as well as my business, Clareo Potential. It's a highly rewarding exercise however, and our primary mission and goal emerges as a result.

'In order to be irreplaceable, one must be different'
– Coco Chanel

I would go on to say, "and others must be aware that you exist." Therefore, what is your own UAP and do others know this too?

Fedelma Good shared with me, *"I have personally been incredibly lucky with my career. Because I have a different name and a different accent, it has also made me stand out in the UK. Think about it. What's the memory you leave people with? I do this instinctively and I always send a follow-up email".*

There are several tools that can help us to understand our strengths and our motivations, including psychometrics. We can also track our career and personal history over time, identifying the highs and the lows to notice important aspects of our leadership. We can also look to people that we admire and identify the components of their work, experience, or style that we admire.

This is not to try to replicate, we know that imitation has the danger of lacking authenticity. It is to continually grow and refine who we are becoming. Squeezing ourselves out of shape does not bring out the best in us. So, for example, as women, we must be able to consider the unique qualities that we bring, rather than adjusting to a pre-defined model of leadership. With an increasingly diverse group with independent economic power and investment capability, traditional methods of attracting customers and doing business are no longer the game of play.

It's also important to gather feedback on ourselves. By understanding others' perceptions of us and their views on our brand, we can pick up some of the patterns that will help define our UAP.

Having done this in the past, I have been genuinely surprised by some consistent themes around my strengths, which I had never realised before. I knew they existed of course, but not to the extent that they made me stand out.

All of these interventions help us to get closer to defining our own unique proposition.

Features and Benefits

Now, if we consider a product, the features of the product are *not* the same as the benefits. A feature of the product is actually the physical property, characteristics and function of a product. The benefit of the product answers the questions, *'Why should I buy you; what's in it for me?'*

It is the same with us: our job description is not the same as the benefits we bring to the organisation. Being clear on our 'benefits' helps us think about our value that we truly bring and gives others a clear perspective too. The spark doesn't occur by describing the 'doing', it fires up when we describe the 'being'. It helps us to shift from getting bogged down with what we know, to, instead, creating a compelling story that is backed up by evidence. A huge amount of power comes from our leadership attributes, ones that create the desired limbic resonance with those we wish to influence.

At times, some opportunities may pass us by, and that's okay too. Have you noticed how, when one door closes, then another even better opportunity opens up? Through the laws of attraction, we will draw people and opportunities to us. As my mother always told me, *"Leigh, what is right for you won't pass you by."* As I reflect back on my life, I realise she was right. It's just taken some initiative and courage on my part.

Raising Our Profile

Fedelma Good shared, *"I'm from Catholic Ireland and my parents had a strong work ethic. Principles about respect and hard work have been drilled into me; these values and principles for living are our foundations. It was not about promoting yourself. I have held leadership positions from a young age. I realised in a male dominated environment, men were getting promoted ahead of me. Unless you are sharing your own virtues, how will people know what you can bring? Working hard, I mistakenly felt I must be doing something right and isn't it obvious to others?"*

Now this is where many leaders shudder at the thought. People tend to get caught up in the semantics regarding 'brand promotion'. They label it as the act of the sycophant, which is lacking substance, self-serving and something they're very uncomfortable with. There is more to getting ahead than simply doing a great job.

At a certain point in our careers, this becomes a natural expectation of us. It then becomes about our leadership profile and image. We do need to be clear on what we bring and how we add value. This means shutting off the internal and external dialogue that holds us back from telling people about what we can offer.

Once we have clarity about our goals, passions and strengths, we then have to make people aware. Strong brands can be created through alternative approaches to building awareness. We can go from the extreme such as Virgin or Rolex to something more low-key like Starbucks; all are successful brands and businesses in their own right, but their approaches to advertising are completely different. This is how we consider ways of raising the profile of our own personal brands. What feels right, or works for some people, may not work for us personally. We can still communicate our UAP in a way that feels genuinely authentic.

We can also afford to stretch ourselves outside of our comfort zones by thinking differently. For example, by the way we can see networking events either as an unfortunate necessity, or as an opportunity to learn about other people.

There are several ways to raise our profile:

- Identify advocates and sponsors*
- Mentoring and Coaching – both receiving and providing
- Internal and External Networking
- Speaking at Forums and Conferences
- Leading high profile initiatives, both internally and externally
- Leveraging social technologies such as Websites, LinkedIn, Facebook, Twitter, On-line forums - all of which extend the potential reach of our personal brand
- Charity work, government projects and community projects
- Demonstrating thought-leadership and getting published/keynote speaking/write a book!
- Workshops and Masterclasses – we're often 'too busy' and yet these have the double-benefit of getting us networked whilst we become less parochial by learning about the latest thinking

Chapter 14: Tools, Techniques and Resources provides further ideas on how to raise your profile.

*One of the most common themes that came through the research was the undoubted value of having strong advocates and sponsors, particularly inside, but also outside the business.

If you were to consider, at this point in your career, who's covering your back, then who would be on the list of your advocates and how are you maintaining these relationships? If they even exist! Of course, there is also the question: who do you actively advocate and support?

Leadership is a lonely place. So the role of the confidante becomes exclusive, and therefore often elusive to many. Consider our governments and executive boards. If we're not taking responsibility as leaders to sponsor others, then now is the time to start.

When Elin Hurvenes, Chair of the Professional Boards Forum, scanned the web for background information on inspiring women for the forums, she was surprised at just how little there was. Mainly we use LinkedIn, possibly Facebook and that was it. Instead of waiting for people to come to us, it's time we take the initiative, think about what we want to achieve and how we want to make ourselves more visible and then go for it.

As humans we are hard-wired to be 'seen'. We are energised by our relationships and connections. It is therefore important that technology does not provide us with the false belief that we are raising our profile sufficiently. The fact is that, with so much content available at the fingertips from around the world, it then becomes harder to differentiate between who are the best people to connect with.

Social media and technologies can make us visible. We must then remember to proactively forge strong relationships at a more personal level with the appropriate people. It's not all about what people see about us, it's about what people feel about us too.

Career Navigation through Experiences

Being relevant has trumped loyalty, therefore, we must respond to the changing nature of work. How do we continuously make ourselves relevant? In today's economy, having a strong track record of success is a basic foundation requirement for opening doors. Understanding what 'a great track record' means and ensuring that it aligns with our own ambitions for our future career is important.

For the big leadership roles, this involves accumulating experience in significant areas of responsibility such as: managing profit and loss accounts, large leadership roles, cross-product/country experience, international exposure, leading in tough environments such as acquisitions, and turnarounds. If we want to successfully manage our careers, then we must be able to understand the opportunities that will help us to develop and, thus, build our career potential even further.

It's important that we make wise and discerning choices when we navigate our career opportunities. Some people will try to 'sell' us a job that that they need to fill, yet it may not be in our best interests. Many leaders have described how the job reality and the original description, which they were sold, have been poles apart. It's important to do our due diligence to ensure it's a good move. Even if we make a mistake and take on our worst nightmare, that's okay. We always have choice. Don't stay in unhealthy, toxic jobs or relationships.

Baroness Margaret Eaton
DBE & DL Life Peer in the House of Lords

Baroness Eaton's leadership is powerful and inspiring, touching on a world that few of us ever experience – the House of Lords.

"I grew up in Yorkshire, England. I never liked my school days; they weren't particularly exciting and vibrant for me. I was quite happy as a small child both inside and outside of school. However, apart from my very earliest experience of my rather artistic infant school, where we did a lot of drama and music, I just found it very grey. I didn't really know what was so uninspiring about the school, but on reflection it had no vibrancy and no challenge and, for me, it was particularly dreary.

"My mother was the youngest and also the only girl in her family, and so she was the apple of everybody's eye. She liked to be the centre of attention; so I'm not sure that she coped that well when she had me. As a young child I would get a lot of attention, which I don't think she liked. She was a particularly intelligent woman although she underachieved. I think I held this against her, because my attitude is that you should do something with your life. I didn't want to be like her, she wasn't a role model for me.

"Then I went to college and found life very exciting, with the right type of challenge and much broader horizons. It took me from the north of England to the south. I had a fantastically interesting Principal, who would put you into socially quite challenging positions. She was well-renowned in many organisations and was very well connected with interesting people in the arts and the BBC. I remember, for example, she said that Michael Peacock (a

British TV executive) was coming to visit and asked me to collect him and give him tea. So you would have to go to collect these people on your own and entertain them. Consequently you learnt a lot of social skills along the way. It also meant that you got some really great insights into worlds that you had never come across before. It was a constantly interesting learning exercise. I liked living where I did in the country.

"In terms of the Principal, she was a very inspiring leader in the way that she was different and challenging. She wasn't the run of the mill and she wasn't boring. Most of the previous educators I had met were very uninspiring people. On the back of these earlier experiences, I had never wanted to be a teacher because my own experiences were so poor. However, I found that when I did go into teaching I absolutely loved it and so I taught for quite some time in Yorkshire. I got married and had a wonderful social life, as well as loving my work. My son became very ill for a long time and on the edge of death, which was a really tough time. Fortunately he got better.

"I started my political career by being elected to Bradford Met District Council and eventually becoming its first woman leader. However, I came to a point where I wanted more. Then my career as the Chairman for the LGA (Local Government Association) took off. Then I moved into my role in the House of Lords.

"I learned that I am very resilient. I can cope very well as a solitary person, but I like other people. I get a lot of pleasure from seeing what makes other people tick. I don't have any expectations, I get more pleasure from creating excitement and inspiration for others. I don't think I'm very self-focused and I don't see the world through what I want. As I have got older, I have learnt to balance this more. So, for example, this morning I got up slightly later and yesterday I worked from the hotel. I realised I can be flexible and that I don't need to be governed by somebody else's routine, but it's taken me a long time to learn that.

"In circumstances where I feel the most challenged, I drive myself incredibly hard. Even when these have been challenges with home, my instinct is not to think, 'How do I give certain things up?' Instead it's, 'How do I manage both?' I don't think I can't do something. It just means that I

have to adapt and make sure that I do right by certain things that are important to me. I manage to do a double-act. The only time I really found it challenging was when I was bitten in the summer time and got a blood infection. I hadn't realised until now how absolutely wretched I felt for four months. I had no energy because I felt so ill and not having the answer to what was causing it. I began to challenge myself as to whether I could continue to do what I was doing, when I didn't have the energy to get through the day to do it. Before I had always felt I had loads of energy to manage things and so it did make me reflect more. Good health is very important to having energy and confidence.

"I largely learned from other women in my life and career how I didn't want to be as a female leader, rather than how I did. If I think back to the Headmistress in my school for example - she was absolutely awful. She was a very strident, unforgiving, unfriendly kind of person. There was no warmth. She talked down to people, as if we were from peasant stock! It didn't go down very well, but, as I look back, I think I felt more socially at ease than she did at that time.

"I can think of leaders where I have not wanted to be like them, but aspects of their leadership have inspired me, such as their intellect. For example, Margaret Thatcher for the things that she was able to achieve; that women hadn't traditionally done. But, there were things about her that I didn't quite like, such as the hardness about her.

"Yet, that wasn't the whole picture, because Margaret Thatcher came to visit Bradford when Yorke, my son, was ill. He should have been having treatment in hospital that day; instead he was in his wheelchair. She spent a lot of time with him - that wouldn't have any benefit for her, only of benefit to Yorke. There was more of that than any of us ever realise from the public persona. In the House of Lords there is some interesting female talent. Even if I don't agree with their politics, they have delightful personalities. The female leaders I do admire have kept their authenticity, despite their status.

"I can honestly say, I have never come across any organisation, or institution, at any point in my political career where I have felt disadvantaged because I am female. The only thing I look on with amusement is the title women have in the Lords; no one quite knows what

Baroness is. It doesn't concern me. The old hereditary members of the House of Lords are very friendly and I feel very involved. I've never felt it a disadvantage being a woman.

"I do think that there are generational shifts. So, now younger women and men make equal contribution both at home and work. Even so, I think women with children have a great issue about guilt. Even now it feels selfish to want to do anything for yourself. So even if it's your career, then it is perceived as your hobby. Whereas bringing up a child is considered extremely important, which I think it is. However, you are made to feel that if you were not there doing all of it, then you are not being particularly successful at home. I think that's a big issue for women: the combined guilt that women feel and their focus on career which may be perceived by others as selfish. This is where it is not quite the same for men, as they are encouraged to define goals and achieve.

"I think you have to approach gender diversity and equality in a balanced way. There is a fine line, and we run the risk of men feeling marginalised, or women getting special treatment. I'm not a great believer in quotas. Ability to me is the most important thing, rather than gender. I suppose it's an easy thing for me to say because I have never personally experienced any discrimination or bias.

"For example, I was the first female leader of Bradford Metropolitan City Council, which is the fourth biggest Met in the UK. There were 90 councillors. That role involved building a group from practically nothing. When I first arrived, there were only 14 members as we were firmly 'in Opposition'. When I became the Leader of the Council there were 40 Conservative Councillors, when every other council was losing Conservative members. I felt very satisfied that whatever it was, it was working at that time.

"Also, when I stood for the candidacy for the Chairman of the national body for Conservative Councils, again it was not easy. When it came to be elected to the chairmanship of the Local Government Association (LGA), I got more votes than all of the men put together. These are three things that I have done where I was the first woman to do them and don't feel I have ever been held back. It just hasn't happened in my career.

"I think strident feminists can, at times, do the agenda and us a bit of disservice. It can become alienating. So it needs to be about what contributions can be made compared to what's there. So it is important to highlight our particular qualities that we can bring to the table. These can often be the softer skills, ones that come with emotional intelligence. The challenge is that in macho cultures it is hard for these skills to be valued and recognised. But I think it is these skills, and not trying to be another man and competing on those terms, that marks out the most successful women.

"One of the things that interests me is when some people set goals for the next ten years, whilst others have a more unstructured approach to their career. I think my experience has been the latter. I have responded to opportunities that have arisen, rather than saying I want to be leader and setting out to achieve this. These things just happened because I was somewhere that has allowed me to put my hat into the ring. I needed a lot of encouragement to do it, as I thought I couldn't really do these kinds of things!

"I do believe that I am living my life with purpose, because at my age many women start to retire and do very little that moves them out of their comfort zone. I feel, as long as I am healthy, that I'm really enjoying what I'm doing. What distresses me is when I look at some of my friends and I see how their health may be deteriorating. So I constantly challenge myself and ask, 'Am I doing what I love, and am I living my life for a purpose?' I met an old friend last night and at 74 he is still a Professor at one of the universities and he and I have a pact that we are not going to retire.

"I don't really have a good work-life balance, and, in all honesty, I don't think I ever will. It becomes a decision about what's important to you and sometimes it is not easy. I do have things that I don't do that I would like to do, and so that is something I need to work on a bit more.

"My advice to other women is to please yourself and go for what you believe is the right thing to do. Don't worry about what other people think about you."

How many of our succession plans are actually realised? As leaders of others, it's important that we build robust succession plans to develop our pipeline of diverse talent. Individual needs are variable, with so many career considerations that take into account both work and home factors. We make assumptions about people's unavailability for certain roles as a result.

Often we purely look at the plans from only the singular perspective of the business need and current incumbent. If we base our decision on traditional structures, then we run the risk of limiting our creativity and forward thinking about the future of work.

We also limit the pool of potentially great talent that we can tap into. If we understand the individual's ambitions and needs (both home and work), then we can affect a new kind of development that becomes the career enabler, rather than a blocker.

Many organisations are improving the employee value proposition, in particular, the language used in areas such as job advertising. However, in our assessment and hiring of great talent we still don't have diverse leadership teams. So what's the missing link? If we continue to use old methods, for example, high potential models to identify future talent, or the same panel of assessors, with their unconscious biases, then we will get what we always got. Unless of course we impose some quotas!

When looking for talent in today's economy, we are looking for something different. When creating job opportunities, we need to respond to the changing market and create more attractive offerings. When designing developmental work experience, we need to put in place the right support mechanisms that increase people's chances of success.

Experience and Track Record

With GenY, in particular but not exclusively, there is a desire to progress quickly through the organisation. It is easier to demonstrate track records at an earlier stage in our careers. However, as our responsibility grows, so does our decision-making power. Our impact becomes more long term, rather than short term. Superficial, or light touch, impact may seem to reap its rewards in the short term. However, as we progress, these will only serve as a disadvantage.

The problem with too much fast-tracking, is that it becomes all 'face and little substance'. It's therefore important to concentrate on the richness of people's experience, the entire stretch and scope of our responsibilities and embed the learning to move forward.

Have we got the impulse control, as ambitious leaders, to make career choices that delay immediate gratification, in order to gain the right experience and make a real difference in the longer term?

Alternatively, there are many of us who take time in making career transitions. We may be so focused on delivering a great job and enjoying the role that we have, that we sometimes forget to think about what's next. Many of the best opportunities arise, and are in the pipeline, long before they are advertised.

Too often when we don't have crucial conversations (those that say we are interested in something new) and then the key decision-makers don't know. When we are too busy to even notice, we fail to raise our antennae to see we what might be coming up.

So, have far more fun with our career routes, navigate opportunities and broaden out our experiences. Some leaders have held themselves back from potential opportunities, with untrue limiting assumptions, fears and uncertainty about what the next role will bring.

Often in our assessment of leadership talent, we find that the leaders who make the selection have a highly parochial view and experience themselves. This can also create some career limitations for us. Through creating broader experiences, both inside and outside of the organisation, we open our minds to fresh knowledge and wisdom.

When I interviewed Chris Sullivan, Chief Executive for the Corporate Banking Division at RBS, he had a confident, energising and very naturally engaging style. I had no doubt that speaking came easily to him, so imagine my surprise when he shared with me: *"I often have to speak at dinners and events. I used to have a pathological fear of doing this. I would turn them down; making excuses as to why I couldn't do them. I realised I couldn't continue to do this for another 35 years– there are only so many excuses! Speaking requires all sorts of skills and it wasn't natural to me to begin with. After a '100' times doing speeches, though, I suddenly realised that I had become a natural at it."*

Whilst we must play to our strengths, it's important that we don't shy away from opportunities to really grow and develop our leadership.

Almost every leader that I have interviewed, coached, or helped to develop has spoken of their apprehension when trying new things. This is particularly pronounced when the practice arena occurs in a public setting, the norm for most leaders! In a feedback-based culture, we have heard "this is what we think you're good at, this is what you're not so good at." Then we get told to focus on our strengths! However, developing in other areas is essential and we know from the Neuroscience and IQ chapters, that it is completely possible. This is about choice and motivation and generally not about ability (within reason, of course). This isn't saying we'll be doing something that goes against the very grain of our being. It is, however, saying that by imposing limitations, based on our fear of failure, it is highly limiting. Saying we are not good at something then becomes our narrative. Given my own upbringing in traditional Catholic Ireland, I hear myself do just that a lot.

Using role models to benchmark ourselves against can become part of the solution and paradoxically part of the problem. I have selected role model motivational speakers in the past like the world-famous Tony Robins. It's like pitching myself against Einstein; there is of course no comparison. There are then no surprises when the result was to feel like a fraud. Jonathan often reminds me, *"Leigh, it's taken me ten years to become an overnight success."* A little bit like exercise, when we are stretched, it can be hard and a little uncomfortable. The important thing is it shouldn't stop us.

It is essential for us to then *own* our ideas, successes and achievements. This is very important, not only for us, but also our teams, who look to our leadership for their own recognition and celebration. People naturally want to be part of a winning team and led by someone they, and others, admire.

Moments of Truth

In terms of the corporate brand, all of the components from marketing to other people also make up the identity and the personality of our organisation. People who are proud to work for us will take personal pride in delivering great customer service. The real sign of our brand comes at the key touch-points with the customer: the moments of truth.

I was recently doing a speaking event for Europe, Middle East and Africa with the Hilton Worldwide Group. I had planned a working holiday in Dubai a couple of weeks before the event. I therefore decided that it was only fitting that I should book into the Hilton's Jumeirah Beach Hotel to get to understand the brand experience and form my own opinion about their reputation.

There were three key moments of truth that made my experience with the hotel an unforgettable one:

1.   I was looking for a place to work on my book whilst at the same time enjoy the nightlife and a glass of wine. We went to check out the Pure Sky Lounge bar at the top of the hotel before it opened. That was where we met Jasmine, the waitress. Having spotted us, without hesitation she stopped what she was doing and showed us around the venue. She introduced us to the staff and chefs and told us about the different events that she knew 'we'd love'. Warm and engaging, she made a real impact on us.

Moment of Truth: Her ability to engage with us made us *want* to return, and we did – three times!

2.   On the final evening, we were looking around the buffet area. That was when we met chefs Stephen, Sunil and Roshan. Stephen called us over and suggested some amazing steaks, which we would love. The chefs involved us in very friendly banter, and their interaction with each other was hilarious! They attracted the attention of other customers. It reminded me of the amazing Seattle Fish Market that attracts customers from all over the world (but our buffet had far more appealing smells!) We had been to the world-famous 7 star Burge Al Arab hotel the evening before and the service didn't even come close to what we experienced at this Hilton hotel! It became clear you don't necessarily have to run a 7 star establishment to deliver 7 star service.

Moment of Truth: The cohesion and spirit of the team is infectious. It reaches far beyond anything we even realise is possible.

3.   On the same evening, at the end of our meal, the Head of Food

and Beverages came to our table to see how we had enjoyed our stay. In our conversation we learned how he'd started as an assistant waiter. It was a robust development programme through their internal university and he had a highly supportive boss. As we finished our main course, he disappeared briefly into the kitchen and returned with a large slice of chocolate cake beautifully presented with the words 'goodbye' piped out in icing sugar.

Moment of Truth: Investment in our people has a huge return at the coalface, making our colleagues loyal and want to go the extra mile for our organisation and our customers.

As a leader, if you were to return to the shop floor in your own business, what would your experience, or moments of truth be like?

Of course, moments of truth also occur for us as leaders. Our own 'leadership shadow' stretches very far and creates the culture, or personality, of the organisation, which we lead. In each interaction, or lack of interaction, we set the tone for the experienced of our leadership and how we work with our teams.

The moments of truth not only occur in structured settings, such as: our board presentations, our team meetings, and our one-to-ones, they also exist in more nebulous ways.

For example, the manner in which we engage with people as part of the relationship, or task completion. Do we constantly criticise, or recognise others and are we present, or elusive? Do we appear hyper-busy and manic, or centred and calm? What happens when we ignore the 'elephant in the room' (the major thing that everyone sees but not naming)? Are we closed, or are we transparent?

All of these moments of truth behaviours affect our own leadership brand and that of the business. I wonder what our people, or customers would say about us when we are not in the room?

It is also important that we completely respect each other's brands. Too many times, reputations have been damaged by the words of others who have inappropriately used a platform to air their opinions.

One inspiring leader spoke of an earlier incident in her career, where she was at an executive meeting. To build her own credibility with the team, she openly gave feedback about another individual who wasn't present; *"When I came out of the meeting, one of the directors pulled me to one side and said never to disrespect another person like that again. It was a totally inappropriate setting and I was humbled by my actions.*

"I knew it wasn't the right thing to do and what I said had affected their career, in all honesty, for my own means. This single act damaged both of us. It was an early learning in my career and something I will never repeat again."

Being clear about who we want to be as leaders and the moments of truth we want to create really helps us with how we actually are experienced as leaders. It defines how others feel about us.

Ask For What You Want

A defining quality of successful leaders is our ability and willingness to take calculated risks, even when it takes us out of our comfort zone and is even a bit unnerving!

It was clear that leaders that I interviewed found their courage to ask for what they wanted and needed. They put their hat in the ring, when opportunities arose. They didn't become stagnant in a position. If they sensed inertia settling in, then they proactively started to look at the next opportunity in the form of experience, responsibility and even new roles.

Rhiannon White said, *"After we won the election I was offered a role in the Prime Minister's office. The problem was, it wasn't a role I wanted. I met with the Campaign Director in the War Room to discuss my career and the role and I just cried as I was exhausted by the campaign I didn't know what to do. He told me everything would be okay and we sat and worked through a plan together. We shaped a proposal, which helped me get a bigger team, double the size of my responsibility and increase my budget. I didn't realise until then the power of asking.*

"A few years on, in a different role and company, the Chief Product Officer was leaving for a new role in San Francisco and I asked 'Can you

take me with you?'

"A different type of role came up and at first I was sceptical, as it was not a straight fit with my background. I felt I wouldn't be good enough. However, I managed to shut myself up and say why I would be good for the role and am having an amazing time contributing to a fantastic company.

"A very wise woman once told me that you need to say what it is you want, to the right person, and then wait patiently. It's all about asking and then timing. It is sometimes the hardest thing to do, to keep saying what you want, in the midst of waiting.

"Waiting patiently doesn't mean you've failed, it just means you need to wait for the right timing."

This does not mean that their careers are always about the next thing and driving forward. The pace and energy matches their focus. However, sometimes the foot has been taken off the accelerator to allow for life's events, or to feel more grounded. They are not constrained by the traditional boundaries of working. They are able to establish what they need to thrive. This is often through being creative and asking for support. They present solutions.

We sometimes hold ourselves back from opportunities because we feel they won't work for us due to the restrictions that we have. When asking for what we need, we must look at the entire support network: spouses, children, friends, boss, and team – whatever it takes. We are not alone and with every possible challenge, there is no end of possibilities.

I was coaching a very successful CEO, and he had an issue with work: life balance. Both he and his wife were workaholics. They were not getting sufficient quality time together, as a family, or even just in their own marriage. When we looked at his working days, we realised that he would be the first to arrive and the last to leave work. Then he would open up his laptop and continue working as soon as he home. There was no 'off' button.

The CEO said, *"It's such a busy time, it's important that people see me in the office whilst they are there. I don't think they will believe I am not a good leader, if I disappear off and they're still there."* He had never asked his team what they thought and felt; he had only made assumptions. We must be prepared to ask for more of what we need from others.

We should also be prepared to listen to what others need from us. Only then will we start to shift from traditional operating structures to ways of working that are more relevant with today's needs.

Positive Power and Influence

Catherine Muirden is an HR Director in the finance sector and has spent her career working with and supporting top talent. She shared, *"In order to lead you have to be able to communicate with people, to enthuse, inspire and motivate them. You have to learn to express yourself publicly, either in written or spoken form.*

"The thing I have learned is to use the language of everyday life, and speak in simple terms, not to over-complicate things. I have a large, dispersed team and I feel comfortable with this. Giving thought to your structure is also important.

"Lastly, when you are in front of people, you need to be seen as authentic. I recently choked up and lost it a bit at the end of a meeting, as I shared my thanks with the team for their donations made to our charity, which held a particular significance for one of our colleagues who was terribly unwell. At the end, when people came up to me I kept apologizing for being so flaky and emotional.

"They all said to not worry and that they believed it was better to be able to show true feelings and be human!"

Although we all have our own Brand UAP (Unique Authentic Proposition), one of the core themes through the research is our ability to act confidently and powerfully in order to influence and inspire others. Confidence and power does not necessarily mean volume, and in fact, volume can have a negative effect.

It is deeper than that: it is about the quality of your wisdom, the timing and the actual content. Although, sometimes you may just need to turn the dial up to be physically heard, or completely down so others can be heard!

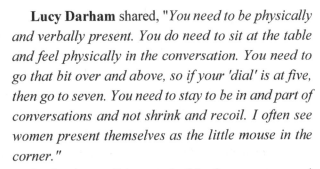

Lucy Darham shared, "*You need to be physically and verbally present. You do need to sit at the table and feel physically in the conversation. You need to go that bit over and above, so if your 'dial' is at five, then go to seven. You need to stay to be in and part of conversations and not shrink and recoil. I often see women present themselves as the little mouse in the corner.*"

It is impossible to build the energy and momentum that is required in others, if we are unable to build their confidence and trust in us. In Robin Kermode's coaching, he shares how our non-verbal signals, created as a result of our thoughts and emotions, subsequently affect our posture. When people observe our leadership, they read the non-verbal body language and don't just listen to our words.

When we are feeling centred and confident as a leader, then this shows through in our breathing and tonality. However, many of us adopt a mind-set, position, and pose that disempowers us.

Personally I have found that, when I became anxious, my neck would go red and I would find myself short of breath. None of this is unusual and it can easily be managed and redressed. Finding the internal confidence and using this as the basis to create a more power-enhancing position is the key that gives us presence. Again, this goes back to dialling up or down dependent on how we are impacting others.

It is worthwhile learning about other people's body language and the messages you are unwittingly transmitting yourself from your own body language. I find that the book *What Every Body is Saying,* by the ex-FBI agent Joe Navarro to be most interesting.

His advice was to establish people's baseline behaviours and to watch out for multiple tells - things that add up to give you a good understanding of what is out of the ordinary and whether people are comfortable or uncomfortable with what is going on. Our limbic system is the part of the brain that cannot lie and our neo-cortex is the part that does, so watch out for some of the following:

- *Feet first?* Consider the position of people's feet – in conversations, are they pointing towards the other person or away from them? Are they engaged and do they want to be part of the conversation, or are the feet indicating that they would rather be somewhere else?

- *Grow or shrink?* The freeze, fight or flight response shows itself in various ways. When people don't want to be in a meeting and feel intimidated, then you can see them visibly shrinking. Joe refers to the 'turtle effect' demonstrated when someone's head begins to disappear down between the shoulders to present a smaller target for attack.

- *Like or dislike?* People lean towards, or away from someone else, depending on whether they feel they can trust them or they are mistrustful of them.

- *Discomfort or comfort?* When people are relaxed and comfortable they are open in their body postures. When they are uncomfortable, then they seek pacifying behaviours. Women touching their neck dimple, playing with a necklace, or their hair, can indicate this. When men are uncomfortable they will touch the back of their neck, play with their ties or stroke their neck.

- *Territorial grabs.* It is interesting to watch people spread themselves out across the back of another chair, place their hands on their hips or on the table as they lean forward. Also it is interesting in meetings to see how some people spread their documents around their place at the meeting table to give themselves more space and perceived power.

This is a complex area, which these examples just give a miniscule taste of, and it is a subject worthy of a great deal of your further study.

Presentation and Impact

Once we have worked on our body language and tone, we need to be clear on the content of our message. There is a known saying, "*Failing to plan is planning to fail*". Our role as leaders is to make the complex simple, and distil the key messages that will inspire people to follow us.

A CEO once said to us, "*We are paid as leaders to make three major decisions each year that will add huge value to the organisation; we just need to decide what these are. If everything is priority one, nothing is priority one. We lose our message. We attempt to attack on a broad front and are worn down. The rule of three can be used to prioritise resources so you attack in just three places. You also have just three points to make and get a consistently clear message across."*

Meetings turn into fascinating events! Whilst they are one of the most powerful 'platforms' for our leadership impact, it is often the place where communication failure occurs at every level; the interplay is very telling. They become the forum for downloading information, often disengaging most of the people at the table in the process. Meetings generate emotions such as anger and frustration, resulting in dominance and outbursts. Out of control discussions mean that the quieter, introverted and more reflective people lose their voices. If we are to consider the effectiveness of our own leadership brand and also of our team's brand, we must develop mechanisms for communicating with a sense of equality, trust and transparency.

Claire Hall shared, *"In this role lots of the value you add is in relationships and team dynamic which isn't instantly obvious. I have been fortunate in my career that people have valued what I bring to the table. There are only two women in a team of eight, so lots of macho opinions at times!*

"Mine is not normally the voice that dominates the discussion and that's fine, but when I do contribute I'm listened to and I have credibility. They see the value and the skills I bring to the team as well as appreciating my own style of leadership."

Situational leadership is essential to today's diverse and fast paced work environments. Exceptional leaders are highly responsive to different needs and styles and are able to adapt accordingly. Therefore, we must be able to communicate in a variety of different ways. Sometimes situations require a more directive style, other times a coaching style, and sometimes a consensual and collaborative style.

We may have personal preferences for specific, habitual styles. However, we need to develop a repertoire of additional styles, which we can call upon. We need to know from experience, which approaches are best suited to the people we are working with and the situation we find ourselves in.

Savvy Politics

Sayyeda Salam believes that, *"Sometimes it's important to put yourself forward so that you can have influence. I've come across people who have not come forward when they should have done, or have been too constrained by bureaucracy, or their cultural setting. I remember when in Sierra Leone I was keen to get a meeting with the First Lady and one of our Vice Presidents. Everyone was really reticent. I realised I was asking the wrong person and so navigated through until I identified the right person who could influence this. It's challenging working across cultural barriers, and some people hold on protectively to their relationship and the power."*

By accepting others' imposed limitations, then we struggle to influence and make an impact. The ability to navigate the politics and the system means that we can intervene and achieve the desired end result.

Organisational politics tends to be a contentious issue and highly debated topic. It is often believed to be manipulative and inauthentic, self-serving and to the detriment of others. Other people have little issue with office politics and see it as an opportunity to positively influence in some way. I believe that both views are right, dependent of course on the lens that you are looking through. We naturally form in-groups (where the rules are very clear) and out-groups. We see this with executive boards and senior leadership that lack any form of diversity. In its most negative form, it shows up as favouritism, taking credit for other's work and becoming sycophantic. In these environments, if we choose not to follow the approved group behaviours, then we fear the implications for our own careers and reputations.

Savvy politics is more positive and productive in nature. There is no doubt, however we feel about it, that political acumen is an essential skill for leaders.

Understanding how to be politically savvy helps with achieving better outcomes. This can be done authentically and positively. It is more about being influential and getting the right resources on board, so our teams can function effectively. It's navigating the complex relationships that exist across highly matrixed, global, cross-cultural structures where others are affected by the decisions we make.

Consequently, as leaders it is important to create safe and collaborative environments that enable people to navigate the organisation in a healthy and constructive, rather than obstructive way. This sometimes means letting go of personal agendas to achieve greater value for the whole business. A lot of energy is exerted when imposing our power and control over others. This has little overall value and is one of the greatest causes of conflict.

Being politically savvy is about how we make decisions, together to achieve a desired outcome of win-win. The components of this skill are key to our leadership and can often be the very thing that derails us.

Our Image

It is important that our own image as ambitious leaders is professional and in keeping with the standards of the businesses we work in or the clients we work with. There has been a significant amount of research on how people make judgements within the first few seconds of meeting.

Image is really is important, not just in our message to others, but also in how we feel ourselves - our psyche. If we want to be taken seriously, then we must be aware of others' perception of us. Whether it be the out of control hair, the too low neckline, or the badly scraped shoes.

As a busy Mum, with image somewhere down the priority list, I too have been an offender! I recall when the hem of my skirt would fall down I would resort to stapling it!

These days, I realise just how important my image is to my career and so give it the necessary attention that it deserves. I have assembled much of my knowledge from experts such as: Inanch for my hair styling, Image Coaches for 'colours' and dress styling and make-up artists to help with the right products.

It is important in our leadership that the only distractions are the verbal messages that we share and not something less flattering! Remember, if our image is unprofessional, or shabby, then people notice this first and not the leader.

When we take care of our image, then we sustain and even enhance our personal power and presence. Consequently, people fully notice the leader, rather than any flaws in our brand or image.

Lou Barber
Chairman, Proximity London
Marketing & Advertising

Lou shared her story: *"My Dad was a doctor and my Mum was a midwife. In my late teens I trained as a nurse for five years. After I got married, I found that my husband worked 9-5 and because I never saw him, I decided to switch careers.*

"I have always been interested in people, particularly what motivates people to buy things. When switching careers, I had no business or commercial experience at the time. However, I was convinced that I had transferrable skills.

"Career advancement - I started as an Account Executive in Advertising, when a group of senior managers decided to set up on their own in the 1990s. It was a real start-up where we sat around a dining table in Gerard's Cross, London. I worked my way up through the organisation and have been very lucky that it's a very supportive agency. It's certainly always been gender neutral and so never an issue. I have always put my hand up and grabbed every possible opportunity.

"I do believe we are in control of our own destiny; it's never a pre-determined road. So if you really want something, then you need to go after it. I always tell my children that it's the whole package that's most important. You can have academic achievement, but there is no point coming out of university if you can't connect with people and communicate what your personal brand is. Your ambition and your desire to get on really help you to be self-motivated. I have built my reputation by setting goals and objectives that are organised around achieving a continual improvement - day by day.

"In 2005, my husband and I gave up our jobs and we went travelling with the kids around the world for a year. The CEO was very supportive at the time and gave me a sabbatical. Sadly other people would often try to talk us out of it, saying, 'What if this disaster occurred, or that drama were to happen?' They would never try to talk us into it. We went anyway. We home-

schooled our children using the school curriculum and taught things like fractions using pizzas and a budget of $100 per day. It was brilliant fun.

"It interests me what people say and the comments they make about other people. They hold back because they know at some point they would also like to have a family.

"It has never occurred to me that I would not work. When my daughter, Lilly, was small she would ask me, 'Mummy why do you go to work when Doris' Mum doesn't'. I started to say things like, 'It is so we can go on holidays and have nice things', but this was really bollocks. It was actually because it gave me independence and satisfaction.

"About 11-12 weeks after giving birth and having maternity leave, then I returned to work. At the time, there was much less acknowledgement and so little support. Not like there is today. So it was very hard juggling full-time work and home life. I couldn't have done this without brilliant nannies and parents.

"My husband is in project management and we would share equally the domestic stuff and childcare. We would look at our diaries and share out the duties. There was no expectation that I would have to be the primary carer of the children. I do think how difficult it must be for single working Mums.

"My key lessons are:

Values -we sell 'people' as part of our business organisational culture. We need to understand what are the healthy behaviours and what do we value as an organisation. We have created a strong culture around doing the right thing. Even if we get a short-term client project, if it clashes with our values and it's not what we should do, then we turn the work down. We do not just pursue for the revenue.

Authenticity - You have to be true to yourself going through the ranks. Changing to be something else is a hide-away to nothing. You need to be consistent and genuine. Your brand and personal reputation are crucial. You need to decide about your view on something and be clear about this. As a leader, you cannot vacillate, chop and change things. This does not mean that you can't bring in other people's thinking.

Be self-aware and aware of the impact you're having on other people. I have always cared about what other people think. You need to put yourself in their shoes, just to understand how things will sound from their perspective: how will it feel and what do I want them to do, as a consequence. I have mostly worked with other females who have not put themselves in others shoes. They've been aggressive, self-serving and not perceptive.

__Vulnerability and Mistakes__ - Recognise when you've made a mistake. I recall when I resigned from my work and five and a half months in to my six month notice period, I decided I didn't want to go. I'd had an offer from another agency, which was in the press and I had to communicate publicly that I no longer wanted to leave. I've learned a lot about saying I've made a mistake and swallowing my pride. It might have been a painful to put it right, but an important thing to do.

How I got through this was to get pragmatic about it all and wrote down the pros and cons with the reasons why. On the face of things, there didn't appear to be much tipping the balance one way or another. It became an emotional decision about what was right for me. A lot of people do things because they feel that they ought to, or because they said that they would. It is important to go with what is instinctively right for the long term.

__Managing time__ - I have a very tight mental timetable in my mind, because of the work I do, and the way I approach it. I have to plan as I find it difficult not to know where I'm going. It can drive my family nuts at times, as I even apply this to when we go on holiday and things!

It goes right back to the times when I was a registered nurse and my training, which was very task based. After years of mental lists and prioritising this has been ingrained in me. In terms of relationships and life, my approach is more 'carpe diem' (seize the day). In terms of money or savings I believe that you can't take it with you, so I make sure that we enjoy our lives by going to the theatre, playing tennis and lots of other things.

__Legacy__ - For me my legacy is in my role as Chairman. I own the agency culture and I believe (Peter Drucker's) quote:'Culture eats strategy for breakfast!' If you don't deliver or buy with transparency, honesty and high integrity then this is an issue. It is important to know *what people care about. I run things like quarterly breakfast clubs for new people in order to get to know them, and find out what they like about our business, what they'd change and any observations and ideas on how to make things better.*

Awareness *- Although I haven't had a 360 feedback for a couple of years, I ask people I work closely "what could I have done better". People tell me that I am genuinely collaborative and live by my values. It's not about what I say; it's about what I do. They see me as the wise old owl, where they can come and ask for advice and opinions.*

Do The Right Thing and Worry Less *- I'm conscious of how much I worried in my early 30s and 40s, I was almost obsessed with what I feel I should say rather than what I believed was the right answer. I really believe that you have to say what you believe in and stick to it.*

It's not trying to say what other people think the right answer is. It doesn't matter whether it is right or wrong. If it's not what people want to hear then invite feedback and if you think it's right, then agree to disagree. If you do the right thing then you will build a reputation as someone who is trustworthy and a brand that people respect. They may not like you but they will respect you."

Inspiring Women Leaders' Words of Wisdom

1. Be Different, For the Right Reasons

"My husband would say to me 'Stop turning into a bloke', as I was trying to fit in and be noticed. I didn't need to curse. You need to focus on the important meetings. Aim to look more feminine, instead of disappearing in a sea of black suits. Visually if you're noticed, then it can help. But make sure it's not for the wrong reasons."

2. Make Sure Your Talents Are Visible

"My strength is understanding patterns and making connections. My coach asked me once 'Do you think others know that?' When you have something, that others don't have, you think it's obvious to everyone. Take time to help others get to know what you bring to the table."

3. Communicating with Impact

"When presenting, or influencing, you need to work the room, so people get your point. It's not to be confused with a show-off moment. Make sure people notice the important points: you want people in the room to be excited by what you have to say and compelled to take action. Unlike a piece of music without any expression, it's the 'tah-dah!' moment!"

4. What People Say When You're Not in the Room

"How you measure great leadership is what your employees say about you around the family dinner table. As a top leader in business, it is our responsibility to do a better job at being effective and a far more inspiring leader and role model for other women."

5. Influencing and Selling Ideas

"I was always a pioneer and visionary, so had to learn the skill of internal selling, as I was always one step ahead. It wasn't so much political play, but just knowing the landscape and how to sell ideas and influence people."

6. Saying What You Want

"I think that women don't always put themselves forward. I think self-confidence has a huge part to play in this. I think that you don't have to be the CEO. But, if you **want** to be the CEO, then you had better speak up and tell somebody that. I think that women are often reticent to ask, and wait for somebody to come and tap them on the shoulder to give them 'permission' to go out and put their name forward."

7. Getting the Most from Networking

"I think that networking works to a degree, but sponsorship works much better. If you want to help people along, then you need to connect them up with potential opportunities. You need to take proactive action, versus just being there for the sake of an event. It's therefore about thinking what you want from the networking in advance."

8. Advocacy

"I have found that sponsors are absolutely vital. I find it difficult to blow my own trumpet. I don't tend to try to dominate the conversation; it's just not me. I don't feel comfortable pretending either, so for me, sponsorship and advocacy are absolutely fundamental. You need sponsors that absolutely go out on a limb to support you. I have had this early on in my career. When the new Director arrived, they believed that I had been in the business a long time, which couldn't be good. One of my sponsors helped to change this view. You need someone who will put himself or herself out for you."

9. Track Record

"You do need to have high work standards, be visible and work hard. All leadership must be underpinned by delivery. Concentrate on what you do really well and get noticed; drive your performance, so senior people can see it, rather than be blinded by PR. I believe too many people are too busy managing their own PR."

10. Being a Role Model to Others

"Many blocks to advancement are not caused by men, but caused by women, who display toxic behaviours yet unbelievably are put on the pedestal as apparent role models. This teaches other women you have to be a certain way in order to succeed. So we will get a repeated cycle, slowing down the whole agenda. Women are our own worst enemy and we must break the patterns."

11. Sharing Your Own and Others' Successes

"I have some career choices that have really accelerated my career. I didn't know this at the time. We don't have bonus structures, and recognising and appreciating your own and other's successes is particularly important. Culturally, we don't do this naturally. You need to find strategies for how to promote yourself and the work that you do. I get frustrated in interviews when people don't share their successes. People want to work for successful teams and managers."

12. Simplification: 'Now say what you said again, but in fewer words'

"Working in a consulting environment you work with hugely bright and intelligent people. I remember getting told once 'If you ever leave a voicemail more than 30 seconds again then I'll delete it.' In an open plan office it was tough and awkward but as a result I learned to get my messages across to people - in a clear way, based on what they really needed to know."

13. Managing the Politics

"Politics is often seen as a negative. However, anything about people requires an understanding of how to manage the politics of people. We also need to compromise. People think these are dirty words but the positive management of human relationships should not be mistaken with bad behaviour."

14. Talk Yourself Into It, Not Out of It

"There's a problem with too much internal dialogue: you go through the first thought, the second thought and so on. By the time you're ready, you shut down and miss out on the opportunity to contribute. You need to talk yourself into contributing and not out of it."

15. Great Job, Great Experience and Realise Your Potential

"Do the best you can in the job that you're in, because that builds your best potential for the future. At the same time don't be bashful in letting people know what you are looking for next. Don't assume they know. "

Chapter Reflection: Brand Presence and Impact

Here are some questions on which you may like to reflect:

- Are you able to bring your authentic self to work?
- What is your track record for success? How can your stretch this further?
- How strong and visible is your brand, both internally and externally?
- How adaptable is your leadership style to suit different needs and contexts?
- How compelling and inspiring is your communication?
- What is the leadership shadow that you cast on your business?
- Is your leadership shadow one that you feel proud of?
- What are your strengths and UAP (unique authentic proposition)?
- How comfortable do you feel raising your profile and sharing successes?
- How comfortable do you feel taking on new and risky challenges and opportunities?
- What are the moments of truth in your organisation?
- Do you know what you want and need?
- Do you ask for what you want?
- What is your Brand image?
- What do people say when you're not in the room?

Chapter 12
LQ: Legacy

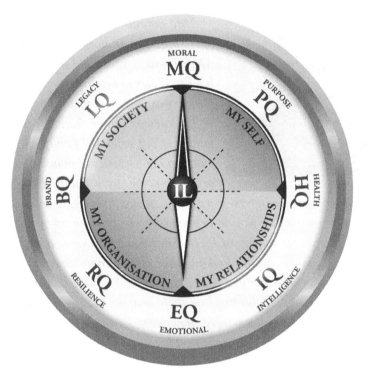

"Above all, she [mother] was very clear that nothing would mean anything if I didn't live a life of use to others. I didn't know what that meant for a long time. I came into this business young and worried about my own experiences and my own pain. And it was only when I began to travel and look and live beyond my home that I understand my responsibility to others. And when I met survivors of war and famine and rape, I learned what life is like for most people in this world. And how fortunate I was to have food to eat, a roof over my head and a safe place to live and the joy of having my family safe and healthy. And I realised how sheltered I have been and I was determined never to be that way again. We are all so fortunate...I will do the best I can with this life to be of use."

**Angelina Jolie - Acceptance Speech, Jean Hersholt Award,
Governor Awards, November 2013**

Lynne Turner
Global Finance Director at Christies

"My parents are both Welsh and Welsh Speaking. I was born in Manchester and when I was 4 years old my parents moved back to Wales to be closer to their family. My father was a Mechanical Engineer at the Wylfa Nuclear Power Station. I have a close family, a big extended family and it's quite matriarchal – sisters, aunts and, cousins organise some great family 'get togethers'.
Both of my grandmothers were very strong influences in my life. My maternal grandmother was an orphan and was brought up by her aunt and went into service at the age of 13/14. She had a great sense of humour and a very caring nature, always looking after other people. She was a fantastic cook and I remember her giving us plates of food to take round to neighbours on the street, people who lived on their own or were going through hard times. I respect her enormously. Whenever I'm doing something that's in conflict with my values, it's her voice I hear in my head, challenging me to do the right thing.

"My paternal grandmother was intelligent and the eldest of ten children. She had had to abandon her own education when her mother died the week she was taking her O levels at 16. She and my grandfather had a strong influence over my education. They believed that the opportunity to learn was a precious gift and gave me a sense of 'standing on the shoulders of giants'. They struggled through their lives and so I feel very lucky to be born into the age and culture that I have. I feel it's my responsibility to take this forward. Both my grandmothers were strong female role models, not in terms of career, but in that they did some amazing things and taught me a lot about my values.

"I grew up in a small fishing village in North Wales. One of my teachers introduced me to Germaine Greer's The Female Eunuch, *which I read when I was about 14. I didn't really understand it all but I remember it being about*

challenging the status quo. This really influenced my outlook, that you didn't have to accept what society determined were traditional roles for women. I found my school environment and living in a small village community quite stifling and couldn't wait to leave to go to university and 'discover the world'.

"My Mum was also an important influence. She's a great homemaker and very active in the local community giving it all her energy and passion. She stayed at home when we were young and then ran the local nursery school in our village. She had dreamt of being a teacher when she was young but for various reasons she got disillusioned with school and left to train as a hairdresser. I remember, when she started the nursery school, seeing her come alive and fulfilling her ambitions and using her talents. It was great to see. She has a real passion for giving children and young people a good start in life.

"I know it not fashionable to describe oneself as a 'feminist' these days but for me it just means every person having the opportunity to fulfil their dreams and their potential. There's a certain injustice about the boxes that we put others and ourselves into. Traditional ideas about the role of women or men constrain us and I still see the legacy of this today. Trying to juggle work, kids and the domestic chores, I feel women are still doing the lion's share of the work and it's tough. I have two boys (21 and 18) and I hope I have brought them up to respect every individual's right to be the best they can be and to help each other.

"My Dad's very adventurous. In the summer we would take a tent, or caravan and travel across continental Europe. I absolutely loved the escape. I loved French literature and films and had a French penfriend called Florence and we would spend our summers together to practice our language skills. My Dad always encouraged us to think and challenge ourselves. We would have lots of debates and discussions with him. Dad was the first of his family to go to university. His parents had ambitions for him to be a minister of the church but he chose engineering. It was something he had to fight for.

"I went to Loughborough University to read Business Studies and French. I loved university and took every opportunity that was offered in my first year doing parachuting, hitch hiking to Paris and much more! I joined an

organisation called AIESEC (Association Internationale des Etudiants en Sciences Economiques et Commerciales). They organised international internships and I went to work for Texaco in Athens with about 70 other students from all over the world. I loved it and found that we were all the same at core - we didn't have any cultural clashes. When I was looking for a job after university, I knew I wanted to work in business and I wanted to travel but didn't know exactly what kind of role. I was good at maths and Accountancy seemed to created lots of options and opened doors. I was probably more focused and thinking ahead in terms of my career than most of my friends. I think it was that sense of responsibility to make the best of the opportunities offered me.

"After I qualified, I joined the Alliance & Leicester Building Society as a Project Accountant. The organisation had been given legal powers to expand into new areas of business and they had very few graduate managers who could evaluate the business cases and make the change happen. I had a very supportive boss. There was no manual to follow and no one else knew what to do, as there were no professional processes in place. At the age of 25, I was operating at board level as the Group Financial Controller. This was a big break in terms of confidence and leadership.

"In the early 90s housing market crisis, the property prices crashed and people had been given excessive mortgage loans and were starting to default because they couldn't afford to pay them. Mortgage repossessions were so rare that we didn't really have proper processes to deal with them. My colleague was on holiday and one of his team members brought me the calculations of the loss provisions, which he didn't believe because the number was so huge. I re-checked his calculation and realised that we potentially had a significant crisis on our hands with unprecedented levels of negative equity. No-one was really taking charge of the situation, or knew quite what to do. I asked for a team to assess a sample of the loans and work the issues through. The regulatory environment was such that any Building Society, which was going to declare a loss in its annual results, would get taken over by another, to maintain confidence in the sector. Because it was a crisis, I lost any self-consciousness I felt about overstepping the mark and focused on what needed to be done.

"Managing in a crisis helps you to cut through politics and flex your leadership muscles. I was six months pregnant with my first child and felt a strong sense of urgency to resolve the issues and get a recovery plan in place before I went on maternity leave.

"I learned from that experience that I'm stronger than I think. I found that by keeping a clear head, I could see a route through and could see the positive outcome that could be achieved from something potentially catastrophic. I realised people will listen to me and that I needed to bring people with me. The emergency and immediacy cut through the petty squabbles and political games. This carries through all aspects of life. The little voice in my head told me not to hold back; holding back on speaking the truth as we see it just doesn't serve us in a crisis. Leadership really shifts during a crisis. That is just because leaders may have a big title, but they are quite often just as lost as those who are following them. Protecting your own back and creating a culture of blame is just not helpful.

"Many years later I worked for another organisation where the culture at board level was toxic. We were doing a significant business migration and had built capacity to handle 5,000 customer calls a day. On the first day we realised we'd been seriously misled and were actually taking 25,000 calls, which we couldn't cope with. We also had some significant IT issues to handle. As a management team we all had to roll our sleeves up and share the problems between us regardless of our job description. One of our board members was a bully and quite obnoxious. He would shout and scream in an incredibly unhelpful way. He would say 'it can't be this bad' and would want us to 'massage' the numbers. He was one of those people who had risen in the organisation by managing the messaging. He had no empathy for people. He told us to just fix the problems or he threatened that someone else would be brought in to do the job instead.

"We ended up having to shield the rest of the team from his toxic influence. The key thing was to fix the IT issues and build the capacity to handle customer calls as quickly as we could but it would take weeks not days. It felt like being caught under the waves. As soon as we fixed one issue and bob our head up to take a breath, another wave would come along and drag us under again. There was a moment when I just wanted to go home,

give up and cry. My boss was a vulnerable leader but also strong, he showed me it was possible to be both. He was completely open and had the courage to say things as they were without any 'spin'. Through all of this, he was thinking about the welfare of his team. He helped me to dig deep to find my strength and resilience.

"In this project, I learned the importance of teams. Some people are going through some really tough personal things and you don't learn about that when things are normal, as people don't share. Instead you learn so much more when in a crisis. We were all in this together, so even if one person is falling, we would help to pick them up and never let them falter. We eventually sold the business. It was important to us to manage the transition well, create redeployment opportunities and make sure that everyone was treated fairly. It was no longer about being a Financial Director, it was more about learning how people were and how to treat people as you would like to be treated yourself.

"I had to think about where to go next in my career and had relocated my family. My husband had given up his job and was a student. We had a big mortgage and I was the main earner. Although I wasn't overly worried, it was a minor anxiety.

"I was offered a Finance Director role, which turned to be quite a stressful job because of the politics and the market circumstances. On reflection I accepted it without doing a proper due diligence on whether I was a good cultural fit with the MD. I would now insist on doing that and would walk away from a role if the chemistry didn't work or there was a mismatch in core values. That's something you only learn with experience. As well as the job not being right for me, my marriage was drifting. In my personal life I felt trapped in a marriage I knew in my heart of hearts was making us both quite miserable. I really learned about vulnerabilities and weaknesses as courage fails you. You need to take time out to say, 'What do I need here?' I had some really tough moments where I was barely holding my head above water at this time. It just got to a certain point where I needed to focus on something good in order to drag me out of my thinking. When it feels like everything in your life is going wrong you have to try and fix one problem at a time, but it can be hard to see a way through.

"Fortunately for me I was offered a different role, which played to my strengths. It involved a significant outsourcing strategy, which needed to be handled with sensitivity due to the impact on people. I was determined to deal with it in the 'right' way as there would be an impact on the working lives of over 100 people. I was not going to be pressured to do things faster than we could handle. Fortunately, my boss was supportive of my philosophy and realised that it was important to bring the team with us on the transformation journey. Our philosophy was that, 'It was a tough job that we'll do well. People may not like us, but they will respect us.' Working with my HR colleagues, we spent time thinking as much about the emotional aspects of the change as well as the more rational and practical aspects. We allowed people time to vent their frustrations, express their anger or sadness that things were changing. It was important to face people in a way that was congruent with our values. It was hard work but I feel quite proud of what we achieved. My team learned new skills. Rather than being the victims of change they managed to learn through the challenging circumstances we were all now facing.

"I was now divorced and had secured a better work-life balance for myself, having been through what was a necessary period of change. But I had the sense that there was more to life than this. With the kids and work, I didn't have much room for anything else. I had very few slots for relaxing or the gym. My boys were getting older and more independent, so life was getting a bit easier as a working mum. One evening I was out with a group of girlfriends and we were day dreaming about having a 'gap year' once our kids had grown up and gone to university. It felt like we were wishing our lives away! One of my friends asked if I fancied doing a sponsored trek for a week in the Namibia desert! I knew it was something I really wanted to do but couldn't imagine how I would fit it in with work and being a single mum. I guess it was a great test of whether my faith would allow such a life changing experience. I found a way of juggling my responsibilities at work and arranged for Mum and Dad to look after the boys. It was such an amazing experience. Fundraising and training for the trek were the real challenge, which started from the moment we signed up for it. The group was all female which was a novelty after working in mostly male dominated

environments. *I have to confess that I had some reservations about this, probably going back to memories of school and how bitchy groups of girls can be to each other. In that environment I learnt quite a lot about how we women have a choice of being our best or worst selves.*

"We were in the middle of the desert and were split into two groups called X and Y. There were quite a few what I'd call 'alpha-females' - very confident and competitive but a bit cliquey. I could see the dynamic developing as they picked their favourites and excluded others. The following day we realised the groups had all shifted around as they'd asked to join their friends in the other group. Suddenly there was a lot more positive energy and fun as everything became calmer and less competitive. We were really starting to gel and everyone was getting on and supporting each other. Fiona and I were slightly older than the others so I think we set the tone for our group. It became a supportive team in what was a very gruelling environment and everyone was opening up. In contrast, the other group were racing ahead, dragging the slower members along and not sharing water and it was getting pretty fraught between them with the physically weaker ones falling behind and getting disillusioned. One particularly gruelling day, we trekked for 10 hours in 40 degree heat. Our group had got through it by composing a motivational marching song which we sang as we walked and sharing our sweets and stories. We had made a pact that the most important thing was for the group to stay together and all of us to make it to camp on foot. In the other group only a few individuals made it with others having to be picked up by the rescue truck en route. Around the campfire later that evening the stories and the sense of achievement were palpably different.

"On the final day we had scrambled to the top of a hill. Our guide told us an inspiring story about a tribe who lived in the North of Namibia by a river. He said that this influenced their sense of time as 'moving backwards, rather than forwards'. He invited us to sit quietly on top of the plateau where we would see how far we had travelled and contemplate the personal journey we had made. He shared the philosophy of this tribe which is: 'Let your memories go, cast them into the river of time until the end of your journey where you will meet them on the shore and you can say to yourself that these are the memories of a life well-lived'. In my moment of quiet reflection,

inspired by this story, I realised just how powerful we women can be if we work together and how destructive and dysfunctional we can also be at times! It made me reflect on just how lucky I am. I also thought about what an adventure life can be if you embrace the opportunities that come up – they don't always come at the most convenient moment but there's never any regret in embracing what life throws up.

"A few months later, I went to a university reunion where I met up with Ed. He was an old boyfriend and we'd split up probably because we were too young to appreciate what we had at the time. He is my soul mate and I'm enormously grateful that we met again.

"Organising the treks came about as I wanted others to also experience what I'd been through. Fiona Aris and myself connected with an entrepreneur and philanthropist who ran a micro-credit charity and was keen help to organise the treks with us. We wanted to do something more in our lives and this felt it could be right. The entrepreneur was a great risk-taker and we really wanted to turn a great idea into action. We paid the flight deposits and started planning; we were aiming for about twenty people in total.

"We launched the Namibia Desert Challenge in January and managed to make a list of about 14 potential participants but by February we only had a list of seven confirmed people when we'd committed to twenty. I remember waking up in a cold sweat; it felt such a crisis moment. We certainly didn't want the charity to be out of pocket. I had to 'silence the voice' of concern and we got on with creating a big recruitment campaign. We ended up getting twenty-one women participants and raised £60k for the charity. This turned out to be 25% of the charity funds for the year, so it made a significant financial impact for them. It really validated the experience. The trek set the tone for women who were put in a position where they were challenged to find out how strong and skilful they really were.

"The company I worked for had a problem of lack of gender diversity at senior management levels. Part of the problem was women not putting themselves forward for promotion because they lacked role models and the networks that men took for granted. After the trekking challenge, I wanted to experiment with taking a group of women from across the company on a

challenge so they would discover their personal potential as well as forming supportive friendships. I approached the HR Director with my idea and it was agreed that the company would sponsor participation as part of a leadership talent development experiment. They agreed to pay half of the costs, with participants paying the remainder. To keep costs down I decided on a 4-day trek in the Atlas mountains of Morocco, the Mount Toubkal Challenge and chose CAMFED (Campaign for Female Education) as our charity. Participation was entirely voluntary and I had hoped for about twenty but was quite nervous as I launched it – what if nobody would come? I was amazed when forty women signed up within the first ten days! I wanted the event to include personal development and so involved a number of executive coaches in the programme. The whole journey required a huge amount of commitment from those who took part. This required a lot of fundraising, also leaving their kids and so the trek was truly a symbolic event at the end of our 9-month development programme. We used the 'Hero's Journey' by Joseph Campbell as a call to action. We created a real sense of the organisation coming together. We linked it back into the organisation and this led to the Women's Network. I was really proud of this work.

"After the trek in the mountains I had arranged for us to visit a women's group which had been established by a small group of Berber women who wanted to challenge the limited role of women in their society and help them develop business skills and provide more education for their girls. I was interested to see what impact this would have on our view of our own opportunities. I was also keen to have a token to celebrate the trip and asked them if they could organise some local crafts as a memento of our trip. We were given such a warm welcome and were greeted by the women who had hand-embroidered hessian bags with our trek logo. This really connected the group and was very touching.

"I think the experience of meeting those Berber women made us think, 'Who am I not to take on challenges and push the boundaries given my opportunities?" People tell me that what we did was life changing and helped them with their bravery to make the shifts they needed to make in their own lives. I believe that we are all bigger than the organization we work for. We all have a part to play in our contribution to the wider world.' I

hear a lot about dead aid and how Micro-credit really works to give poor women the opportunity to build businesses and work their way out of poverty to feed and educate their children. It unblocks opportunities for women to create a sustainable living for themselves and their families."

Fiona and Lynne also shared the following key insights from these experiences:

- *"I left my work on a sabbatical after we did the trek. In fact, quite a lot of women ended up changing or leaving their jobs at this time. The challenge for organisations is to really think about what diversity means and if you're serious about it to accept that it involves embracing different ideas. I think the ones who came back with a new outlook and confidence felt uninspired by what they had previously been doing and the opportunities available to them so they tended to leave to get more meaning and purpose in their lives. Others were able to make it work more constructively."*
- *"On the treks we took calculated risks. On the most dangerous days, that's when we really felt the 'wow' moments. Every night we would sit around the campfire, with the trek leader and guides and discuss issues and share stories. It was important for everybody to have the best experience whilst they were there. Everyone had a different story for why they want to join the challenge, each was powerful and very liberating."*
- *"We would have 20 minutes of 'QM' - 'Quiet Moments' to allow us time to reflect on the experience. This helped to bring powerful energy back into the group and created a sort of spiritual moment."*
- *"We had a common purpose which created a real connection; deeper than the one you would get normally. This empowering experience that all of us went through meant that nobody came out of the other side the same. We all became different people; far stronger, having grown with the courage and confidence to renegotiate the boundaries in our lives."*
- *"It is important for us to be role model for our children. Now I have*

something in the photograph album to look back on. I had kick-started something that took me out of my routine of life, I had never thought of myself as an adventurer. One friend said to me, "I remember you coming back from the trek and I had never seen such a change."

The lesson is that you just have to take one courageous step and then things evolve from there. There is an expression, *'Every trip of 1,000 miles starts with a single step'*. It can be tough being a woman in a leadership position, and you must have the right character. There are as many bad leaders, as there are good leaders. The culture of any organisation has huge implications for the quality of our leadership. It has implications for health, communications and relationships. It is so important to be yourself in business and not create a false persona. It all comes back to the compass - moral integrity, purpose and the shadow we cast as leaders.

Definition of LQ: Legacy

In the research that I've been doing, as well as my development work with leaders, many have shared how they have wanted to live lives that hold greater purpose and meaning and, consequently, make a real difference. Interestingly, I hear how this grows in importance later on in our lives, as we search for real meaning and legacy. At earlier stages in our careers we are driven by a desire to grow and succeed. Legacy therefore becomes something to give focus to in the future, rather than an opportunity for us to make a difference today. Although many are actively involved in some way, there is a general sense that more can be done.

There is also a lack of clarity about what kind of difference we can really make, as the challenges presented to us can be somewhat overwhelming. Where do we begin? There is often a sense of fear, as what needs to be done feels beyond our capabilities. Some are equally concerned about focusing beyond their own immediate needs of money, career, or security. They tell me, *"I really want to make a difference, but I am not quite sure where to start."* In a hyper-busy world, our thoughts and actions required in order to create our own legacy become a plan for the future.

We often make the excuse that we will do it, but only when things are little less manic, or a little bit more secure. Our job is not to be perfect; our job is to be human. One deep question is, 'How do we sustain our humanity and existence?' We also ponder on another question, 'What do we want to be remembered for?' Through all of our experiences, what is most evident is that leadership is at the very heart of LQ.

We will all leave a legacy, whether we decide to take action to do so, or not. It is just a question of, 'What kind of legacy are we going to leave and is this one that we are happy with?' In Rick Warren's inspiring book and subsequent TED Talk, *The Purpose Driven Life: What on Earth Am I Here For?* he shares how he believes that spiritual emptiness is a universal disease. He describes three levels of living: the survival level, the success level, and the significance level. This is where you figure out *why* you actually matter, what you are actually here to do. He has coined the notion that leadership is in fact *stewardship*, we don't own what we are leading, we are only the steward to look after it during our tenure. We are tasked with the responsibility for caring for that which we lead, in order to make it better than when we first inherited it. He goes on to share that the good life is not about looking good, feeling good, or having all the good – it's about being and doing good.

This, for me, has been one of the most compelling and enlightening articles I have read because it takes the whole concept of overcoming the need of our own ego. Instead he inspires us to be selflessly courageous and influential in the service to others.

I have also been hugely inspired by Mary Robinson, whether as president for Ireland, or as the UN rights Commissioner. In her powerful book, *Everybody Matters – A Memoir*, I was typically moved by her vast amount of courage, illustrated in the following paragraph:

"On the evening of the event, the hall was absolutely full. There was a terrific buzz of excitement. For a moment I felt a surge of anxiety and nervousness, remembering JM Kelly's admonition that mine was not an appropriate topic. What I was about to say was radical; I would be attacking some sacred cows, and I had no idea how my idea would be received. As soon as I started speaking, the adrenaline helped me find my voice. I spoke

about the 'special position' of the Roman Catholic Church in the Irish constitution, and how the laws were enforcing Catholic morality, mistakenly equating 'sin' with 'crime'. I espoused removing from the constitution the prohibition on divorce, lifting the ban on use of contraceptives, and decriminalising homosexuality and suicide, on the basis that these were personal moral issues that should not be subject to the law of the state but should be up to the individual to choose, based on his or her own moral and religious code. When I finished speaking there was a prolonged silence, and then came great applause. This was a seminal moment for me, a moment of validation. This was why I had studied so hard; this was what law was about. There was no overt dissension at the time; that would come later, so I sought to implement these ideas."

Therefore, I define LQ, a legacy, as:

Daring to live a life that combines courage and inspiration, transcending far beyond serving oneself, to all that we could possibly influence. It does not matter how large or small the act, only that it positively lasts beyond our tenure.

Many readers and I are very fortunate to live in an economy of capitalism and democracy, which in some respects works, although it has its pitfalls. In essence we see extreme wealth and power in its broadest meaning. This is experienced by comparatively few people and, so, extreme responsibility goes with this. It's important that those of us, who are fortunate enough to be in these positions, help to tackle the issues that are affecting our world today.

In what is fast becoming a connected and transparent world, where information is shared freely, we have seen powerful momentum built to tackle some of the toughest issues. As a result, much is already happening to reduce: our mortality rates, pollution, inequality, and improve the general standards of living. These things don't happen on their own, it needs people with the power and the influence to make the required change happen. Whilst there are many issues, it is also the case that some of the greatest injustices and inequalities exist right on our doorsteps, in our communities, and in our workplaces. Therefore the opportunity to make a difference is far closer than we think. It does not matter the size, or the scale of our contribution, only that we leave something behind, or that we enhance something so that it's in a better place than before we came along.

Legacy also requires us to be proactive: it is the capacity, courage and willingness to notice the issues and effect change. We therefore have responsibility for the decisions we make and the influence of the legacy that we leave behind. The impacts of our decisions ripple far beyond our teams, organisation and even tenure. It is the shadow that we cast that has implications, long after we left the room or our organisation. I believe that most leaders want to have a positive impact through their organisation. There comes a point where it is no longer about power and financial gain. A true inspiring leader longs to add real value and leave a legacy - one that doesn't die, but stands the test of time. As one witty friend remarked, *"Aim to be a legend in your lifetime and not just in your lunchtime."*

LQ is not something that is beyond us, or bigger than us, and it can occur in our simple daily acts. There is a saying *'words create worlds'*. We should be very aware of the words in the language we use. Often as leaders we barely even notice these acts and yet the affects can be life-changing for the those we lead. A legacy therefore is something that we can simply integrate into our day-to-day behaviours. It can be demonstrated in each interaction we choose to have, or not to have, each decision we take or not to take. This is not about how valuable we are, but the value that we add that ensures a positive difference.

Consequences of Lack of LQ

The true power of a diverse world is the concept that we are all born equal. Our contexts, cultures and lives may differ but our basic fundamental rights should be the same. However, this perspective undoubtedly depends on people believing in it, wanting it and – most of all – protecting it. Powerful leadership does not necessarily equate to inspiring leadership. I believe that one of the biggest diseases in our society today is that of power – another narcissism. We see too often the trade-off between basic humanistic values and compassion for greater power, control and status, and so equality becomes far more challenging for this to be realised.

It is hard to believe that widespread discrimination and, even oppression, continues on the basis of gender, ethnicity, religious belief and sexual orientation. We continue to see personal gain at the expense of others. Why is it that minority groups are still oppressed by traditions and culture, at times quite viciously? For me, these malicious or extreme acts are not only the overt ones that we see and hear about.

They can also be the psychological bullying that takes place in many of our organisations today. They can be borne out of the subconscious biases that seep through to our behaviours and make our organisational cultures toxic.

The story of Lady Ashton, who has been credited with playing a key role in pulling off one of the 'biggest diplomatic coup in the history of EU foreign policy' – the landmark deal with Iran to rein in its nuclear ambitions. Yet, her appointment was greeted with a mixture of male condescension and ill-concealed derision. The French dubbed her 'Lady Qui?' implying they don't know who she is. At societal levels, we also see acts of bullying and aggression at their most extreme. Take, for example, the story of Malala Yousafzai, the young Pakistani girl who was shot in the head by the Taliban gunmen. Her 'crime'? Having spoken up about the right girls to be educated. After weeks in intensive care she fortunately survived, and is now a beacon of courage and hope.

There is an expression, *'Go on, try and impress me; you walk the gauntlet of my scorn, while I pass judgement on you and your ideas'*. It's the cynics, sceptics and fearful that use tactics to demean, undermine and ridicule those who go against the flow. They sit in judgement about everyone else, but fail to have the humility to admit their own failings. The funny thing is, these pre-historic attitudes make dinosaurs of such leaders, demonstrating their irrelevance and disconnection in a modern-day society.

I also spoke earlier in the book about delayed gratification. Yet, our performance and reward systems measure us on instant results and respond to our desire for instant gratification. We are most commonly measured through a 'balanced' scorecard of results based on: profitability, employee engagement, strategic intent, and delivering shareholder value. The question is, who are we answerable to and in service of? As executive boards, our responsibility to our shareholders is focused on delivering short-term results and assuring the long-term health of the company. With the fleeting nature of C-Suite job tenures, their impact ripples through beyond their time in the organisation.

On the positive side, we have seen some shifts where organisations have restructured bonus systems to mitigate the risks and have delayed the benefit of their compensation. Sadly, we also hear examples of the return to the days of high risk and high short-term reward, yet long-term significant damage to their clients and, potentially, the economy. Despite a heavy emphasis by our media to demonise particular sectors, such as the bankers and politicians, it is fair to say that it is not exclusive to them. Nor does it mean that the majority are corrupt. In fact, to give perspective it is a very small minority who gain such high profile benefits and negative media coverage. The vast majority of people in business and politics are hard-working, honest and well-intentioned individuals who go to work each day intending to do a great job.

Leadership gives power and responsibility to influence change. Too often we have seen leaders abuse this power. There is no doubt that creating more diverse leadership will affect positive change. By addressing cultures and tradition as influential forces, we are able to re-frame gender roles in society. We cannot get ahead if half the population don't hold positions of influence. It is essential for our economic growth, stability and security.

However, this is not the answer to everything that goes wrong! I believe we must also be more considered in the content of our debate. I often hear sentiments that corruption would not exist or unspeakable atrocities would not be possible if women were in charge.

Women are more likely to rise to positions of power in open and democratic systems, which are less tolerant of abuse. Our history has shown evidence of equally bad behaviour by women and men. If you recall from chapter on IQ, there is a biological implication when they gain stature. The sense of power produces the dopamine and testosterone, or our own fears cause an amygdala hijack, or our own hardwiring based on past patterns and belief systems, resulting in us acting differently than would be expected. These gender generalisations that suggest 'Women are good and men are bad', can be very misleading.

Brutal bullying and atrocities are not only the prerogative of a few bad men. They can be committed, or even encouraged, by women too.

We have witnessed this in one of the most horrific cases in Rwanda, where Agnes Ntamabyariro reportedly became one of the most influential perpetrators in the genocide. Whilst again extreme in nature, it is a demonstration of the devastating impact of excessive status, power and emotion at its most destructive.

What is more common and clearly less extreme, and yet unpleasant to be on the receiving end of, are the alpha-female behaviours. One frequent issue we hear about are women leaders who are trying to emulate alpha-males and consequently they have diminished their natural empathy and humility. For example, one female leader was brusque to the point of rudeness, dismissive of colleagues and alternating between being a bully and a charmer. She would later apologise for her outbursts and give presents to make up for it. The telling sign was the numerous presents around the office, which indicated the trail of destruction she left behind her.

With three cases of bullying against her, she agreed to a compromise agreement and moved on. The concern is that her conduct was not fully addressed and so the likelihood is not much will change in her behaviour as she moves to a new organisation.

So, the question really is, how can we, both male and female leaders, maintain our authenticity and compassion at whichever level we are operating?

In this transparent world enhanced by social media, disclosure and access to facts, we are fortunately able to gain insight to moral and ethical injustices in order to take positive, corrective action.

When something has gone wrong we have vigilant custodians who have a voice that is heard and understood such as stakeholders, customers, employees and constituents.

Leadership firmly places us in the public arena, where a strong moral code and leadership by example is demanded.

There is a consequence, however. Our judgements and perceptions of other's failings have become the modern spectator sport. As we respond with emotional outrage and commentary, with a passive and often virtual contribution we should not confuse that with affecting real change. Stepping into a position of leadership and finding one's voice is tough. Leadership is often lonely and not for the faint-hearted.

Take for example, the polarised responses when strong independent women or men with a voice find courage to speak up against certain issues. For example, when Sheryl Sandberg wrote the book 'Lean In', there is no doubt she prepared herself for mixed opinions and most certainly a backlash. Now, why on earth is this the case?

We often ask of others to walk the talk. We can only have credibility as leaders if we are leading by example. If we redefine what is inertia and what is movement, maybe we will start to unlock the potential that is within us all to affect change.

President Theodore Roosevelt's quote from a speech in 1907 at the Sorbonne in Paris is just as relevant today for women and men:

"It's not the critic who counts. It's not the man who points out how the strong man stumbled. Credit belongs to the man who really was in the arena, his face marred by dust, sweat, and blood, who strives valiantly, who errs to come short and short again, because there is no effort without error and shortcoming.

"It is the man who actually strives to do the deeds, who knows the great enthusiasm and knows the great devotion, who spends himself on a worthy cause, who at best, knows in the end the triumph of great achievement. And, who at worst, if he fails, at least fails while daring greatly, so that his place shall never be with those cold and cruel souls who know neither victory nor defeat."

As we gain powerful leadership positions within our organisations and society the question is, what kind of legacy do we want to be responsible for leaving behind?

How can LQ help you as a Leader?

Some consider that Eleanor Roosevelt was the power behind the throne of the US president himself. However, I believe that belittles her contribution as a significant female leader in her own right, as witnessed by her statement made at the United Nations in New York:

"Where, after all, do universal rights begin? In small places, close to home – so close and so small that they cannot be seen on any maps of the world. Yet they are the world of the individual person; the neighbourhood he lives in; the school and college he attends; the factory, farm or office where he works. Such are the places where every man, woman, and child seeks justice, equal opportunity, equal dignity without discrimination.

"Unless rights have meaning there, they have little meaning anywhere. Without concerted citizen action to uphold them close to home, we shall look in vain for progress in the larger world."

Through the distorted filter of stories that we hear through social media, it is sometimes difficult to see the true results of the hard work by many inspiring leaders over the decades.

By way of illustration, in Bono's enlightening TED Talk (www.ted.com), he describes how the sharing of information, which is now technologically available to us, is so powerful that it can challenge inequality. He states that, *"Facts, like people, want to be free; and when they're free, liberty is just around the corner."* He explores how, when facts are presented to us they challenge apathetic behaviours that eventually lead to inertia.

What is most compelling are the stories of progress and achievement. In our efforts to tackle issues of inequality in some of the most deprived places, we have significantly reduced issues such as death rates, child mortality and severe poverty whilst increasing access to education.

Bono stresses what drives him 'nuts' is that most people seem unaware of this progress.

With so much attention on what's not working with gender parity and equality, it is easy to miss the great progress that is actually being made. Inspiring male and female leaders *are* making a difference and leaving a sustainable legacy.

Messages of 'disappointment' belie the reality. We are tackling some of the toughest challenges that shake our cultures, traditions and infrastructures to the very core. It is not for me to define what our own personal legacy must be. These stories are the legacy. They stand in their own right as an example and inspiration to us.

Rewiring the Organisation

When I interviewed **Chris Sullivan** it was clear he was a part of the new breed of leadership. Passionate, yet humble, he has a well-respected reputation and his team hugely admire him. As a result, they have nominated him for various awards.

Chris shared with me, *"I am inspired by the extent of my role which combines the ability to run a huge organisation and fuel the engine that affects our external customers, whilst working with the broadest mass-markets. I believe it is not enough to say we deliver customer service. We need to find specific things that create enough value for the customer. Customers are looking for a return to the old-fashioned bank, with managers who understand their needs and can build relationships with them.*

"We need to get back to professional banking standards and regain the trust of our customers and our people. This means that we don't just take short-term actions that damage things for the long term. Banks are omnipresent and have, for years, facilitated bad decisions. It's wrong and society bites back. We should not make decisions that are to the detriment of our customers or to society. We need to understand the organisation as part of society, we need to build to underpin society and look for the opportunities to role model and influence.

"To become more customer-centric we need to encourage more qualified women through to senior positions and get them economically active. We need to attack each of the barriers that are preventing this from happening.

"There are not enough positive role models, mentors, networks and group interventions to facilitate this. There are many small and medium sized businesses led by women. The gender challenge is a very powerful one. This links back to purpose and legacy in that it must become the mission and vision for the organisation. Corporate Social Responsibility has got itself a bad name. It is not embedded in commercial reality. Our next generation and graduates are more resourceful and aware of the societal agenda. Our efforts to act as guardians and influence must be genuine and sustainable."

Organisations and employees, more than ever before, are getting actively involved in their communities. It's no longer just the business agenda: leaders want to feel they are making a real and sustainable difference in the world. People in organisations are taking up the gauntlet and getting involved in charitable fundraising, where they feel greater fulfilment through extending their contribution to society.

Stronger Communities

I also feel fortunate that I live in a society where the leadership does work extremely hard to ensure basic human rights, not just in our own country, but also with our international neighbours. These rights ensure everyone has access to education, health and opportunities. Whilst we will all note there is more to be done at every level, there is a significant amount that has already been achieved. Not every person around the world has these same basic privileges. For example, I would highlight the influence of Naomi Eisenstadt who led Sure Start and the Social Exclusion Taskforce. She and her team, supported by government, made a deep and positive impact affecting those who come from disadvantaged backgrounds.

I also had the pleasure of interviewing **Baroness Stedman-Scott OBE, DL** CEO of Tomorrow's People. She has a very natural, easy and down to earth leadership style, combined with both a passion and compassion for her work. Baroness Stedman-Scott shared: *"Tomorrow's People has gone from strength to strength since our foundation in 1984. In that time we've helped over 465,000 disadvantaged people on their journey into employment. I feel really passionate about the work that I do. How could I not be?*

"What drives me is very simple – to get up each morning and help our clients to get and keep a job! Running an organisation like Tomorrow's People is challenging and demanding, as it would be for any business of our size. Leading a charity is no different from leading any other business – we have ambitions and a firm view of where we want to get to, the only difference is that our profits are reinvested so that we can do more for the people we are here to serve, rather than distributing dividends to shareholders."

When we constantly notice all of the things that need to be fixed, we often miss or ignore the great progress that is being achieved.

The Greater Good

I was extremely impressed by the personal strength of **Claire Hall,** an HRD at Centrica. Ignoring advice from family and friends, she pursued her dream to make a highly positive impact and difference.

"I had been arranging a charity bike ride involving over 760 miles with 600 people, 50 of whom rode the whole way. We raised £750,000 for Great Ormond Street Children's Hospital. Our Managing Director spoke about 'Everyone getting over the finish line safely and encouraged us to all look after one another.' He was a very experienced cyclist, so cycled at the back of the group. He could easily have crossed the finish line in the top three every day. But to him it wasn't about winning, it was about everyone getting through each day safely and as a team. No one was ever left behind. This truly is 'leading from the back'. You feel so much better when you cross the line as a team.

"We were due to ride on the Saturday, but the Tuesday before I was diagnosed with cancer. People closest to me didn't want me to go ahead with the ride saying, 'You should be saving your energy for the treatment' which was totally understandable. It was all well-meaning advice with sound logic, as I needed to be fit for the operation, but I felt compelled to do the charity bike ride. At a time when I felt like so much was being taken away from me, I wanted to do this. I didn't want to lose this too. I felt this was something I had control over and it was a good distraction to be part of something so special.

"When your life is turned upside down like this, it really gives you perspective about what's important. Before it happened I was always concerned with the future and not what was happening in the here and now. I've learned to live 'in the moment' more. People are constantly moving onto the next thing and missing what's happening. The downside is I've lost discipline when it comes to buying handbags and shoes that I love. I think, why wait!"

Pay it Forward

Lucy Ndungu from Kenya shared with me how important that it was that, after her own career success, she returned to her home village to make a positive difference. She established Hope for Teenage Mothers to provide care and counselling within schools located in the slums, with a focus on teenage pregnancies. Breaking down the stigma of rape and pregnancy, she developed a programme that enabled 150 young girls to return to school. She offered them another chance to break free of victimisation and provide a non-judgemental supportive environment. The programme aimed to 'Rewrite the Future' of the teenage mothers and their children. Since then the charity has impacted on hundreds of girls, children and families, helping to eradicate poverty amongst the most vulnerable.

Courage to Fight for Justice

Manal al-Sharif filmed herself driving a car in Saudi Arabia, where women are prohibited from driving. She posted the video on YouTube, called on women to participate in a Women2Drive campaign. It attracted 12,000 fans to a Facebook page, which she'd collaborated in producing called 'Teach Me How to Drive So I Can Protect Myself'. She was arrested and nine days later, amongst a groundswell of protest, she was released from jail. Such courageous acts challenge the status quo that reinforces inequality and lack of fairness.

Words Shifting Worlds

Sophie Perreard shared, *"I was working in Darfur, Sudan, as Senior Protection and Advocacy Manager for women and children programmes. Consider, normally you would have villages of 5000 people, but here with the conflict the villages turned into camps of up to 80000 people. Gender-based violence was happening on daily basis, including domestic violence inside the camp, but*

also sexual violence, mainly outside the camps. Women and girls as young as 5 or 6 years old, would leave the camp to collect firewood to cook. This is when most of the sexual assaults would take place. Rape of women and girls had become a common form of violence in this conflict, which started in 2003.

"Part of our humanitarian intervention was to set up centres where women would meet and develop life-skills through various activities. They were leading their projects and were involved in all stages of the project cycle: it was not what we wanted them to do, it was what they wanted to do - even if they chose projects which subsequently failed. This was part of the learning and the ownership approach we decided to use. They would make some handicraft that they would then sell at the airport shop or in the market, which would provide them with a small income. Part of the earning would also go to the centre's social fund to support survivors of gender based violence. In the centers, they learned how to read and write their language - Arabic; they were so proud as they learnt how to read the Koran, which is a very important part of their culture (before they would learn it by heart but were not able to read). Literacy classes allowed them to read stories to their children. Women would develop books based on their culture, which is so important to them.

"Just to be clear, the conflict was at its peak in the entire Darfur region and consequently there was a lot of sensitivity, especially with the militia groups (Janjaweeds). Security of these women was our priority. We had some high profile visitors coming over to see what was really the situation in Darfur. We regularly organised for them to meet with the women but the local people would hardly speak out, fearing reprisal by the militias. The usual approach when foreigners would ask the question: 'What are the issues you face?' would be to get the standard answers 'Women get raped if they go out of the camps' but not the full stories. So we organized some workshops and some of them focused on how to pass on messages; how to have an impact. We shared tools and they adapted them to what they felt was most relevant to their context. One thing they did not appreciate was meeting people who would pretend to listen and immediately try to impose on them solutions from other countries, which were not adapted to the current

conflict situation or not in line with their culture.

"There was an average of four women's centres per camp, and women from the displaced community and host community would elect women committees for each centre who would then elect women leaders for each camp. Women committees were also endorsed by the overall camp committee, which would include some women leaders as representatives of some specific sectors. We worked intensively together on capacity building and women empowerment.

"At one stage, the United Nations Under-Secretary-General for Humanitarian Affairs and Emergency Relief Coordinator – Jan Egeland – managed to get approval by the Government to visit Darfur and part of his agenda was to meet the women of Darfur and hear directly from them what was happening. Security was clearly very tight and the Government had already refused granting him access a number of times. So this was a great opportunity for the women to be heard by one of the most influential people from the International Community. To avoid putting those women at risk, we had to organise a secret meeting as part of his tour. We arranged for the women representatives to come from each camp very early and prepare their meeting. We created a secured lunch where he could meet the women with no media or anyone else apart from the women, his translator and us. The head of the women leaders was nine months pregnant and started to have contractions!

"Jan Egeland thanked them for agreeing to meet with him and asked them to explain what the situation was right now for women and girls.

"At that moment the head of the Sheikhas (women leader) told him: 'Instead of us telling you we have prepared a poem for you to describe what's happening'. Poetry plays a very important role of the Darfuri culture. My team and I didn't know that they had prepared this. The head of the Sheikhas read the poem, which was three pages long, sharing all the incidents that had happened in the camps and surrounding during the last two weeks. Instead of just describing the issues, the poem was divided in three sections: description of the situation, what was being done at the time and what we wanted him to do to help them.

"They shared about the fact that they made fuel-efficient stoves, which

reduced the number of trip outside the camps for search of firewood and therefore reduced the risk of being attacked by Jenjaweeds; they explained the women's groups, the support to survivors and what the NGOs and UN were doing to help. They shared that they didn't want UNAMID armed forces 'to be with us when we go outside the camp collect firewood, but instead to secure the area'. It was very compelling. The leader, who was having her contractions, handed the poem to the UN Under-Secretary-General for Humanitarian Affairs and said, 'This is for you to put in your office on display, so that every day you will remember the women of Darfur.' This was a real achievement. They kept their culture and they passed on the messages of what they wanted to see happening to one of the most influential people in the world at the time, in order to assist the displaced population and particularly women and girls from Darfur.

"These are the women who influence; they are really strong and inspirational. They manage to pass on very important messages in the most memorable way."

When more is not about having, it's about being

Linda Cruse, a nurse and single Mum, changed her life completely, most eloquently described in her book, *Machine Guns and Marmalade*. She was determined to make a difference when the 2004 Tsunami hit killing 230,000 and took immediate action to help. With a backpack and plane ticket, she gave up everything to enter a whole new word devastated by the tragic aftermath of the tsunami. She has since embarked on an unusual journey, moving from project to project around the world, assisting in some of the most catastrophic disasters. She has brought aid and teaching skills to the victims, from war-torn refugees to the most poverty stricken areas in the world. She has faced some of the most horrific and even life threatening situations, yet continues to work on helping communities.

Giving back with no expectation

Shola Awolesi of Save the Children shared how generous people were in using their skills to support charitable projects. She described, *"In the last couple of years I have been developing the coaching agenda and creating*

431

partnerships. We evaluated our programmes and found we have delivered £500,000 of pro-bono coaching. My experience of working with the charity is the passion for making a difference.

"I see a lot of reluctant leaders, not interested in the labels, just the agenda. There are a lot of unsung heroes that just get on with the day to day. Embarking on my coaching qualifications provided a real 'Aha!' moment for me. As a leader it all boiled down to the one-to-one skills, which has validated what's important. The time and space that coaching gives you is amazing and something that we can really harness. In addition to this, I've seen the value and impact of engaging with young people providing mentoring, and coaching."

Leading the Way

Debrah Dhugga is the successful General Manager at the Dukes Hotel in the heart of London. As an inspiring and talented leader, I asked about her leadership style, *"Be in Control to Control. If you expect your team to work hard and produce quality content, you're going to need to lead by example. There is no greater motivation than seeing the boss as keen as everyone else, showing that hard work is being done on all levels. We all carry luggage! Knowing what you want, sharing the idea and giving the team drive to get on and deliver, it makes it exciting for everyone. Like any business you have to stand out from the crowd to get talked about. Reach for the stars!"*

As an advocate for diversity, she recognised the growing need for creating a female friendly customer environment. Appreciating that travelling for women can be an intimidating experience, she has developed tailored services to meet their needs. For example, female members of staff handle all room service and housekeeping requirements to creating a more inclusive vibe and ambience to areas like the bar and lounge. This sensitive insight into the needs of the customer has seen positive results and increased their revenues. Debrah is also keen to encourage women in hospitality careers and sees LQ as core to her values. When asked about career advice she would give to other women Debrah said, *"I remember being told over and over again I would never make money in the hospitality industry [because] it's a job, not a career. My message, especially to women in the industry, is to be strong, live your dream, do what you believe is right, work hard, share success, and don't be afraid to ask questions along the way."* Outside of work Debrah enjoys helping others and supporting people less fortunate than herself.

These success stories are not unique. Around the world we are seeing the courageous acts of individuals helping to make a greater difference for humanity and society. Organisations are taking positive steps to affect change and assume greater responsibility for driving value beyond the immediate shareholder. More than ever before, we see societal issues of sustainability, legacy and stewardship becoming even more main-stream. All of the inspiring leaders in this book are actively involved in various causes, whether it's helping to bring greater equality, a variety of charity and local community work through events and fundraising, campaigning to raise awareness, mentoring, or even micro-financing.

When we make choices about the trade negotiations we make, the suppliers and the products that we use and the partnerships that we engage with, we must ask ourselves are we doing the right thing. Are we sourcing and behaving ethically? Are we helping others to be the best that they can possibly be, helping them to realise their own full potential?

I have been personally inspired by Rick Warren who, based on the concept of 'tithing', gives a percentage of his earnings back into charitable programmes. This has helped form the basis for how we manage Clareo Potential and the resources we use. In our partnerships with independent consultants and coaches, we have agreed to contribute a percentage of our time, resources and profits back into our selected charitable projects to helped disadvantaged young people and minority groups. Working with the inspiring women, we are launching new programmes and expeditions to support the fundraising, which is being launched alongside the book. Book profits will be donated to selected charitable projects too (if you would like to know more or get involved, please do visit my website). I have been very passionate about helping others, particularly given my own personal circumstances. It's something that is hugely rewarding and meaningful. It can consume us, however, and an early lesson for me has been to balance my desire to give in abundance with staying afloat: physically, financially and emotionally. So, I've personally found it's important to manage both effectively so it can be sustainable.

Giving something back, or paying-it-forward, does not have to be a major thing. It can be in its most basic form and yet have a huge impact. When it comes to a legacy, this is absolutely nothing to do with oneself and one's needs. It is everything to do with abundance, stewardship and making a positive difference.

People often think, 'How can I, as just one individual, make a difference when others before me haven't?' However, on studying history we can clearly see that all of the major changes have been initiated by a single individual or small group of determined men and women intent on fighting for human rights. I'm reminded of the parable of 'The Starfish Story', which has been told in a number of different versions. Here is one I find captures the essence of LQ:

The Starfish

A young man is walking along the ocean and sees a beach on which thousands and thousands of starfish have washed ashore. Further along he sees an old woman, walking slowly and stooping often, picking up one starfish after another and tossing each one gently into the ocean.

"Why are you throwing starfish into the ocean?" he asks.

"Because the sun is up and the tide is going out and if I don't throw them back in they will die."

"But, old woman, don't you realise there are miles and miles of beach and starfish all along it! You can't possibly save them all. You can't even save one-tenth of them. In fact, even if you work all day, your efforts won't make any difference at all."

The old woman listened calmly and then bent down to pick up another starfish and threw it into the sea. "It made a difference to that one", she softly replied.

Author's Note: Please be aware that the following inspiring woman's story contains issues of abuse and the resulting pain and how she overcame this to become a successful woman with an agenda for paying-it-forward.

Kezi Silverstone
Musician, Entrepreneur and Philanthropist

"A few months after I was born, my father left the country to go to the USA. My mother struggled to cope; she was vulnerable, fragile and trying hard to fight the emotions of my father's sudden departure. Amongst her confusion, she would leave me with friends and acquaintances, just a few days at a time at first, but the pattern kept repeating itself. She would leave me, come back for me and take me home, but eventually the length of time that passed grew. A few days became a week, a week became two and two became three. One day she left me with a woman she barely knew who expected her to come back for me after a few days. Three or four weeks passed and the woman, who was advanced in years, couldn't continue to take care of me. She called the social services and Barnardo's took me into care. I was about 13 months old.

"My mother spent the next few years trying to get her life together. I spent the next few years in several different foster homes, not really knowing where I would be from one day to the next. I would wake up with a different family on a regular basis, never really knowing who would be my 'mum and dad' next. Eventually I went to live with a family who had other foster children a lot older than me. I was very quiet and withdrawn but eventually I took to one of the older boys and 'clung' to him.

"Our foster parents had marital issues and needed time out to try to fix them. We had a foster 'aunt and uncle'– the aunt was the sister of our foster father. One day they came to the house and told us that the older children were going to stay with them for a holiday. They were foster parents themselves and over the years many children had passed through their care.

Because I was tiny and the foster aunt and uncle were progressed in years, they decided that I should stay where I was. When I discovered my foster brother was leaving, I was very distressed, crying and shouting 'and me'. Little did I know that I sealed my fate that day, because they agreed to take me with them...

"We were meant to stay for two weeks, but we never went back and instead remained with our foster aunt and uncle. So bizarrely, our foster parents became our aunt and uncle and our foster aunt and uncle became our foster parents. A truly difficult and confusing transition to make yet again.

"On several occasions over the next couple of years, my natural mother got in touch with the social services. She felt she wanted me back. Because I had been placed in care, court dates were set for my mother to appear in order to prove that she could take care of me. Sadly on every occasion my mother didn't show. A final court date was set and they advised her that if she didn't attend, all rights to me would be taken from her by the courts. She didn't turn up...

"When I was about 5 or 6 years old we moved from the south of London to just south of the Midlands to accommodate my foster father's job. Very soon after this, the sexual abuse began. I don't remember the exact moment, but as the years passed I was very aware of what was happening to me. I was insular, quiet and withdrawn as a young child, very isolated and surrounded by fear. When I was 9 years old my foster mum got very sick. She died when I was just 10 ½ years old. It was crushing because she was one of the small good parts in it all, her and my foster brothers and sister. I loved them deeply and as they were much older, with families of their own in most cases (some of them still living in the South of London), being with them was my respite.

"She died at home and on the day she died, my foster father wasn't in the house so my foster sister gave me the news that my mother had died. Then I walked to school, alone. I remember this so vividly and the sadness of that experience has never truly left me. When I came home from school, nobody was there, just a woman who I had never seen before. She made me tea and looked after me. I wasn't allowed to go to the funeral and was instead sent off

to school as though nothing had happened.

"For all of my traumatic early experiences, my foster mother's death is one of the most painful long-term memories. No one was there to pick me up, hold me and rescue me. I remember such isolation and loneliness. By the time I was 12 years old I was practically running the house. Left alone whilst my foster father worked, I made dinner and did chores when I got home from school. I don't remember going out with my friends a great deal. My foster father restricted my movements and so for the best part, I was imprisoned in the house with that awful man. Not having anybody to turn to because I couldn't speak of the terrible things that were happening to me.

"After my mother died, he also began to physically abuse me. I'm not sure why he started to hit me; I think he was caught up in the trauma and frustration of being left alone when his wife died. The sexual abuse got worse as I got older, more and more regular and more and more invasive. I couldn't escape it. He said that if I told anyone, he would send me away, take my brothers away from me; I adored them so I was scared into silence. He used it as ammunition to control me; it worked. There was also a part of me that was scared that nobody would believe me…

"I had never known what it was like to be loved, shown affection and to live a happy life like other children. My self-esteem was virtually non-existent and I had never known any other life than this, so, consequently, part of me felt that if he sent me away, I could actually end up somewhere even worse than the abusive life I was already in. Better the devil you know…

"When I started secondary school I came out of myself a little, because I had a great love of food and the arts. I started home economics, cooking and drama. Then, a year or so in, things got very confusing. A roller coaster of emotions, the abuse, and loss of a mother, coupled with adolescence had me go off the rails a little. I played truant from school and when pushed by school friends, started stealing little things from the local newsagents. Friends would bait me and although I would be scared it was an adrenaline rush. Mostly a big part of me thought it was a way of fitting in with the other kids. I played truant more and more, going to the school register and then leaving to hang out with my friends.

"One day I woke up to myself and thought, 'If I don't change this I'm

destined for the scrapheap.' I was very strong in English and literature and naturally quite academic. I was pretty crap at maths and science and had no real enthusiasm for those subjects. But I did know that I had to fight this roller coaster of fear, confusion and bad behaviour. I was 14 years old and I needed to do something positive with my life. I needed to find a channel for the bad energy and somehow turn it into something good.

"I joined a local theatre group, in the first instance because I quite fancied one of the young leading actors there. He was confident, outgoing and extremely talented. I was very drawn to him as he was everything I wasn't and felt I could never be. But, ironically, I shone. It was the strangest thing. When I threw myself into a role I became that character and got to leave 'me' behind and be 'someone else'. A revelation, a form of escapism and most of all it took me out of the house away from that abusive man.

"Within months I was taking lead roles and went on to win 'most promising young actress of the year' in a National play festival for my role in an Alan Ayckbourn play, ironically called In Need of Care. *My school careers adviser told me I should go to drama school but my response was that acting was unpredictable and that I needed to focus on a more stable career. I had grown up before my time. I wanted to be a social worker, or a probation officer. But my love of the arts never faded...*

"As my confidence in the arts grew, my love of music developed and I forced myself to make the positives out-weigh the negatives. I was 16 when I secured my first modelling contract, working part time for a fashion house. Then I started my own band. I decided I could either be the victim of my childhood and circumstances, or I could be a survivor. I had reached a crossroads in my life and knew I had to find a way out. I no longer wanted to be a victim; I wanted to be a survivor.

"So I did find a way...

"I left and I never came back. I started a whole new life.

"I was no longer the child trapped in a world with no voice, I had reached a place in my life where I felt I could survive. My work in theatre had given me some of the confidence that I had so deeply lacked. My love of animals helped me to find strength too. They are so vulnerable, so dependent and so unconditional and when I was really sad and lonely I found solace in them. I

would pick the animals up, hold them close to me and when I put them back down they would run off and find their 'place'. I think that's what I felt like, the little kitten that really wanted to be picked up and held. But if you put me down I would run away and find my 'place', because life had taught me to survive in that way. As I grew, my love of animals and their welfare became an important part of my life. I channelled time into animal welfare and I am patron of an animal sanctuary in Kent.

"And so, at 16 years old, I had to make a success of my life, on my own. And I did, I made my own way. At 17 I was running my own business, had a modelling contract; from which I was earning good money and I was the leader of a band. I set it up, created it, marketed it and employed all the musicians. The band became one of the most successful acts on the military circuit throughout the UK and Europe and, ironically, I became a modern day forces sweetheart! I was literally focusing my energies on succeeding, not depending on anyone else. I have never allowed myself to be dependent on anyone financially. I always wanted to be safe in the knowledge that if 'the shit hit the fan', then I would still manage somehow. I didn't have parents to cushion my falls, or to act as my safety net. When I looked behind me, there was nobody there to catch me; the only person there to save me was myself. I owned my first home when I was 18 and I set up my life so that I would never be trapped, because I had spent so much of my childhood trapped. Emotionally, I'm different because I'm very tactile, a very emotive person. If I love, I have no problem showing that love.

"Everything that had happened in my life didn't stop me letting people in. I didn't stop trusting people, I did the reverse; I wanted to be the exact mirror opposite of what people would expect given my chequered beginnings. I didn't want to be the cliché, the girl who shut down and didn't know how to connect, or show her feelings. If I let that happen to me, then it had beaten me. It had won.

"I set out on a mission to connect with people, to let them into my life and trust them. I didn't want to be the stereotypical cold, messed up, dysfunctional girl who couldn't love or be loved and was shut down emotionally. I didn't want to spend the rest of my life hating everything and everybody, blaming my childhood for a million sins and a million bad

personality traits. I didn't want to be devoured by it all.

"That's not to say that I haven't made bad decisions about people who have entered my life. There are times when my deep-rooted insecurities and fears have led me to make very bad decisions. I spent a vast amount of my life being afraid of people leaving me. I would grieve over everyone who left, whether they were good or bad; a separation dependency that stemmed from never knowing where I would wake up as a child. I've now learned to walk away from people who are bad for you because you spend years recovering from friendships and relationships that fundamentally suck.

"It took me many years to learn that we shouldn't concern ourselves too much with the people from our past, there's a reason why they didn't make it to our future. If people walk away for seemingly little reason, they were never good people in the first place and didn't deserve your love.

"My foster father died of cancer when I was in my late teens. He called me to his bedside and told me he hadn't been a good father, which was, quite frankly, the understatement of the year. He obviously wanted me to grant him some sort of absolution. When he died, it opened a can of worms for me. I went into turmoil. I think it was the realisation that I had no reason to keep the secret anymore. Perhaps I was afraid of what the consequences of opening up this dark secret would be...

"After my foster father died, I wanted to understand more about my biological parents so I went to Barnardo's. They gave me counselling and told me that my father, based in the United States, had in fact looked for me. I was a child at the time when he wrote to Barnardo's and they were not obliged to give him information about my whereabouts. I had to be the one to initiate contact by law. My father had become a very successful man in the USA, as a Realtor (real estate agent). He owned one of the largest real estate businesses in California. Our lives were so diametrically opposed...

"Sadly, my mother's life was a different story and the ravages of time had truly taken their toll...

"My career? I worked really hard for it. I loved my work as a theatre actress and thought that that would be where my life would take me primarily. I occasionally took musical lead roles in theatre but never considered myself a singer as such, although my directors told me

differently. They told me I had heart when I sang and that rode above technique. To be fair, in my opinion, I'm an all-rounder; I like to balance everything. I'm not the most technically skilled singer; I've never really gone for the big knockout punch. I never had vocal classes, however, when I sing I wear my heart on my sleeve. My life experiences have brought that to the surface, so, combined with the acting and creating the role, I become the girl in the story when she sings. Then I got into writing, poetry, song-writing, journalism and realised that the literacy talent I had shown in school had followed me. I wrote songs from a young age and found it a very important and cathartic experience. I got my first recording contract when I was still in my teens.

"I consider myself an average singer, an okay songwriter, a fairly good producer and not a bad composer. I know my limitations and never set my sights too high above those but I never stop learning, listening and creating and I always work towards the next small achievement. When I won my Faberge modelling contract it pushed my career forward a great deal but that came as a result of bloody hard work and commitment, treading the boards and taking the knocks. At 16/17, I was having an education, in a band travelling all over the UK and Europe. I was out on my own and paying my own bills. I had to take a lot of jobs, singing in the band, modelling, secretarial work, which I would do from home. I did anything I could to make money so I could pay my bills. When I was 18 I bought my own house. I had learned that I was not good at change, so I built a nest around myself and that was my safety and security. My home, the place where my stuff is...

"My career brought success both as a singer songwriter/composer and model. Faberge made me a well-recognised face and my music led me to work with some of the most prestigious songwriters and producers in the UK. My first single was number 5 across three national charts and was a success in both Europe and the United States and further releases have been a great success for me too. I have been fortunate enough to perform in stadiums, on national television, national radio and acclaimed venues across the UK, Ireland and China. I am proud of what I have created and for making the choice to fight for my dream and not let my past devour me. The girl on stage is my alter ego. The girl on stage has none of my insecurities. She turns into

a vivacious performer and off stage people expect her to be the same, but I'm not. I'm a real home person. I love animals, I love cooking, being with friends and loved ones and simply just being at peace with myself. People who meet me would never know that behind the seemingly confident person that walks into the room, that in my own little life, I am completely different. I didn't enjoy the media wheel that I had to inevitably get on when my career started to go forward. But I dealt with it with as much grace as I could muster. When it got too oppressive and too fake for me, then I got off. Instead, I focused my life on the quieter side of the industry, like film composing, music management and most of all, my charities.

"What has my life taught me and what have I witnessed? My natural mother, who had wrestled with herself over me for many years, wanted to find a way to keep me in her life but found it all too much to cope with. She thought I would be better off with another family who would raise me properly and give me security and safety. She could never have known the set of circumstances I would end up in. My circumstances were unfortunate and unusual – many kids go into families with loving and wonderful foster parents.

"There is a very small window in which a child will confess abuse. If there isn't someone there to hear those words, at that moment, there is a very good chance that the child will shut down and be forever trapped in a childhood, which will ultimately become adulthood.

"Being believed is the scariest part of this confession, which is why the confession doesn't come readily. People who do listen are the 'keepers'. But you need to find the courage to share and take the risk. Some people are naive about abuse, so it's our job to educate them. Others choose not to see it, to be in denial. Not being believed is one of the biggest stumbling blocks for any child or adult who has lived through abuse.

"I experienced this. Not being believed. I found a way through that, but then later being ostracised by the people who I thought had loved me, who I had sacrificed a great deal in my childhood to keep in my life, was and still remains one of the hardest blows. The people who ostracised me were a huge contributory factor to my insecurities and fears; they are responsible for the demons that still occasionally raise their heads. Betrayal is one of the

442

hardest things to deal with and to move on from...

"I wish more than anything that I hadn't trapped the story inside of me for so many years. But I felt I had no choice. I didn't want to risk not being believed again. My journey has been longer as a result, but I did it all by myself. I didn't seek therapy or counselling, I just found a way to channel the bad stuff and make it into something good. I have no one to thank for my recovery but me. In my latter years, ghosts still reared their heads occasionally and sporadic insecurities led me to make bad decisions, or not speak out when things hurt me. Equally when people took advantage of my non-confrontational nature and my eagerness to please, then my special people taught me to be strong enough to take the risk and put a hand up to people and say, 'stop, enough'.

*"As an abused child you feel shame. You think you must have done something very bad and been a terrible child to deserve that. It's our job to teach a child that it was **never** their fault.*

"Maybe my recovery is a bit of a revelation for me. I created little boxes in my head, put all the bad stuff in the boxes and put the lid on oh so tightly. As a teenager I started to wonder why my cunning plan wasn't truly working. With time I realised that you can't pretend it didn't happen, that it would all just simply go away. And so, I rethought those little boxes of mine. I left the stuff inside them, but I never put the lids on so tightly. Then once in a while, I would open a box, take a peek inside and then put the lid back on loosely. Thus, I controlled the boxes, they didn't control me. I chose when to look at my past and accept that it was there and I chose when not to.

"The first time Barnardo's approached me to come on-board as a role model, I turned them down. I wasn't ready. Although I'd moved on from my experiences, I wasn't ready to talk about them publicly. The second time they approached me I felt I was ready. I have nothing to be ashamed of. I wasn't the perpetrator; I was the victim. You spend a lot of your life trying to figure that out.

"I've come through those traumatic childhood experiences, I survived and I made something of my life. When I talk about my story, it's not about going into the detail. I do believe that less is more. I think body language says a lot. You can say something very simple and yet it can make a huge impact. The

story I'm sharing with you is far more than I would normally share.

"I created the Kezi Silverstone Trust because I wanted to continue to make a difference in a far more hands-on and organic way. I spent many years raising funds and awareness for charities and I decided it was time for me to make the decisions about what I was funding. It's very important for me to know exactly how the funds raised are being spent. So, we focus our efforts on very hands-on projects that make a real difference. I dedicate a large part of my life to vulnerable children because, when I think back, if someone had been there for me to help me to fix things and understand my innocence, then my journey wouldn't have been so immeasurably hard. If I change one child's life then that's incredible for me and I know that I have helped give that child their life back. If I can stop things in their tracks, whilst bad things are happening to them, help them to find courage and recovery so they never reach adulthood weighed down by the demons, then that is what I wish for them. We don't have to end up where we started. My journey was a hell of a lot longer and a hell of a lot tougher than it should have been, but I got there. I want to shorten that journey considerably for other vulnerable children.

"So you may look at me and say, 'Kezi, look at where you are now' and for that I thank you. But I am where I am in part because I was fortunate enough to be 'built' a fundamentally strong and robust person. But it's not acceptable for me to assume that everybody else is built that way. My mother wasn't. Some people need that big helping hand and that's where charities like The Kezi Silverstone Trust are so crucial. My strength has been a huge advantage for my recovery but there were times when I didn't believe it was there, didn't see it. My mission with the charity is to take my knowledge and teach children self-esteem, that someone believes in you, that deep down you have the strength, we just have to find it together. I don't want them to be 27 before that happens.

"London Rocks, staged at The Café de Paris in Piccadilly is in its fifth year and is an annual awareness and fundraising event with a very arty twist. It showcases some extraordinary talent, some high profile and some very new and fresh and combines with glitz and glamour, wonderful food and lots of fun. The Kezi Silverstone Trust is now the benefactor of London

Rocks.

"The Kezi Silverstone Trust pledges to help protect and rehabilitate children who are victims/survivors of sexual abuse, sexual exploitation, physical abuse, neglect, domestic violence and mental cruelty. It also pledges to provide support for children who are victims of poverty, protect and lend support to children who live with parents who have alcohol/drug addictions or mental health issues, provide support for child carers and lend support to children who are victims of bullying/cyber bullying.

"What have I learned from life? Love is a two way street, only cross the road for people who will meet you halfway and value you as much as you value them. Don't waste your time, energy and heart on people that are fundamentally toxic. Find a place where you are happy and content, with a few good people around you that love you for you and who care for you unconditionally. I've learned to figure out the good people. That's taken a great deal of time. Be true to yourself always and never regret the decisions you make in your life, because there's always a reason for those decisions at the time.

"Sometimes I would think that if one more bad thing happened, then I would never recover. Yet somehow I do find the strength. My cousin, who was also my best friend, was killed in the World Trade Centre attack. I recently lost my foster brother, who was very special to me; he died of cancer.

"I have suffered from Crohn's disease since I was 19 years old, quite probably brought about by stress as a child/teenager. I love food but have to eat healthy as much as possible in order to keep myself on an even keel and give me the vitality I need to juggle my life which is full of so many demanding projects. I set up Kezi's Veggie Kitchen with my business partner Helen who has food intolerances. KVK is primarily a vegetarian food company delivering to local homes and businesses alongside our dietary consultancy, but we also specialise in intolerance foods and foods that help people going through recovery from body damaging treatment for illnesses, such as chemotherapy. I also have an event company with Helen called Live & Loud Events, a music consultancy company and a music management company called JAKrock Music with another wonderful colleague. Live &

Loud Events is the creator of London Rocks and JAKrock Music collaborates with us to make the event the spectacular that it is today.

"Children should be cherished, loved and nurtured. But, the harsh reality is that for some children this will never be. Abuse comes in many guises and can touch anyone in any walk of life, rich or poor. It's never as far away from you as you think...".

Chapter Reflection:
Making a Positive Difference and Leaving a Sustainable Legacy

Myself:
- Is my life about having, or being?
- Am I living a life of survival, or significance?

My Relationships:
- How do I preserve and nurture my most cherished relationships?
- In the Starfish Story, how will I make a difference to that 'one'?

My Organisation:
- How can I be the steward, or guardian for the work that I do?
- What opportunities can I create to 'pay-it-forward'?

My Society:
- Which charitable or humanitarian causes do I wish to champion?
- How can I move from observing to taking positive action?

Chapter 13
Inspiring Leadership Integration

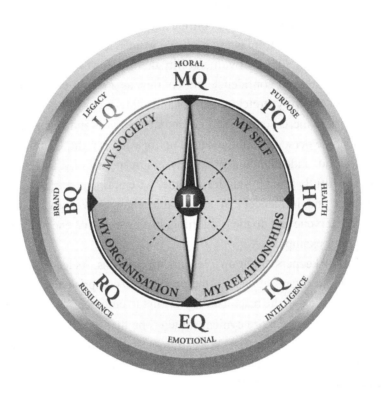

"I learned that courage was not the absence of fear, but the triumph over it. The brave man is not he who does not feel afraid, but he who conquers that fear."

Nelson Mandela (1918 -2013)

Author's Note: It was a poignant moment, as I finished writing *Inspiring Women Leaders*, Nelson Mandela passed away. He was a truly inspirational leader, who not only moved a nation but enlightened a world.

We need a new kind of inspirational and moral leadership in our world today.

As humans we have the wonderful capacity for combining logic and emotion – each has the power to confine and control us or, to set us free. We have heard the stories from many inspiring women leaders. They have shared willingly and with a level of vulnerability that we don't normally get access to. We can build our confidence and courage as a result, taking calculated risks, in order to truly stretch ourselves and achieve our full potential.

We see how increasing the level of moral standards and change can occur just by a single person's action to stand up for what is right. Communicating our truth, and understanding others, is our responsibility as leaders; we cannot be wilfully blind bystanders. Rather we can find power in our roles as the shapers and influencers of sustainable change. We always have the choice to intervene and do the right thing, in a manner that encourages others to follow our example.

We are the keepers of our own leadership compass. As leaders we are the stewards of our organisations and the people who comprise it. The decisions are ours to make and the responsibility is ours to embrace. We can choose to take an easier road, a more cynical route – one that holds onto old patterns and the experience of the past. We can immerse ourselves in our fears, our sense of injustices and become angry for what is, or might be. We can continue this road of self-preservation, playing small and focussing internally.

Or, we can take a more challenging path of transformation and abundance. By finding our courage to follow and nurture what we believe in our hearts to be right, then we can hold a steady course.

Our aspirations are deeply personal, our purpose too. Even if others attempt to impose limitations upon us, we know that they serve no one - apart from the egos of the insecure. We know that judgements are prone to subjectivity and bias. Yet squeezing ourselves out of shape because of this, will only be to the detriment of our authenticity. By reminding ourselves, *"We are good enough, we are clever enough, we are worthy enough"*, then we will not compromise ourselves.

Instead, we must search for compassionate wisdom that is discerning, avoiding the pitfalls of being judgemental of others and ourselves. We do not know the full picture, only the limited area of one's life, where the spotlight shines. The choices we make belong to ourselves and ourselves alone; all are completely relevant. That is as long, of course, as we adhere to basic humanist principles and rights.

Know that our mistakes do not define us, and, instead, become our route to new learning and wisdom. It is then that we will open our minds to the full power of freedom of thought. By believing that each and every one of us comes from the same place of good intent, we will open our hearts to greater collaboration, gratitude and compassion. By choosing people who give us energy, rather than drain energy from us, we will travel far easier and happier journeys.

Nothing important happens in life, without some form of compromise – not in work, nor relationships, love, or even progress. Nothing transformational in life occurs without some form of courage. We must talk about the sacrifices in real terms and make sure that the price is worth paying. Can we live with the consequences? We must appreciate the gains of bringing others on to achieve true equality, without fearing that in some way we will become disempowered. No true power emerges from fear, only from inspiration.

Now that we understand, more than ever before from the neurobiological evidence, that the patterns of our past do not define our future, we *know* we can affect change. We have choices – *always*. What is clear is that we are not alone. We have a sophisticated support system in our relationships and we are hugely resourceful. Our evolution confirms this. We just need to reach out and ask.

In our hyper-busy world, how do we *also* leverage the best of our past traditions and values? A return to a sense of community can only make us stronger. What effort does it *actually* take to care and reach out to others?

In a world of transparency, turbo-charged by new technologies, where the data presented to us tells the true story, inertia cannot serve us. With the growing momentum for doing what is right – not just for today but also for future generations – then ignorance and greed can only become yesterday's leadership.

In our institutions, we have the opportunity to transform from old traditions, cultures and models. These no longer serve this new kind of leadership. Being responsive and more creative to the changes in a free market will help us to attract and retain people and customers, whilst making a sustainable difference.

Metrics and statistics will not get us there. The real change will occur when our infrastructures respect and embrace diverse cultures and styles. This is not an issue of gender. This is an issue of inclusion. Through addressing the injustices of the minority as a result of dominant powers, we can leverage the opportunity for all of us to participate and collaborate in creating positive change.

We need to honour those who are making progress and it is only when we celebrate their successes and give them status that change will really occur.

By approaching this agenda with humility, compassion and courage, we create momentum, excitement and followership.

This is 21st century leadership, this is...

'Inspiring Leadership'

Chapter 14
Tools, Resources and Interventions

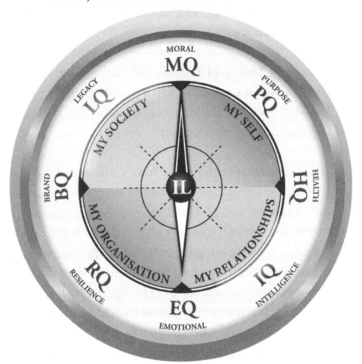

"I had a great leader who was pretty much a pitch master, exceptional at storytelling and how to communicate. I picked up many techniques from him. I learned that you can continue to have fun when even when it gets tough and that you also need to take people with you. It's important to understand what's important to business and people, using your own talents and authenticity to best effect and not be someone you're not. You don't have the room or space to be different – just do what you do, and well. I have been given the space to be who I really am. All of the opportunities have now cemented the experience for the role and helped me with self-belief."

Jo Whitfield
Finance Director

About This Chapter

This chapter contains a set of simple tools, resources and interventions to support you in your personal, and career, development. The chapter is divided into three sections:

Part 1:   **'Inspiring Tools and Techniques'** – a combination of simple tools and techniques related to each of the components of the Inspiring Leadership model. Building our self-awareness is the starting point for all successful development.

Part 2:   **'Inspiring Interventions'** – I have collaborated with some of the book's contributors and independent suppliers to share some of the fun, inspiring and powerful interventions to support you, your teams and, even, your personal relationships. These include retreats, team development, women's programmes, leadership expeditions (for the adventurous among you) and more. We have all agreed to the concept of 'Tithings': a traditional concept of giving a percentage of our profits back to vulnerable groups.

This is evolving all of the time so please my website **www.leighbowmanperks.com** for more information on products and details of the great projects and how you can get involved.

Part 3:   **Recommended Resources** – I have recommended some books, on-line resources including TED Talks and references to give you more information and inspiration about different topics.

Part One: Tools and Techniques

Building Self Awareness

1. Johari's Window

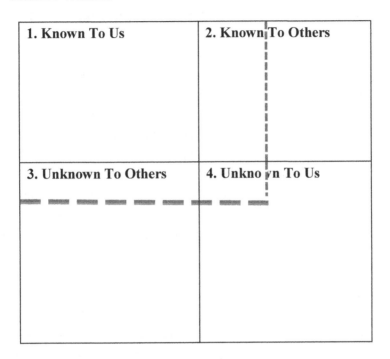

1. Known To Us	2. Known To Others
3. Unknown To Others	4. Unknown To Us

The purpose of the Johari's window technique is to create greater self-awareness. It helps you to build stronger and more trusting relationships, often achieved through controlled and relevant disclosure. Joseph Luft and Harrington Ingham in USA, 1955, designed this simple for box model and the model takes the first few letters of each of the first name and hence it is called 'Jo-hari'.

Charles Handy described it as being like a house with four rooms:

- **Room 1** is the open arena, which both we and other people know about ourselves.

- **Room 2** is our blind side, where others can see a lot about us, but we are not yet aware of it.
- **Room 3** is our hidden area or our façade, where we keep private things about ourselves which others don't yet know.
- **Room 4** is the unknown area, which neither we, nor others know about ourselves yet, but we can discover together.

Your aim is to extend the dotted line, so you can gain more insights into others' perceptions, help others' to know more about you and your life so you can build trusting relationships and also negotiate for what you need. Sometimes we put barriers up to protect ourselves or seem professional – this can sometimes feel disconnected from the people you work with.

Alternatively, too much vulnerability and disclosure can send different messages to your team. At times, be clear on what is relevant. As a leader, consider how you can also extend the dotted line for others too. From experience we have found that when you increase the size of your open arena you make yourselves more trustworthy and are likely to be a more inspiring leader.

2. Psychometrics

There are a number of psychometrics that create a wealth of insight about your: preferences and motivations, strengths, intellectual horsepower, emotional intelligence, leadership style, team effectiveness, and leadership derailers (such as your overdone strengths).

I would recommend working with a qualified psychometric assessor who is also an exceptional and accredited coach to facilitate the process. Often organisations use psychologists. However, this may provide the insight without the development to enable transformational shifts. For example, leaders have often fed back to me how they've undergone a rigorous assessment process, but there has been very little support afterwards. This is costly for the organisation and very frustrating for the individual. We all have something to bring to jobs and so putting the insights into context is extremely important. I fundamentally believe in the quality and sensitivity of feedback with someone who can support you as you do something about it.

3. Giving and Receiving Feedback

'Stop, Start, Same'; the Three S's are a quick and simple way to get some great feedback. This helps you to collate a clear set of feedback. You can be use this effectively with the team, in a one-to-one meeting or even with your key stakeholders.

4. WWW and EBI

WWW = What's Working Well and EBI = Even Better If. This is a very positive forward thinking way of how to deliver and receive feedback. I've often used this as part of team events when greater trust needs to be built, whilst also naming the 'elephant in the room'.

The 'elephant in the room' is the problem, which is stopping progress in the team, whilst everybody is being wilfully blind to it and pretending that it is not there.

MQ: Morality and Ethics

1. What You Value

What would be your answers to the following questions?

- What were the top 3 values you were taught, when growing up by someone you loved or admired?
- How far are you living those values?
- Where are you falling short?
- If they were with you now, what advice would they give you today?

As you build relationships with others, find out what they value most and how these values have been shaped by their life experiences.

This is very powerful in the early stages of building relationships with your team. Many inspiring leaders make special efforts to hold one-to-one meetings to explore these with their employees, peers, bosses and even their customers.

2. Become the Interrupter!

Know when, where and how to take a stance. But do find the courage to take a stance. In my research, many leaders recounted how people were hired for their voices and opinions and yet, for a variety of reasons, they held back. So ask yourself, *"As an inspiring leader, am I playing the part of the 'bystander', 'persecutor' and 'interrupter'?"*

Feeling comfortable that we take on a role that reflects our values and beliefs is critical to our own sense of wellbeing. As we have seen, in many cases over recent years, this is also true for the wellbeing of others too.

3. Chain Reaction

Aspire to make decisions that have no detrimental affect on you and others. When we consider the suppliers we use, our purchasing choices, the products, the people and customers affected by these decisions, do we feel confident in the ethical choices that we make? 'Making a deal with the devil' can only result in consequences later on down the line. Unfortunately, we have often seen this negatively impact beyond the leaders' tenures.

In the interest of sustainability, ethics and integrity, consider the 'end-to-end supply/value chain' to address the rotten and broken links. As described in the MQ chapter, the Dove Brand has had a profound influence of purchasing choices and brand integrity.

4. The Power of Influence

There is no doubt that with the beauty of power comes the potential to influence, making a positive or negative impact on those who follow a powerful leader. In popular belief The Roman Senators provided their successful Generals with a 'Triumph' – a grand procession of a scale, wealth and power that few would ever see in their lifetimes.

They also ensured that a servant travelled with the General whispering in their ear, 'Memento Mori'. This is loosely translated from Latin into "remember you are mortal". Such a reminder was to point out to leaders that whilst they were victorious and successful, they can equally face setbacks and disappointments in the following weeks. Remember it may be possible that you are wrong! Keeping our humanity and our humility are the marks of a truly inspiring leader.

PQ: Purpose and Meaning

1. Create Your 'Bucket List'

The 'bucket list' is my own personal favourite and I tell everyone and anyone about it. Years later, people still ask me, "Leigh, how's your bucket list coming along?"

As a result of my own bucket list, my life has been transformed. I've experienced things, which I've only ever dreamt of in the past. It's also brought out the less serious and far more fun and adventurous side of me. Also the list keeps building, which is so exciting. When you give focus to what you want to be and do, by the laws of attraction, you find the opportunities suddenly start rolling through!

We often dream about the things that we want to do in our lives. However, in our hyper-busyness we forget to build them in. So, here's the deal. Get your phone out now, or a notepad – I mean _NOW_ – and make a list of all the places you want to visit, sights you want to see and experiences you want to have before you die (kick the bucket).

Find your youth, find your energy and find your happiness. Have fun with your bucket list. And if you're feeling a bit nervy about what it contains, then contract with someone to do it together. You see, the bucket list can be part of a collaborative action plan, as well as a personal one. Trust me, if you take it seriously (and, paradoxically, not seriously at all) you will turn your dreams into reality. Now start making these dreams happen.

I enjoy the quote by the Himalayan explorer Murray, incorrectly attributed to the Poet Goethe:

"Until one is committed, there is hesitancy, the chance to draw back. Concerning all acts of initiative (and creation), there is one elementary truth, the ignorance of which kills countless ideas and splendid plans: that the moment one definitely commits oneself, then Providence moves too. All sorts of things occur to help one that would never otherwise have occurred.

"A whole stream of events issues from the decision, raising in one's favor all manner of unforeseen incidents and meetings and material assistance, *which no man could have dreamed would have come his way.*

"Whatever you can do, or dream you can do, begin it. Boldness has genius, power, and magic in it. Begin it now."

2. Living Your Life 'On Purpose'

What will you be doing if you are really to live your life "on purpose"?

- What will people say about you?
- How will you feel?
- What will you have achieved?
- How will you behaving?
- Where will you be living?

These questions are far from simple. They require an in-depth soul search and are often taken too lightly. Or, the lives we lead are based on someone else's pre-defined expectations. This exercise may even evolve over time. I found this as I went through major transitions in my life and had to recalibrate.

I have one of the most inspiring coaches that I have ever met in my career - Carolyn Free-Pearce. In one of my toughest periods in my life and work, she encouraged me to take comfort in the transition, embracing this precious time as a chance to take the foot off the accelerator and re-evaluate. She encouraged me to find the metaphorical, or even real, rock to sit on. Away from everyone and everything, what are the real thoughts, feelings, emotions, desires? What's working and what isn't?

The metaphorical 'warm rock' can be a different for us all, yet it's purpose is completely the same.

3. Gaining a Time Perspective

Use the '10-10-10 Exercise' when you have a difficult decision to make that has emotional content. Step back and consider how you will I feel about it in: ten minutes from now, in ten hours from now and in ten months from now. We often get caught up in our anxieties and fears. By putting things into a time perspective, we can determine how important something *really* is.

There have been times in my career and life where I've felt, 'Oh no, this is it. I've screwed up big time!' As a consequence, I've self-flagellated and fretted over the consequences. It turns out that my imagination has been far more melodramatic than the reality.

4. Facing Difficult Decisions – What Would You Advise Your Best Friend?

When facing a difficult emotional decision, if your best friend had the same problem, then what advice would you give them? Write down the answer. Then take that same advice for yourself.

5. Defining Your Life Purpose - Questions to Ponder

- In one sentence define your life purpose. Then answer the following personal questions.
- Your success and happiness:
    o What are your top 10 goals in your life? Be clear on why you do what you do and the resulting benefits.
    o What are your real priorities? What are you willing to give up to achieve your goals and life purpose?
    o Check your reality. How realistic are your top priorities and how focused are you to achieve them?

- Your positive contagion. Choose with whom you spend your precious time. Select people who add to (not detract from) your quality of life. Seek radiators and avoid drains.
- What is your identity and what are your roles in life?
- What are your top 10 goals for this year?
- What is your brand?
- Where do you add value for other people?
- What are your top 10 life values?

HQ: Health and Wellbeing

1. Health

How will you balance having fun and keeping healthy? Draw a line down the middle of a blank page; on one side put the title 'fun' and on the other put 'keeping healthy'. List the things that put fun in your life and list the things that give you longevity and health. Notice the overlaps and the gaps.

2. Boundary Creation

With the ubiquitous technologies, such as mobile phones and laptops, creating blurred boundary lines, we can now work anytime and anywhere in the world. We are fully immersed in our personal and work life. Work with those important to you to agree priorities and boundaries.

By creating rules, such as the work-phone gets switched off at a certain time and it certainly doesn't make its way to the bedroom, you start to take control of your work rather than it controlling you.

3. 'Me' time

Go on this as the exercise where you can spoil yourself! Inspiring leaders are not selfish, indeed they give so much of themselves to their families, friends, colleagues, clients that often there is little time or energy left for themselves. But they know how important it is to look after their own health and well-being mentally and physically by giving themselves time for renewal and regeneration.

Equally, as we'll discuss in the mindfulness paragraph, it's important to have quiet, downtime with time to reflect on what really matters.

In the airline safety video, when the cabin pressure drops in an emergency, oxygen masks fall down from the bulkhead. The recommendation is that you put on your own mask first before putting on the mask for your infant. That way you are conscious enough to do the right thing.

The same is true about you as a leader: you must look after your own health and well-being to be up to lead others properly.

4. **Mindfulness Practice**

Dr. Henry Ford states that Mindfulness has been shown to improve clarity of thought, personal presence, perspective and creativity, with positive impacts on relationships, authenticity and emotional intelligence, all of which are a benefit to leaders. Further it has been shown to create specific peripheral benefits for those in leadership roles, including improved emotional well-being, reduced physiological stress and job satisfaction. Even learning to breathe in five seconds and out five seconds using your belly rather than your rib cage and generating a feeling of positive emotion can be a major enhancement.

To experience the 1 minute Mind-Body connection for yourself, try the following simple exercise:

Stand comfortably with your hands hanging at your sides and, as you bring the following emotions into your mind, take 5 seconds to express these feelings each with your hands and body:

- Joy
- Anger
- Anticipation
- Sadness
- Boredom
- Fear
- Calmness

When you have cycled through the emotions, take 15 seconds to pause, scan your body, and take a weather report on your internal pattern: energy, tension and feelings which are manifest

IQ: Cognitive Intelligence and Wisdom

1. **Get The Basics Right - Qualifications and Experience**

Ensure that you can demonstrate on your CV all the basic building blocks of your career. Create a powerful enough CV that will get you through to the crucial interview. Deliberately acquire a whole range of experiences;

accumulating breadth and depth is important. Don't get stuck in a rut. It isn't just a ladder, you often benefit from going sideways as well as up. Wherever possible acquire profit and loss management experience, lead teams, travel and get a mass of experience. Once you have accumulated that experience then don't talk yourself down once you reach the interview. Time again men overstate their experiences, whilst women modestly understate what they have actually achieved. Don't undersell yourself!

2. Mental Exercises

More mental focus, discipline, determination and willpower will help you succeed in life. Willpower acts like a muscle, it gets stronger the more you exercise it. Tackling even a tiny challenge without giving up, and finding tips and techniques to help you keep your resolve will make you stronger. It is crucial that we avoid getting stuck in mental ruts doing the same thing day after day and thinking in the same ways. Seek mental stimulation, which will help generate new neural connections. Travel widely and volunteer for exchanges with other organisations. Be a corporate magpie: learn, absorb and reflect on whatever you're observing, reading and hearing.

3. The TGROW Coaching Model (By Myles Downey)

The TGROW coaching model is a variation of the GROW model, adapted by my good friend Myles Downey and explained in his excellent book, *Effective Coaching*. His TGROW model works in so many different situations and taps into the wisdom of the person who has the problem. You bring the skills of asking great questions and a simple disciplined framework to allow them to think for themselves. Myles's advice is as follows:

T stands for **Topic**, in other words it is the broad area that your coachee wants to address. It would make sense, at the start of the conversation, to understand and clarify the topic and its scale, understanding the bigger picture in terms of why this is important to the coachee and perhaps their longer term vision. At this stage you may uncover issues which are different to those that the coachee came to the table with and the focus of the conversation may be re-prioritised.

By having this Topic stage before and separate from the Goal stage, it helps to differentiate the bigger picture from the specific goals that may arise from it. It also helps to form a solid foundation and ensure that goals are not set prematurely before the bigger picture is clarified. For example setting goals before the motivation behind it is checked can lead to irrelevant goals, which the coachee may not be committed to.

Some of the questions you may be asking at this stage are:

- What would you like to talk about?
- What is important to you?
- What areas do you want to address?
- What is behind this?
- What would this mean to you?

The rest of the TGROW coaching model follows the traditional GROW structure so in summary:

Topic: Clarification and exploration of the topic.

Goal: Setting of specific goals – long/medium/short term and for the session itself.

Reality: Understanding where the coachee is now in relation to their goals?

Option: Exploring options for moving forward.

Wrap Up: Identifying and agreeing specific action

4. Mentoring

Successful leaders often cite that mentoring is very influential in their career development. Mentoring is a personal development relationship where one with more experience and knowledge helps to guide a less experienced person. They have benefited from the sharing of ideas and asking questions, drawing from the wisdom and experience of the mentor.

The conversation allows for discussion, and even challenge, in a safe environment. In a knowledge-based world, it's invaluable as a source of social capital and mentors can be the expert guides around the corporate politics snares!

Here are some tips to help you create a successful mentoring relationship:

- Be clear on the purpose of the mentoring. Mentor relationships fail, when there is a lack of clarity about the value of the relationship. Mentoring works really well, for example, when you start a new role such as on-boarding, if you're considered high potential and you are learning new and stretching skills.

- Match the right mentor with mentee, by having a conversation to ensure that the right chemistry exists between you both. Contract around the mentoring programme so you are both clear on how you want to work together. It is important to select a mentor that is different too, so you get the opportunity to learn different styles and perspectives. For example, base selection on knowledge and chemistry, not using criteria like gender.

- Set up review points, so you can evaluate the on-going value of the relationship. It is often the case that there is a natural endpoint to the mentoring.

- In a reverse mentoring situation, the mentee has more overall experience than the mentor. However the mentor or has knowledge in a particular area such as gender diversity or millennial generation. This form of mentoring is becoming extremely popular in today's business, encouraging overall learning from each other.

5. Coaching

When we first start developing, interventions such as training are helpful in learning fundamental knowledge and skills. As we grow in our leadership careers, coaching is recognised as a method of development that causes dramatic, positive shifts. Many leaders shared how executive coaching creates a strong sounding board, helps to bring out the best thinking, builds confidence and creates a safe environment for practising leadership techniques.

The best approach to coaching is to receive it over a period of time to help to transfer and embed the learning. There are also some great specialist coaches, such as Robin Kermode mentioned earlier in this book, who offer specific development of communication skills, presentation skills, image, speech training and PR and media training, to name just a few.

It is important to feel comfortable with the coach that you choose, so I would recommend meeting two or three highly recommended coaches and seeing where you have the best chemistry.

6. Role models

In order for us to understand and appreciate what great leadership looks like, we need to identify role models around us that espouse attributes and skills that we admire is an important part of our learning. However, it is important for us to remain authentic and value what we bring and who we are. Therefore, it is best to base our own personal development around the specific areas that we admire in others and not try to emulate them.

EQ: Emotional and Social Competence

1. Identify The Emotional Hooks

The first step in developing emotional agility is to notice when you've been 'hooked' by your thoughts and feelings. That's hard to do, but there are certain tell-tale signs. One is that your thinking becomes rigid and repetitive. Notice your emotional hooks and patterns in the moment. Identify the unhelpful ones such as guilt, shame, or fear. Highlight the empowering ones that bring you joy, pride and excitement. Create a label for them. Mentally unhook the recurring emotional patterns that don't serve you well. Maintain and nurture the ones that move you forward.

Remember, this not only improves behaviours and wellbeing, but also promotes biological changes in the brain that are very beneficial.

2. Accepting Emotions

Accepting the emotion with an open attitude of 'it is what it is' you can pay attention to what's occurring for you. Take 10 deep breaths and notice what's happening in the moment. This can bring relief, but it won't necessarily make you feel good. In fact, you may realise just how upset you really are.

The important thing is to acknowledge both internally and externally what's happening for you. Now, intervene: how can you think differently, take an alternative perspective or even the complete opposite? How can you let go of the unhelpful emotions and look at the situation through a new lens?

It is the Buddhists who have that very calming attitude that 'it is what it is'. The skill, once you accept what already is and that you can't change what has happened, is to think about what you're going to do next.

3. 'Reality TV' Training – Reading Emotion

With a friend, watch a reality TV show on television with the sound switched on for a while, then switch off the sound and continue watching the TV show. What do you notice? What did you pick up from the body language? Had you been following the story? How accurately did you pick up the emotions? You can then go back to the start of the part you watched on mute and re-watch it with the sound on to see what you missed. You start to learn some real skills of reading body language.

Alternatively, stop and take a good look around the office or in a team meeting. Observing what's happening, paying attention to the intricate detail of interactions, the energy and the environment. What are you noticing?

4. In-Group And Out-Group Bias

One of the downsides of group biases is the need to improve reduced self-esteem. This gets severely eroded when we feel 'informally excluded' from a group. It is the real skill of a leader to know how to enter the in-group, when you are on the outside of it. Equally, as an inspiring leader, it's just as important to know how you bring people into your in-group. Make a point of getting to know people who are not in your dominant group. It is a natural human trait and failure to want 'people like me' around you, as you feel you can then trust them more and you know 'where they are coming from'. The danger is you are closing your minds off to innovation and new ideas and making your organisation less future proof and robust.

Work consciously to bring diverse, out-group colleagues into your in-group, by making them feel welcome and valuing their differences. It is an unfortunate habit of humans that, while we want to be included in prestigious and exclusive groups, once we finally overcome the obstacles and get into the exclusive group, then many of us don't want anybody else to join, especially if we don't know them!

So if you're part of a minority group and are feeling like an outsider, consider what you can do to engage with the in-group and find common connections. Study the participants carefully and seek to be interested in what they're interested in.

Remember the saying, '*Everybody has something to teach you, if only you would listen*'. It's not about presenting a façade of perfection; rather it is about getting behind the façade and getting to know the real man and woman behind it.

In its rawest form it involves asking great open questions to begin a conversation with someone and then you just listen really well. Be curious about what you'll learn from them and keep checking with yourself mentally to ensure you drop any assumptions, prejudices and biases you have about people who appear different from you.

5. Cultural Awareness

Work hard to the research into the different cultures with whom you're working. There is a mass of information available for you on the internet, there are programmes on building greater cultural awareness and you can spend time with people from their culture to understand them better.

Make a point of understanding the traditions, styles, etiquette and taboos of their culture. Have an appreciation of the difference between cultural stereotypes and learn what is unique to the individual you are working with.

6. Positive To Negative Ratio

Go out and catch people *doing things right* in your organisation - every day. Tell them what it is you appreciate and value about them using the three S's -be sincere, be specific and be short. Aim to experience five positive emotions for every one negative emotion, and then you dramatically improve your health and your ability to deal with challenges.

7. Increasing Oxytocin

Shake someone's hand for six seconds, or send someone you know a message of appreciation and love. You get more strength from your friends, your neighbours, your family, and your community when you make a real personal connection with them.

A great way to boost your social resilience is gratitude, and touching someone (appropriately) is even better. By, for example, shaking someone's hand for just six seconds dramatically raises the level of oxytocin in your blood stream, which is the trust hormone. That means that you are biochemically primed to want to like and help each other.

8. Decreasing the Stress Hormone, Cortisol, while Increasing Oxytocin

The other exercise, which is enormous fun, is to ask everyone to stand shoulder to shoulder in a circle. Then get them to turn to their right and then, (with the permission of the person in front of them) place their hands on the shoulders of the person in front. Then gently massage with both your hands in the area of the neck, which is where we store most of our tension in stressful situations, which generate high levels of the stress hormone, cortisol.

This massage exercise raises the level of energy in the room, causes a lot of humour, releases tension, whilst also increasing oxytocin plus generating other beneficial hormones such as endorphins, dopamine and serotonin.

RQ: Resilience and Coping with Adversity

1. Positive Framing or Reframing

When we are feeling negative, fearful or are prone to worrying we tend to over-exaggerate the issues and implications of conflict. It may even be our own pride or egos that are preventing us from seeing things clearly. This pride or pressure affects our ability to view these situations from multiple perspectives and, therefore, think more creatively around possible solutions. We can make assumptions and assertions that are deeply biased and parochial. This is not just exclusive to the distinct more pronounced situations, it also very relevant for simple thoughts, worries and concerns that

470

soon become a repeated pattern.

Positive reframing for yourself and for others will strengthen your position as a leader. You will be able to confront the toughest situations in a positive and constructive way.

Try the following:

- If you are prone to being particularly impulsive, reacting in the moment and emotional outbursts, then STOP! Many leaders use public displays of outbursts to reinforce their own power. However, all it does is destroy your reputation and the trust of your team. Remember from the EQ and Neuroscience chapters, you *always* have CHOICE.

  o Identify the emotions in the moment and INTERRUPT yourself. Take time out in a quiet zone, such as get a breath of fresh air. This way you can do your finest thinking in a calm environment and return to the discussion when you are ready.

- If you are prone to more negative framing of any situations or people, in other words 'the glass is half empty", you may be distorting the reality. Look through an alternative lens to help you look at this from different angles. Look at the facts, analyse your assumptions and biases and consider alternative perspectives. Pessimism is often triggered by our own past experiences, causing us to ruminate or react. So it's essential to understand what's occurring for you and why. If it's about people, place yourself in their situation. If it's about situations, look for alternative possibilities. You may benefit from making a list. For example:

  o What is my desired outcome? (or variations of)
  o What is their desired outcome? (or variations of)
  o What are the hard facts / evidence?
  o What are my views and feelings?

471

- o What are their views and feelings?
- o What are my limiting assumptions that I am living as true?
- o What questions do I need to ask to find out important answers that will help to move this situation/relationship forward?
- o How do I want to be as a leader when I am dealing with this situation?

One point to note is that framing ideas, thoughts and actions in a positive way leads to greater success and outcomes. It not only enhances your own abilities to think and communicate, but your impact as a leader becomes far more powerful and influential. It also has the added benefit of improving your health and wellbeing.

2. Personal Resilience Stock Take - My Strengths, Weaknesses Opportunities And Threats

Complete this exercise for yourself:

My Personal SWOT

- • What I have going for me is:
- • I limit myself by:
- • I could choose to:
- • I need to be aware and alert to:

My Personal beliefs

- • I currently believe I can:
- • I currently don't believe I:
- • I could believe I:

3. Tools to give you greater resilience

Many of my coaches have found significant value and transformation in the excellent book, *The Tools*, by Phil Stutz, M.D. and Barry Michaels, where they share some visualization exercises that they regularly use in their practices to help people break out of stalled thinking and emotions. These visualizations include:

a) **Reversal of desire** to overcome discomfort at doing what needs to be.
b) **Active love** to overcome your anger trapping you in the past
c) **Inner authority** to overcome feeling intimidated
d) **Grateful flow** is to get rid of worry, self-hatred, and negative thinking.
e) **Jeopardy** is used to help you keep applying the first four tools.

My recommendation is to read this insightful book and practice the tools.

BQ: Brand Impact

1. Voice

Our voice is very much part of our personal brand. The skill is to have a voice, which is appealing to listen to, clear and gives us credibility. Robin Kermode gives some wonderful tips and advice in his book, *Speak*, about lowering our centre of gravity, exercising the muscles around our throat, tongue and chest. For example:

- Channel nervous energy by squeezing your butt cheeks tightly and pressing your foot firmly to the ground.
- Pause briefly and take a few deep breaths before you start to speak.

Some simple actions, yet very affective!

2. Presence

Developing a calmness and quiet presence is a goal worth aspiring to. True presence comes from being attentive and curious about whomever we are with and being comfortable in our own skin.

One sound piece of advice is given in the following quote, '*If you are worried what other people think about you, then you would be surprised how little they do.*' Presence comes from a quiet passion, focus and attentiveness as well as being sufficiently assertive to get your point across at the appropriate moment.

Try some of the following techniques to help you:

- If someone would like to talk with you but you are busy, politely say so. You can either offer them, for example, 10 minutes so you are both completely focused or schedule some time in so you can be completely present.
- Change the environment, for example, try being outside in the fresh air and giving your complete focus away from other distractions.
- With your family, create focused time where your full attention is on them without distractions of home, work and whatever else is on your agenda. Set boundaries around what you feel is right for you and your relationships. When you feel you have been completely present, it's far easier to feel less guilty!
- We all have the ability to think and communicate. Trust the person or team in front of you as an equal thinking peer, and be completely present with them. This means turning off the internal dialogue and the desire to jump in, waiting for their in-breath, drowning out others' thinking! Inspiring leadership is not about being the only one who thinks and makes decisions, but being an expert facilitator of others' finest thinking too.

3. Somatic

Somatic Psychology is the study of our mind-body interface, our energy and our physical manifestations of our thoughts and anxieties. There is a view that the body never lies and it gives away a lot about ourselves; consequently we should become skilled at reading body language and emotional signals we and others emit.

There is so much that we can pick up from the sounds other people give out when they mirror behaviour, and the pace and depth of breathing and our own and their body movement.

Examples include when we notice shallow breathing, the tapping foot and pickup what is happening within our own body to indicate possible signs of nerves and anxiety.

After awareness comes the action and we can then intervene to manage what we have just read such as slowing and calming our breathing when we are stressed and anxious.

4. Meeting Confidence

We know that we have been hired because of what we bring, which is different to everyone else at the table. We don't need to be the same, say the same, or act the same.

To add value we can bring our full talents to the room by being authentic. What's the worst that could happen?

If you're a leader of a team, it's important to maximise the full capability within it, here are a few strategies that can help:

- Turn your meetings into a decision-making forum and not a communications download
- Have the right people in the room, and use your resource wisely. This also means you too. Some leaders attend far too many meetings and like to micro-manage or retain power. Let go, and delegate more.
- If meetings aren't productive, change them or stop them all together.
- Start with recognition, successes – the things that will generate serotonin/DHEA and other great hormones that will encourage creative relationships and not alert the amygdalae creating fight/flight/freeze!
- Structure your meetings so no-one dominates and no-one is unheard.
- Introduce a system where everyone gets to show you whether they're in agreement with decisions. We often use thumb-voting: if the thumb is up, they agree; thumb down they don't agree; and if mid-way, they're unsure. Ask individuals what it would take to get a thumbs-up!

If you are fearful of speaking up, here are a few strategies to help:

- Be as prepared as you can be by being clear on the agenda, gathering knowledge through conversations/reading and consider or solicit a few key points or ideas in advance.

- Speak up for something that you feel passionate about and manage your openness to feedback. Remember, less is more! Get the balance between talking and listening and be succinct in your messages. You can always expand when asked, and best not to
- At the start, take a few deep, slow breaths, which will control your body and mind. As a result you will think more clearly and you won't sound like Minnie Mouse on helium when you do speak up! This will centre you and you will appear calmer in your delivery and, interestingly, your voice tone will change slightly too.

5. Personal Histories Exercise - Building Your Brand with Your Team

This exercise is great for team offsite. Please explain to your team members three things about yourself:

- Where did you grow up?
- How many children were there in your family?
- What was the most difficult or important challenge in your childhood?

In that way they will get to learn about you as a leader; what motivates and drives you; how you build your reputation, and what you would wish your brand to be.

6. Feedback on Brands and Reputations & The Impacts on the Team

Get your team to complete a table with two columns and a row for each member of the team. Use this by way of a feedback session as a team offsite. Give answers to the following two questions:

- "What is the **single** most important behavioural characteristic, or quality demonstrated by this person that **contributes to the strength** of this team?"
- "What is the **single** most important behavioural characteristic, or quality demonstrated by this person that **can sometimes derail** this team?"

476

7. Stakeholder Relationships

It's important to evaluate the quality of our stakeholder relationships and to ensure we are spending sufficient time engaging with the right people that have influence over the work we do or our careers.

Start by identifying what it is you want to focus on, for example, the work that you do or the career that you want to develop. Then map all of your stakeholders and relationships.

Sort the relationships into two categories; (1) those who have high influence and power and (2) those with low power and influence. Selecting those individuals with high power and influence, map the quality of the relationship using the scale below. If this is the person you duck away from when you see them walking down the corridor, you would put them at -5. If you have a strong healthy relationship with the person you would movement towards +5.

Knowing where each person sits on scale, you can then start to develop some strategies for managing the relationships. Maybe some relationships that, no matter how much effort and time you put into them, you will never be up to get them up to the desired level.

You then have to evaluate if this is where your energy is best spent. *Identify your sponsors, or potential sponsors, as this is one of the most cited positive influences for unblocking careers.*

Where your relationships are strong, you have clear advocates within the organisation, and it is important to maintain and nurture these relationships.

8. How visible are you?

With sophisticated headhunting techniques and organisations desire to tap into the best talent, it is important for you to the as visible as possible. Here are just a few simple ways you can achieve this:

- Networking - become a savvy socialiser. Look at the quality of the networking events that you are going to at the moment. Are they getting you introduced to the right people, learning about your topic of interest, even stretching you outside of your comfort zone?

We don't have a finite amount of time, it is really important to identify the types of events and workshops that are really going to work in your favour. Identify the type of people that you want to meet and make it your task to connect with these people when you're there.

If you feel uncomfortable about attending networking events, bring a friend or colleague.

- Online - If you did an Internet search under your name, what would appear? Craft a great profile on LinkedIn, which is becoming a major source of information for recruiters.
- Thought leadership - Get recognised as a thought leader and take time to write some articles, maybe even write a book! It not only enhances your visibility, but your own learning too. Find your niche, and become the speaker at events or sit on panels and forums.

LQ: Legacy

1. If You Had Only 12 Months Left To Live

Consider that you learnt from the doctor that you had only had 12 months left to live, and would die on the final night having been healthy up to that point, how would you live those 12 months, how would you behave with other people? What things would you tell the people you love, which you've previously held back from saying? What unfinished business do you need to resolve to get closure in your life? Now pick out three things and do them.

2. Leadership Logical Levels

I first came across this concept with the ideas from Robert Dilts and it's based on a simple pyramid built from the top-down as follows:

- Your Purpose
- Your Identity

- Your Values And Beliefs
- Your Capabilities And Skills
- Your Behaviours
- Your Environment

Work with your coach and lay out six markers on the floor, beginning with Your Environment and ending at Your Purpose. Firstly step onto the marker for Your Environment.

The coach then asks you, "*What is your current environment like? Describe it to me - both at work and home.*" After you have spoken for a while, then the coach could ask you, "*If you were to describe your environment in three words what would they be?*" Your coach then captures those words on a sheet for you.

You then step onto the next marker and repeat the process. So for example the coach may ask you, "*How are you behaving in your current environment? How are you behaving at work and how are you behaving at home?*" Again you will be asked to summarise that in three words, which will be captured on a sheet for you to use later.

Carry on up the pyramid until you reach Your Purpose. Here you will be asked, "*What is your life purpose?*" This is often a hard one for people. The aim is to capture it in a clear sentence for you. Once you have distilled your purpose, and you may need to revisit this a couple of times on different occasions, after you have had time to reflect, then you can move onto part two.

In part two you then go down the pyramid through each stage. So for example your coach might ask you, "*If that is now your clear purpose, what do you wish your identity to be and who will you be differently from how you were before?*" Again your response can be captured in a few simple words. You repeat this through all the stages and now have a far clearer idea of what you want for your life going forward and the sustainable legacy you intend to leave.

3. Creating a Sustainable Legacy With Less, Not More

I'm very grateful to our friend, Oliver Johnson, who brings considerable experience and wisdom to the field of development.

Oliver has started a campaign to encourage people to focus on wanting and living with *less* not more. Less is an inside-out process, which is definitely about building a sustainable legacy in our personal lives, relationships, our organisations and our society.

Too often advertising encourages us that will only be happy when we have more of things, rather than being content with what we already have. Our consumer society pushes us to believe that, for example, one handbag is not enough.

They make us believe that we need to have minimum of five or six. However, we can only use one handbag at a time sensibly!

I like this definition of the difference between success and happiness:

> *'Success is getting what you want;*
> *happiness is wanting what you <u>already</u> have.'*

Maybe we need to start with ourselves first. So here are six questions that Oliver believes might be useful to you and subsequently to those you lead:

- To what extent is **more** your default mindset?
- What are your **more** habits?
- What is the impact of your **more** habits on the things most important to you?
- What benefits might come from experimenting with **less**?
- What could get in the way of experimenting with **less**?
- So, what is your next step?

4. Creating a Legacy in Your Own Lifetime - Journal For Opening & Closing The Day

I'm very grateful to a fellow coach who shared this generic approach that they used to creating a journal of your personal learning. This will allow you to think about the legacy you're creating in your own lifetime and how sustainable it is. It is far more inspiring to think about creating a legacy in your own lifetime, rather than after your death.

Open the day asking

- 'Will what I'm going to do today, *best serve*, my talent and ambition, my needs and the needs of those I care about?'

At the end of the day ask yourself

- 'Did what I did today, *best serve*, my talent and ambition, my needs and the needs of those I care about?'

Based on what I've learnt, what do I need to:

- Do more of?
- Do less of?
- Do the same?
- Do new or differently?

When you complete your journal ask yourself:

Learning

- What did I learn today?
- What did I enjoy?
- How much did I enjoy my day overall? (1% - 100%)
- What can I do to improve it?

Achieving

- What was challenging and why?
- What did I achieve?

Challenges

- What did I aim to finish today but didn't?
- Why?

What got in my way?

- What worked for me?
- What didn't work for me?
- What did I do that got in my way?
- What did others do that got in my way?
- What did the organisation do that put things in my way?
- How did life, the universe support me?

Giving and Receiving
- Who did I help today?
- Who helped me?
- What did I give?
- What did I receive?
- What am I proud of today?
- What am I grateful for today?
- How did life, the universe support me?

What did I contribute that made a worthwhile difference:
- For me?
- For others?
- For those I care about?

Collaboration and co-operation
Who did I collaborate with:
- Why?
- How can I do more?
- Do less?

Who did I co-operate with:
- Why?
- How can I do more?
- Do less?

Health
What did I do that maintained or improved my health:
- Physically?
- Mentally?
- Emotionally?
- Spiritually?

Relationships
- What did I do today that created, maintained or developed the

relationships that matter to me?

- What did I learn today about my key stakeholders? How can I apply this to benefit me?

The list of questions is by no means exhaustive, I encourage you to create your own and use them to shape and give focus to your thoughts and actions.

5. Reciprocity

Remember Pinky Lilani's advice to giving back without any expectation of anything in return; it's not about keeping score, it's giving in abundance to others. Here are some examples of how:

- Offer to mentor / coach / sponsor others inside and outside of the organisation, help to bring on new talent both male and female.
- Open up your networks to people and create connections between people. Often the people that can help each other are within our networks or their networks
- Make the effort to give others feedback that will help them sustain great behaviours and manage blind-sides. Remember 5:1 ratio of appreciation versus constructive feedback and also WWW and EBI
- Your time is invaluable and a gift to others. Whilst being realistic consider how you can help others.

  The inspiring women in my book were extremely generous with their time for this book and the topic, and I will always be truly thankful.
- Focus on your relationships and those that matter most. Reconnect with friends, create special family time and with partners too. At the end of the day, the quality of this time will create your most treasured moments.
- Being resourceful and creative. Some of the most wonderful visions and innovations have emerged from dialogue – instead of closing things down, try opening them up.

Part Two: Inspiring Leadership Interventions

We have established new collaborations with a number of great independent leadership coaches, facilitators, expedition guides and experts to deliver inspiring leadership interventions.

Our 'tithings' commitment means that we donate a percentage of our profits and/or time back into selected charitable projects. Below are just a few of the interventions we do.

To find out about more interventions and also the difference we are making, check out my website **www.leighbowmanperks.com**.

- **'Inspiring Leaders' and 'Inspiring Women Leaders' Programmes**
  Customised programmes and events based on the components of inspiring leadership model: MQ - Morality and Ethics, PQ – Purpose and Meaning, HQ – Health and Wellbeing, IQ  – Cognitive Intelligence and Wisdom, EQ – Emotional and Social Competence, RQ – Resilience, BQ – Brand Presence and Impact, and LQ – Legacy.

  The programme can include a range of interventions including top key-note speakers, psychometrics and assessments (such as using the IL-i^{TM}) development workshops, executive coaching and mentoring and supporting discussion forums and networks. Facilitated by topic experts and led by Jonathan Bowman-Perks MBE, Leigh Bowman-Perks, and Dr. Reuven Bar-On.

- **'Presenting You'** – Working with a specialist team, you will receive the full make-over customised to requirements. Aimed at bringing out the best in you and retaining your authenticity, for example:

  o   Presenting and Communicating with Impact Coaching
  o   Personal Brand Image and Style
  o   Professional Photography (Including make-over)

- o Social Media Presence
- o Filming and Production

- **'Inspiration 4000'** – If you're feeling particularly adventurous and looking to make a difference, why not join us on one of our leadership adventures that combines fundraising, adventure, team development and coaching, plus lots more! By getting  focused on a project you can make a real different to others and to your own health.

  Working with experts including, Isabelle Santoire (inspiring female mountain guide whose story is in this book), we run a variety of 3-day discovery weekends throughout the year that are designed to: inspire; create an incentive to get fit; give a confidence boost; help find the right balance – equilibrium, and help with making a commitment.

  With lots of on-line support and fixed events to keep the motivation up, using fitness and training centres including The Altitude Centre (**https://www.altitudecentre.com/**)

- **Inspiration Retreat, Ireland** - held over a weekend away from the hustle and bustle of everyday life in the quietness of rural County Donegal, Ireland.

  The retreat is facilitated by Kerry Cullen  who has been working with leaders in her capacity as a Chartered Business Psychologist for over 15 years.

  She blends her knowledge of the business world with her experience of teaching mindfulness and yoga. You will be welcomed and nurtured with wholesome food, big open fires, being by the ocean, country walks and Irish hospitality.

- **Leadership Retreat, France** - Named after Chekhov's play, The Cherry Orchard is a beautiful, newly renovated stone farmhouse and ski chalet located in the Grand Massif, France's fourth  largest linked ski area, and is just over 1 hour from Geneva Airport. A customised retreat facilitated by Sally-Anne Airey, to meet yours and your team/family's needs and can include coaching, leadership development as well as exciting activities to appreciate the beauty of the skiing resort.

- **Beyond the Barriers: Building Your Personal Resilience Workshop** While we can't often change our external environment, we can train ourselves to better manage our inner state and build our capacity to thrive in the most difficult circumstances and emerge healthier, happier and stronger. In this two day programme, you will learn how to:

  o Build capacity to be flexible in the face of change and prepare challenging situations.
  o Improve concentration and energy levels and reduce the propensity to make mistakes by understanding the role of nutrition, fitness and recovery and developing personal energy management strategy.
  o Increase cognitive performance, creativity and emotional clarity with scientifically proven methods that will enable you to see through problems in a calm and effective manner, creating a greater sense of well-being.
  o Be less reactive, think more clearly and make the decisions under pressure.
  o Prevent stress before it happens by understanding the physiology of stress, resilience and performance and retraining your stress responses.
  o Enhance energy and vitality – build your resilience capacity each day, instead of letting life's challenges drain your reserves.

- **Beyond the Barriers: HeartMath Workshop**
  We live in arguably the most challenging economic era of our lifetime. Uncertainty about the future is creating significant levels of anxiety, relenting pressure, and increasing health problems. The HeartMath System is a comprehensive set of highly effective, scientifically-validated practical solutions for reducing stress, anxiety, sleeplessness, and increasing resilience and performance. Not surprisingly, a decrease in stress and anxiety is directly linked to a substantial increase in performance, health and well-being. HeartMath clinical studies have demonstrated the critical link between emotion, cardiac function and cognitive performance. Facilitated by Anna Hemmings MBE (one of our inspiring leaders in the HQ chapter), this 1-day programme will present simple, proven tools and technologies that can be implemented in real time to reduce stress and help build your personal resilience and well-being, by retraining the human stress response and organising your innate emotional power to perform on demand.

- **'Inspiring Boards' Assessments** - In recent years there has been an increasing focus on the boardroom and increasing pressure on individual board members. Their role has been made more demanding by such matters as technology, both in companies' strategy and potential IT risks; crisis management and reputational risk, particularly during a period of economic difficulty; and how they communicate with stakeholders, alongside an increase in boardroom-stakeholder (particularly shareholder) engagement. Boards are now required to evaluate how effective they are in dealing with these and other matters. This may be accomplished by an internal review, but, increasingly, an external evaluator is called in to conduct an independent external review. Board Assessments cover:

  o Board structure and composition
  o Collective and individual board capabilities

- o Formal operation and effectiveness of the board and its Committees and their effectiveness
- o Where appropriate psychometric testing of board members
- o Observation of board/committee meetings

Part 3: Recommended Resources & References

Books & Presentations

Beautiful	Katie Piper
Brain Rules	John Medina
Career Distinction	William Arruda & Kirsten Dixson
Careers Advice for Ambitious Women	Mrs Moneypenny
Daring Greatly	Brené Brown (also see TED Talk)
David and Goliath	Malcolm Gladwell
Decisive	Chip Heath & Dan Heath
Effective Coaching	Myles Downey
Ethicability	Roger Steare
Everybody Matters: A Memoir	Mary Robinson
Feel the Fear and Do It Anyway	Susan Jeffers
Giant Steps	Anthony Robbins
Inspiring Leadership	Jonathan Bowman-Perks MBE
Lean In	Sheryl Sandberg (also see TED Talk)
Man's Search for Meaning	Viktor E Frankl
Mindful Coaching	Liz Hall
Mindsight	Dr. Daniel Siegel
Now, Discover Your Strengths	Marcus Buckingham & Donald O. Clifton
Screw Business as Usual	Richard Branson
Snakes in Suits	Paul Babiak, Ph.D. & Robert D. Hare, Ph.D.
SPEAK, So Your Audience Will Listen	Robin Kermode
Start with Why	Simon Sinek (also see TED Talk)

Success Intelligence	Robert Holden
The 7 Habits	Stephen Covey
The Accidental Mind	David J Linden
The EQ Edge	Steven J. Stein, PH.D. & Howard E. Book, M.D.
The First 90 Days	Michael Watkins
The Inner Game of Tennis	W. Timothy Gallwey
The Naked Truth	Margaret Heffernan (also see TED Talk)
The Purpose Driven Life	Rick Warren (also see TED Talk)
The Speed of Trust	Stephen Covey
The Tools	Phil Stutz & Barry Michels
Time to Think	Nancy Kline
Walking Tall	Lesley Everett
What Every Body is Saying	Joe Navarro

References

Prologue – My Story

1. Brown, Brené, (2012). *Daring Greatly: How the Courage to Be Vulnerable Transforms the Way We Live, Love, Parent and Lead.* Gotham.
2. Covey, Stephen R, (1989). *The 7 Habits of Highly Effective People.* Franklin Covey.

Introduction to Inspiring Women Leaders

1. Sandberg, Sheryl, (2013). *Lean In: Women, Work, and the Will to Lead.* Allen.
2. Katz, Jackson, (2013). *'Violence Against Women — It's a Men's Issue'.* www.ted.com
3. Heffernan, Margaret, (2011). *Willful Blindness: Why We Ignore the Obvious at Our Peril.* New York: Walker

Chapter 1 – Defining Inspiration

1. Bowman-Perks, Jonathan, (2015). *Inspiring Leadership.* Fisher King Publishing.
2. Heffernan, Margaret, (2011). *Willful Blindness: Why We Ignore the Obvious at Our Peril.* New York: Walker
3. Twenge, Jean M. and Campbell, W. Keith, (2009). *The Narcissism Epidemic: Living in the Age of Entitlement.* New York: Simon & Schuster.
4. Maccoby, Michael, (2009). *The Leader We Need: Leadership Insights.* Harvard Business School Press.
5. Babiak, Paul & Hare, Robert, (2009). *Snakes in Suits: When Psychopaths Go to Work.* New York: Harper

Chapter 2 – Overview of the Inspiring Leadership Model

1. Changeboard, (2013). The Lost Generation of Talent (4.12.2013)
2. Robinson, Mary. *Everybody Matters – A Memoir.* Hodder.
3. Tabachnick, B. G., & Fidell, L. S. (2001). *Using multivariate*

statistics 4th edition. Needham Heights, Massachusetts (US): Allyn and Bacon.

4. Hill, T., & Lewicki, P. (2006). *Statistics methods and applications*: *A comprehensive reference for science, industry, and data mining.* Tulsa, Oklahoma (US): StatSoft.

5. Bowman-Perks, Jonathan, (2015). *Inspiring Leadership.* Fisher King Publishing.

6. Anastasi. A., & Urbina, S. (1997). *Psychological testing 7th edition.* Upper Saddle River, New Jersey (US): Pearson.

7. Bar-On, R. (1997). *The Bar-On Emotional Quotient Inventory (EQ-i): Technical manual.* Toronto, Canada: Multi-Health Systems.

8. Bar-On, R. (2004). The Bar-On Emotional Quotient Inventory (EQ-i): Rationale, description, and summary of psychometric properties. In Glenn Geher (Ed.), *Measuring emotional intelligence: Common ground and controversy.* Hauppauge, New York (US): Nova Science Publishers, pp. 111-142.

9. Bar-On, R. (2006). The Bar-On model of emotional-social intelligence. *Psicothema, 18,* 13-25.

Chapter 3 – The Research Behind Inspiring Leadership

1. Bowman-Perks, Jonathan, (2015). *Inspiring Leadership.* Fisher King Publishing.

2. Anastasi. A., & Urbina, S. (1997). *Psychological testing 7th edition.* Upper Saddle River, New Jersey (US): Pearson.

3. Bar-On, R. (1997) *The Bar-On Emotional Quotient Inventory (EQ-i): Technical manual.* Toronto, Canada: Multi-Health Systems.

4. Bar-On, R. (2004). *The Bar-On Emotional Quotient Inventory (EQ-i): Rationale, description, and summary of psychometric properties.*

5. Bar-On, R. (2006). *The Bar-On model of emotional-social intelligence.*

6. Anastasi. A., & Urbina, S. (1997). *Psychological testing 7th*

edition. Upper Saddle River, New Jersey (US): Pearson.

7. Tabachnick, B. G. & Fidell, L. S. (2001). *Using multivariate statistics 4th edition.* Needham Heights, Massachusetts (US): Allyn and Bacon.

8. Anastasi. A., & Urbina, S. (1997). *Psychological testing 7th edition.* Upper Saddle River, New Jersey (US): Pearson.

9. Hill, T., & Lewicki, P. (2006) *Statistics methods and applications: A comprehensive reference for science, industry, and data mining.* Tulsa, Oklahoma (US): StatSoft.

10. Tabachnick, B. G., & Fidell, L. S. (2001). *Using multivariate statistics 4th edition.* Needham Heights, Massachusetts (US): Allyn and Bacon.

11. Tabachnick, B. G., & Fidell, L. S. (2001). *Using multivariate statistics 4th edition.* Needham Heights, Massachusetts (US): Allyn and Bacon.

12. Tabachnick, B. G., & Fidell, L. S. (2001). *Using multivariate statistics 4th edition.* Needham Heights, Massachusetts (US): Allyn and Bacon.

13. Hill, T., & Lewicki, P. (2006). *Statistics methods and applications: A comprehensive reference for science, industry, and data mining.* Tulsa, Oklahoma (US): StatSoft.

14. Anastasi. A., & Urbina, S. (1997). *Psychological testing 7th edition.* Upper Saddle River, New Jersey (US): Pearson.

15. Tabachnick, B. G., & Fidell, L. S. (2001). *Using multivariate statistics 4th edition.* Needham Heights, Massachusetts (US): Allyn and Bacon.

16. Tabachnick, B. G., & Fidell, L. S. (2001). *Using multivariate statistics 4th edition.* Needham Heights, Massachusetts (US): Allyn and Bacon.

17. Tabachnick, B. G., & Fidell, L. S. (2001). *Using multivariate statistics 4th edition.* Needham Heights, Massachusetts (US): Allyn and Bacon.

18. Bowman-Perks, Jonathan, (2015). *Inspiring Leadership.* Fisher King Publishing.

19. Mirza Davies, James (Sept 2013). Topic: Economic Situation, Unemployment. *NEETs: Young People Not in Education, Employment or Training - Commons Library Standard Note.*

20. 'Project 28 – 40' by Opportunity Now (Gender Equality Campaign by Business in the Community) and sponsored by r2i, PWC's market research centre. *Study into women's experiences in the workplace in the UK, final results to be published Spring 2014.*

21. Hays Global Skills Index 2013 (produced in collaboration with Oxford Economics). A comprehensive global indicator of the state of the market for skilled labour.

22. Global Entrepreneurship Monitor (GEM) 2012. *The largest ongoing study of entrepreneurial dynamics in relation to economic growth in the world.*

23. RBS Group 2013, 'Women in Enterprise: A Different Perspective'. *Study conducted by Aston Business School.*

24. Cameron David, British Prime Minister, BBC politics news Summit in Sweden, 2012.

25. Anastasi. A., & Urbina, S. (1997). *Psychological testing 7th edition.* Upper Saddle River, New Jersey (US): Pearson.

Chapter 4 – The Neuroscience Behind Inspiring Leadership

1. Brown, Paul, (2012). *Neuropsychology for Coaches.* England: McGraw-Hill.

2. Bird, Geoff, (2012). Neuroscientist and friend from University College London in a series of talks and discussions.

3. Kline, Nancy, (1998). *Time to Think: Listening to Ignite the Human Mind.* Castell.

4. Rock, David, (2009). *Your Brain at Work - Strategies for Overcoming Distraction, Regaining Focus and Working Smarter All Day Long.* Harper Collins.

5. Heming, Anna, (2013). *Beyond the Barriers* tips and guidance from her training on behalf of the Heart Math Institute in America.

6. Navarro, Joe, (2008). *What Every Body is Saying.* New York:

Harper Collins.

7. Siegel, Daniel, (2010). *Mindsight: The New Science of Personal Transformation*. England: OneWorld Press.
8. Peters, Steve, (2012). *The Chimp Paradox*. Vermillion.

Chapter 5 - MQ

1. Katz, Jackson, (2013). *Violence Against Women — It's a Men's Issue*. www.ted.com
2. Heffernan, Margaret, (2011). *Willful Blindness: Why We Ignore the Obvious at Our Peril l*. New York: Walker.
3. Covey, Stephen M. R., (2006) *The Speed of Trust: The One Thing That Changes Everything*. Franklin Covey.
4. Kline, Nancy, (1998). *Time to Think: Listening to Ignite the Human Mind*. Castell.

Chapter 6 – PQ

1. Bowman-Perks, Jonathan, (2015). *Inspiring Leadership*. Fisher King Publishing.
2. Capodagli, Bill & Jackson, Lynn, (1999). *The Disney Way*. McGraw Hill Professional.
3. Frankl, Viktor E., (2004). *Man's Search For Meaning*. Ebury Publishing.
4. Carlzon, Jan, (1989). *Moments of Truth*. Harper Collins.
5. Maccoby, Michael, (2009). *The Leader We Need: Leadership Insights*. Harvard Business School Press.
6. De Posada, Joachim, (2009). *Don't Eat the Marshmallow*. www.ted.com
7. Holden, Robert, (2009). *Success Intelligence: Essential Lessons and Practices from the World's leading Coaching Programme on Authentic Success*. Hay House.
8. Fonda, Jane, (2011). www.ted.com
9. Zohar, Danah & Marshall, Ian, (2004). *Spiritual Capital: Wealth We Can Live By*. Berrett-Koehler.
10. Sinek, Simon, (2010). *How Great Leaders Inspire Action*.

www.ted.com

Chapter 7 – HQ
1. Bean, Tim & Laing, Anne, (2009). *Turn Back Your Age Clock.* Hamlyn.
2. Loehr, Jim & Schwartz, Tony, (2001). *The Making of the Corporate Athlete.* Harvard Business Review.
3. Holden, Robert, (2009). *Success Intelligence.* Hay House.
4. Dalio, Ray (2011), *Ray Dalio's Principles.*

Chapter 8 – IQ
1. Kline, Nancy, (2009). *More Time to Think: A Way of Being in the World.* Fisher King Publishing.
2. Bowman-Perks, Jonathan, (2015). *Inspiring Leadership.* Fisher King Publishing.
3. Dotlich, David & Cairo, Peter, (2003). *Why CEO's Fail: The 11 Behaviours That Can Derail Your Climb to the Top and How to Manage Them.* Jossey Bass.
4. Lockwood, Lisa, (2013). *Reinventing You.* Author House.
5. Kline, Nancy, (1998). *Time to Think: Listening to Ignite the Human Mind.* Castell.
6. Holden, Robert, (2009). *Success Intelligence: Essential Lessons and Practices from the World's leading Coaching Programme on Authentic Success.* Hay House.

Chapter 9- EQ
1. Bar-On, Reuven, (1997). The Bar-On Emotional Quotient Inventory (EQ-i) Manual, Toronto: Multi-Health Systems.
2. Bechara, A., Damasio, A., & Bar-On, R. (2007). The anatomy of emotional intelligence and the implications for educating people to be emotionally intelligent. In R. Bar-On, J. G. Maree, & M. Elias (Eds.), *Educating people to be emotionally intelligent.* Westport, CT: Praeger, pp. 273-290.
3. Bar-On, R. (2006). *EQ-i Leadership user's guide.* Toronto,

Canada: Multi-Health Systems.

4. Tuckman, Bruce, (1965). 'Developmental sequence in small groups' in *Psychological Bulletin.*

5. Stutz, Phil & Michaels, Barry, (2013). *The Tools: Five Tools to Help You Find Courage, Creativity and Willpower.* Random House.

6. Jeffers, Susan, (1987). *Feel The Fear And Do It Anyway: How to Turn Your Fear and Indecision into Confidence and Action.* Vermillion.

7. Kline, Nancy, (1998) *Time to Think: Listening to Ignite the Human Mind.* Castell.

8. Bowman-Perks, Jonathan, (2015). *Inspiring Leadership.* Fisher King Publishing.

9. Buckingham, Marcus, & Coffman, CW (1999) *First Break All the Rules: Gallup Study into Managers,* Simon & Schuster, London.

10. Kline, Nancy, (1998), *Time to Think: Listening to Ignite the Human Mind.* Castell.

Chapter 10 – RQ

1. Pink, Daniel, (2013). *To Sell is Human.* Cannongate Books.

2. Frankl, Viktor E., (2004). *Man's Search For Meaning*, Ebury Publishing.

3. Rosenbloom & William. From Dr. Donald Bosch research.

4. Karpman, Stephen. *Drama Triangle.*

5. Lockwood, Lisa. *Reinventing You,* Morgan James Publishing.

Chapter 11 - BQ

1. Everett, Lesley, (2004). *Walking Tall: Key Steps to Total Image Impact.*

2. Arruda, William & Dixon, Kirsten, (2007). *Career Distinction: Stand Out by Building Your Brand.* John Wiley & Sons.

3. Kermode, Robin, (2013). *Speak – So Your Audience Will Listen.*

4. Navarro, Joe, (2008). *What Every Body is Saying.* New York: Harper Collins.

Chapter 12 – LQ

1. Warren, Rick, (2012). *The Purpose Driven Life: What On Earth Am I Here for?* Zondervan.
2. Robinson, Mary, (2012). *Everybody Matters: A Memoir.* Hodder
3. Cruse, Linda, (2012). *Marmalade & Machine Guns.* John Blake Publishing Ltd.

With special thanks to the inspiring leaders that generously gave their time and effort to be interviewed for this book. Some leaders have chosen to remain anonymous and so their names have not been included in the following list.

Inspiring Leader	Role	Sector
Alison Hutchinson	CEO, NED and Trustee	Charity & NED
Alison Ramsden	Managing Director	Financial Services
Alison Traversoni	Career Break (Former CEO)	Property Services
Alix Pryde	Director	Media & Entertainment
Andi Keeling	Director Women's Markets	Financial Services
Andrea Berkeley	Education Director	Charity
Anna Hemmings MBE	Ex-Olympian and Director	Consulting
Anna Mallett	CEO Studios and Productions	Media & Entertainment
Annalisa Bicknell	Head of Sales and CRM	Financial Services
Anne MacPherson	MD, Diversity in Business	Financial Services
Dame Anne Pringle	British Diplomat	Government
Ann Francke	Chief Executive Officer	Adult Education
Bob Bond	Ex-Chief Distribution Officer	Financial Services
Carol Nicholls CBE	Head Teacher	Education
Catherine Muirden	HR Director	Financial Services

Inspiring Leader	Role	Sector
Chris Sullivan	Chief Executive, UK Corporate	Financial Services
Cilla Snowball CBE	Group Chairman & Group CEO	Marketing & Advertising
Claire A-Lina	Head of HR (ER & Support Svcs)	Retail
Claire Dale	Director	Consulting
Claire Hall	HR Director	Energy
Clare Harty	Global Diversity and Inclusion	Technology
Deanna Oppenheimer	CEO and NED	Consulting & NED
Baroness Deborah Stedman-Scott OBE, DL	CEO & Member of the House of Lords	Charity and Government
Debra Channon	Communications Consultant	Telecommunications
Debrah Dhugga	General Manager	Hospitality
Ed Fox	Head of Talent	Financial Services
Elin Hurvenes	Founder & Chair	Consulting
Elizabeth Corley	CEO	Financial Services
Eva Eisenschimmel	Group Marketing Director	Financial Services
Fedelma Good	Director of Information Policy & Strategy	Financial Services
Fiona Aris	Business Development Director	Media
Georgina Cavaliere	Learning & Development Director	Charity

Inspiring Leader	Role	Sector
Heather Melville	Global HR Manager	Oil & Gas
Helen Sachdev	Director of Strategy	Financial Services
Holly Goodier	Director of Mktg & Future Media	Media & Entertainment
Inanch Emir	Entrepreneur & Hair Extentionist	Fashion & Image
Isabelle Santoire	Professional Mountain Guide	Extreme Expeditions
Joe Emir	Entrepreneur/Marketing Director	Fashion & Image
Jackie Gittins	Consultant	Consulting
Jackie Uhi	Managing Director	Financial Services
Jane Parry	Director of Marketing & BD	Financial Services
Jaz Rabadia	Energy Manager	Retail
Jean Chandler	Corporate Media Relations	Financial Services
Jill Leonard	Group Head of Resourcing	Travel
Jill Shedden	Group HR Director	Energy
Jim Devine	Group HR Director	Defence
Jo Whitfield	Retail and International Director	Retail
Judith McGregor	British High Commissioner (SA)	Government (FCO)
Julia Zingu	Managing Partner	Consulting
Julie Roddy	Senior Executive, Banking	Financial Services

Inspiring Leader	Role	Sector
Kezi Silverstone	Singer, Songwriter and Philanthropist	Entertainment & Charity
Kim Morrish	Director & Entrepreneur	Ground Services
Latha Caleb	Director of Programmes, India	Charity NGO
Laura Birrell	Head of HR	Media & Entertainment
Lesley King-Lewis	Chief Executive Officer	Charity Education
Lisa Lockwood	Consultant, Speaker and Author	Consulting
Liz Satow	H-DME Regional Advisor - Asia Pacific	Charity NGO
Lizzie Dale	Head of Talent Management	Oil & Gas
Lou Barber	Chairman	Advertising & Marketing
Lucy Darham	Head of OD	Media & Entertainment
Lucy Ndungu	Operations Management	Charity NGO
Lynne Graham	HR Director	Services and Hospitality
Lynne Turner	Global Finance Director	Elite Auctioneers
Baroness Margaret Eaton DBE, DL	Member of the House of Lords	Government
Mariam Elsamny	Chief Marketing Officer, UAE	Financial
Marie Nassor	Deputy Headteacher	Education
Mark Edwards	General Counsel	Financial Services
Mary Edmunds	Group HR and Engagement	Consulting

Inspiring Leader	Role	Sector
Menaca Calyaneratne	Child Safeguarding Director	Charity NGO
Menna Rawlings	Director of Human Resources	Government
Minaz Sherazee	Vice President, UAE	Financial Services
Monica Singer	Chief Executive Officer	Financial Services
Nadia Younes	Group Adviser, D&I	Mining
Naomi Eisenstadt CB	Senior Research Fellow – Education & Social Policy	Oxford University
Nikki Flanders	Managing Director	Telecommunications
Olivia Byrne	General Manager	Hospitality
Patty Farmer	Marketing & Media Strategist	Consulting
Paula Quintana	Customer Performance Director	Financial Services
Pavita Cooper	Founder & Director	Consulting
Penelope Biggs	Head, Institutional Investor Group	Financial Services
Pinky Lelani OBE	Chairman, Women of the Future	Consulting
Rania Ahmed	Director, Finance & Support Svcs	Charity NGO
Rebecca James	Head of Strategic Transformation	Financial Services
Rhiannon White	Director	Media & Entertainment
Rita Ross	Head Of Diversity & Inclusion	Financial Services
Sally-Anne Airey	Executive and Life Coach	Consulting

Inspiring Leader	Role	Sector
Sandi Rhys Jones OBE	Advocate and Change Manager, Engineering & Construction	Engineering & Construction
Sarah Clarke	Head of Talent & Development	Financial Services
Sarah Gregory	Enrichment Programme Manager	Charity NGO
Sayyeda Salam	Deputy Philanthropy Director	Charity NGO
Shola Awolesi	Global Leadership Development	Charity NGO
Sophie Perreard	Lecturer, Humanitarian Assistance	Adult Education
Sonia Sedler	Vice President	HCL Technologies
Susan Hooper	Chief Executive Officer	Travel & Tourism
Lady Susan Rice CBE	Managing Director	Financial Services
Svetlana Khmyrova	Global Operations Manager	Consulting
Dame Tessa Jowell DBE	Member of Parliament	Government
Tracy Cunningham	Corporate Responsibility Manager	Energy
Wang Le	Director, China	Charity

About the Author

Leigh Bowman-Perks
CEO of Clareo Potential Executive
Coach, Motivational Speaker and
Top Team Facilitator Author of
Inspiring Women Leaders

As a certified Executive Coach, Facilitator and Speaker, Leigh brings more than twenty years of leadership experience in developing executives and leaders with global FTSE organisations including: BP, Unilever, HSBC, Barclays, RBS, Centrica, Hilton Worldwide Group and Scandinavian Airlines. Leigh draws from lessons in her strategic and operational leadership experience, as well as her work as a coach, facilitator and speaker around the world. Leigh combines her own 8-point Inspiring Leadership model, leading coaching methods and the latest research in neuroscience to create insight, support and challenge leaders to make behavioural change and a positive impact. Leigh brings practical tools and techniques for immediate transferrable skills to create authentic leaders that successfully inspire others and build high performing teams and businesses.

Leigh has a particular passion for changing the landscape for developing women in the workplace. Leigh continues with her on-going research on the topic of *"Inspiring Leadership"* and *"Inspiring Women Leaders"*, developing programmes tools and initiatives to drive greater leadership excellence.

As CEO of Clareo Potential, Leigh sources top executive coaches, Business Psychologists and Leadership Consultants to deliver world class Talent, C-Suite and Executive Development solutions. She has led the design and delivery of global high-flier development programmes, leadership benchmarking and assessment.

As a keen philanthropist, Leigh has founded her own charity, the Inspiring Leadership Trust to help develop and empower vulnerable women and young people from the poorest communities around the world. Aspiring and inspiring leaders, like you, that are keen to use their skills to 'pay it forward' are getting involved and make a difference. Profits from the Inspiring Leadership books and tools are donated to the projects

Contributing Authors

Jonathan Bowman-Perks MBE
Neuroscience and Inspiring Leadership

Jonathan has had more than his fair share of challenges, anxious moments and setbacks as a leader over 33 years. The immense learning from these 'crucible moments' has shaped him as a trusted leadership advisor and Master Coach to global CEOs. He is powerfully motivated to continue in his father's footsteps with a life purpose of 'Inspiring leadership - so that you lead to succeed'.

He works with executive clients and top teams at: Sainsbury's, HSBC, Asda, Nestle, Christies, KPMG, RBS, Rio Tinto, Lloyds, Barclays, The Welcome Trust, Wincor Nixdorf, Mars Inc., Telefonica/O2, Travelex, Cambridge and other Universities, Governments and successful Entrepreneurs.

Jonathan passes on practical tips and skills from his inspirational speeches, his book and audio called *Inspiring Leadership*. He brings a breadth and depth of raw leadership experience in the British Army, PwC, IBM and as Penna PLC's MD of Board and Executive Coaching.

Jonathan is one of only 22 Master Certified Coaches (MCC) in the United Kingdom and is qualified in many of the major psychometric tools. He was Assistant to the Head of the British Army, Chief of Staff of the Army's largest Brigade and commanded his Company on three operational tours.

He is the Honorary Visiting Professor in Leadership at Cass Business School. HM the Queen awarded him the MBE for his services to live leadership. In addition he has a passion for learning and research that led to his MA and MBA.

Dr Reuven Bar-On
PhD – IL-i^{TM} and Research

Dr Bar-On has worked as a psychologist for government and private organisations since 1972. He received his doctorate from Rhodes University, and has held an adjunct professorship in the Faculty of Education at the University of Pretoria and an adjunct faculty appointment in the School of Medicine at the University of Texas. He was accepted into the Consortium for Research on Emotional Intelligence in Organizations as the first non-founding member. Dr Bar-On is also a member of the Association for Coaching and the Association of Business Psychologists in the UK, as well as a member in the Global Mastermind Group, which is a think-tank for advancing leadership development in the US. Involved in emotional intelligence since 1980, he is acknowledged as one of the leading theorists, researchers and practitioners in this field.

The 'Bar-On Model of Emotional Intelligence' is one of three leading approaches to this concept. He coined the term 'EQ' ('Emotional Quotient') to describe his approach to assessing emotional intelligence. Dr Bar-On also created the *Emotional Quotient Inventory* (the *EQ-i*), which is the first test of this concept to be published. The *EQ-i* has been translated into more than 30 languages and passed the one million mark within five years after it was published, making it the most popularly-used measure of emotional intelligence. Dr Bar-On co-edited *The Handbook of Emotional Intelligence*, which is one of the first textbooks on this topic to be published. He co-edited an additional book titled *Educating People to Be Emotionally Intelligent*. At the Center for Creative Leadership in the US, he conducted a ground-breaking study confirming the ability of emotional intelligence to predict successful leadership. Dr Bar-On has also studied the neurological basis of emotional intelligence as well as its impact on health and well-being. Together with Prof Antonio Damasio and his colleagues, he published the first peer-reviewed article on the neurology of emotional intelligence. Dr Bar-On's work has been described in encyclopaedias, books and journals, as well as in numerous newspaper, radio and television interviews. He has nearly 50 publications in the area of emotional intelligence alone and has delivered more than 25 presentations at conferences. His work is cited in more than 4,800 scientific publications.

Dr Henry Ford
Mindfulness

Henry is an inspirational coach with a quarter century of experience working with leaders to bring the best out of their teams and themselves. He helps managers and leaders to define their leadership presence based on authentic character strengths and calm self-awareness, using positive psychology and applying mindfulness to achieve results.

His work as executive coach is informed by his roles as Moderator of the Investment Committee and Head of Professional Development for a €10B PE Fund, at Citigroup as MD Global Head of Quantitative Analysis and with J P Morgan, Sovereign Markets, where he served as officer in the JPM Holding Company. Henry currently is Trustee for €2B UK Pension Scheme and serves on the board of a charitable trust which supports research to address women's breast cancer.

Henry provides the space and discipline to create success. He helps leaders and managers to focus on achieving authentic goals by developing a sustainable leadership style based on clear self-awareness and mindful application of personal values.

Dr Donald Bosch
The Headington Institute: Resilience

Dr. Donald S. Bosch is Director of Clinical Services, overseeing all training and counseling work. As a licensed clinical psychologist and psychoanalyst with 35 years of experience, Don understands human behavior and brain function.

Don is often in the field doing debriefs, working with global response teams, and providing psychological support for security trainings.

Robin Kermode
Communications Skills and Author of 'Speak So Your Audience Will Listen'

Robin has been coaching personal and public communication skills for the last ten years and is now one of Europe's leading communication coaches, working with senior executives, entrepreneurs, politicians, auctioneers, charities, corporate teams, professionals and media personalities.

He originally trained at the Central School of Speech and Drama and has been an actor for over 25 years. He is a well-known face to audiences on television and the London stage; a popular voice-over artist and presenter; he narrates audiobooks and regularly speaks at conferences and corporate Away Days.

He works with companies on all forms of their communication, from Sales and After Sales to Customer Service and internal communication and is quickly able to identify how clients can improve their communication skills, helping them gain confidence, clarity and impact.

He is experienced in working within a range of settings, from large conferences to small meetings, from television and radio to telephone and conference calls. His cross-cultural experience is invaluable to international organizations.

As a professional writer, Robin is able to advise clients on the structure and content of their message, working 1-1 or with teams on the preparation and delivery of specific talks, presentations and pitches. His input into pitch preparation has helped many companies win new business.

Robin's experience, enthusiasm and sense of humour make his sessions memorable, fun and, above all, highly effective. He is a speaker for Speakers for Schools and is an associate of the Global Leaders Academy.

Lightning Source UK Ltd.
Milton Keynes UK
UKOW06f2123010615

252720UK00003B/37/P